Shapers of
Early Christianity

ALSO BY ROLAND H. WORTH, JR.
AND FROM MCFARLAND

Biblical Studies on the Internet: A Resource Guide, 2d ed. (2008)

Messiahs and Messianic Movements through 1899 (2005)

Congress Declares War: December 8–11, 1941 (2004)

Alternative Lives of Jesus: Noncanonical Accounts through the Early Middle Ages (2003)

Biblical Studies on the Internet: A Resource Guide (2002)

World War II Resources on the Internet (2002)

Secret Allies in the Pacific: Covert Intelligence and Code Breaking Cooperation Between the United States, Great Britain, and Other Nations Prior to the Attack on Pearl Harbor (2001)

Church, Monarch and Bible in Sixteenth Century England: The Political Context of Biblical Translation (2000)

No Choice but War: The United States Embargo Against Japan and the Eruption of War in the Pacific (1995)

Pearl Harbor: Selected Testimonies, Fully Indexed, from the Congressional Hearings (1945–1946) and Prior Investigations of the Events Leading Up to the Attack (1993)

Bible Translations: A History Through Source Documents (1992)

Shapers of Early Christianity

52 Biographies, A.D. 100–400

Roland H. Worth, Jr.

McFarland & Company, Inc., Publishers
Jefferson, North Carolina, and London

The present work is a reprint of the illustrated case bound edition of Shapers of Early Christianity: 52 Biographies, A.D. 100–400, *first published in 2007 by McFarland.*

LIBRARY OF CONGRESS CATALOGUING-IN-PUBLICATION DATA

Worth, Roland H., Jr., 1943–
Shapers of early Christianity : 52 biographies,
A.D. 100–400 / Roland H. Worth, Jr.
p.   cm.
Includes bibliographical references and index.

ISBN 978-0-7864-6942-0
softcover : acid free paper ∞

1. Christian biography.   2. Church history—
Primitive and early church, ca. 30–600.   I. Title.
BR1700.3.W67 2012   270.1092'2—dc22   [B]   2007000274

BRITISH LIBRARY CATALOGUING DATA ARE AVAILABLE

© 2007 Roland H. Worth, Jr. All rights reserved

No part of this book may be reproduced or transmitted in any form or by any means, electronic or mechanical, including photocopying or recording, or by any information storage and retrieval system, without permission in writing from the publisher.

Cover art: *St. Jerome,* Matteo di Giovanni, tempera on wood, 16½" × 25", 1460s

Manufactured in the United States of America

*McFarland & Company, Inc., Publishers
Box 611, Jefferson, North Carolina 28640
www.mcfarlandpub.com*

Table of Contents

Preface 1
Introduction 3

1. SECOND CENTURY CHRISTIANITY
The "Apostolic Fathers" Context 7
Clement of Rome 8
Second Clement 10
Ignatius of Antioch 12
Justin Martyr 15
Hermas 18
Papias 22
Polycarp 23
Melito 27
Bishop Victor of Rome 30
Irenaeus, Bishop of Lyons 32
Perpetua and Felicity 34
Clement of Alexandria 37

2. FAITH AND IMPERIAL GOVERNMENT
Constantine the Great 40
Flavius Julius Constantius 47
Julian the Apostate 49
Thundering Legion 53
Pammachius 54

3. THE CHRISTIAN INTELLECTUAL TRADITION
Julius Africanus 58
Gregory of Neocaesarea 60
Eusebius of Caesarea 62
Faltonia Proba 66
Firmicus Maternus 67
Aurelius Clemens Prudentius 69

    Ephraem 71
    Epiphanius of Salamis 72

4. **BIBLICAL TRANSLATORS AND TEXTUAL SCHOLARS**
    Tatian 75
    Origen 79
    Ulfilas 84
    Jerome 87

5. **DEFENDERS OF ORTHODOXY**
    Cyprian of Carthage 92
    Athanasius 97
    Gregory of Nazianzus 103
    Basil the Great 105
    Ambrose 107
    John Chrysostom 111
    Hilary of Poitiers 113
    Augustine of Hippo 114

6. **PROPONENTS OF "HERETICAL" ALTERNATIVES**
    Marcion 121
    Tertullian 125
    Valentinus 128
    Felicissimus 131
    Arius 133
    Montanus, Maximilla, and Priscilla 138
    Donatus 143
    Jovinianus 145
    Bonosus 147

7. **ALTERNATIVE ROUTES TO HOLINESS**
    Antony 149
    Pachomius 154
    Marcellina 158
    Paula 160

Chapter Notes 165
Bibliography 181
Index 193

Preface

I remain endlessly fascinated by the process of change — why it occurs, the ways and rationales by which it is promoted, and the reasons and justifications why it is opposed. In the last forty-five years of my adult life I have seen my own religion change dramatically. Some of these changes have been for the better; others, in my judgment, have been destructive.

Regardless of one's individual judgment on such matters, the most frustrating thing is how many *don't realize major change has occurred at all.* To them it's been that way "all the time" (effectively defined as the last two decades or less), their personal experience not being able to reach any further back. Even those who have helped bring about the alterations have often become so accustomed to them that they would be reluctant to admit there was a day when those changes were bitterly controversial, vigorously opposed, and the subject of intense debate.

Having preached the gospel for more than two decades (everything from occasional to full time) I have a special interest not only in the changes that Christianity has undergone in my own lifetime, but also in changes that it underwent when it was freed from the presence of the first two generations of Jesus' disciples. The modern blindness to the fact that customs, practices and beliefs of the relatively recent past have been significantly altered was often missed by them as well. Just as it is today, the newest set of changes had become so customary that to question them was to be perceived as undermining loyalty to the apostolic tradition itself.

One of the purposes of studying history is to expose the fallacy of that common human failing. Good history should show what once was, how things were changed and by whom, and what things were changed to, as well as to analyze the forces encouraging those changes. If the work is of an "apologetic" nature it goes beyond this to either defend or repudiate the changed order. In regard to the latter, since this is a historical analysis, such concerns are of only peripheral concern — we are interested in "who, what, where, when" and (at least to some extent) "why" the process occurred.

Hence, the purpose of this book is to understand the beliefs and behavior of both key and representative figures in the crucial transitional phase from primitive Christianity to early medieval Catholicism. Some of the seeds had certainly been present a decade or more before the earliest individuals discussed in this volume rose to prominence, but in the centuries covered a range of new, previously unthought-of controversies and issues were raised, discussed and debated. These divided the community of faith along lines that ultimately became unbridgeable. To understand how these divisions occurred and how different personalities reacted to them can provide a useful lesson in how such matters evolve and take on a life of their own even among those with — initially — very similar convictions.

A few words need to be said about the terminology of our discussion. The title "saint" was later bestowed upon many of those later regarded as "orthodox"— by virtue of having come out of the controversies as the dominant faction — but they certainly did not wear the title at the time. Hence we have usually avoided such expressions (never mind the fact that certain of these were clearly less than "saintly" where significant parts of their character and behavior are concerned).

Likewise a caveat must be given in regard to the terms "orthodox" and "heretic," both of which should be taken with a grain of salt. Just as the victors write the history when it comes to military warfare, the same is equally true in regard to the winners in theological conflict: they become the "orthodox" because they won. Yet the terms are so well established that they can hardly be ignored in their entirety. Hence it is only proper to use both terms as blunt descriptive terms of the ultimate outcome (and not necessarily as an endorsement of their respective claims to truth) *and* to periodically utilize "hedging rhetoric" to show even more clearly that we are not necessarily endorsing either side in the religious controversies that are described.

In some of the controversies (to express a personal religious judgment based upon my own decades of scripture study), the heretics were in the right and in others the orthodox were right. Furthermore, some of the disagreements are so complex and theologically long-winded that few except the most well versed specialist would even want to make an effort to determine where they belong in regard to the various camps.

To provide my own experience as an illustration: Decades ago I was asked my opinion of the "godhead" by two sets of visiting Jehovah's Witnesses, a group well known for its anti-trinitarianism. One set announced I was Trinitarian (or Nicene in the historical context we will be studying); the other decided I was not Trinitarian (or roughly Arian in the period covered by this work). Personally I would not even attempt to place myself in either camp except when in one of my periods of playful efforts to be annoying. It is likely that the majority in the ancient world would have been equally difficult to precisely situate in the theological landscape of their day, though most seem to have solved the problem by loyalty to a leadership with a firmly established doctrinal persona. Such esoteric issues were for those with the time and temperament and not for the everyday Christian simply trying to survive.

Hence we are unconcerned with any other elaborate analyses of the details of the various religious debates. Instead, we limit ourselves to sketching out the broad outline of what the competing theories were about so we can evaluate the behavior and attitudes of those in the various warring camps.

As in the past, a deep debt of gratitude is owed to the William Smith Morton Library of the Union Theological Seminary in Richmond, Virginia. Their vast resources provide access to obscure sources of information that are available in few other places. Special thanks are due to Roger B. Pittard, circulation librarian, who solved a major problem with book-borrowing privileges that grew out of a transition in management personnel.

Introduction

The period from about A.D. 100 to 400 saw the dramatic transformation of early Christianity both outwardly and inwardly. Outwardly, it moved from oppressed minority to officially approved minority and then, rapidly, to majority status. Inwardly, it underwent the evolution from highly decentralized, essentially independent congregations into local and regionally supervised groups with a leadership that gradually linked their own aspirations to authority to that of the apostles. These and other fundamental and profound changes in practice and attitude produced a very different church than that which had earlier existed.

Why did these changes occur? Who brought them about? And what was the reasoning of those who did? The purpose of this volume is to provide at least a partial answer to such questions by examining the lives, teachings, and assumptions of those who played a role in the evolution.

It is impossible to treat within the bounds of one short volume all the significant personalities who shaped and reshaped post-apostolic early Christianity. Hence we have limited ourselves to a survey of some of the most significant individuals, supplemented by a study of representative ones who are typical of a given mind-frame, societal position, or office. Even reducing the boundaries of our study by such a drastic step, there is still no way to provide a comprehensive analysis of each individual, as entire books much longer than this one have been written on many of them.

Hence we usually settle for an overview of each person's life and a more in-depth treatment of one or two narrow areas. Even so, some of these people appear in a variety of contexts beyond that of their own life. For example, of Jerome's many endeavors, we have selected his Bible translation work to emphasize. Yet due to his personality, influence, and variety of writings, his name and actions are introduced in regard to the development of the monastic movement and religious controversies of his age as well. Such will also be true of several other individuals.

Although a strict chronological study of the period has often proven useful to students of the subject, we believe that the needs of a short analysis are far better served if we utilize this approach only for our first chapter ("Second Century Christianity") and substitute what might be called a "conceptual" method in the remaining six, in which we trace representative examples of the different *categories* of individuals who comprised the community of faith in that period.

Some are important because they played a key role in shaping the convictions of others. Some are significant organizationally in expanding the power of the church leadership, others due to their *opposition* to both the gradually defining "orthodoxy" of the era as well as to the power of specific individual church officials. Finally, there are those who were not necessarily overly significant in their own right but can be treated as embodiments of a specific aspect of changing church thought and action.

In Chapter 1 we examine a variety of second century Christians, beginning with those who came to prominence just before or after the century began. These span the spectrum from church leaders to propagandists for the new faith to martyrs.

In Chapter 2 we turn to "Faith and Imperial Government." At the apex of the political hierarchy, of course, were the "Christian Emperors." All of these appeared in the last century of the period we are concerned with and they exhibit three of the different relationships to Christianity that powerful individuals can embrace. The first of these was Constantine the Great, who utilized his imperial power to help shape the faith and obtain the triumph of what later generations deemed mainstream orthodoxy. The second was Flavius Julius Constantius who came to the throne after Constantine the Great's death and threw the weight of imperial influence on the side of Arianism. There was one final option available and the very next emperor, Julian, embraced that one: wash one's hands entirely of Christianity and energetically embrace a revival of old-fashioned polytheism. Hence the traditional appellation of Julian as "the Apostate."

During these centuries, the number of Christians who entered (or were converted while in) the military grew significantly. The most famous unit with a large number of them was the "Thundering Legion." During a period of despair and imminent disaster, the army was suffering from extreme thirst and exhaustion and a victory by the enemy was all but certain. They prayed for relief and a major thunderstorm shocked the enemy into breaking off its advance.

These men were, so to speak, at the bottom of the social totem pole yet essential to the survival of the imperial government. As an example of a Christian in the higher ranks, we study Pammachius (died c. 409), who was a senator. After the death of his wife, he put behind his prerogatives of rank and spent the remainder of his life engaged in works of charity.

In Chapter 3 we turn to "The Christian Intellectual Tradition." This is not to say that these men were uninterested in Biblical or religious matters, but because they also carved out roles that we today would be more likely to class under the heading of intellectual (rather than strictly spiritual) endeavors. Among the historians were Julius Africanus (who integrated Christian, Jewish, and pagan history), Eusebius of Caesarea (who is considered the inventor of church history), and Epiphanius of Salamis (who was deep into both church history and religious controversy).

Firmicus Maternus is valuable to posterity for his description of fourth century polytheism. Gregory of Neocaesarea provides an early (third century) example of Christian autobiography. Poetry was far more popular than in our age and we provide three examples of such individuals: the Spanish poet Aurelius Clemens Prudentius, the biblical commentary and poet-hymn writer Ephraem, and the female poetess Flatonia Proba.

Chapter 4 centers on "Biblical Translators and Textual Scholars." The heretic Tatian pioneered the "editing" of the gospels into one intermingled narrative, a form of approach still appreciated by many. The doctrinally controversial Origen gained lasting renown for his scholarly compilation of the *Hexapla* which provided both a Hebrew Old Testament text as well as multiple contemporary Greek translations of it. The Arian Ulfilas appears here not because of his Arianism but because of his role in translating the Bible for the Goths. Finally there is the eminent Jerome, who translated the Latin Vulgate, at its time a bitterly controversial endeavor.

Chapter 5's discussion of various "Defenders of Orthodoxy" includes some of the most famous names of the era. Athanasius became known as the "Father of Orthodoxy." Basil the Great gained more regional fame as preeminent defender of Eastern Christianity. Ambrose (temporarily) seemed a bridge between orthodoxy and Arianism but soon came down firmly against the latter. Hilary of Poitiers similarly seemed to have some concern for legitimate nonorthodox concerns, stressing that words should not be magnified beyond their true intention in the interest of obtaining doctrinal victories but similarly crusaded hard against the Arian dissenters. Cyprian of Carthage is connected, in contrast, with the struggle against Novatianism.

Some individuals gained fame not merely for their struggle against doctrinal nonconformity but for the skill and power of their preaching. Two examples of this were Gregory of Nazianzus and John Chrysostom. Finally there was Augustine of Hippo: not a particularly prestigious man in his own time but one who gained fame for the breadth and eventual impact of his theological writings and for his *Confessions* of how, reluctantly, he became a Christian.

We turn to "Proponents of 'Heretical' Alternatives to the Evolving Orthodoxy" in Chapter 6. Marcion pioneered a vigorous Gnostic system in which the temporal world was evil and the God of the New Testament was not the God of the Old Testament. His followers created their rival church to oppose the orthodox. In contrast, Valentinus formed a Gnostic movement that was quite content to remain within the bosom of the church.

Arius unintentionally created the Arian movement, which prospered even better (and in more forms) after his death than during his life. The New Prophetic movement (Montanism) had its three great prophets, Montanus, Maximilia, and Priscilla. Tertullian (known as a notable apologist) drifted into the movement and championed it just as vigorously as he had "orthodoxy" in his earlier work.

To some, would-be orthodoxy marked itself as apostate because it was too lenient. Hence Marcellinus initiated the Donatist schism over the premise that an apostate Christian could never again be readmitted to fellowship even after the period of persecution was over and he or she claimed to repent.

As early as the mid–third century, Felicissimus built a reputation (or became infamous, if one was on the side of centralization) by championing presbyterial authority as opposed to that of the episcopate. The fourth century in particular saw the blossoming of asceticism in popularity and prestige and the accompanying growing assumption that the honorability of even married sexuality must be accepted only cautiously and grudgingly. Hence Jovinianus gained condemnation for his opposition to asceticism and Bonosus created horror among many by daring to suggest that the virgin Mary had not remained a virgin throughout her entire married life.

In our final chapter we analyze "Alternate Routes to Holiness." Pride of place (both because of his importance and chronological priority) goes to Antony, the founder of Christian monasticism. A little later comes Pachomius, who pioneered the cenobitic (collective) form of monastic life. In regard to the female effort to find new ways to express their spirituality we study Marcellina (who advocated a life of perpetual virginity) and Paula, who was a pioneer of female monasticism.

By becoming familiar with this cross section of personalities and attitudes, we gain insight into the rival approaches to Christian faith that warred during the first few centuries after Christ. Whether we regard the ultimate outcomes as the triumph of greater spirituality or as a dramatic drift from a simpler and less demanding Christianity, there is no question that a massive change had clearly occurred within the movement. And these men and women — and those like them — made it happen.

Chapter 1

Second Century Christianity

The "Apostolic Fathers" Context

The term "apostolic fathers" came to be applied in the seventeenth century to a collection of ancient works that originated beginning shortly before A.D. 100. Because they were considered to be second generation Christians, the term "apostolic" seemed fitting to describe individuals who would have been either students of the apostles or of those who had worked with the apostles. In actual fact some of these were likely *third* generation Christians, but due to the early origin of the material the nomenclature has remained in use.

The collection originally included six writers. Two go by the shared name of "Clement," though style argues strongly for different individuals to have written the two letters bearing the name. Hermas writes in the prophetic tradition of providing "visions" of the future. Ignatius and Polycarp represented Near Eastern Christianity of the period. Finally there was pseudo–Barnabas, attributed from the third century, at least, to the traveling companion of Paul.

A few other works from this era were later discovered, including the *Didache* (*Teaching of the Twelve Apostles*), which surfaced in 1873, and these were also lumped into this category. The *Didache* itself is a collection of instructions regulating church practices, though a significant amount of moral instruction is also included as well as some apocalyptic teaching. Rather than being apostolic in origin, it is a systematic attempt to compile the ideas that the apostles had allegedly originated. As part of this synthesis, it adds its own interpretive glosses on such matters as urging baptism in running water (hardly possible in Jerusalem in Acts 2 or in the desert with the Ethiopian eunuch in Acts 8:26, 36–39) and in advocating an obligatory one or two day fast prior to baptism (in contrast to the pattern in Acts of prompt and immediate baptism rather than a period of delay). Because of the fictitious nature of both *Barnabas* and the *Didache* (and for space reasons as well) we have omitted these second century works from our analysis.

Some of these works were deeply revered in the early centuries. The popularity among Christians of the codex (book) rather than the scroll form to contain their sacred writings not only permitted all or most of them to be put within a single volume, it also required the editorial judgment of *which* gospels and epistles were to be regarded as so uniquely authoritative that they merited inclusion.[1]

Of course the books regarded as norm-setting were incorporated, but there was also now space to include at least some additional works of superior value. The problem arises, of course, as to where the manuscript copiers drew the line between the two types of material. Their inclusion *could* indicate a perceived authoritative canonicity, or simply respect for a widely admired work not recognized as having that high a status.

For example, *Codex Sinaiticus* dates to the fourth century and includes both *Barnabas* and a partial text of the *Shepherd of Hermas*. The Codex Alexandrius from the following century has *First Clement* as well as *Second Clement*. At the very minimum, the inclusion represents a high degree of reverence for their contents in the areas from which the manuscripts originated.

CLEMENT OF ROME (writing c. 96)
Peacemaker for the Corinthian Church

Oddly enough, the epistle does not contain Clement's name at any point. The assumption that he was the author, however, is based on two pieces of significant evidence. First is the fact that manuscripts containing the text explicitly attribute the authorship to him. The second is that a bishop Dionysius refers to a letter as coming from Clement and notes that it was continuing to be read in Corinthian church services in his day. It is *assumed* that this letter is our First Clement[2]; yet unless one is to postulate a missing Clement-Corinthian letter one is hard pressed to avoid accepting the connection.

Assuming that the author's name actually was Clement, some have speculated that he was a freedman of the house of Titus Flavius Clemens, a prominent Roman executed by Domitian. Either a Jew or a Christian (possibly both), Clemens' household likely contained a number of similarly spiritually minded individuals. As a freedman of this house, it would have been quite natural for this church leader to take on the household name when being freed. On the other hand this was by no means an inevitable name choice for a freed servant.[3] Furthermore, it has been argued that the strength of this purported family relationship is weak because it originally grew out of the story painted of Flavius Clemens in the pseudo–Clementine *Homilies* and *Recognitions*.[4] Be that as it may, a large body of later speculative literature grew up around him, which included his having a personal knowledge of the apostle Peter.

Clement's Post in the Roman Church

Adopting the name "Clement" for convenience as well as its likelihood, it seems clear that whoever composed and sent this letter was clearly a respected figure in the Roman church to have been given this responsibility. At what point the monarchical episcopate was established in Rome (i.e., a single bishop with a body of presbyters as clearly subordinate) is unknown. It was quite likely much later than this letter, however.

In chapter 42 of the epistle, the apostles are said to have appointed *episkopoi* (bishops) as well as *diakonoi* (deacons). The Septuagint form of Isaiah 60:17 is cited as a prophetic proof that the establishment of such officers was part of the divine plan. In this Old Testament text, however, the term used is *presbyteroi* (presbyters), which most naturally indicates that to Clement his "bishops" are still synonymous with "presbyters" rather than distinct from the class.[5]

Without such incidental evidence, Rome could reasonably be assumed to have become an early bastion of this centralized approach to church government since it was the seat of the Roman government and it would be a quite human tendency to gradually claim on a spiritual level what the Roman government did on a political one. The apparent reluctance to make such a power grab argues powerfully for the integrity of the church office holders of the time since such an evolution would have been in the interest of the very position(s) they held.

The silence of the author as to his identity argues that he is not writing as an expression of personal authority but simply in behalf of the entire congregation.[6] Nor was it meddling by the congregation and its leadership to send the letter. As W. Jaeger observes, "The authority assumed in the letter by those who are talking to the Corinthian church rests on the hypothesis that this is not an act of arrogance on the part of the Roman church, but the fulfillment of their duty as Christians toward their brothers whom they see go astray."[7] He and they wished to assist and correct not rule. They are not laying down law nor giving orders;[8] they are pleading, arguing (in the positive sense of the term), imploring that the Corinthians set aright the unsettling situation that has left them in ongoing unrest and turmoil. They wish to be honest brokers and fair-minded mediators of the dispute.

After all, it was natural for the Romans to be concerned about what was happening. Both the city and its church were important in their own right. Furthermore, many people moved around and there was the real possibility that this could result in the root Corinthian problems being eventually transferred to Rome to plague them as well.[9] To help them was to help themselves.

Date of the Letter

First Clement (1:1) seems to clearly refer to the Roman congregation as recently undergoing a period of adversity. This would unquestionably fit Nero's notorious bloodbath as he attempted to divert onto Christians the responsibility for the great fire that burned much of the city. Most scholars find this far too early a date, though there is nothing in the epistle that explicitly excludes it.

If Nero's hostility is not under consideration, then the severe persecution under Domitian (c. A.D. 96) has been preferred. Of course in recent decades the severity and even the existence of any significant persecution by him has been seriously questioned. (My own studies lead me to conclude that there was a "moderate" persecution at the time, but nowhere near as severe as the one traditionally attributed to this emperor.) Be that as it may a date of 98, plus or minus a few years, is the dominant one.

But does the text actually refer to a period of persecution in the recent past at all? (If not, the primary underpinning for any date is removed.) In a typical rendition of 1:1, the epistle describes their adversity as the "sudden and repeated misfortunes and hindrances which have befallen us."[10] This has been criticized as an "over translation" of the Greek and that the words used do not necessarily have to refer to a period of government imposed oppression. The language is taken as not necessarily anything more than a polite excuse to explain the delay in responding at an earlier date. To the extent that there had been difficulties, the words refer to "internal dissensions" rather than government action.[11] Even the advocates of this alternative concede that this scenario has not gained much support.[12]

The Problem in Corinth and Clement's Plea for Reconciliation

The historical context of the letter involves a serious power struggle going on in Corinth that Clement wished to discourage[13]:

> We are of the opinion, therefore, that those appointed by [the apostles], or afterwards by other eminent men with the consent of the whole church, and who have blamelessly served the flock of Christ in a humble, peaceable, and disinterested spirit, and have for a long time possessed the good opinion of all, cannot be justly dismissed from the ministry. For our sin will not be small, if we eject from the episcopate those who blamelessly and holily fulfilled its duties.

Presumably echoing the practice of his own congregation, it required the general "consent of the whole church" for the appointment to the episcopate. Charisma, even supposed miraculous abilities, did not automatically create the a priori right to hold office. That required formal congregational approval so far as Clement was concerned.[14] The appointment is to be a permanent one, assuming good behavior: although he does not mention grounds for removal, the fact that he heavily stressed that these particular individuals had honorably discharged their duties would imply that if they had *not,* then the admonition to maintain them in office might not be applicable. Because they have not betrayed their trust, however, there can be no legitimate reason to remove them.

Hence the epistle urges the Corinthians to respect their existing church leaders, rather than yield to the movement underway to replace them. Such an effort could have grown out of the availability of new (or relatively new) members who had greater wealth or social prestige.[15] Alternatively there may have been local problems that the leadership was attempting to resolve and that those supporting the dissidents had been stirring up trouble to prevent them.[16]

There is no reason to believe this was doctrinal as opposed to a matter of personalities and individual power struggles. Since the epistle repeatedly criticizes jealousy, Simon Tugwell reasonably argues that envy either lay at the foundation of the division or was a major contributor to it.[17]

SECOND CLEMENT (date unknown)

This "homily," or "sermon," is the earliest such Christian one to survive in its entirety. (Some suspect that the New Testament book of Hebrews likely deserves that honor,[18] in which case this would be the second oldest surviving sermon.)

It should be noted that although it is a sermon it is the record of a *previously prepared* sermon that is to be read to the people after an introduction from an appropriate scriptural text: "Wherefore, my brethren and sisters, after the reading of the words of the God of truth, I read also unto you an exhortation, to the end that ye should attend to what has been written, that ye may both save yourselves and him who preacheth among you; for I ask of you, as my reward, that ye should repent with your whole heart, gaining for yourselves salvation and life" (19:1).[19]

There is no indication of the authorship, but various manuscripts circulated with both First and Second Clement together.[20] This could argue for a long-standing tradition of joint authorship, an origin and original preservation in the same place (i.e., Rome), or that the two are interlocked in some other manner.

Some have considered Second Clement a sermon preached in 120 or the two decades thereafter by someone in Corinth. Others have considered it as originally a letter by Rome's bishop Sorer (c. 170). Others date it A.D. 98–100 on the assumption that it is an admonitory sermon prepared by church leaders in Corinth as a response to First Clement. Because of the exchange of letters between Corinth and Rome (leading to the writing of First Clement), one could imagine any one of these scenarios resulting in a copy being retained in Rome and the two documents being circulated together. The fourth option as to place of origin places it in Alexandria, Egypt, at an unknown time in the second century. This reconstruction leaves unexplained the linkage of First and Second Clement that was not uncommon in the ancient church, while the other three scenarios provide a more obvious connection.

The author is almost certainly a Gentile, for he speaks of how they had previously worshipped idols: "for we were maimed in our understanding, worshipping sticks and stones, and gold and silver and iron, the work of men, and our whole life was nothing but death" (1:6).

The sermon (as do so many today) had multiple goals. One major purpose was to criticize complacency and its dangers: "My brethren, let us therefore repent forthwith; let us be sober and followers of what is good, for we are burdened with much folly and wickedness. Let us wipe out from among us our former sins, and repent sincerely and be saved. And let us not be pleasers of men, nor let us wish to please one another alone, but let us also please them that are without by our righteous conduct, that the Divine name may not be blasphemed on our account" (13:1).

Yet this is not his only theme. Hughes O. Old puts the emphasis on how the sermon stresses that church members are to live lives of continuous joy in their service to God even when obstacles and difficulties come their way. Since the lesson cites Matthew 9:17 about calling sinners to repentance, Old finds a secondary intent in teaching non–Christians who were present about the fulfillment of the Old Testament prophets in Jesus and the responsibilities of discipleship.[21] If so, then the listeners are assumed to be individuals who already have had an introduction to certain of the first principles of the gospel and who are viewed as being willing to consider the duties and potential difficulties if they leave either traditional Judaism or polytheism behind.

Jesus' Teaching in the Work

In explaining the meaning of the Old Testament, the personal teaching of Jesus is repeatedly referred to. The document quotes Jesus in a varying manner. On the one hand it can quote verbatim "No servant can serve two masters" from Luke 16:13.[22] Yet it can also attribute to Jesus words that are not found in the canonical gospels at all: "For when someone asked the Lord when His kingdom was going to come, he said, 'When the two shall be one, and the outside like the inside, and the male with the female, neither male nor female.'"[23] The "neither male nor female" certainly sounds Pauline in phraseology. The remainder seems simply varying ways of stressing the need for reconciliation with others (including the other gender) and with oneself (inner versus outer conduct)—sentiments that are certainly fully consistent with Jesus' attitude and teaching but never found expressed in canonical sources in this manner.[24]

Likewise Jesus is quoted as warning the apostles that "You will be like lambs among wolves." When Peter asks about the danger of the wolves destroying the lambs, Jesus responds, "After their death the lambs should not fear the wolves, nor should you fear those who kill you and can do nothing more to you. But fear him who, when you are dead, has power over soul and body to cast them into the flames of hell."[25] The lambs/wolves analogy is utilized in Luke 10:3 to warn the disciples of the dangers they face. Similarly the warning to fear the one who can cast you into eternal punishment rather than merely kill the body comes from Matthew 5:29–30. Hence the individual conceptual *pieces* are canonical but not the way Second Clement puts them together into one thought.

IGNATIUS OF ANTIOCH (c. 50–c. 110)
Bishop, Letter Writer, Martyr

Eusebius of Caesarea claims that Ignatius was the third man to serve as bishop in Antioch and that he gained the post while Trajan was emperor (98–117). Later during the same reign he was arrested for being a Christian and sent to Rome for execution. Beyond this, virtually nothing is known of his life except for what clues may be drawn from the seven letters he wrote while on the way to Rome. Further limiting the data is the fact that these were composed over a short period of time (it has reasonably been speculated that several weeks represents the maximum time range[26]), meaning that matters that might be brought up in retrospection at some different point in his life escape mention entirely.

Although certainly a Gentile, what was the religious background of his parents? Was he raised in the faith or was he converted independently or simultaneously with them? What kind of education did he have? Was he trained with some specific career in mind, such as lawyer or an educator? Even in regard to his arrest the details are conjectural. Why was he singled out? Were others maltreated and punished locally? How long had he served in his post as church leader? Such are some of the unknowns that confront us.

The general, but not specific, time of the letters can reasonably be estimated: They can't be any later than Trajan's death in 117 and are typically dated at c. 110, though some favor as much as three years later.

As to his arrest, Ignatius indicates that his home church had significant internal cleavages. Hence it has been speculated that one or more faction might have been accused of real or imagined unsettling of law and order and that he became the governmental target as the congregation's most visible personality and leader.[27] Working from the reality of those divisions, however, one might equally well conjecture that a hostile faction had used the internal contentions as an excuse to stir up suspicion and hostility by the governor at the official leader of their church. Indeed, the probability for such is increased if we accept that an open split had developed among them,[28] which would legitimize or at least rationalize (in the eyes of those invoking state power) taking such an extreme step against the official bishop.

However he got into his situation (and for whatever reasons the local governor did not feel it appropriate to execute him in Antioch), he underwent actual execution in Rome, where he became one of the "entertainments" provided the citizenry through publicly executing prisoners by having them mauled and killed by wild animals.

From the standpoint of church history, he is most important as an early example of how ecclesiastical structure was shifting: He is the first documentable instance of the "bishop" being distinct from the broader category of presbyters. Indeed, at this early stage the phenomena seems to have been limited to only a very few churches.[29] Of the seven letters he wrote, only the one to Polycarp of Smyrna was addressed to a specific individual designated the "bishop," which argues that he was passing through a region where the new custom of church organization was only beginning to be established. It is intriguing that even this pioneer in claiming enhanced power for the episcopate makes no claim that the "bishop" has his superior position due to having "apostolic succession" to the authority of the twelve apostles, an assertion that later generations utilized to justify the centralization of control in their hands.[30]

Ignatius makes claims to having at least limited and sporadic supernatural gifts. In writing to Philadelphia he speaks of how certain people suspected that he rebuked church conflict because "I knew in advance about the division caused by certain people." He insists that this was not the case but "the Spirit itself was preaching" to and through him about the harm of the divisiveness.[31] In a similar vein he promised the Ephesians that, if he could, he would write again to them "especially if the Lord reveals anything to me" concerning "the divine plan with respect to the new man [in] Christ Jesus."[32]

The perception or claim that he had such supernatural gifts might well explain his advancement to the post of bishop in Antioch.[33] If he *also* used such revelatory claims to justify claiming superiority to the presbytery or if he *assumed* that because he had such gifts he *had* to be justified in asserting superior status, one can easily imagine how less receptive individuals in the congregation might have come to the conclusion that he was self-deluded by power seeking rather than being truly Spirit led. This could easily have fueled major intra-church problems and even efforts to depose him.

The Letters of Ignatius

During the journey to Rome, Ignatius was permitted access to visitors from various congregations in cities he passed through. In turn he was given access to writing materials and he composed letters to Polycarp, who was serving as bishop in Smyrna, as well as to seven churches. The seven letters survived in three forms: a short version (referring to textual length) preserved three epistles in Syriac. The middle (length) recension contained all of the seven mentioned by Eusebius and was preserved in both Greek and Latin. The long version contained an expanded text of all seven letters as well as six additional ones.[34] An alternative nomenclature has also been used to describe the three text types: describing them in the same order just summarized, they become "the Syrian abridgement," the "short recension," and the "long recension."[35]

During the 1870s and 1880s a powerful case was made for the middle recension representing the original text. This theory was forcefully challenged beginning in 1979, but the earlier consensus soon reestablished itself.[36]

Contributions of the Letters to the Development of Christian Thought[37]

Acts 11:26 states that the name "Christian" was first used to describe believers in Antioch, which was Ignatius' home. Ignatius expands the use of this word — a noun — in his letters. He utilizes it in adjective form, speaking of "Christian nourishment" in particular.[38] He also coins the term (literally rendered) "Christianism," an obvious parallelism to the well known contemporary term "Judaism," and which has continued to be utilized in the form "Christianity."[39]

Nor was this the only case of linguistic innovation in his writings. Speaking to Smyrna (which had its own bishop as distinct from the presbyters) he pled, "Wherever the bishop appears, there let the congregation be; just as wherever Jesus is, there is the catholic church. It is not permissible to baptize or to hold a love feast without the bishop. But whatever he approves is also pleasing to God, in order that everything you do may be trustworthy and valid."[40] The word "catholic church" here means universal, as distinct from the local congregation. It represents the first known use of the term to describe the entire church throughout the world.[41]

It has been reasonably speculated that some important individual (a presbyter?) had been daring to baptize or hold charitable love feasts when bishop Polycarp could not be present, refused to come, or even was not invited.[42] This instruction was clearly designed to arm Polycarp in his demand that the validity of all such activities hinged upon his personal participation. In those congregations where the "bishop" had begun to evolve a de facto or de jure supremacy over the rest of the presbytery, the acceptance of this principle would considerably further the transition of informal leadership into one of official status.

In some sense, Ignatius felt he could claim to the Ephesians that there were bishops "appointed throughout the world."[43] Some have denied the authenticity of the Ignatian letters because they believed (correctly) that this was untrue. Others have assumed that he intentionally overstated the case, such as by blurring the distinction between bishops and presbyters that he actually preferred to promote — there were "bishops" everywhere because there were "presbyters" everywhere. Another possibility is that the dynamics of interpersonal relationships virtually inevitably results in one individual assuming the primary effective leadership even when the official power relationship is collegial in nature. Hence it is quite possible that "bishop" is used in this de facto sense, though with the hope that others would come to his more "advanced" understanding of the term in time.

JUSTIN MARTYR (c. 100–c. 165)
Apologist against Polytheism and Traditional Judaism

Justin's reputation was high among both contemporaries and those who came afterwards. Tatian described him as "the most admirable Justin." The fact that he died for his faith further enhanced his standing. As a result, Hippolytus labeled him as "the martyr" and that appellation henceforth became part of his name.[44] Born in Palestine at about the beginning of the new century, he worked his way through four separate systems of Greek philosophy before turning his attention to Christianity. This life-shaping decision may have occurred while he was at Ephesus. Afterwards he moved to Rome and formed a study circle around himself.[45]

More than one thing may provoke the interest of an outsider in becoming intrigued and then converted to a new faith. In his second *Apology* (the first is more than four times longer), Justin implies that even when he was a dedicated Platonist, he was convinced that the character libels aimed at Christians were manifest exaggerations. Furthermore, there was a clear-cut bravery in their willingness to die for their faith. In his *Dialogue*, he emphasized how discussion with a certain elderly Christian had led him to realize that in Christianity — through its Hebrew Torah and prophetic roots — that there was a system of spiritual perception that antedated even that of the Greeks and which was deserving of the highest reverence and allegiance.[46] This is done in the context of discussing with Trypho — a traditionalist Jew who rejected the claims of and for Jesus — the validity of Christian faith.

Having become a Christian, Justin devoted his considerable intellectual talents to defending Christianity. Much of his work, however, has perished. This includes all his sermons, though we know he wrote a number of them.[47]

Critic of Polytheism: His "Apologies"

His two *Apologies* (defenses of his faith) were the work of the early 150s and in them he targets contemporary Gentiles. He argued that the worthiest and most noble of Greek philosophical aspirations were fulfilled within Jesus Christ and His teaching. Hence he attempts to integrate Christian thought with Greek thinking into a synthesis rather than treating them as totally opposed and irreconcilable systems.[48] In effect, he argued that one did not have to totally repudiate the best of the past but had the option of integrating it into a new mixture.

Although the main agenda of the apologies was establishing the credibility of the Christian religion to the imperial leadership, the work was also clearly designed for circulation among polytheists in general as well as Christians. For the latter, he goes out of his way to implicitly repudiate Marcion's teaching by throwing in descriptive phrases referring to God's role in creating the physical universe, thereby rejecting Marcion's denial.[49]

Trypho the Jew: Was He Real?

The character of Trypho has been the subject of great disagreement. Some regard him as fully historical, others that he is a literary invention but embodies the typical arguments of the era, and yet others that there is minimal connection between him and any genuine historical personality. As to the discussion or debate itself, some regard it as a literal rendition of one, while others think that it is invented out of whole cloth. A third school opts for its being the expanded version of a genuine discussion.[50]

The fact that Trypho effectively presents his own case against the followers of Jesus — rather than being just a straw man with arguments that can be dismissed virtually without thinking about them — argues that he both represents a genuine historical personality and the form (if not the literal words) of the contemporary arguments being lodged against Christianity. Even conceding that there are places where Trypho does not effectively present his case, there are far more instances where he makes arguments known to be contemporary with this period, which is the kind of mixture of strong and inadequate argumentation not unknown even in religious debates in the nineteenth and twentieth centuries. Furthermore there are little human touches — such as individuals smiling — that would occur in real life but which would tend to be ignored in a work with a strictly theological purpose and no historical roots.[51]

Whether intended primarily for a traditional Jewish audience or not (even today it is often hard to get someone to read literature critical of his or her own group's religious convictions), it was certainly a useful discussion to show less informed Christians how to go about defending their faith. In addition, it provided any Gentile attracted to Judaism an explanation of why Christianity should be regarded as its monotheistic superior alternative.[52]

Dialogue with Trypho the Jew: Justin's Arguments

Prior to Justin, Christians had tended to view the church as a *continuation* of Israel.[53] Indeed, the apostle Paul argues that some (i.e., converted Gentiles) deserved to be counted as part of Israel though they were not such biologically (Romans 9:6) and that the true Jew was determined by behavior not ethnicity (Romans 2:28–29). Within that view was the implicit claim to the collective right to be regarded *as* Israel, either partially (if Israel accepted Jesus as Messiah, which it mainly did not) or exclusively (if the bulk remained in rejection).

What with two major unsuccessful insurrections against Rome (in the late 60s and then in the 130s) and the continued unwillingness of the bulk of ethnic Jews to embrace Christianity, the sense of alienation became unbridgeable on both sides.[54] Those who wished to be regarded as Jewish and Christian simultaneously became an isolated minority within the two communities. Even as late as Jerome we read of segment of Christians who worshipped in the synagogue and were viewed with contempt by traditional Jews and with suspicion by Christians at large.[55]

Within this historical context of the religious cleavage being set in theological concrete on both sides, it is not surprising that Christianity now moved to the position of regarding itself exclusively as the true Israel and conventional Jews as no longer worthy of being regarded as such in any meaningful sense. The rhetoric of the New Testament criticizing Jews was transformed from intramural criticism of one group of Jews rebuking another into criticism by a Gentile dominated church of Jews who were now total outsiders.[56]

Justin manifests this changed outlook in his rhetoric. In utilizing the Old Testament, he insists that they are "not yours, but ours."[57] In a parallel vein, in pseudo–Barnabas, which might be earlier than Justin, Christians are warned, "Take heed to yourselves now, and be not made like unto some, heaping up your sins and saying that the covenant is both theirs [Jews] and ours. It is ours."[58] In a very real sense, the Torah was no longer the authority for either Jew or Gentile, for Jesus' law superceded it. As Justin argued to Trypho, "the law given at Horeb is already antiquated…. A law set over against a law has made the one before it to cease, and a testament coming into existence later has limited any previous one."[59] Hebrews 8:13 had spoken of such a day; Justin proclaims it had arrived.

The destruction of the Temple in A.D. 70 and the second conquest of Palestine in the 130s by the Romans were viewed by Justin as a pattern of spiritual insurrection against God that had brought its just and proper punishment. The banning of Jews from Jerusalem after the second revolt, argues Justin, was the justified repercussion of traditionalist Jews having "slain the Just One and His prophets before Him; and now you reject those who hope in Him."[60]

The *Dialogue* provides the first extensive post–New Testament detailed exegesis of the Old Testament as Julian's contemporaries were making it. In other sources the Christian interpretation is mentioned in passing, but here it becomes lengthy and detailed.[61] Depending upon how many texts one understands as direct quotations rather than interpretive textual allusions, one close student of the subject arrives at 76 direct quotations, of which 39 refer to Isaiah in the context of making the citation.[62]

Justin heavily emphasizes how the Old Testament spoke of certain events happening in the future and how these occurred in the life and time of Jesus. Sometimes they are passages like Isaiah 7:14 (the miraculous birth).[63] Here the wording of the Septuagint was critical, for the Greek clearly refers to a virgin, while in the Hebrew it speaks of a "young woman." Since the Christians found it far easier to justify their claims from the Septuagint — not to mention that for the ever growing Gentile contingent of church members Hebrew was an alien language — it became their de facto standard text. Because of, at least in large part, the Christian preference for that version, it was increasingly rejected by the Jews among whom it had enjoyed a multi-century usage.[64]

Justin also appeals liberally to texts where the wording may fit but which were clearly not written with the events they are applied to specifically in mind. This is called the "typological" argument. Hence the offering given in the Temple to indicate purification from leprosy is introduced as finding fulfillment in the communion. The scarlet cord hung by Rahab at Jericho becomes a prophetic "type" for the shed blood of Jesus. This type of argument obviously varies greatly in its impact: when the wording verbally fits well with the event concerning Jesus it is certainly germane to mention. Yet, as seen from these particular examples, it can easily open the door to such fanciful parallelism that "special pleading" and "total irrelevancies" are the terms most likely to come to mind to those reading them today. In such cases, they may work effectively as *sermonic illustrations* but to introduce them as serious argument to actually *prove* that a point borders on the ludicrous. The distinction was clearly "fudged" by many ancients, including Justin, in the interest of maximizing the number and power of their arguments.

HERMAS (writing c. 140)
The Shepherd

Although a very few date this work (*Hermas the Shepherd*, or simply *The Shepherd*) as early as the 60s or 70s,[65] the generally accepted dating would be between A.D. 100 and 150. A dating sometime in the second quarter of that century dominates.

A large number believe that the writing of Hermas is actually the work of multiple authors, writing over a period of decades.[66] The alternative is that it is all by the same individual, who added new materials over an extended period of time. In this scenario the similarities in underlying subject matter and attitude argues for one writer throughout.[67]

Hermas: The Man

This diversity of opinion about authorship raises the question of why it was attributed to Hermas and who, if he was a single individual, he was. The Muratorian Fragment (which includes the canon of the New Testament) dates from c. A.D. 170–175, and speaks of this work having been recently written. It attributes it to one Hermas, who was a member of the congregation in Rome and who wrote it while his brother Pius was its bishop (i.e., 140–154).

Some dismiss this attribution as a legend because the Fragment wishes to reject the work as part of scripture.[68] On the other hand the Fragment does not deny that the man was a prophet nor deny that the book was useful. Indeed the identification of the author as brother of Rome's bishop would surely have increased its prestige, especially among the Romans. If the author was pursuing a strategy of unjust discreditation he would surely have branded it as the work of a heretic or some obscure and little known individual. By linking the work to the brother of a prominent individual, he gives implicit credit to it and its virtues while making plain that neither justifies its being counted part of scripture.

Even so, the work was highly regarded in the following several centuries. Origen went so far as to describe it as "divinely inspired,"[69] a description fully in tune with the book's description of itself as recording divinely given revelation. This would not necessarily imply a claim to canonicity, since even in Paul's 1 Corinthians there are references to such gifts being exercised without any claim made or inferred that such "revelations" were to be regarded as on a par with apostolic ones. Irenaeus explicitly described Hermas as Scripture, because of its purported prophetic origin.[70] Eusebius speaks of how it was still being read in the church assemblies of his day.[71] The allegations of an Arian Christology, however, apparently served to undercut its reputation as such issues became more dominant.[72]

It has been speculated (from the wording of his teaching) that Hermas was not a particularly well-educated individual,[73] but that would not be all that surprising since he is self-described as coming from a slave background. After gaining his freedom, his personal income was based upon agricultural pursuits, since the text speaks of his being personally involved in such matters. Some passages have been read as implying that he had lost much (though not necessarily all) of what had once been, for him, a considerable piece of money. Possibly he had been among those whose properties had been seized by the anti–Christian Domitian and recompensed by a grant of new land under Trajan.[74] However exaggerated Domitian's persecution has often been presented, there is no doubt that he was one spiteful individual, quite as willing to use a religious pretext as any other to repress potential foes and enhance his treasury. That a specific individual might have run afoul of him or his bureaucracy is a quite rational scenario regardless of whether there was any systematic religious oppression at the time.

The probability of Hermas retaining a significant body of holdings is particularly relevant to his teaching: when he preaches about the responsibilities of those with significant earthly possessions, he is not speaking as an "outsider" whose possessions are minimal but one who has them and must utilize them in the very manner he is advocating if he is to be regarded as consistent and not a hypocrite. (And when is it more tempting to minimize one's financial helpfulness than when one has personally undergone financial reverses?) This does not mean that he was of the true upper class; just that he was blessed with above average property and prosperity.[75]

His Message: The Revelatory Means and Places

Oddly enough Jesus' name is totally missing from the work and the title "Christ" occurs only once, and that is in a highly challengeable variant reading.[76] The three divisions of the work (according to the wording utilized in a particular translation) are the five "Visions," a dozen "Commandments" or "Mandates," and ten "Parables" or "Similitudes."

These visions are described as occurring in a variety of places. The first occurs "as I was walking on my road to the villages" and he stopped, rested, and fell asleep and had a dream (1.1). The second vision occurs "as I was going to the country about the same time as on the previous year, in my walk I recalled to memory the vision of that year. And again the Spirit carried me away, and took me to the same place where I had been the year before" (2.1). The fifth vision occurs "after I had been praying at home, and had sat down on my couch, there entered a man of glorious aspect, dressed like a shepherd, with a white goat's skin." In short, to the extent that the "revelations" can be placed, they do not occur in a church worship context but outside them and typically during sleep or near-sleep.[77]

He was to communicate the various teachings and visions he received through the means of the pen: "Accordingly I wrote down the commandments and similitudes, exactly as he had ordered me. If then, when you have heard these, ye keep them and walk in them, and practice them with pure minds, you will receive from the Lord all that He has promised to you" (5:1).

The means of revelation to him are varied: in places, he receives it through the form of an old woman who comes to him to instruct him about proper moral behavior.[78] Although some see this as an allegorical presentation of the church,[79] Hermas' use of the image varies from place to place.[80] The church as symbolic of an authoritative teacher is one that fits better with several centuries later. In this early context, the allusion is far more likely to be to wisdom (or the Holy Spirit) personified as a woman. The fact that it is an *old* woman makes her equivalent to being mature, wise, and perceptive, traditional attributes of old age. The age reference may also allude to the fact that the instructions he received about behavior are firmly rooted in an "old," long lasting moral tradition. Be that as it may, it is this revelatory work that both creates and builds the church and provides the church the teaching to instruct its members.

"Angels" are also used to instruct Hermas. These have been interpreted symbolically as his better moral instincts holding him to account.[81] This self-conjured method of internal rebuke was not uncommon among some. In the third century one heretic, according to Eusebius, dreamt so vividly of angels holding him to account that the next day he had visible bruises and publicly repudiated his past teaching.[82] Jerome speaks of a dream in which a "judge" beats him for his love of traditional pagan literature.[83] In such cases a guilty conscience had incorporated its concerns in image-dream form.

In other places the authoritative teacher is a radiant new bride or a teaching shepherd. Yet whatever their form and however much the images of individual teachers sometimes become blurred (the shepherd being identified as different types of angels for example),[84] they all ultimately become means to instruct the shepherd and, through him, all who would listen.

His Message: Repentance and Morality in the Christian Lifestyle

Hermas' visions were, initially at least, a response to sexual guilt: He had seen (presumably while a young slave) his owner naked getting out of the river after bathing. He recognized her beauty and wished that he could have a wife as good looking as her. "This was the only thought that passed through me: this and nothing more," he wrote. No sexual fantasizing, no effort to seduce her or any other woman. Only a quite human (and seemingly innocent) recognition of her sexual appeal and attractiveness. He wanted a woman *like* her, *not her.*

Presumably he recalled this event at a much later date, for we read that it was only a "short time" later that an old woman appears in a dream-vision and rebukes him for having sinned. He insists that, "Lady, have I sinned against you? How? Or when spoke I an unseemly word to you? Did I not always think of you as a lady? Did I not always respect you as a sister? Why do you falsely accuse me of this wickedness and impurity?"

Yet, she insists he *had* sinned and, coming immediately after the reference to seeing the nude owner, how else can it be anything but *sexual* sin he is accused of? (Vision 1.1) *Hence even a recognition of beauty and the desire to have such a spouse is considered sinful.* This confirms a religio-moral context in the Christian community of Rome in which even the most innocent recognition of human sexuality could be considered immoral. In such a context, is it any surprise that the approximately contemporary Tatian of the same city would react by advocating an extreme asceticism?

The rebuke of his sexuality sends Hermas into a period of immense grief and guilt (Vision 1.2) and he then is visited by the old woman again. She expands the condemnation to one of having failed as a father as well: though his sons had done evil against him, he had not rebuked their sins the way he should have (Vision 1.3).

Building on the allusion to his offsprings' evil, the elderly woman proceeds in Vision 2 to censure the excesses of his wife as well. The purpose was not mere condemnation but to urge Hermas to plead with them all to change their lives and repent — a message, she makes plain, that is applicable to the entire church. The Lord will forgive, but there is a point where His patience comes to an end: "For the Lord has sworn by His glory, in regard to His elect, that if any one of them sin after a certain day which has been fixed, he shall not be saved. For the repentance of the righteous has limits" (2.2).

The drift away from faith might be caused by many different factors. The one immediately involved in Vision 2 is ethical failure. Yet lapses might also be caused by either yielding to false doctrine or being driven away by persecution (both of which are repeatedly referred to in the work).[85] Carolyn Osiek points out that there is also a heavy emphasis on Christians having their values warped by wealth and the search for business success,[86] thereby suggesting these as the root of apostasy for a significant number of contemporaries as well.

Yet not all can or will take advantage of the call to reform. Simon Tugwell notes that the book is not so much concerned with the fact that renewed salvation is "limited" but with joy over the fact that it was possible at all.[87] Stumbling was one thing and constant repetition another. Hermas asks whether he must he forgive a spouse's sexual misconduct? He is told, "He ought to take back the sinner who has repented. But not frequently. For there is but one repentance to the servants of God."[88]

On the other hand, later there is the more restrictive statement, as if trying to say the opposite: "There is no other repentance than that which takes place, when we descended into the water, and received remission of our former sins."[89] There seems a clear tension between these two assertions. The latter implicitly forbids any restoration to either marriage or church while the former speaks of how "the servants of God" (i.e., those already baptized) had "one repentance" opportunity open to them. Either way, there would be minimal tolerance for human weakness in Hermas' ideal church, even if the problem were corrected and eliminated.

Those places where Hermas was held in the highest regard appear to have been the places most inclined to limit believers to one and only one opportunity for setting their lives aright and being restored to acceptable membership in the believing community.[90] On the other hand, the absolutist hard-liners regarded Hermas as a terrible compromiser. Tertullian pointedly compares this "adulterous shepherd" with the divine Shepherd of scripture and argues that the two were in irreconcilable conflict.[91]

PAPIAS (died c. 150)
Pioneer of Premillennialism

Although Papias' name is compatible with a Jewish background, others speculate that he is far more likely to have been a Gentile of Phrygia.[92] He made no claim to being a prophet; instead, he is portrayed by the ancient authorities as a dedicated compiler of data concerning the life of Jesus from first and second-hand sources.

The writings of Papias become important in regard to a number of New Testament authorship and interpretive controversies. To more than briefly summarize key ones is impossible: Between 1960 and 1981 over 3,700 published articles and monographs plumbed the various individual issues that flow out of his surviving remarks[93] and came to a variety of often contradictory and mutually exclusive conclusions.

As to specific interpretive issues we can begin with three related to the apostle John: (1) Which John wrote the gospel? (2) Which John wrote the three epistles carrying that name? and (3) Which John wrote the Apocalypse? The apostle in all three cases? "John the elder" in all three examples? Or are the works somehow divided between the two different men? The strongest case for the elder/presbyter authorship obviously comes in regard to Second and Third John, because both epistles use that label to designate the author, although even that would not rule out the title's simply being an alternative manner of referring to the apostle.

In regard to the writing of the four gospels, Papias' remarks become battlegrounds as his references are invoked as to authorship of Matthew and Mark, the intent of the gospel writers, the original language (was Matthew in Hebrew—or does Papias really mean Aramaic?), and in regard to whether there was an earlier collection of "logia" (sayings) of Christ independent of the gospels we have today.

Some find him relevant to a major issue of textual integrity. In regard to the disputed genuineness of John 7:53–8:11 concerning the woman taken in adultery—one of the two long disputed texts in the New Testament (the other being Mark 16:9–20)—Papias refers to a woman guilty of *many* sins, which may or may not have any bearing on John 8, which singles out the single sin of adultery.[94] Eusebius throws in his own added obscurity: he mentions the fact that the incident about the many sins woman was also found in the "Gospel of the Hebrews."[95] Is this one of the canonical gospels or one that has vanished?

Although one may argue at length whether premillennialism has any genuine Biblical root (as recently as the 1950s the bulk of religious Christian conservatives would have denied it), it certainly represented an interpretation of the scriptural texts that enjoyed a significant appeal from an early date. Of the individuals who mentioned the idea during the second century, Papias is of special interest because premillennialism was a pivotal part of his religious beliefs. Indeed, some go so far as to argue that he may fairly be given credit as the person who first interpreted the Apocalypse as requiring a thousand year rule of Jesus on earth.[96]

What was this period to be like? Although Irenaeus does not explicitly refer the following to Papias' teaching about the earthly millennium it is hard to conceive what other period Papias could have had in mind[97]:

> The days will come in which vines shall grow, each having ten thousand branches, and on each branch ten thousand twigs, and on each true twig ten thousand shoots, and on every

one of the shoots ten thousand clusters, and on every one of the clusters ten thousand grapes, and every grape when pressed will give twenty-five measures of wine.

And when any one of the saints takes hold of any one of their clusters, another will cry out, "I am a better cluster, take me; bless the Lord through me."

In like manner, a grain of wheat would produce ten thousand ears, and every ear would have ten thousand grains, and every grain would yield ten pounds of clear, pure, fine flour; and apples and seeds and grass will produce in similar proportions; and all animals, feeding then only on all these products of the earth, will become peaceable and friendly to each other, and be in perfect subjection to man.

Even as hyperbolic exaggeration of an idealic and peaceful earth, the language seems excessive. Yet Papias presents this as the personal teaching of Jesus as Papias received it through others.[98]

Perhaps if more survived of Papias' works, it would be easier to make a fair judgment of his intellect and use of his resources. With what modest amounts survive, however, it seems reasonable to give him higher marks on good intentions than on strict accuracy. Eusebius, who had access to the works we lack, argued that "as is clear from his books, he was a man of very little intelligence."[99] Although many have taken this cynicism to grow out of Papias' embracing of an earthly millennium,[100] Eusebius speaks of "books" in general and not of one specific repugnant idea or misapprehension. Hence it seems far more likely that he viewed this as merely one of an alarming number of failures of perception upon Papias' part: Good intentions had not made up for a lack of interpretive astuteness.

Papias was not the only individual influenced by apocalyptic literalism. Not long afterwards Justin Martyr insisted, "But I, and others, who are right-minded Christians on all points, are assured that there will be a resurrection of the dead, and a thousand years in Jerusalem, which will then be built, adorned, and enlarged [as] the prophets Ezekiel and Isaiah and others declare...." This, he insisted, was rooted in the teachings of the man "whose name was John, one of the apostles of Christ, who prophesied by a revelation that was made to him, that those who believed in our Christ would dwell a thousand years in Jerusalem...."[101] The reference to how he is in agreement with "right-minded Christians on all points" sounds highly defensive, as if there were many who would *not* agree that they were either correct or "right-minded."

Others were emphatic in their repudiation of the concept. Bishop Dionysius went so far as to deny the apostolic origin of the Apocalypse (which still wouldn't necessarily deny that it had a non-apostolic prophetic authorship) but conceded that "many brethren were enthusiastic about it."[102] Origen dismissed such millennial enthusiasts as those "who refused to work intellectually, preferring to dream in joy and peace; interpreting scripture literally after the manner of the Jews."[103]

POLYCARP (69–c. 160)
Early Christian Martyr

Whether he was a native of the seacoast town of Smyrna in Turkey or had come there sometime in his youth is unknown.[104] At some point prior to Ignatius' letter to him in A.D. 110, he had risen to the post of its bishop. His adult life seems to have revolved exclusively around Smyrna except for limited travel elsewhere in connection with the office he came to occupy.

The so-called *Life of Polycarp* comes from a minimum of a century or more later and provides the story of how he had been adopted by a wealthy woman in response to a divine revelation. He grew into the post of her household steward and nearly destroyed its solvency through ultra-generosity to the poor. Bishop Bucolis took a liking to him and his clear talents. Under his guidance Polycamp was made deacon, then presbyter, and (on the bishop's deathbed) became his designated successor as bishop — a decision that the congregation enthusiastically backed. Although some have counted the narrative as largely reliable, the bulk of critics have concluded that any isolated tidbits of history cannot be separated from the unreliable sea in which they float.[105]

According to Irenaeus, Polycarp was a direct link back into the apostolic age and maintained a reputation for reliance on the apostolic tradition to his death, "Now Polycarp was not only taught by apostles and hung out with many who had seen the Lord, but he was also appointed bishop by apostles in Asia in the church of Smyrna. We even saw him in our early years, for he lived a long time and passed from this life in extreme old age, an honored and illustrious martyr. He always taught those things which he had also learned from the apostles, which are the traditions of the church, those things alone which are true."[106]

Most scholars are extremely cynical about the reliability of this testimony.[107] For one thing the plural "apostles" is far more unlikely than his meeting a single apostle. Also, the claim that he had received teaching from the "apostles" is linked with (implicitly) hearing details of Jesus' life — not from the apostles — but from "many who had seen the Lord." Should he not have said the apostles *and* these individuals since the apostles would have been the more authoritative source? Or is this a case of puffery in which Irenaeus really *means* (rather than says) that Polycarp had been taught by the apostles *through* the teaching he had received from the "many who had seen the Lord" and that his association with the apostles had been by this indirect method?

Although it is certainly not impossible that an apostle had appointed him to be a bishop (the plural "apostles" stands out like an illogical sore thumb at the date required), it should be remembered that the monarchical episcopate was nearly nonexistent at the time and that Polycarp (initially at least) would have been but one of several presbyters. Of course by the time Irenaeus wrote, Polycarp had successfully established superiority over the others. It is likely that the verbal linkage of the apostles and Polycarp is intended to "prove" that they had endorsed the newer system. Either Irenaeus preferred to gloss over the older arrangement of presbyterial equality as a passing stage or he assumed that since Polycarp *had* been apostolically ordained and since he *had* gained authority as bishop superior to the presbyters, that his very success in doing so argued for divine foreknowledge and approval of that step. (The issue is further complicated due to the difficulty in determining to what extent Polycarp actually claimed a personal organizational preeminence of the kind championed by his contemporary Ignatius and is itself a subject of lively debate.)[108]

The issue is further clouded because in Eusebius' *Church History* (also known as the

Ecclesiastical History, according to what translation one is utilizing) (V.20), there is a letter extract from Irenaeus on the same subject.[109] He refers to how Polycarp had learned from "John" and "the others who had seen the Lord." He conspicuously does *not* describe John as an apostle nor the "others" as such. So one has a version in which apostles (plural) were in contact with Polycarp at least briefly and one in which the implication can be either that the single apostle "John" was known by him or that an eyewitness by that name was in contact. The truth of the matter is that, though Irenaeus surely meant well, his memory has distorted one account or both. In the letter found in Eusebius, Irenaeus described himself as a "boy" at the time of meeting Polycarp, using a Greek term usually indicating someone just twelve years of age or less.[110]

At some point, Polycarp made a journey to Rome to meet with bishop Anicetus. Whatever other issues may or may not have been discussed, the one that was remembered was the question of the proper date for Easter. Polycarp supported following the Jewish calendar and observing the event on the 14th of Nisan regardless of which calendar day it occurred. (Anicetus wanted it to always be on a Sunday.) They both agreed to accept the propriety of either practice and not to insist on their own preference.[111]

Polycarp also had to deal with the Valentinian heresy during his life and, reading between the lines of Polycarp's letter to the Philippians, perhaps some form of the Montanist movement — or, at least, the theological assumptions later embodied in it.[112]

Ignatius' Letter to Polycarp

In his one personal letter on the way to Rome, Ignatius provides Polycarp with advice on the best administration of the congregation and the encouragement of believers in proper Christian values. Some find it significant that though Ignatius stresses the need to teach married couples to love each other, that the husbandly "headship" of the family is conspicuously missing. With a single exception in First Clement, it is noted that this teaching is totally absent in the "apostolic fathers" period and writings. Instead the language of leadership and authority is transferred from husbands toward wives to church leaders exercising authority over their congregations.[113]

It should be stressed, however, that this should not be permitted to carry the implicit baggage that the earlier family "power" relationships had been repudiated, for which there is no evidence. Instead we are faced with a clever and useful rhetorical tool that could be used by bishops in order to increase their own prestige and leadership prerogatives. Since the rhetoric of the traditional family "authority" relationships was long established, the more advocates of episcopate power could convince others to apply the same language to the people's relationship to the church, the greater the probability that they would actually be permitted to exercise the unilateral authority men such as Ignatius were demanding.

Of course, the new power was supposed to be utilized in a constructive and positive manner. In writing this letter, he repeatedly speaks of the need for a bishop to be like a medical doctor and be long-suffering and patient with those needing his spiritual ministrations. This has been taken as a not-so-subtle suggestion that Polycarp was known, at least upon too many occasions, to roll over opposition and impose his will arbitrarily and by coercion rather than by attempting to win the willing compliance of those under his authority.[114] Or, for that matter, it may even be an implicit self-criticism of Ignatius for not having learned the lesson earlier.

Polycarp's Letter to Philippi

The sole correspondence of Polycarp that has survived is his letter to Philippi. Some have postulated that this document is actually an amalgamation of two separate epistles: chapters 13 and 14, written first, and chapters 1 through 12, which were written two decades later. Although some scholars introduce alleged differences between the two sections, the main pillar of support comes from the fact that in chapter 13 Polycarp speaks of Ignatius as if he were still alive, while in nine he speaks of him as "with the Lord," i.e., dead. Barring an unexpected repudiation of his decades of faith, Polycarp could be certain that Ignatius was *going* to be executed (hence "with the Lord"—if not currently then in the very near future). while yet not knowing for certain whether it had yet occurred (hence the remarks as if he were still alive later in the epistle). The varying language likely conveys nothing more than the uncertainty as to Ignatius' exact fate as of the moment.[115]

Polycarp makes mention of how they were governed by "presbyters" and conspicuously does not suggest that they had adopted the monoepiscopate he practiced in Smyrna. Indeed, he does not utilize the term bishop to describe himself and rhetorically minimizes the difference by introducing the letter as from "Polycarp and the presbyters with him."[116] If the absence of a superior bishop over inferior presbyters was a temporary one, perhaps due to death—rather than the "superior" office being totally nonexistent—then some passing reference to the post and, perhaps, advice as to the type of individual to choose as a replacement, would have been expected.[117]

Polycarp's Martyrdom

Polycarp's death occurred sometime between 155 and 167.[118] Described in detail in the *Martyrdom of Polycarp,* the record originated as a letter sent from the Smyrnian church to a congregation in Phrygia. From these two cities it was spread far and wide. This is not surprising since it is the oldest surviving post–New Testament detailed account of the death of a martyr[119] and may, indeed, have been the very first. Furthermore, since Polycarp had served as bishop for more than forty years, the circumstances were inherently dramatic, and he was likely one of the last living individuals who could claim to personal knowledge of one of the original twelve apostles of Jesus (or at least His immediate disciples), there would be an inherent broad appeal in learning of the circumstances of his death. A miraculous element exists in the telling but is remarkably limited in comparison with some of the tales that sprang up of later victims of Roman anti–Christian repression.

Faced with arrest, Polycarp learned of the danger but declined to flee. After insistence from his compatriots, he finally agreed to do so and took refuge in a farmhouse where it was hoped he would remain undetected. One day he went into a trance while praying and saw the pillow he was using catch fire. He explained to those hiding him that this meant that he would ultimately have to undergo such a death by fire himself.

After reluctantly agreeing to move on to a new rural hiding place, the first one was raided and torture utilized to discover where he had gone. Fearing that their leader would be traced, his disciples implored him to change hiding places yet again. Enough was enough, he decided. Hearing his pursuers break in on the first floor, he went down and instructed that a meal be prepared for them. For himself he simply requested an hour for prayer before they left. No doubt feeling considerably embarrassed by his cooperativeness and great age, they concurred.

Presumably because of his bodily infirmities, they permitted him to utilize a donkey for transport into the city. The official in charge of ordering the arrest met him at the entrance and pleaded with him to offer his token worship to Caesar, but he firmly refused. Taken into the stadium, the hostile roar of the crowd seemed to drown out all competing noise, but an equally loud voice cried out, "Polycarp, play the man!" The proconsul demanded he recant and proclaim, "away with the atheists" (i.e., Christians who denied the existence of the polytheist gods). He did so, but with a wave to the audience, making *them* the "atheists" he wished to see vanish. Threatened with being torn apart by wild beasts, he refused to back down. Threatened with being burned alive, Polycarp warned that even a more deadly "fire" awaited those who did him harm. He insisted that if they were to do anything that they should get on with it.

Piles of wood were brought out to burn him and they prepared to nail him to an execution stake. He asked to be tied to it instead and they granted his request because he insisted that his God would give him the strength not to flee the flames. The flames seemed merely to darken his skin rather than burn them — an optical illusion or was the wood ill-arranged for this manner of death? A knife was then used to put him to death, but, it was claimed, the blood seemed to have put out the fire. Whatever exaggeration is here he was still quite dead, for a witness spoke of hearing a loud roar proclaiming that the crowd had got its wish: "Polycarp is martyred!"[120]

What happened next clearly reflects the quite tentative early stirrings of what one day became full-fledged martyr cults. After securing his bones, the Christians placed them in a "fitting" site (*Martyrdom,* 18:2). Annually they then began to gather on that day to celebrate what they called "his birthday" (18:3), presumably his "birth" into the eternal kingdom of heaven that they all sought. The annual gathering is described as "a commemoration of those who have fought the good fight in the past and as training and preparation for the coming generations" (18:3).[121] Note the plural "those": it was not yet centered exclusively on just the memory of the one man whose bones they had, but upon that of all who perished in behalf of their faith.

MELITO (flourished 160s–170s)
Second Century Apologist

The primary ancient source for Melito's life are the references to him in Eusebius' *Church History.* Although other ancient sources discuss him, what they say is often considered to be primarily deductions they made from information Eusebius provided.[122]

The year of his birth is pure guess work, though he seems to have been of Jewish ethnic heritage. Whether he came from a slave background or from an established family is unknown. He was described as a "eunuch" who, in spite of this, became bishop of Sardis and remained in that post till he died. The term "eunuch" has been interpreted by some, however, to simply mean that he was living celibate at a time when married bishops were still customary.[123] On the other hand, "eunuch" is an unusually strong term to use — standing alone as it does — if some less literal usage is intended.

Jerome quotes Tertullian as referring to Melito's "ingenuity" and "elegance," which argues for a man of considerable intelligence — perhaps inherent, or, more probably, enhanced by a decent education.[124] The description certainly argues that he did his best to fully develop his intellectual ability.

A Christian by the name of Onesimus sought from him a collection of proof text passages "from both the law and the prophets concerning the Savior and our faith," something which obviously had major apologetic usefulness. He also wished to have a list of all the books belonging to the Old Testament.[125] The subject of differences between Diaspora Judaism and Palestinian Judaism of the era is a vexed one, though virtually all scholars would concede that there were significant variations in emphasis and behavior between the two regions. The desire for an accepted canonical list in Sardis (and its local unavailability) would seemingly argue that there was no absolute consensus in the Jewish community of the city that the Christian community could rely on so that their arguments could not be dismissed as coming from noncanonical sources — possibly even that there was disagreement among the Christians themselves as to the exact extent of that canon.

Whatever the cause of the lack of a canon and collection of proof texts, Melito was determined to provide them. Hence he journeyed "back to the east and reaching the place where it was proclaimed and done [i.e., Palestine] I got precise information about the books of the Old Covenant."[126] As to the proof text collection, he used the text of the canonical books as recognized in Palestine to compile it: "From these I have also made the extracts, dividing them into six books."[127] Interestingly, he does not take over a preexisting compilation, which likely indicates that even in Palestine itself this was either literally the first effort to prepare such a work or one of the very first. Certainly it is the first explicit mention of an individual compiling such a collection.[128]

To defend the faith before polytheists, he addressed an *Apology* to Marcus Aurelius. This was likely composed somewhere between 169 and 177. It represented considerable intellectual sophistication and has been viewed as manifesting a clear knowledge of stoic ways of thinking.[129] His character assault on existing contemporary Judaism, however, has eclipsed these other achievements.

Savaging Traditional Judaism

The standard dating for Melito's *Peri Pascha (Homily on the Passover)* is sometime during the 160s. It was not until the nineteenth century that major fragments were discovered of this work, and 1940 when a nearly complete text finally appeared. The work is one of the most venomous assaults on Judaism of the period. Indeed, one has to go to the period of Constantine and beyond before there is anything more intense.[130]

In one place Melito writes (in a theme that he goes to repeatedly), "Thou didst bind the beautiful hands with which he shaped thee from the earth; and his beautiful mouth, the mouth that fed thee with life, thou hast fed with gall, and thou hast slain the Lord in the great feast." By killing Jesus, man's creator had Himself been killed. Or as Melito says in another place, "God has been murdered, the King of Israel has been slain by an Israelitish hand!"[131]

Hence he is the first to speak not just of Jews murdering Jesus but of defining this as also murdering *God,* i.e., deicide.[132] As a rhetorical tool to bloody one's foe this was surely quite useful; to the degree to which the language ultimately began to be taken literally it unleashed its own demonic forces into the world to justify bloody repression and even extermination. At the time, such would have been regarded as fantasy; unfortunately some fantasies become reality.

The reason for this venom is usually considered to lie in the fact that the church in his community was weak numerically and in influence, while the traditional Jewish community, unlike so many other places, enjoyed an influential and well-established reputation in the Gentile community.[133] In short, in any conflict, the Christians were far more likely to come up on the losing side and the very respectability and acceptance by their foes may well have encouraged the dominant monotheist group to utilize such influence far more freely than in cities where their own favorable reception was far more marginal.

Miriam S. Taylor rejects this popular analysis of Melito's psychological motivation. She effectively argues that the roughly contemporary Theophilus of Antioch was faced with an equally impressive influential local Jewish community but did not react with the stringent rhetoric Melito utilizes.[134] This may only argue, however, that local circumstances and individual personalities are equally pivotal in determining how a minority group reacts to a more influential segment of the population. That, in part, also hinges upon how that more significant group uses its power and how it is perceived as using it (which are not always the same or even fairly based).

Other factors could well have played a supportive role in inflaming the language of Melito. Some have speculated, for example, that with his own apparent Jewish background and his insistence that Easter retain its chronological linkage with the Jewish observance of Passover — not to mention possible other "Jewish" influences ethnically or theologically within his congregation — that these cumulatively resulted in both him and his flock being viewed as far too "Jewishly influenced" for most Gentile Christians to be comfortable with. Hence the criticism he levels would also represent an effort to prove the orthodoxy of himself and his Christian community by pouring out disproportionate venom on their traditionalist foes.[135]

Theological concepts do not remain static — they evolve and encourage or discourage alternative ways of thought. Hence if the killing of the man Jesus could be considered "the murder of God," it should not be surprising if the mother of the boy Jesus could similarly be transformed into "the mother of God." To the extent that either of these rhetorical descriptions gained popularity, it encouraged the adoption of the other since

BISHOP VICTOR OF ROME (c. 190)
Advocate of Roman Supremacy over Regional Church Practices

Although the Roman bishop enjoyed prestige beginning much earlier, only as we enter the late second century do we find him demanding that his decisions be accepted as authoritative and binding even in other regions of the world and in defiance of local preference and precedent and custom. The issue of the correct (or, at least, best) date for Easter had arisen before. About 155–160 Polycarp of Smyrna had traveled to Rome and the current bishop of the city had agreed not to demand uniformity of practice. Whether this was done out of respect for rival customs, personal regard for Polycarp, or the lack of perceived power to make any regulation prevail in other parts of the empire, such moderation now came under attack by Bishop Victor.

Polycrates of Ephesus is considered the leader of the easterners favoring calculating Easter on the same Jewish calendar as that in use in Jesus' day (maintaining its original chronological connection), even when that resulted in the resurrection being remembered on a day other than that which the gospels record it as having happened (the first day of the week, Sunday). Whether he was recognized by easterners as leader is unknown, but the fact that he wrote Victor of Rome on behalf of a regional synod that upheld the linkage caused his name to be irrevocably linked to its advocatacy so far as western Christianity was concerned. To the eastern believers, however, the Roman custom was an external western regional deviation.[136]

The church historian Socrates noted that these advocates claimed that they had inherited their doctrine from the apostle John; those who followed the Roman custom insisted *their* doctrine also had an apostolic linkage, in this case Peter and Paul. (To find anything in the New Testament suggesting that there was an annual memorial at all requires a very creative mind. The custom spoken of there is of a weekly remembrance through the communion rather than a yearly one (Acts 20:7; 1 Corinthians 10:18–26; 16:1–4). Socrates hit on the core problem both sides faced: "Neither of these parties, however, can produce any written testimony in confirmation of what they assert."[137]

Eusebius speaks of how Victor responded with an excommunication of all those who adopted this "Quartodeciman" view, as it was called. In spite of this, there is widespread suspicion that Victor never went beyond anger and planning for such an act into actually carrying it out. Certainly Eusebius speaks of how church moderates pled with Victor to back off from this retribution, but Eusebius gives no indication that they were successful. Even Irenaeus—a man whose very name is virtually synonymous with heresy hunting—pled for Victor to restrain his repressive intention.[138]

In behalf of the scenario that a tacit understanding was reached, one can introduce the words of the later church historian Sozomen, who speaks of how "they unanimously agreed [which sounds more like a church council or de facto consensus than a backing down by Victor] to continue in the observance of the festival according to their respective customs, without separation from communion with each other."[139] The fact that Sozomen misidentifies the conflict as between Victor and Polycarp argues that he has confused the earlier controversy that *was* amicably resolved with the one where Victor insisted upon having his way. In fact, in pleading for restraint, Irenaeus introduced this earlier conflict as the model that should be followed.[140]

Hence it seems best to conclude that Victor did act against his foes to the extent that was practical and that any retreat was due to inability to enforce his edict rather than any moderation in stance. And that may have been over a far wider area that he at first realized. He discovered that not even everyone locally yielded to his demand. One Blastus openly formed a congregation of dissenters that refused to comply.[141] If Victor couldn't compel full uniformity locally, it was hardly likely that his demands would meet a friendlier reception in the east, where resistance would have been even deeper and backed by the power of traditional practice — and that of well established church leaders.

This leaves us with the question of why Victor chose the path of confrontation and at least attempted to act forcefully and unilaterally. Though it is hard to avoid the conclusion that there was more than a little ecclesiastical power-building in his action,[142] some prefer the more positive interpretation that he acted out of a sense of the responsibility of his office.[143] It had certainly become clear that he was not going to get voluntary compliance with his wishes: synods had met in four places in the east and none of them had adopted his stance on the date for Easter.[144] Surrender, compromise, or compel? He chose the last.

Other factors may have come into play to motivate action, of course. Rome was an international city, with people regularly coming to it from throughout the known world. It is quite likely that there were those already present in the city who insisted on following the eastern rather than the local custom. Hence Victor could well have been responding, in part, to a rival tradition existing on his home ground. The fact that it was a competing custom would have been annoying enough; if it was growing in popularity he may have felt even more defensive and felt compelled to act forcefully to maintain the local norm.

Yet there is another possibility that has been suggested to explain his behavior: That the observance of an annual memorial of Jesus' resurrection in Rome was a relatively recent phenomenon and that Victor was hypersensitive because of that. Approached this way, it can be argued that the earlier disagreement between Anicetus and Polycarp was the one that centered on this issue — one of observance (Polycarp) versus nonobservance (Anicetus). In the intervening years, however, Easter had come to be practiced in Rome as well. In this reconstruction, it is argued, one can best explain Irenaeus' insistence to Victor that the current controversy was far less significant than the earlier one: If even whether to observe Easter or not was one that could be amicably resolved, why draw a line over the specific date?[145]

However one reads this aspect of the issue, the question of episcopate power — and that of the Roman bishop in particular — remained pivotal. Francis A. Sullivan, in his study of the development of the episcopate, rightly notes the significance of Victor's stance: he was claiming that there had to be "not only agreement in faith but uniformity in *practice* as well" with that recognized by the bishop of Rome.[146]

Having claimed a universal jurisdiction, the bishop of Rome never repudiated it,[147] though that does not mean that it was consistently insisted upon over every issue. What made it possible to establish the expansion of authority was the fact that, by and large, matters were "permitted" to continue in accordance with local custom, with the "veto" power existing primarily in theory rather than practice. Only when and if Rome chose to do battle did confrontation become inescapable and, with each Roman victory, the precedent for Roman supremacy on the *next* contentious question became that much more probable.

IRENAEUS, BISHOP OF LYONS (died c. 200)
Critic of Unorthodoxy

Irenaeus was born prior to c. A.D. 150 (estimates have run the gamut from 98 to 147), and the general assumption is that he was a native either of Smyrna in modern-day Turkey (where Polycarp was bishop and whom he knew briefly while very young) or of nearby Asia Minor. His fluency in Greek argues for having enjoyed some type of advanced education.[148] At an unknown date, he literally moved to the other end of the Roman Empire, taking his religious interests to what is today Lyons, France.

In Lyons, he was appointed presbyter and in 177 charged with the responsibility of carrying a congregational letter concerning Montanism to Rome. He returned to find his adopted city without a bishop and with a significant number of the church having perished in the persecution while he was away. Recognizing his talents, the survivors promptly selected him as the replacement bishop and he remained in Lyons for the remainder of his life. The proviso should be added that though the letter he carried to Rome refers to him as a presbyter, neither he nor any other contemporary document refers to his becoming a bishop,[149] so his assumption of superior authority in Lyons could well have been more de facto rather than de jure.

He was a pivotal figure in publicly opposing both Marcion and the Gnostic movement. His was not a mere intellectual interest in opposing what he regarded as blatant error; there were advocates of such approaches in the nearby region and opposing their principles was a means of dealing with them before they became a serious local problem for him and the church.[150]

Jerome refers to his dying c. 202 as a martyr, but since an earlier and more detailed biographical account Jerome had written of him omits this, the claim has left many unconvinced.[151] Although it would provide a particularly dramatic ending to his life, the fact that he was able to carry a letter to Rome during a persecution should remind us that most Christians at this time were able to escape governmental wrath even when their specific church was under assault. If there was a violent end for him, it could just as easily have been due to his being one of those who died or were killed during the conquest of Septimus Severus, who defeated his rival for the imperial office in 197. Lyons was sacked afterwards and the previously flourishing city went into abrupt decline.[152]

Irenaeus' letters and most of his writings have vanished. Only in the modern era was an Armenian translation discovered of his *Demonstration (Proof) of Apostolic Teaching.* The first section of this is a sketch of history from the creation of Adam to the ministry of Jesus. The second introduces various prophecies about Jesus and explains how they found their fulfillment within the confines of His life.[153] Irenaeus' most well known work was his extensive *Against the Heresies,* a work that so impressed later scholars and theologians that they often quoted from it, thereby preserving much of the Greek form of a work preserved in its entirety only in a later Latin translation.[154]

His writings are the first where we can document a shift in the nature of the source for scriptural citations: While earlier writers quoted the Old Testament on a regular basis, quotations (rather than allusions) are found from the gospels and New Testament epistles only on an occasional basis. With Irenaeus, not only is the New Testament quoted some 1,000 times, it is quoted twice as often as the Old Testament.[155]

In spite of its broader title, *Against the Heresies* is actually a sustained history and rebuttal of Gnosticism in its various forms. The historical comments provided the only detailed account of these movements and their theology until Gnostic source documents were discovered after World War II.[156]

It is uncertain whether the *Heresies* volume was simply a gradual accumulation (and revision) of notes over a period of years or whether Irenaeus worked from a basic conceptual outline from the inception of the project. Certainly the work is loosely organized, as if the author was far more interested in laying the case out than in organizing it in a carefully planned manner. As a result, it shifts from description to refutation and varies the type of argument used in an inconsistent manner. Irenaeus will write at length on one theme or another and then hammer together a transitional section to join it roughly with his next subject.[157] How much of his argument is original and how much is actually an adaptation and, perhaps, polishing and improvement of arguments of others is uncertain,[158] though his passion to throw every conceivable argument against the heretics would argue that he freely utilized earlier resources to the extent that they were available.

To him all heresies are interlocked, with their origin in Simon Magus, the Samaritan magician described in the book of Acts. He accomplishes this by pointing out one or more points of alleged similar teaching between various repudiated groups and Simon Magus' alleged teaching.[159] In some cases he does not make the effort at all, suggesting that even for Irenaeus' creative mind the case for conceptual linkages would have been difficult to make. Even assuming that he had any real idea of what his prototype heretic had really taught — rather than his name simply being a convenient theological dumping ground used to encompass later heretical ideas — dissimilarities in development of those "shared" concepts would be equally important in evaluating whether there were meaningful historical and theological connections. In the modern world, it would rather be like taking the similarities between Presbyterians and Baptists in America and arguing that the refutation of one of these group's beliefs *a century earlier* refuted those of both today.

Even so, he was convinced that by refuting even one heresy he had, effectively, overthrown all later ones. In regard to Valentinus, for example, he wrote, "Since those who are of the school of Valentinus have been refuted, the whole multitude of heretics are in fact also overthrown."[160] Of course this logic only works if the doctrinal beliefs were, overall, the same in substance rather than having mainly superficial resemblances.

PERPETUA AND FELICITY (died 203)
Visionaries and Martyrs

The *Passion of Perpetua and Felicity* is the autobiographical account of Perpetua of Carthage and is the earliest surviving Christian work to have been penned by a woman under her own name.[161] The insight into the nature of martyrdom and the pressures that accompanied the preliminaries to death are especially significant because, unlike so many other ancient accounts of such individuals, this is not a fictitious embellishment loosely based upon what little was known of the death of an individual, but came (at least in significant part) from one of those who was executed and was supplemented by the firsthand account of the deaths.[162]

The language is direct and to the point. There is no attempt to be "literary" in either the narrative of what happens to her or in the four visions she narrates. Although later church writers of the early centuries provide detailed allegorical applications of the language — the ladder she sees becomes "Jacob's ladder" of the Old Testament and the shepherd becomes the "Good Shepherd" of Jesus' parables — there is nothing in the text to suggest that such concepts were present in her consciousness. To her it was simply the record of what she was seeing and enduring.[163] Indeed, some have argued that, to whatever extent these images were conjured up on the basis of her past learning, her discipleship was at such an early stage that the *pagan* use of such imagery as ladder and shepherd would have been even more in her mind than any distinctly Christian application.[164]

That material was added to the narrative is clear and how much of the text actually goes back to Perpetua has been the subject of great debate. Although generally accepted as essentially originating with her in both the ancient and medieval church, there were a few (overlooked) doubters. Augustine leaves the question open: he cites from the *Passion* on a doctrinal issue and notes that the work "is not itself a canonical writing, whether she herself wrote it or whether anyone else wrote it."[165] The generally scholarly evaluation is that the alleged firsthand narrative (either totally or mainly) does, indeed, reach back to the martyr herself.[166] Even if someone else actually composed even the "autobiographical" section, the repeated access that church members had to her would have provided abundant opportunity for a detailed account to have been passed on and for someone else to have had more than adequate accurate data from which to compose the work.

The arrest and persecution of these two young Roman women occurred in Carthage in North Africa about 202 or 203. At the time, Carthage was one of the major urban centers of the Empire, with a population around 400,000.[167] Perpetua and a brother were converted to Christianity though the reasons and motivations are not spelled out. Certainly she lived in an age when political affairs had become unsettled, most emperors died by violence rather than of natural causes, and the military dominated the government, a time in which it would be less than human not to seek out psychological comfort that neither personal prosperity nor position could any longer adequately provide.[168]

Contrary to the image of the ideal or heroic female believer that had begun to be popular, Perpetua stands out by virtue of *not* being ascetic. She was, instead, an example of the typical adult woman of the period: married and with children.[169] Whether Perpetua married before or after the conversion is unknown but the marriage resulted in the birth of a child who was two years old at the time persecution disrupted her life.

Arrested with her was the slave Felicity (hence the inclusion of her name in the title of the narrative) as well as at least five other believers. Felicity (because a slave) could not legally be married, but was pregnant at the time of the incarceration. Since there is nothing critical of her on this score and since she is pictured as a person attempting to be a faithful Christian, it seems best to assume that she was in a standing relationship somewhat analogous to common law marriage in twentieth century America. (The possibility of being a forced concubine of her owner, of course, can't be ruled out.)

Technically, at this time Perpetua was only a "catechumen" (one receiving instruction prior to baptism) but emperor Septimius Severus issued an order in 202 prohibiting conversion and this was interpreted as applying to those at this step in the process of conversion as well as to those having completed it.[170]

Somehow her brother escaped arrest for unknown reasons and by unknown means. By and large most senior church leaders were likewise spared seizure, both here and in contemporary persecutions in Alexandria, Corinth, and Rome.[171] Instead, the targets were usually those who were recent converts or intending to become such. Quite possibly they were regarded as the weakest element in the church and most vulnerable to coercion, while those with an established record as long-term believers were considered far less so. Also the hope may have been that by halting new additions, the church would die a slow death as its older members were not replaced by a new generation.

Hurriedly baptized after their arrest, the prison conditions were miserable, but bribery resulted in at least some necessities being brought in to them. Her two-year-old child was still nursing and the jailers permitted her to temporarily tend him before returning him to her family. Later they relented and permitted the child to return to the prison to stay a second time, but the conditions under which she lived broke Perpetua's health.

Her slave Felicity was well along in her pregnancy at the time and bore a girl while imprisoned. If the imprisonment and threat of death were not enough to break her heart, the emotional anguish was that much worse as she needed to pass the baby on to a fellow church member so the baby could survive her death.

Perpetua faced her own anguish due to her own offspring as well. Her father viciously assaulted her verbally for her conversion. Genuine anger or humiliation of being socially "stained" by her actions? Perhaps both were involved. Appearing for judgment before the governor, he even held the baby out to her and pleaded for both his sake and the child's that she offer the required sacrifice. She refused. (Oddly enough, her husband is totally absent from the work. Equally strangely, his support or animosity does not even merit a mention.)

Her faith was reinforced by several factors during these trying days. For one thing she had access to her child and for another she had repeated visits by church members and her converted brother. Furthermore, there seemed to be a "supernatural" reassurance from four visions she had, including one the night before her death at the hands of wild beasts. (Others would see her psyche conjuring up inner support for her via her visions.)[172]

In one vision, she saw herself facing death and then climbing a bronze ladder to heaven and seeing what the long-promised world would be like[173]:

> And I went up, and I saw a very great space of garden, and in the midst a man sitting, white-headed, in shepherd's clothing, tall, milking his sheep; and standing around in white were many thousands. And he raised his head and beheld me and said to me: Welcome, child. And he cried to me, and from the curd he had from the milk he gave me as it were a morsel; and I took it with joined hands and ate it up; and all that stood around said, "Amen."

Her fellow prisoner, Saturus, also provided an account — more fully developed — of the beauty and glory of the next life that awaited them (11–13). Although we have called each of these, accounts *visions* (for that is the normal nomenclature), more properly they are *dreams* or *dream-visions*. At the end of Perpetua's vision above, "at the sound of that word I awoke" (4), after two dream-visions concerning a brother she is self-described again as one who "awoke" afterwards (7, 8), and after one in which she becomes a gladiator and defeats her foe she again "awoke" (10). Saturus also saw a vision of the next life and afterwards; "then in joy I awoke" (13). However we describe them, to those who underwent the experience they were clearly the voice of God and vastly reassured them as they awaited their fate.

When that day came, Perpetua entered the arena and steadfastly stared at the crowds without casting her look away in embarrassment or shame. On the symbolic level, this conveyed both her resolve conviction and her lack of being cowed into terror. This was the kind of self-assuredness that the onlookers were well acquainted with among gladiators.[174]

The governor selected a mad cow as the instrument to stomp and injure the two of them as they were women. Since its attack was unsuccessful, Perpetua literally uncovered her neck for the executioner so he could have an unimpeded visible access — also a symbolic act, one expressing both her own willingness to die and also the kind of bravery gladiators were expected to manifest when facing death, both of which would certainly have been understood by onlookers.[175]

Five died that day. At least one soldier involved as a guard in carrying out the deaths was converted as well as some of the others who witnessed what happened. Not for the first time nor for the last had bravery in facing unjust death resulted in new converts to take the place of those who perished.

Impact of the Account

The event and its account made a vast impact upon Christians of the era. During Constantine's reign, the anniversary of her death was remembered annually in Rome. In the 300s a church was built in her honor in Carthage. Augustine preached repeated sermons on her death and utilized the record of it that has survived.[176]

In spite of these early indications of importance, the work later faded into lesser significance. The fact that Perpetua engages in repeated bouts of prophecy opens her to the accusation of being Montanist in sentiment,[177] an accusation that would drastically undermine the document's acceptability at a later date.

If, as some suspect, it was Tertullian who prepared the final text of the work, his own Montanist participation would have further increased the suspicion of the propriety of either using or, at the minimum, *encouraging* the use of the work.[178] The most powerful argument against his having had any significant influence is that the language used and the style is distinctly different from that of his own.[179] If he worked on the *Passion* at all, it was with an unusually light and restrained touch.

CLEMENT OF ALEXANDRIA (c. 150–c. 215)
Lecturer on Christian Faith

Born around 150, Clement utilized Alexandrian sources and philosophical attitudes as well as the allegorical method that was so popular there. These factors make it more likely than not that he was a native of that city, though some even in the ancient world thought he had been born and raised in Athens. Unquestionably he did not limit himself to Alexandria and was engaged in wide travels during his educational years and rubbed elbows with a cross section of the scholarly elite of the time. Unfortunately, he omits ever identifying exactly who these individuals had been.[180]

Clement eventually became interested in Christianity though a means and manner unknown. The fact that Clement wrote of how conversion made him feel young again argues that he was middle-aged by the time it occurred.[181] He appears to have come under the influence of Pantaenus, a philosopher and then head of the catechetical instruction program in Alexandria, Egypt. (Whether there was a *formal* catechetical school at this time has been questioned and what we may actually be speaking of is a far more informal system. By the time of Origen it certainly had evolved into a fully developed system, however.)[182]

When Pantaenus died in 200, Clement was so well respected that he soon was designated his instructor's replacement. His service in the post ended abruptly in 203 when a wave of severe persecution broke out. To survive, he fled to Cappadocia and remained there until he died about a decade later. Even away from Alexandria he remained active in the religious education of fellow Christians. Alexander of Cappadocia was serving as bishop in Caesarea and he wrote of how Clement was contributing greatly to the growth of the church in his own city by his role in such endeavors.[183]

He was not only interested in scripture, he was quite interested in philosophy as well. Although many other early churchmen were skeptical or even hostile to philosophy, Clement was convinced that if one properly applied its tenets, that one's insight into Christian truths would be usefully deepened.[184]

He was also out of step with contemporary trends in other areas as well. For example he was quite firm in his praise of marriage and his view that celibacy was definitely inferior to it. Likewise, he regarded the communion as a "memorial" of the crucified Jesus rather than a "sacrifice" being reenacted.[185]

Of most concern was his possible flirtation with quasi-gnosticism. His affection for their style language made him potentially suspect, but the clear endorsement of Eusebius in his *Church History* gave Clement sufficient prestige to assure his being counted on the orthodox side of the religious spectrum.[186]

Of ten works of his that Eusebius lists,[187] two minor ones and three major works have survived the passage of time and anti–Christian persecution. In his *Exhortation to the Greeks* he vigorously critiques the mythological stories that were at the root of contemporary polytheism. In the *Tutor (Paedagogus)*, he provides a kind of introductory guide to Christian living for converts. In the first part he stresses the nature and fruit of love. In the remainder he deals with what it should mean in behavior and attitude to live as a believer in his age.[188]

In the *Stromata* he weaves together a discussion of various specific themes that were loosely connected to each other. Hence the title that literally means "carpets," the rhetorical "weaving" allusion being one applied to various other works of this type in his era.[189] He introduces the work by a defense of circulating a written discussion on the subjects he examines. Late in the third century Plotinus dismissed the teacher who used the written word as typically inferior to those who did not. Presumably this bias in favor of the spoken word as the sole ideal means of teaching had long been a factor in Alexandrian education and Clement is reacting, at least in part, to this assumption.[190]

He presents his teaching as that of the third generation of Christians: the apostles had instructed his teachers and, through them, he had learned the spiritual insights that they had shared with both the public at large and the spiritually advanced — truths that were not contradictory but supplemental in nature.[191] By this late in the second century it would seem more likely that one would be speaking, at the minimum, in terms of being a *fourth* generation Christian; the attempt to lessen the chronological gap between Jesus and his age was presumably to enhance the authoritativeness and reliability of his teaching.

So far as Clement was concerned, the knowledge level for outsiders and even new converts should be kept at a minimum. Even when one could answer a question more fully, it was better to be obscure "so that the discovery of the sacred traditions may not be easy to any of the uninitiated."[192] In a very real sense a kind of "mystery religion" mentality was being cultivated in which only the fully initiated were deemed qualified and acceptable to have a full knowledge of the Christian religious system.

It appears that Clement prepared commentary style discussions on various selected texts, but these have not survived. In the ninth century Photius critiqued them for being extremely allegorical and for presenting imaginative exegesis that had no real root in the wording being commented upon.[193] This certainly fits Clement's approach in the *Stromata* and the known preferences in Alexandria for symbolic interpretations over literal ones, though some have stressed that in actual practice early exponents of both views recognized the usefulness of the other alternative.[194] In Clement's practice, the allegorical application was clearly considered far more important and it usually involved working the Christ-church relationship into texts that had nothing obviously requiring or implying such a reference.[195]

As an example of his interpretive approach, he wrote in regard to the Jewish temple, "Now, connected with the concealment is the special meaning of what is told among the Hebrews about the seven circuits around the old temple, and also the equipment on the robe [of the high priest], whose multicolored symbols allude to celestial phenomena, which indicate the agreement from heaven down to earth."[196] The Christological aspect is of even greater importance: "the robe prophesied the ministry in the flesh by which he was made visible to the world directly."[197] To us such claims may seem fanciful at the most generous; to Clement (and many others) it manifested spiritual insight.

Chapter 2

Faith and Imperial Government

CONSTANTINE THE GREAT (died 337)
Shaper of Orthodox Faith through Imperial Power

To make the needs of administering a major empire more practical the emperor Diocletian decided to divide power between four regional leaders. The theory was that they were all *inter*dependent rather than *in*dependent, ultimate precedence among the four still being in the hands of Diocletian himself. Going into voluntary retirement (likely motivated by a lengthy illness), Diocletian forced Maximian to do so as well.

In the new arrangement, Constantine's father now held the rank of one of the four emperors. At that point he successfully sought agreement from Galerius, the Eastern Emperor, to let his son return to the west. Reluctant permission was granted and Constantine joined his father in Britain. When his father died in October 306, the troops immediately embraced him as both leader and Caesar. Wisely Constantine postponed any immediate action to widen his personal scope of power as rival claimants for leadership busied themselves seizing control in various places and warring with their closest rivals.

When it became clear in 311 and 312 that the would-be Caesar in Rome, Maxentius, was determined on a policy of no compromise with him, Constantine acted boldly to seize the initiative. Although he had an army outmanned at least two to one (100,000 versus 190,000) and quite possibly far more than that, he marched into Italy during the spring of 312 and defeated two major opposing armies by skill and daring. Then, at Rome itself, he defeated the forces that were directly under Maxentius.

Constantine did this under the claimed conviction that he had seen a vision that assured him it was the God of the Christians who would give him his victory (see following section). Considering the great dangers he had faced, he showed remarkable restraint in dealing with those who had supported Maxentius and avoided the massive retaliation that could easily have been expected both out of personal anger and as a "prudential" means to avoid potential challengers. He reached an accommodation with Augustus Licinius, who received Constantine's sister as wife to seal the pact and who agreed to grant Christians freedom of worship in the East. Presumably out of respect for

Diocletian's tetrarch concept for the empire (i.e., rule by four individuals) and because Licinius was the only one of the original four still alive (thereby creating at least a paper link with the legalities of the past), Constantine had good reason to preserve the peace with this coruler.

Ultimately viewing Licinius as having betrayed their relationship, however, Constantine moved against him in 316. Though the first resulting battle was a clear win for Constantine, the second forced both sides to recognize that it was in neither's interest to continue the conflict if an agreement could be reached. Licinius, however, paid the greater price by forfeiting most of his European territory to Constantine.

This time the peace lasted until approximately 322, when Licinius went out of his way to anger Constantine. Included in the new policies was a vigorous persecution of Christianity, an escalation of his earlier steps to curb their religious rights and liberties.[1] Constantine's pride probably interpreted — and rightly so — Licinius' suppression as a way of indirectly insulting him by striking out at his rival's preferred religion. From the standpoint of Licinius, these people were likely considered a potential "fifth-column" whose loyalty could not be trusted.[2]

The two armies that collided at Adrianople in July 324 were both large, with a significant but not necessarily decisive edge in Licinius' hands. In spite of being at a numerical disadvantage, Constantine's troops routed those of his opponent. Licinius reacted by so buttressing the Byzantium garrison that it became clear that the only way to take it would be by wearing it down through a prolonged land and naval siege. A naval engagement at one end of the Dardanelles was indecisive, but Constantine's forces retreated and rejoined the rest of his navy. Sensing opportunity, the Licinian naval forces attempted to overtake the enemy and bring them to combat. Unfortunately for them, a fierce storm intervened and they lost a large percentage of their ships.

Leaving behind a besieging force at Byzantium, Constantine pursued the retreating Licinius and decisively defeated him. Inflicting 25,000 casualties, the bulk of Licinius' remaining forces fled. Surrendering, Licinius was granted his life but a year later he made a new thrust for leadership and was executed in retaliation.

With Licinius out of the way, all power was now once again in the hands of a single ruler. Constantine made the policy decision to move his capital to Constantinople and spent the following decade building up its physical and economic assets to befit that new role.

The Persian king Shapur decided to challenge Constantine and the Roman mobilized his own resources to deal with the threat. Before he was ready to lead his army out, illness struck him and death ensued in May 337. It was only during this ultimately fatal illness that he was actually baptized.

The Claimed Dream-Vision and How It Has Been Interpreted

As was his custom before beginning a great endeavor or undertaking a potentially risky course, Constantine sought to invoke the deities to provide him with forewarning of the future. The pagan haruspices were unanimous: If he marched against Maxentius (see previous section) he would bring upon himself a disaster. It was the Christians' deity that assured him the opposite would be the case and this brought about his conversion.

There are two basic accounts of how this came about. In the first he had a dream involving the symbol of Christ. The second was that he had a vision and saw the cross in the sky. Some prefer one version, some the other; yet others believe that some form of both events occurred (though differing as to the order) and that one phenomenon worked to strengthen the motivation provided by the other. Those seeking a physical explanation can find at least a partial one for the day and time of the event. The "halo phenomenon" can result in a cross-like image forming from the sun. As to vision-dreams, these were in keeping with a "real" but subjective origin. In his own earlier life there had been a polytheist dream about the future which had warned him of an alleged plot against his life. For that matter even Tertullian speaks of how common (be they good or bad) such events were, "It is to dreams that the majority of humankind owe their knowledge of God."[3]

As the result of the events, the symbol of the two overlapping letters X and P that stood for Christ (*Chi-Rho*) was ordered placed on the standards of his army, though the practical exigencies of the moment may have limited how widespread that was immediately done. To the army, the act simply meant that the emperor supported the deity it symbolized and that it was right and proper to pray to that God for support for their leader. This in no way required a change in their own private religious allegiances.[4] Furthermore, in a traditional polytheist and secular context, the two letters had been used as a contraction for the Greek word for "good" and the sign denoted texts of special value to the reader. Hence it could be used without any exclusively Christian connotation, a not inappropriate caution in an empire still predominantly polytheistic.[5]

Having gained new confidence, Constantine successfully defeated his foe and collected the power into his own hands. Reflecting upon his victory and his vision afterwards he was convinced that he had not just seen a cross but the very *words* on it: *hoc vinces* ("in this sign wilt you conquer"). He erected a statue of himself and on the pedestal had the words inscribed, "By the aid of this salutary token of strength I have freed my city from the yoke of tyranny and restored to the Roman Senate and People the ancient splendor and glory."[6]

Toleration and Encouragement of Christianity

When imperial power (except that exercised by Licinius) had been consolidated in his hands, Constantine unilaterally decreed that Christians should be tolerated. As part of a meeting with Licinius in 313, they jointly issued the Edict of Milan, which extended that toleration to the entire Empire. This did not revoke the rights of rival systems; it simply extended to the Christians the rights that others already enjoyed. The language used of the divine was broad enough to cover all systems of religious belief. This made great sense because the goal was to heal divisions that might divide the empire (and hence contribute to its diminishment or collapse) rather than to create new excuses for internal turmoil.

If the toleration decision seemed a tremendous blessing, the idea of a Caesar being a Christian had to be even more challenging. Tertullian spoke of how inconceivable such an idea was: "the Caesars too would have believed on Christ, if either the Caesars had not been necessary for the world, or if Christians could have been Caesars."[7] To him, the two ideas of supreme leadership and being a disciple were incompatible. (Those skeptical of the actions taken by the state in the following centuries might well feel similarly, as probably did the intra-church victims of various "Christianified" emperors.)

Constantine also took steps that directly benefited the church and its leadership. In about 313, for example, he granted church office holders exemption from paying taxes. He was even willing to tolerate some very *un*–Roman practices that were becoming popular in the church. Celibacy had been the subject of legal penalties all the way back to the days of Augustus. Under Constantine, the law was removed from the books.[8]

If he benefited the church, certain influential personalities within it began to have a major influence on him as well. Bishop Ossius of Cordova in particular became one of his most respected advisers.[9] The old adage "you become like the people you like being around" has more than a little validity. Certainly they are in a position to bring the greatest influence to bear upon the individual and in this case the individual was not a mere common citizen but the emperor himself. In encouraging regal intervention in behalf of the "right" church faction, this would prove particularly useful.

Discouragement and Repression of Rival Systems

Being emperor and favorable to Christianity posed practical difficulties for Constantine since the rival systems were still dominant and active persecution a legacy of the recent past. Hence Constantine followed a policy essentially respectful of both the monotheistic and polytheistic traditions. At most, the latter seemingly were inconvenienced rather than seriously challenged. Indeed, in regard to paganism, he remained titular leader of the cults, had theoretical control over them, and was obligated to assure that they were treated with respect and tolerance.

What unquestionable repressive steps he took had firm roots in the past. Magic and divination had traditionally been viewed as potential security threats. The predictions of divination could be used against any Caesar and magic could be used as a weapon to cause harm to the emperor (or so many believed). Hence in 320 Constantine adopted the firm policy of suppression that predecessors periodically embraced. Both the diviner and the person who hired him were equally subjected to the death penalty. If that were not enough, the client's possessions were to be seized by the state, thereby imposing potentially serious financial loss to any family members left behind. The nasty (and financially rewarding) practice of offering rewards to informers encouraged the violations to be reported.

In the same year, Constantine required that all polytheistic worship be public and adopted a regulation that could be read as banning all private pagan sacrifices. This seems unlikely to have been his true intent since it would seemingly be impossible to prohibit a *private* practice while permitting *public* sacrifices. Such a ban would have also been incredibly socially disruptive because the nature of social and religious custom resulted in most such observances being done in a private setting.

Eusebius claimed that Constantine went so far as to totally abolish the legality of pagan sacrifice.[10] This claim has been both defended and dismissed by modern scholars. Certainly it is possible that some ambiguously worded decree was issued that might (or might not) be interpreted in such a manner. On the other hand, the increased tensions and needless provocation of the still majority polytheistic citizenry would surely have restrained any explicit action of such a draconian nature.

What Eusebius may actually be referring to was the fact that sacrifices by government officials was no longer being practiced in a significant number of places due to the advancement of Christians to many public offices of responsibility. Also Constantine was on public record indicating disdain for animal sacrifices,[11] creating a kind of de facto repudiation of the practice.

In the past, government closure days had been scattered throughout the year in order to coincide with special religious and civic occasions. Hence, if one were Jewish or Christian, one's day of worship had to be sandwiched in between or after events of what was normally a typical workday. In A.D. 321, Constantine ordered that all courts be closed every Sunday, thereby setting the precedent for it to be observed as a weekly day of worship. He called it *dies Solis* ("day of the Sun") in his legislation and, though it was a well established polytheist term, his actions gave it a distinctive Christian connotation.

In addition to government courts being closed, soldiers were given time off to attend Christian worship. Those who did not opt to do so were required to participate in gatherings at which their unit recited an imperially established prayer that referred to the "Highest Deity," clearly code language to describe the Christian God though still sufficiently ambiguous to avoid open repudiation or embracing of any specific deity.[12]

Constantine and Intra-Church Divisions

Regardless of how deep Constantine's Christianity actually went, his recognition of the havoc that needless division could produce in the secular realm made him only too aware of its potential danger in the religious: beyond a certain point it challenged the very stability of the Christianity he had embraced. Hence, confronted with rival Christian systems, he faced the need to either work out an accommodation between the sides or intervene on behalf of one.

The first of the two fundamentally different world view divisions concerned proper church order. This was in regard to the hard-line Donatists who insisted that they represented the true faith which countenanced no lapses during persecution. Since the "Catholic" faction more or less readily granted more leeway, they were automatically proved to be apostate and unworthy of support in the eyes of the Donatists. The Donatists requested that Constantine transfer into their hands the financial perquisites being given their opponents because of this blatant apostasy.

Although personally preferring the "Catholic" side (perhaps out of a "real world" recognition of how even a strong person may break under the stress of conflict), Constantine ordered synods to meet to consider and judge the Donatists' case. When several came out against them, this only angered them further. Carthage was gripped by riots in 317 when the two sides took to the streets to settle the matter by violence. The need to preserve public order, anger at the side that had not won the synod debates, and the need to assure stability in Africa for its grain and other exports resulted in Constantine ordering strong military intervention against the Donatists. He won the streets and the "orthodox" the religious edifices, but the Donatists dug in and set up their own rival church. When both his efforts at peace-making (via the synods) and his efforts at suppression (via the military) had clearly failed, he washed his hands of the matter and left the two factions to argue it out.[13]

The Arian conflict with the Nicene faction was even more divisive and explosive. The Donatist controversy was one over hierarchical and institutional legitimacy. This was vital to the self-respect and egos of those involved, of course. But the Arian controversy was one that was doctrinal at its core: what was the relationship of the Son to the Father. In what sense was the son "one" with the Father (in appearance, in nature, in essence, in some other manner)? In what sense was he "equal" and in what sense was he "lesser"? Was He eternal or was He a created being? And if the latter, how could he possibly have produced the redemption of the human race when the death of dedicated, fervent, and even divinely inspired prophets in the past had not? The future Nicenes insisted on the identicalness of the two both as to divine nature and eternality; the Arians denied both.

Arianism quickly gained a multitude of supporters and sympathizers and many who did not agree with their terminology believed they were closer to the right underlying idea than their opponents. This fact argues that, however unpleasant the notion was to the other side, that *even before the controversy erupted* there was a widespread support for an Arian-type interpretation among both church leaders in the East and the rank and file there as well.[14] Hence to many it was the (future) Nicene faction that was guilty of doctrinal innovation and church division in pushing the controversy and insisting on the legitimacy of only their party.

Whichever side one favored, there could be no question this represented an issue of real substance that hit at the heart of the definition of the supernatural world. Hence it would be one that Constantine could not overlook even if the hair-splitting language used by the two sides probably made him wish he could. Economics once again had a supporting role to play: it was no secret that the overwhelming bulk of Alexandrian, Egypt, dockworkers favored the Arian side and the ultimate political nightmare was for these religious issues to spill over into civil unrest and the elimination of vital Egyptian exports to the rest of the empire.[15]

This time he decided to bring issues to a head by calling a massive assembly of bishops for the spring of 325, which he would attend to assure that a solution was worked out. After assembling, Constantine took his place in front of the gathering. Eusebius of Nicomedia gave the opening statement, full of generous words of praise for the emperor who had called the meeting. Constantine responded with a piece of rhetorical exaggeration common to politicians by stressing that he counted the opportunity to meet with the leaders of the church as the greatest blessing of his life. He gave thanks for the ending of persecution against the faith and stressed his desire that "all [be] united in one judgment and in that common spirit of peace and concord ... which becomes those consecrated to the service of God." To show his own determination to let the past stay in the past he took various letters of complaint that he had received from various bishops about each other and publicly burned them. In case they could not grasp the symbolism he spelled it out: "Christ enjoins him who is anxious to obtain forgiveness to forgive his brother."[16]

Constantine directed Ossius to preside over this and future sessions but conspicuously retained his seat in the front to maintain his own authority over the convocation and to intervene when he thought things were getting out of hand or going in the wrong direction. Even granting him the greatest sincerity, it is hard to believe that he fully understood the fine points of the debate; after all most people today do not.

He endorsed that the relationship of Father and Son was one of *homoousios,* a term stressing their absolute and full identicalness — in the understanding of the term by what afterwards became the Nicene faction. The Arians could theoretically argue for a looser definition of the expression, but the Nicenes stoutly insisted it meant "absolutely the same in all ways"[17] and anything significantly less than this was never a viable option: the language was inherently far more congenial to the Nicene approach and, for that matter, Arius had earlier rejected the propriety of the term.

The result of the church council was the Nicene Creed, which differed from earlier efforts at creedal-style statements in that it was not an effort to sum up what was generally agreed to already. Rather it was an attempt to authoritatively *define* what must *in the future* be believed — in this case, on the contentious issue of the relationship of Father and Son.[18] It marked a critical step to the church as authoritative lawgiver. In one sense such was inevitable if councils were to be held at all since the nature of the controversy was one difficult to verbally plaster over and, even if attempted, would almost certainly have been doomed to failure at the hands of zealots on both sides. On the other hand, it did nothing to convince the losing side that they were in the wrong. To lose because of being outnumbered — or due to the invocation of government power — was far from being convinced that one was in error.

Impact of Constantine on the Church's Real and Perceived Status

For purposes of brevity we might summarize the socio-cultural-religious impact of Constantine's policies under three major headings:

(1) Transforming the church into a pillar of government encouraged society. The opening of the imperial treasury to expanding existing and building new structures provided public evidence that Constantine's new policy was not merely one of verbal acquiescence to Christianity's existence but of personal approval and encouragement as well. Such actions moved the church from the marginal edge of societal existence significantly toward its being recognized as one of its core institutions. These expenditures also vastly facilitated the ability of the church to expose its message to a larger listening audience since previous space limitations — due to lack of funds, the use of private facilities, and marginal legal existence — had imposed inherent practical restrictions that no longer existed.[19]

The flip side of encouragement was, at the minimum, that polytheism had to share its claim to state approval and endorsement. The resources diverted from it by the government to Christianity, however, could easily convey the message that in actuality the government no longer considered the traditional ancient gods as essential either to the government or to the empire's well-being.[20] In effect, to be ignored was to be repudiated.

(2) The growing acceptability of the Christian option among those of the upper strata. A reading of the sermons delivered by John Chrysostom and others of that period carry repeated indications that those who attended the sermons and lectures of the era were increasingly part of the higher class of society, individuals who had the leisure time to attend such activities on an ongoing basis without risking economic loss due to time away from work. Hence the church shifted from a relatively lower class basis to one in which even the "poor" became relatively prosperous by the standards that would have been used a few decades earlier.[21]

The growing upper class membership of the church inevitably included members of the Roman Senate. In 384 Ambrose asserted that "the curia is crowded with a majority of Christians."[22] Although the literal accuracy of this claim has been questioned, it certainly indicates a sufficiently large number of Christian members to make the exaggeration credible.

(3) The growing numerical strength of the church. Bruce J. Malina estimates that at the time of the Council of Nicaea in 325 there were about 880,000 Christians out of a Roman Empire population of 60 million. He arrives at the Christian figure by multiplying the number of bishops who attended the Council (220) by the approximate number of individuals such an individual could reasonably directly interact with in a nontechnological society (4,000 each).[23] This assumes the nonexistence of additional bishops and that there were no groups of smaller size who existed independent of the centralization trend that placed most under local and regional bishops.

Thomas M. Finn provides the far higher estimate that there were approximately 6,300,000 Christians out of the 60 million population in the year 300 and that it skyrocketed to over 33,880,000 in 350—an absolute majority of the citizenry.[24]

These and all other numbers can be only rough estimates, but even without being able to give exact numbers, the evidence clearly argues that the number of Christians vastly multiplied after the religion's legalization and encouragement by the government. If being a marginal body created its own set of problems, being at the heart of society would create a different set.

FLAVIUS JULIUS CONSTANTIUS (ruled 337–361)
Imperial Authority on behalf of "Heretical" Arianism

Second son of Constantine the Great, Constantius had demonstrated military skill on the battlefield during his father's lifetime. He oversaw the funeral ceremonies upon his father's death and is suspected of arranging the ensuing bloodbath that swept away all of the brother of Constantine's male relatives except Julian and Julian's half-brother Gallus — potential challengers to his own rise and that of his own brothers.[25] The other sons of Constantine received their own major areas to govern and after their deaths control of the entire undivided empire passed into Constantius' hands in 353.

Although he was repeatedly engaged in various wars against "barbarians" and to protect his rule against internal challengers, he was cautious in pushing his luck against the Persians.[26] Although this brought him the censure of some, the simple fact was that the Persians were a sufficiently dangerous foe that prudence required caution lest he compromise not only his own part of the empire but that of his brothers as well.

Constantine's sons, who moved into leadership upon his death, came down on opposite sides of the Arian controversy. Constantine II and Constans were firmly in the Nicene camp; Constantinus II was Arian. Constantine II restored Athanasius to his old episcopate position; Contantinus made the Arian Eusebius of Nicomedia bishop of Constantinople.

In 338 the Council of Antioch was held. Constantinus imitated his father by being personally present but the decisions that were made endorsed Arian beliefs instead of those preferred by his father. The synod also denounced Athanasius for returning to his post in Alexandria without the proper authorization and replaced him with their own choice. Backed by 5,000 troops, the new bishop carried out the council's replacement decision, action made easier by the fact that Athanasius had prudently chosen to flee the city.

In response, Rome's bishop, Julius, became the leader of the pro-Nicene faction and zealously defended Athanasius' right to his office. A synod in late 340 and early 341 backed this position. During the summer of 341 a synod was held in Antioch, however, that rejected the right of either Rome or the councils it set up to decide such matters.

The death of Eusebius of Nicomedia removed a key Arian leader. The Nicene bishop Paul made a bid for power in Constantinople and the military officer in charge of the forces sent to depose him was murdered during a riot by pro-Nicenes. Constantinus naturally took this as a deep personal affront and took charge of the units that then proceeded to depose the orthodox leader. He wasn't particularly thrilled by the Arian appointment of Macedonius as new bishop, however, since it had been done without his endorsement and the action had played no small role in the civic hostilities that had ultimately resulted in the death of his cavalry leader. Hence he declared the post vacant and refused to appoint any replacement at all. To drive home his anger on a level that everyone could feel, he ordered the allotment of corn sent to Constantinople cut in half.[27]

(Constantius was a dangerous man to cross except when circumstances hindered his reacting as he wished. As one ancient historian put it, "No one easily recalls the acquittal of anyone in the time of Constantius when an accusation against him had even been whispered."[28] Of course this mentality of deep suspicion was quite common among Roman rulers and encouraged by the reports of a multitude of informers hoping to incur royal pleasure or avenge real or imagined slights.[29])

The deposed Paul took refuge in Rome. By then Constans had replaced Constantine II and was dedicated to the Nicene order. The Council of Serdica was held (perhaps in 343) by joint decision of Constans and Constantius in a hope that a reconciliation of the two theological parties could be worked out. This failed amidst bitter recriminations. The Arians proceeded to hold a council at Philippopolis in Greece while the now rump Nicenian Council of Serdica went about its business. Both sides denounced the other, adopted doctrinal stances thoroughly at variance, and issued decrees deposing bishops of the opposing side.

Constantius and Constans both pushed the council decrees of their respective factions. Constans threatened open invasion of the Eastern Empire to restore the deposed bishops and, rather than risk the damage war would do, Constantius permitted the Nicene factionalists to retake their posts. After Constans died, Constantius moved west against Magnentius. Trusting the skill and leadership of his commanders, he remained at prayer at the grave of a martyr while his army defeated the would-be Western leader. In an act symbolically appropriate, word of their triumph was brought by the Arian bishop outside of whose city the battle was waged.

Having tolerated the pressured restoration of Nicenian bishops in his own region and ultimately having to fight a war that he would have preferred to avoid, he was determined to crush that faction once and for all. The personification of purported orthodoxy, Athanasius, was in hiding by the end of 356. Others had either been arrested or gone into "voluntary" exile to avoid retribution. If the Arian faction had endured violence in the past it was now the turn of the "orthodox" to pay in blood — too often literally as efforts to install and maintain Arian supporters was opposed and violently resisted.

Needless to say these policies thoroughly outraged the losers. Hilary of Poitiers described Constantius as a pseudo–Christian, an *apparent* advocate of the faith who was really its bitter enemy: an "impious person who does not know what is sacred, who drives the good from the dioceses in order to give these to the wicked, who by intrigues encourages discord, who hates yet wishes to avoid suspicion, who lies but wishes no one to see it, who is outwardly friendly but within lacks all kindness of heart, who in reality does only what he wishes yet wishes to conceal from everyone what it is that he wishes."[30]

The cynic cannot help but wonder if the character faults attributed to Constantius would have been regarded as so unforgivable if that power had been used to further Hilary and the orthodox agenda. "All fair in love and war," is, alas, a philosophy too often found in theological warfare as well.

This period of Arian ascendancy was marked by the not unexpected continued failure to find some type of doctrinal consensus that could permit both sides to live in peace. Having endured so much adversity, a more militant and stringent form of Arianism simultaneously vied to gain dominance within their own faction. This not only reduced what modest chance there was at reconciliation but also permitted the "orthodox" to contrast their more or less united front behind the *homoousios* definition of the godhead and the divisions among their opponents. Hence when Constantius died in 361 (like Constantine he had postponed his actual baptism until near death), he left behind a divided Arian movement.[31] Although a few other Arian rulers arose, their numbers and successes were inadequate to secure the victory of their preferred theology.

JULIAN THE APOSTATE (ruled 361–363)
A Return to Polytheism

Flavius Claudius Julianus, known commonly, because of his rejection of Christianity, as Julian the Apostate, was born in 331 to the half brother of Constantine the Great. Escaping the effort to wipe out this line of the family after Constantine had died, he was raised in a rural area where polytheism remained strong. Several factors may have predisposed him in the direction of traditional polytheism. As an outcast and always in danger of death at a "Christian" emperor's hands (though for political reasons rather than religious ones) he would have been less than human if some of the hostility did not rub off on the empire's new endorsed religion. It has been speculated that the most influential of his teachers also encouraged him in that direction as well, more than counterbalancing those advocating monotheism. Perhaps the Nicenian form of Christianity (or its Arian alternative) simply grated on his emotions and intellect. Human attitudes are typically the outgrowth of multiple reasons, with the core motivation being reinforced by auxiliary arguments and influences and this was likely the case here as well.

According to his *Hymn to King Helios,* he saw the roots of his reversion not in some human annoyance at particular rulers and their religion or even at Christianity, but in an emotional-psychological inclination toward reverence for the cosmos: "From my childhood a strange yearning for the rays of the [sun] god sank deep into my soul; and from my earliest years my mind was so completely possessed by the light of heaven that not only did I desire to gaze intently at the sun, but whenever I went forth at night, when the sky was clear and cloudless, I abandoned all else and devoted myself to the beauties of the heaven."[32] The polytheist rites gave him a sense of uniting with nature and the cosmos that Christianity did not

Unquestionably as he grew older he founded himself intrigued by Neoplatonism rather than Christianity. Maximus of Ephesus thoroughly enchanted this powerless young man with the prediction that he would restore polytheism to its rightful place in the Empire in place of the usurper Christian religion.[33] When he was permitted to travel to Athens in 355 to further his studies, the area was undergoing a burst of renewed enthusiasm for traditional multi-theism and his own convictions were growing even more intense. He was permitted (and, no doubt, felt honored) to undergo the initiation rituals of the Eleusinian mysteries.

His fortunes now took a dramatic turn for the better. Marrying the Emperor Constantius' sister Helena, he was given a major military command in Gaul as well as rule over the region. He proved to be an able governor and repeatedly displayed on the battlefield superior leadership and the ability to defeat a determined foe even when outnumbered.

Always nervous about his cousin, the successes enhanced Constantius' concerns as to Julian's real intentions.[34] In response, Constantius ordered him to send many of his soldiers to join in a war in the Armenia-Mesopotamia area. He unwillingly gave these forces to Decentius. Since these men had signed on only for war in Gaul, they were more than a little angry at this determination to thrust them into yet a different war in a far off section of the empire.[35] When they reached Paris, they mutinied and informed Julian that they wanted him to be Caesar. Desiring to avoid a civil war, Julian attempted to negotiate an arrangement under which he would acknowledge the superior authority of Constantius. Refusing this compromise, Constantinus demanded that Julian step down as governor and repudiate any claim to authority. There was no support for this in his army and Julian himself would have had to be incredibly naïve not to fear that the next step after yielding would have been his own execution.

Julian gives every indication that he was well aware of the forces at work and was encouraging them to his own end. He avoided negotiations with Constantius (normally always useful if only for the purpose of buying time) and distributed letters from his rival that seemed to implicitly encourage an attack upon Julian.[36] Julian moved swiftly to war and yet, arriving unexpectedly at virtually every place he went, the communities mysteriously praised and embraced him most extravagantly — a most odd series of events unless the groundwork had already been covertly laid.[37] An internal civil war was avoided in November 361 when Constantius died while en route to do battle. Ironically, his will conveyed the throne to his rival.

Repudiating the Recent Past

However much the Christian elements in the Empire were happy with their official recognition, it had not existed all that long. Superficially, Julian's rise should not have changed anything. Outwardly still an observant Christian,[38] his true inclinations and hidden animosities were soon to emerge.

Quickly after gaining power he ordered all closed temples to be reopened and proudly resumed the traditional religious role of the emperor as Pontifex Maximus. If things had not gone much further than the reestablishment of polytheism as the preferred government religious choice, things might not have been so bad. Instead he was determined to make the Christians pay for their relatively short period of ascendancy.

That "pay" was, partly, quite literal. All the state funds given the churches had to be returned to the state treasury. His retribution also involved other matters than those directly monetary: All grants of property and special rights were revoked.

If the church's rights *as an institution* had been the only target that would have made things much easier for the rank and file members. Instead, Julian targeted them as well as the hierarchy and its status symbols. For example, believers were prohibited from being teachers. Even some prominent pagans were appalled at this demand. Although this protest may well have been due to the proportion of Christians now in the educational community[39] it also likely grew out of a recognition that both sides used many of the same basic educational texts. In short, polytheist teachers found sufficient shared intellectual ground with the monotheists that an attack on one was regarded as a potential threat to them all. Of all Julian's measures this was clearly one of the most controversial and, not surprisingly, one of the earliest to be repudiated after his death.[40]

Julian was quite capable of subtlety in his efforts to undermine Christianity. On the one hand, he permitted exiled bishops to return and this might be interpreted as an act of broad-mindedness. On the other hand, it also permitted the return of dissident Arian and other clergy who would not willingly submit to "orthodoxy" and who would undermine the ability of the Christian community to present a united front.[41]

Another two-edged sword was found in Julian's attitude toward Judaism. Anything he did to make life easier for the Jews represented that much larger a "thorn in the flesh" to their monotheist rivals in Christianity. Furthermore, his announcement that he would support the rebuilding of the Jewish temple in Jerusalem deeply annoyed the Christians: the destruction of the temple was interpreted as evidence of Divine wrath on unbelieving Jews and here it was being rebuilt! The brevity of Julian's reign and the fact that his successors reverted to Christianity kept the temple building effort from ever bearing fruit, however.[42]

Julian avoided open persecution that would result in martyrdom. Anything short of that — to harass and undermine the church — was considered quite acceptable.[43] Local anti–Christian zealots, however, regarded this as an opportune time to strike out and execute a limited number of believers in various cities of the empire. Julian's response was more than a slap on the wrist and less that equitable retribution: in one case he wrote a letter criticizing what had been done; in another he removed the governor.[44] Most polytheists probably deduced from this restraint that, on balance, the emperor would be tolerant of their excesses as long as they did not carry them out in too brazen a manner.

Julian recognized that if paganism was to be a moral alternative to Christianity, the ethical integrity of its leaders had to be assured. In the past, various priesthoods were the reward and responsibility of those who held certain specific government positions. So long as they had the financial wherewithal to provide the necessary attending sacrifices and activities, personal character was virtually an irrelevancy. The poor need not apply, no matter how great their personal character and virtue. Julian insisted that this be changed. As he wrote in one of his letters, "I say that the best men in every city, especially those who show most love for the gods, and next those who show most love for their fellow men [must be chosen], whether they are poor or rich."[45]

Priests, he insisted, should have a deep interest in the best of philosophy. They must stay out of the theater (with its typically obscene productions) and scorn animal hunts that were performed in the arena for public entertainment. They must avoid drunkenness and assure that their children were raised to live by such standards as well.[46]

In the past, humanitarianism (such as feeding the needy and helping the parentless) had conspicuously not been associated with pagan religion. Julian insisted that this be changed: "It is disgraceful that, when none of the Jews has to beg, and the impious Galileans [Christians] maintain not only their own poor but ours as well, our people are seen to lack assistance from us." Furthermore, "Why do we not notice that it is their benevolence to strangers, their care for the graves of the dead and their feigned holiness of life that have done most to increase" that monotheist movement?[47]

He took this as a personal crusade. During late 362 and early 363 he wrote a treatise against the "Galileans" as he prepared to renew war with Persia. He found irony and absurdity in the strange fetish of the Christians worshipping a mere dead Jew (Jesus) while rejecting the respected and renowned Roman deities. True, He healed the sick and cast out demons but what did Jesus ever do that was of *real* value to the world?[48]

The decision to settle old scores with the Persians was his fatal miscalculation. After initial success, he burned his boats (certainly to protect against any temptation to retreat) and pushed deep into the country. The Persians, however, adopted a policy of burning and destroying everything of use and Julian was ultimately forced into an embarrassing retreat. Although the Persians did not feel adequate for an all-out attack, they regularly harassed the retreating Romans at every opportunity. During one of these assaults either time was too pressing or the heat simply insufferable and Julian did not put on his breastplate; the result was that an enemy spear sent him to his death. There were some suspicions that the Christians he had opposed were behind it and the report of at least one such conspiracy back in Antioch gave some credibility to the possibility. The circumstances of his death, however, virtually ruled out such an explanation.[49]

THUNDERING LEGION (170s)
Christians as Soldiers

While the Roman army was at war in A.D. 172 the legions were within an inch of complete defeat when a massive thunderstorm saved the day. Eusebius and Tertullian speak of how Christian prayers from within the Twelfth Legion brought about the foul weather that prevented their annihilation as a fighting force. It became part of the established church tradition that a majority of the legion was Christian.[50]

On the polytheist side, Dio Cassius also explains the salvation of the forces as being due to a miraculous thunderstorm and concurs that it occurred because of prayers—though those of a pagan magician, presumably joined by the soldiers: "Indeed, there is a story to the effect that Arnuphis, an Egyptian magician, who was a companion of Marcus [their leader], had invoked by means of enchantments various deities and in particular Mercury, the god of the air, and by this means attracted the rain."[51] He conspicuously omits any mention of *Christian* prayers being involved, however.[52]

He may have intentionally glossed over that potential embarrassment to a polytheist or it may be that the Christian contingent remembered what *they* were doing and later members of their faith either did not know or dismissed the prayers of the polytheists: the blunt reality is that under such severe combat conditions the twentieth century adage "there are no atheists in foxholes" is psychologically true and there were doubtless hurried prayers from many a desperate heart regardless of their religion.

Later claims that this was the time the legion received its appellation "Thundering" ("Fulminata" more properly means "thunderstruck") are clearly wrong. The name had been applied to the unit as far back as the days of Augustus and was based on the emblem they bore on their crests.[53] In this original context the symbolism surely represented the frightening impact they intended to make on Rome's enemies. Of course after the rescue from catastrophe, soldiers of the legion probably linked it with that memorable event as well, since it had been a day, so to speak, when celestial "thundering" had saved the "thundering" legion.

The fact that the legion retained a significant Christian element through the following 150 years did not assure even its members safety from government repression. In A.D. 320 at Sebase (Lower Armenia) forty were executed by being stripped naked and freezing to death on a small lake.[54] By the standards of raw brutality that could be and were sometimes exercised against Christians this was, oddly enough, a merciful death.

Christians and War

That there were Christians from early on who were in the military is unquestionable. Even in the book of Acts of the New Testament we read of the conversion of the centurion Cornelius. When conversion, as with Cornelius, occurred while in the service there was no way short of desertion out of the commitment. Since Roman service was for a minimum of twenty years (in actual practice it could be continued longer)[55] a man was likely "locked in" for another decade or so before he had any realistic option for another way of life.

What becomes speculative is how many Christians *became* soldiers (rather than being converted while in the service) and how great a percentage they were of the combatant force. What is certain is that the first clear-cut evidence of a unit with a major Christian contingent occurs in A.D. 172 — the actual date may be as much as two years before or later — in connection with the Thundering Legion.[56]

There were three basic reasons why Christians might not want to serve in the military. The two most often mentioned motives are the idolatrous practices that were the norm in the legions, including emperor worship, and the other the belief that military force was inherently sinful.[57] The third was utilitarian: if one were part of an unwillingly subject people (such as the Jews were in the first century) one would be giving support to the "oppressor." In times of real or attempted national independence, however, that would not rule out service in one's own forces, so it could not be called "pacifism" in the true sense.

It was only in 212 that citizenship was granted to all residents within the boundaries of the Roman Empire. (This applied to the free class; it did not apply to those who were slaves.)[58] Until then it was a hard won right that was then passed down to one's children. But with the creation of universal citizenship came the explicit claim to compel military service from one and all.[59] Prior to then, the morality of military service was an irrelevancy to anyone who wished it to be such. One might volunteer for service if one desired and thought it proper, but there was no threat of involuntary service to compel consideration of how one should respond.

PAMMACHIUS (died c. 409)
Senator, Humanitarian, Anti-Heretic

Pammachius' service in the Roman senate was during a period in which there were bitter rival claims as to whether pagans or Christians were in the majority. The extremely effective leadership of Symmachus certainly gave the polytheists an edge in the battle for ongoing control, regardless of where pure numbers lay. In spite of his possible minority status, Pammachius was noted for steadfastness in his chosen religious profession,[60] not an easy position for anyone in cases like this when the other side was manifesting enthusiasm and were in (or near) control of the situation.

In 385 he married a woman from a family appropriate to his own rank as senator. Pauline had wedded rather unwillingly, having preferred to live a life of perpetual virginity, and had even hoped to live such a lifestyle within the boundaries of official marriage to Pammachius. Seeing that was not to be the case, she made her primary goal that of having and raising children to be faithful Christians. These efforts repeatedly failed as infant after infant was lost in miscarriage; the final loss also resulted in her own death as well.[61]

Word was spread widely of the funeral Pammachius had planned for her and what was to happen afterwards. After the funeral service at the Church of St. Peter, a massive feast was held within the edifice for all who wished to attend. As each group finished their meal, another was brought in in its place and then yet another. As they parted, each participant was given a generous gift of alms and a new robe to wear.[62] Paulinus of Nola wrote him a letter praising the humanitarianism of this generous act and making the point that, "O Rome, you wouldn't have to fear those threats laid out in the Apocalypse, if your senators always produced such gifts."[63]

After the death of his wife Pammachius also took the step of becoming a monk and devoting himself to charity. For someone of this rank to take such a dramatic step was, of course, startling to most of society — even to many Christians. As Jerome wrote, "Who would have believed that a last descendant of the consuls, an ornament of the race of Camillus, could make up his mind to traverse the city in the black robe of a monk, and should not blush to appear thus clad in the midst of senators?"[64]

Although Pammachius proceeded to give away an immense amount of money in charitable and other activities, he was always careful to retain at least the minimal amount — which was extremely large — necessary to keep his status as Senator. This caution simultaneously assured he would continue to have financial resources for his good works and also provided the protective advantages of continued senatorial membership. Only after his death were these core assets disposed of.[65]

Pioneer of Christian Humanitarianism

Pammachius' humanitarian works included working with (future Saint) Fabiola in 398 to establish a combined hospital-inn to provide services to both local poor believers and pilgrims to Rome. This they established in the community of Porto, part of Ostia, the harbor for Rome. Visitors from far and wide utilized it heavily because it was free of the moral corruption of most lodging facilities and because it provided a friendly welcome to coreligionists from anywhere and everywhere.[66]

Living quarters for the ill were also part of the complex, providing concerned care for ill Christians who could not afford it and, because illness was preventing them from working and earning a living, who would otherwise not have had a roof over their heads at all. In the annals of Christian humanitarianism this institution was important because it was the first such hospital established by and for Christians in the Western part of the empire.[67] (We have stressed that it was a dual use facility because the term "hospital" as a strictly medical facility became clearly differentiated from this broader purpose institution only in the twelfth century.)[68]

The facility also marked an important breakthrough in societal (or, at least, religious) consciousness of the need to provide for the less fortunate. The only organized medical services that existed were for the military; civilians who could afford it could bring doctors to their private home. The poor went ill or made do the best they could. Fabiola recruited a dozen other prominent women, who joined her in regular service, personally providing as they could for the medical needs of the underprivileged who were sick and ailing. So well did they perform this work that Jerome could write with complimentary exaggeration, "The poor wished to be sick if only to be under [Fabiola's] care."[69]

Opponent of Heresy and Friend of Jerome

Due to the prestige of his senatorial office and his dedication to good works, Pammachius was in a pivotal position to discourage heretical alternatives by rallying opposition to them. Three major examples of this provide an insight into his varying interests.

(1) Against the Donatists. Pammachius was prepared to bring to bear whatever influence he had to undercut their influence. Owning property in Numidia, where the movement had considerable strength, he wrote his friends and associates there imploring them to wash their hands of any role in the movement.[70] Augustine wrote of his success in language derogatory of the intelligence of the dissenters, speaking of how Pammachius had "chased up those peasants of yours in Numidia."[71]

(2) Critic of Jovinian. Pammachius took the lead in placing the alleged heretical works of Jovinian before the Roman bishop, Siricius. Obviously wishing to see Jovinian condemned, he was successful in this lobbying effort because an official condemnation came within a few years from councils meeting both in Rome itself and in Milan.[72]

Not only did he seek out episcopate condemnation, he appealed to his old friend Jerome for assistance as well. Jerome and Pammachius had struck up their lasting friendship while Jerome had served and taught in Rome, and Jerome was clearly one of his closer associates.[73] (This acquaintance grew, at least in part, out of marriage to a woman of a family which provided one of Jerome's strongest bases of financial and emotional support while living in the city.)[74]

When Jerome moved out to the distant provinces, they lost contact for a number of years until a letter reached him from Pammachius urging him to take up pen and ink to refute the errors Jovinian was teaching about the virgin Mary and human sexuality. From then on Pammachius received Jerome's various materials and arranged for them to be copied and widely distributed, thereby increasing and broadening the impact of his friend. He propagandized for Jerome and his own personal prestige added to the authority and impact of his associate's writings.[75]

Jerome's initial response to Jovinian poured out his anger in ways that were all too likely to gain the foe sympathizers rather than condemnation. For one thing its glorification of virginity was so intense it could — and was — often read as a rebuke of marriage itself. Indeed, it required an unusually friendly audience for it to be read as anything short of a denigration of married sexuality. If this was not sufficient to annoy and outrage married men and women, the intense disdainful rhetoric used to describe the man's followers was guaranteed to inflame those local individuals already inclined to sympathy toward Jovinian.[76] So intense was the hostile response that Pammachius attempted to purchase as many copies of the very Jeromian rebuttal that he himself had circulated as he tried to keep the backlash from growing even worse.[77]

(3) Critic of Origen. Well aware of the vivid differences of opinion about the orthodoxy of Origen, Pammachius was quite upset with Rufinus' translation of *De Principiis*

and the implication that Jerome shared Rufinus' endorsement of Origen's orthodoxy. Hence he joined Oceanus in writing to their mutual friend and urging him to deal with this misrepresentation. In response, Jerome prepared his own translation, allegedly more accurate and reliable than that of Rufinus, and sent it to Rome. Pammachius had only one copy made,[78] unlike his customary policy of providing a widespread distribution. It is unknown whether he regarded Origen's work as too heretical to be given widespread circulation (even when rendered by an "orthodox" translator) or whether he was concerned that Jerome might himself have played too fast and loose in translating the work. Answer the question however one may, in one significant way Rufinus had the final word: it is *his* translation that has survived and not that of Jerome.[79]

Even Pammachius recognized that his friend sometimes had a bad case of what our age would call "runaway mouth," overstating, exaggerating, and vilifying the opponent. Hence he interceded with Jerome to urge him to rein in some of his rhetoric against Rufinus.[80] Not that this or any other criticism ever seemed to restrain Jerome but for so long.

Psychologically it must have been heartbreaking during Pammachius' final days. In spite of all the glory and accomplishments Rome had produced in past centuries one could hardly ignore the dramatic decline of her fortunes during his own lifetime. Vivid testimony was literally at the doors that its greatness had passed: Pammachius died during the siege of Rome by the Goths in 410.

Chapter 3

The Christian Intellectual Tradition

JULIUS AFRICANUS (c. 160–c. 240)
Integrator of Christian, Jewish and Pagan History

Africanus was born in the Roman town of Aelia Capitolina, the exclusively Gentile city that Emperor Hadrian erected on the site of Jerusalem. Due to the nature of this ethnic restriction, one must assume that Africanus was of Gentile rather than Jewish ancestry.[1] With this as his home, he was in a position to pick up stories related to Jesus, the apostles, and regional history. For example, he claimed that King Herod "had no drop of Israelitish blood." Unlikely though that seems, traditional Jewish sources spoke cynically of his ethnic roots as well: Josephus calls him a mere "half-Jew,"[2] so this likely reflects yet another version of the stories then circulating.

Africanus was educated in Alexandria and came to know the great scholar Origen at that time.[3] He traveled widely, including making a journey to Mount Ararat in an effort to uncover possible remains of Noah's Ark.[4] In spite of the time devoted to such travels, he spent a large part of his life in Rome.

One of the unresolved issues surrounding the man is whether he was an architect, a librarian, or both. In a fragment of his "encyclopedia" (*Kestoi*) that has survived, he speaks of how a text of Homer he was discussing had been read "in Rome at the baths of Alexander in the beautiful library in the Pantheon which I myself designed for the Augustus."[5] Since there is no other reference to his alleged design talents, some have preferred to interpret the text to mean that he "built" the collection of books that the facility contained, an act which would bring it directly in line with his clear intellectual talents.[6]

Be that as it may, the library was important historically because it was the last identifiable one to have been built in ancient Rome.[7] (By the time of Constantine, the total number of such facilities had grown to twenty-nine, but only a third are identifiable as to name or location.)[8] Africanus apparently was in charge of running it whether or not he was also architect, a clear indication of his personal knowledge and reputation as a bibliophile.

On the premises was allegedly a major statue whose identity is far from certain. Some have speculated that it was there to honor Christ and Christians.[9] Not the least problem with this enticing scenario is that the statue was apparently female rather than the male figure we would anticipate as a representation of Jesus.[10]

In his old age he retired to Palestine, taking up residence in Emmaus (Nicopolis).[11] There he became a prominent official and even journeyed back to Rome to represent the interests of his community.[12] He serves as a useful example of how incongruous being an early Christian could be: though anyone *could* be a victim of persecution, there is no hint that the threat of it ever came his way even though he was, at times, in personal contact with the emperor.[13]

The "Chronologies"

Africanus assumed that the history of the world would mirror that of creation, with its length being a thousand years for each day of the Genesis narrative. As scriptural substantiation for the day/thousand years correlation, he appealed to Psalms 90:4, "For a thousand years in Your sight, are like yesterday when it is past, and like a watch in the night" (New King James Version). Jesus was born 5,500 years into the 7,000 year cycle, two hundred more years had passed, which left three hundred years before the end millennium, which would occur c. A.D. 500.[14] Hence any tragedies that occurred during the reign of the current rulers could safely be regarded not as signs of an imminent end — or of divine wrath against the regime — but simply as those recurring problems that erupt throughout history.[15]

In contrast to such "literalism," Augustine disconnected the six "days" from any strict calendar correlation: though there would be six "days" prior to the return of Christ (in the sense of eras or chronological periods), each of these was of indeterminate length. The reason that terrible things were occurring (and would occur) was not necessarily tied at all to the final end. Instead, they were the result of how long the world had existed: "If a man grows old he is full of tribulations; if the world grows old it is full of disasters."[16] Afterwards comes the "millennium" a figurative term for the joys of heaven. As Augustine explained it, "If 'a hundred' sometimes be used to designate perfection ... why, then, may not 'one thousand' represent consummation...?"[17] Augustine's scenario ultimately triumphed because calendar predictions of the end date proved themselves false.

Within the seven-day conceptual framework, Africanus compiled a world history utilizing abundant quotations from prior authors he deemed most reliable. It included lengthy lists of past rulers and events among Hebrews and Greeks. This represented a major step forward because in the past historiography was heavy on the events and the personalities, but very light on the comparative time frame of those matters, especially as they interlocked with other individuals and nations.[18]

Hence Africanus represented a major step forward in the effort to set events in their historical/chronological context, an approach Eusebius of Caesarea carried even further in his own comparative world chronology. Whether Africanus be credited with inventing the idea[19] or whether Eusebius' work be regarded as so superior that he should be given that honor,[20] it is extremely hard not to give at least partial credit to Eusebius' predecessor. Africanus may not have perfected the concept, but he unquestionably inspired its further development.

Africanus is especially interesting because he included a bit of everything. True, he includes lists of such "important" things (to Christians, at least) of known bishops in such cities as Alexandria, Egypt.[21] Yet he also included everything from rulers to more mundane affairs, such as athletic events. For example, under the year 664, he speaks of the Olympics of that year and how "Chionis of Sparta won the *stadion* race; his jump was fifty-two feet."[22]

Five books were required to contain this extensive material. In large part because of its length (and the resulting difficulty and great time required to copy it), it is one of the many ancient works that survive only in extracts from later writers. In this case the preservation was accomplished through Origen, who compiled his own comparative chronology of the Jewish, and other, peoples of the known world.[23]

The "Encyclopedia"

The second major work associated with Africanus is the *Kestoi* (*Embroideries,* roughly equivalent in intent to the modern "encyclopedia"). This consisted of twenty-four volumes of which only extracts have survived.[24] The encyclopedia covered a bit of everything: subjects as varied as the magical arts, war-making skills, healing of the sick and hurting, and farming.[25] The magic charms he speaks of would serve a wide variety of functions, from assuring that one's loved one would reciprocate the feeling, to successfully destroying one's opposing army, to guaranteeing that crops would abundantly grow and produce a superior yield. (This receptive attitude toward magic is quite different from the dominant Christian one then and later in which supposed successful wonders are typically considered as far more likely demonic or intentionally fraudulent.)[26]

GREGORY OF NEOCAESAREA (c. 213–c. 275)
The First Christian Autobiographer

Gregory was born into a prestigious and influential local family in the province of Pontus (within modern Turkey) about A.D. 210. His town was the proverbial big fish in a small pond since the area consisted of only smallish towns; its moderately prosperous economy flourished based upon agriculture and fishing in the adjoining Black Sea.[27]

Sent to Beirut to study, Gregory underwent the conventional education that would lead to a career in law or related public service. He met Origen and was so impressed by him that he remained five years studying under his tutelage in Caesarea of Palestine. Gregory's father had died when he was only fourteen, and Gregory came to regard Origen as "our true father."[28]

Gregory: The Writer

Gregory's *The Oration and Panegyric Addressed to Origen* not only praises his teacher but also represents the first effort at autobiography among Christians that has survived. From this author's standpoint it suffers a critical lack of completeness due to when it was written: it was composed in his early mature Christian years as he ended his period of study under Origen. Though it provides interesting insights into how he viewed his life to that point, the very timing of its preparation meant that the equally important subject of his work as bishop in Pontus goes completely unmentioned. As he saw it, the key element in his life up to then was how God's benevolent providence had altered his career plans and brought him into contact with Origen under circumstances that totally changed his plans and goals.[29]

After his years with Origen, he returned to Pontus and with his new set of spiritual priorities was promptly selected as bishop of the capital city of Neocaesarea. He served in that post until he died about 270. Holding together the church was no small accomplishment. There was a vicious imperial persecution waged by Decius (249–251) and this was followed only years later by barbarian incursions that disrupted the life and economy of the region.[30] Afterwards he wrote what has come to be called his *Canonical Letter*, giving advice, counsel, and instruction to Christians facing the varied side effects of the incursion. These ranged from rape, to eating leftover animal sacrifices originally offered to idols, to the seizure of property by those who had no right to it.[31]

Gregory also composed a paraphrase of Ecclesiastes that has survived. This was likely written during his earlier years with Origen.[32] The blatant misunderstanding and "misreading" of the intent of the text that some have stressed[33] also fit well with such an early date or, alternatively, may simply reflect his preference for spiritual "truths" and "insights" regardless of how well grounded they were in the actual texts being studied.

Gregory: The Advocate of Perpetuating Orthodoxy

As bishop, he was a firm advocate of formal creedal loyalty: after constructing a new edifice for the local Christians, he inscribed on the walls — Gregory of Nyssa says he did it personally — a statement of beliefs that all local Christians were expected to adhere to.[34] Whether some or much of the contents actually dated to his time has been challenged on the grounds that some of its wording seems to have been a tad too useful to protagonists a half-century later to have originated at an earlier date.[35]

Oddly enough, in spite of the reverence in which he was clearly held, his actual ability to establish a spiritually authoritative standard for the next generation may have been considerably overstated. The locals, of course, felt they were the steadfast upholders of his tradition. Basil, however, caused to be introduced such innovations as psalm singing in a manner different from what had been their practice and was appalled at the audacity of their rejection. He insisted that "even the Litanies which you now used were not used in his time." Indeed, "You have kept none of his customs up to the present time."[36] Gregory had become the "pretext" rather than the "text," if you will, for the new local orthodoxy.

Gregory Thaumaturgos (Wonder/Miracle Worker)

In a memorial sermon delivered a century after his death, Gregory of Nyssa speaks of the stories and teachings passed down in his family about his namesake. The tales are full of legendary exaggerations and hyperbole.

For example, there is the matter of the conversion of Pontus. The latter Gregory claimed that the earlier one faced a diocese with only seventeen Christians; when he was through there were only seventeen polytheists. One can't help but suspect that listeners smiled at the hyperbole, since significant polytheist observances are known to have persisted long afterwards.[37] One also can hardly avoid suspecting that listeners of earlier versions of the stories would have been similarly amused (in a low-key fashion) at the exaggeration of their revered leader's reputed miracles — not dismissing them totally, but recognizing their exaggeration.

Some miracles required him to be nothing more than an astute observer: the prediction of a plague could be nothing more than a perceptive recognition that plague-like conditions had arisen. Others sound like "micracleizations" of more down-to-earth phenomena: when we read of the exorcism of a reputed demon that just happens to be within a false teacher, it is easy to suspect that we are really faced with a case of a man being convinced of the error of his ways. Some actions can hardly be called more than idle wonders — drying up a lake that was the subject of conflict between brothers, for example.

In other cases we have an undertone of mocking foes: when a demonic "god" is accepted as objectively genuine and summoned back to its temple to prove Gregory's authority over it, this logically could open Gregory to the dangerous charge of recognizing the objective reality of actual "gods" rather than being a strict monotheist. It is likely that such stories were told and retold at first with fond amusement — much like the modern Paul Bunyan tales — and were transformed into literal historical reality many decades later by those who were no longer acquainted with the original events or their witnesses.

However much we dismiss these accretions, Gregory of Neocaesarea's lifetime unquestionably marked the pivotal turning point in Pontus' religious evolution: the Christian community went within a single lifetime from being a token to being a major player in the social and religious life of the province. Whether we consider this the result of a conscious missionary campaign by Gregory or not (and there are those who vigorously repudiate the idea), the province was unquestionably one of smallish cities: in such cases urban areas could not exist in social and cultural isolation from the countryside as they might in Rome or Alexandria. Hence there would be inevitable major interaction, and the obvious increase in converts in Neocaesarea and other cities would have an inevitable "spillover" effect to the extent that would not occur in major urban centers of the empire.[38]

EUSEBIUS OF CAESAREA (c. 260–c. 340)
"Father of Church History"

It is customarily assumed that Eusebius spent virtually his entire life in or near Caesarea, though there is really no evidence with which to reconstruct the matter. His works indicate that he had received at least a passable education by the standards of the day, including enough Latin that he could, if necessary, translate documents from that language into Greek. Based upon a birth in the early 260s, that education would have been finished by the early 280s when the scholar Pamphilus moved to Caesarea.

Eusebius came to describe Pamphilus in terms of being both his "son" and "master."

Both expressions have been "literalized" by some. Although creative, neither is likely to be true.[39] In light of the affectionate terminology, however, it is hardly surprising that the most important churchman to have an impact upon him was this very man — a scholar who had a deep rooted desire to perpetuate and defend the reputation of Origen. This was done by writing a *Defense of Origen*, which Eusebius himself completed after Pamphilus had been executed for his Christianity. So great was his respect for his tutor that he began to describe himself as "*his* Eusebius," hence, "Eusebius Pamphili."[40]

Eusebius advanced through the clerical ranks, becoming bishop c. 313 and serving in that post until his death. Passing remarks of his provide a few details of his life: we know he met both Constantine and Diocletian. He was a close friend of his educator, the wealthy presbyter-philanthropist Pamphilus. During persecution he avoided doing anything that would force the government to take hostile recognition of his faith and imprison or execute him. Yet he visited Pamphilus in prison and the two worked together on the manuscript defending Origen during that time. He also visited prisoners being punished with forced labor in the copper mines. These actions argue he was no coward but simply exercising caution in contrast to certain others who courted martyrdom.

His prudence, however, was open to censure and hostile suspicion by those who had suffered, and by their families and friends, as well as by those seeking a tool to use against him. At the Council of Tyre, for example, one such individual used this "failure" as a jumping off point for challenging his right to be bishop. Eusebius did not so much answer as find grounds on which to counterattack his opponents. If someone was going to throw verbal stones at him, he was quite prepared to throw his own selection of stones back at them. Beyond trying to shift the issue by such counterattacks, there was little he could say except to stress his abiding respect for the imprisoned and martyrs as well as to emphasize that he had demonstrated the genuineness of this attitude by his emphasis on martyrdoms in his *Church History*.[41]

Biblical and Apologetic Writings

Although his role as historian no doubt was one of which he was proud, his position as church leader made scriptural exegesis more immediately important. His commentary on Isaiah, however, only reappeared in 1934. Although enthusiastic about Origen (whose flights of fancy were only loosely built on anything concrete in the text), this almost complete volume reveals a far more down-to-earth interpretation than one would anticipate. He is far more concerned with the text's historical meaning than with any grander philosophical or theological theme.[42]

He was also a writer of lengthy apologetic literature, though only part of it has survived. In it he reflects a mind-frame like that of his *History:* he carefully cites at length the individuals whose beliefs, concerns, attitudes, or actions he is concerned with. Just as the *History* provides the only source for much information about the details of earlier Christians, in his apologetic work he preserves large segments of the writings of polytheist philosophers whose work is otherwise unknown.[43] Eusebius has the purpose of vindicating Christianity; hence, these excerpts also show how the Christianity of this age blended traditional polytheist texts into arguments for its own monotheism. It is, of course, not history for history's sake (nor philosophy for philosophy's sake), but when source material is rare or nonexistent one remains thankful for its survival regardless of the specific agenda a given writer is serving.

Eusebius and Arianism

Eusebius was opposed to the branding of Arius as a heretic, and himself held ideas that have been considered a modified form of his thought. He spoke of how Jesus described the Father as superior citing the text, "The Father who sent me is greater than I." Furthermore, had not Jesus addressed His own prayers to "the only true God"? And how were those who wished to dissolve the two personalities into one to deal with Paul's solemn profession about there being "the one mediator between God and man, the man Christ Jesus"? Fifty years later these words still angered Athanasius.[44]

Because of the fine distinctions involved in the rhetoric, placing his convictions in a specific, narrow theological niche has resulted in varying descriptions of where he belongs.[45] On the one hand he did not regard the Son as created and yet He believed that the Son has not eternally been in existence. The Son lacked a soul as humans have because His uniqueness did not require Him to have one. He was Himself the Creator of the Holy Spirit.[46]

The 325 synod of Antioch repudiated Eusebius because of his failure to join the crusade against Arius. At the subsequent Council of Nicaea the same year, he managed to salvage his reputation and escape censure. At Nicaea he publicly avowed his full loyalty to the traditional creed of Caesarea which included the belief that Jesus was "the only-begotten Son" and was "begotten of God the Father before all ages."[47] Although there was adequate maneuvering room to put an Arian interpretation upon the words, they met the verbal demands of "orthodoxy" and the acceptance of them by Constantine meant that no one at the council was about to openly challenge the language and their ruler's embracing of him as orthodox.[48]

The emperor, however, said he wished to add the word *homoousios* to the formulation of the relationship of Father and Son that Eusebius had endorsed and advocated. Although the bishop was not enthused by it, he was willing to accept it. This was likely viewed as a face-saving move by both Eusebius (who avoided the danger of being viewed as divisively insistent upon vagueness that might hide unorthodoxy) and by Constantine (who believed that if Eusebius could accept it, that it was a way of splitting off many of the Arian-inclined and vastly reducing the number of open dissidents). Ossius quickly moved to appoint a committee to write a creedal statement that included both these doctrinal sentiments, and it produced the Nicene Creed a matter of days later.

Constantine made it implicitly clear that anyone who was unwilling to sign the new creed would be stripped of his church office. The document was presented to each individual for signature in the emperor's presence, thereby adding yet more pressure. The only two who were not coerced were Secundus of Ptolemais and Theonas of Marmarcia, who were promptly punished with exile.[49] There remained the not-so-covert lingering problem of those who had signed only because of the pressure — some out of concern to maintain their office and others surely out of the fear that someone of vigorous anti–Arian sentiment would take their place. Would they quietly acquiesce or would they attempt to obstruct the new orthodoxy? Many, it turned out, were passive rebels. But, so far as Eusebius went, he could now be counted among the "orthodox," however many remained suspicious of what was in his heart.

His Church History *and* Chronicle

The fact that his *Church History* has survived pays more tribute to Eusebius' pivotal role in providing a readily usable survey of church history than it does to any admiration for the man himself in the dominant pro–Nicene faction of the church. Even into the late fourth century, it is unlikely that either side could really be said to be in clear-cut control over anything other than certain communities and regions. Yet by ultimately winning the theological and political brass-knuckles fighting for dominancy, the Nicene position made itself the orthodox side so far as determining what was generally described as valid versus heretical.

Although there were others who had written church history earlier (we have discussed Julius Africanus above), Eusebius conceived of himself as marking a turning point in just such efforts. He described himself as the "first to enter on the undertaking, as travelers do on some desolate and untrodden way."[50] It was not only that sufficient time had gone by that events could be set in a broader context, it was also that his very approach marked a major shift in how history writing was conceived of among Romans. Traditional historiography had suffered from two major defects: Inventiveness (i.e., the imagination) had traditionally been given wide scope in the presentation of the supposed words of those being discussed, while the quotation of genuine historical records was commonly kept to a minimum. Eusebius reversed these priorities, taking pride in quoting not just occasionally but on an abundant basis what those of earlier generations had said.[51] In short, he was "obsessed" (for lack of a better word) in getting his facts right

In spite of the great value of his handiwork, he was still limited by his literary resources. Hence eastern Christianity becomes the focus far more than western Christianity and its Latin orientated religious scholarship.[52] He never stopped trying to improve the work, however. It was both expanded and edited as to contents through various revised "editions" he brought out during his lifetime.[53]

Before he undertook his *Church History* he had completed a *Chronicle* that was centered on the history of the various ancient peoples. He began with brief surveys of Roman, Greek, Egyptian, Jewish and other histories but the bulk of the work consists of a year by year chronology. This puts the events of each of six peoples in separate columns so that an individual can see what was happening at the same time in each group. Eusebius recognized that the data for a chronology — even his own — was limited and therefore absolute accuracy impossible: "Neither from the Greeks, nor from the barbarians, nor of any others, not even from the Hebrews, can one learn with security the general chronography of the world."[54] Although the analysis is conceptually built on work by such individuals as Julius Africanus, he so broadened the scope of the effort and put such a deep personal impress on the concept that he became the inventor of the writing of "world history" as it would be conceived of for the following millennium.[55]

FALTONIA PROBA (mid– to late 300s)
Female Poet Who "Christianized" Virgil

Although works by other ancient Christian women are known to have existed, Proba's is the only poetic effort to have survived in its entirety.[56] There were three women known to be of her Anicii family that shared the name "Proba" and there has been great uncertainty which of them was the woman whose poetry has survived.[57] In manuscripts of a late date her first name is given as either "Falconia" or "Faltonia." The early monastic copies are simply content to call her "Proba."[58] The dominant view is that Faltonia Betitia Proba was the author and, if so, that carries with it the requirement of a composition date by 370 A.D. at the latest. (A date in the 350s is most common.)

When she was converted to Christianity is unknown, though some have speculated it was midway through her life.[59] Coming from a leading senatorial family, there is no data to suggest that she chose the ascetic-aristocratic lifestyle that became a respected upper class way for Christian women to manifest their faith. Instead she continued her everyday Roman manner of life — well-to-do, pursing studies of Roman literature, and living a life of leisure.[60]

The only direct personal contribution by Proba to the work is her introduction, in which she explains why she has prepared it.[61] She begins by referring to how she had "once" written of the bloody wars and conflicts that characterized the human species. The reference is commonly taken to refer to a poem describing the A.D. 353 civil war.[62] Presumably she had distributed it to those she thought would share an interest in its subject matter.

That was the past. Now she prayed that God would "unlock the innermost chamber of my heart, that I, Proba, the prophet might reveal its secrets" and show, through the use of his words, "how Virgil sang the offices of Christ." Since she is clearly defensive about her previous poetry, Anita Obermeier may well be right in speaking of how she is trying to offer a kind of "atonement" for her earlier literary effort.[63]

The work gained an ongoing audience though it had its critics as well. The most famous was Jerome, who loved Virgil; indeed he quotes this pagan poet more than all rival poets combined.[64] Even so, he severely lashed out at Proba's work (which is grounded in Virgil), though not identifying her by name.[65]

In 496 Bishop Gelasius of Rome lumped it in with those works that could only be read in private rather than in a public religious setting. Even so, it continued to be widely copied in monastic libraries through the 1100s. It also continued as an educational resource that was often utilized significantly into the Middle Ages.[66]

It first appeared in print in 1472, making it one of the first — arguably *the* first — work by a woman writer to appear in the new communications media made possible by the printing press.[67]

Christianizing the Virgilian Mythology in the "Cento"

By our standards the work is blatantly plagiaristic, utilizing selected partial and full lines from the respected poet Virgil. They are melded together to create her *own* distinctive meaning and impact.[68] To the modern taste, such an amalgamation seems uncreative and not worth the effort; the ancients however put a much higher value on such attempts and often deeply appreciated them.[69] Indeed, the very *act* of relying on an acknowledged earlier source was regarded as bestowing respect and praise upon it.[70] Unquestionably the composition of the *Cento* required a minute and detailed mastery of Virgil,[71] which simultaneously conveys Proba's own great admiration for the work.

The poem centers on the two broad areas: first, the divine creation and the human fall into sin that is described in the first three chapters of Genesis and, secondly, on selected incidents from Jesus' life. As Virgil used Aeneas as the model for a hero appropriate to Roman (rather than Greek) interests, so Proba pictures Jesus as a laudable role model for a different set of virtues. Heroic in physical appearance and bodily strength, He yet embodied piety incarnated in human form. Except for the emphasis on personal spirituality, the canonical gospels depict Jesus as "Suffering Servant" (an imagery adopted from the book of Isaiah) rather than impressive in bodily stature or form. Also departing from the Biblical tradition, she depicts Jesus on the cross not as a forgiving individual, but as one threatening retribution on those responsible for His unjust death.[72] Yet these dramatic shifts in emphasis permit Proba to craft a modern Jesus for her own age, one that her readers would see as manifesting the qualities and aspirations that Virgil had spoken of in a worldly rather than spiritual context.[73]

Some have suspected that she wrote the work so that Christians could have a "sanitized" Virgil, one without its polytheist elements.[74] Approached this way, the compilation has been interpreted as destroying Virgil in order to save him.[75] This attitude, however, assumes that a literary work should be immune to adaptation by a later audience with different interests and aspirations. Indeed, by adopting a Christocentric usage of Virgil, Proba and others assured its preservation and usage by later generations centuries after overt polytheism vanished.[76]

Rather than trying to "sanitize" Virgil per se, it seems far more likely that it was her intention to adapt Virgil to Christian purposes and prove that his rhetoric could properly be given a monotheist "spin" rather than have to retain its original polytheist setting. In other words an apologetic motive lies behind it rather than concern with hyperactive Christian scruples about utilizing the original work.

FIRMICUS MATERNUS (flourished c. 340s)
Describer of Fourth Century Polytheism

Only one work from this fourth century Christian writer's monotheist period has survived, and that in a single manuscript: *De errore profanarum religionum* (*The Error of the Pagan Religions*). It was dedicated to the emperors Constantius II and Constans I and makes references to the Persian War that occurred during their reign from 337 to 350, which argues that this was also the period of its composition.[77] As part of its effort to prove that Christianity is superior to all other religious systems, the author spells out a large number of details about the cults being practiced contemporaneously and provides us with the kind of specific information otherwise lacking, especially in the case of the "mystery" cults.[78] Even so, his material must be used with care and in light of more recently discovered data. For one thing, at times he assumes a similarity between sects that simply did not exist.[79]

Lactantius and Tertullian had opposed coercion of others into accepting Christianity because an involuntary conversion could not be counted as a genuine one; hence it would only produce the delusion of salvation rather than the reality. In vivid contrast, Maternus considered polytheism such a fount of inevitable moral corruption that it was imperative for the government to bring the full force of its coercive power to suppress its very existence.[80] Although the earlier apologists would not have demurred on the corrupting power of polytheism—whose very gods too often embodied the worst moral faults of the human race—they had not embraced compulsion as the means to remedy the problem.

Although his reasoning would increasingly appeal to Christian rulers of a certain disposition, he mixed in an appeal to their greed that enhanced the power of his argument immensely: "Be not afraid to strip the temples of their ornaments. May these gods melt in the fire for the minting of your coins, and in the flames of your lead-mines. Confiscate for your own benefit all their gifts; make it your own property!"[81] This was, of course, a formula that cash-pressed rulers could readily embrace.

The Astrologer: Julius Firmicus Maternus Siculus

The case for the Christian Firmicus Maternus being the same as the astrologer Julius Firmicus Maternus Siculus begins with their shared names. In addition, the astrologer published his work within about a decade of the Christian, in the 330s.[82] The connection is further reinforced by a compatible writing style between the two individuals.[83]

Yet if the language and writing patterns are similar, the tone is unquestionably different. As Robert Browning effectively summarizes it, "The astrologer is solemn and composed, the Christian fiery and combative." He suggests that if the two are the same (and he concedes that there are no linguistic arguments from their texts against it) that the latter may be accounted for by post-conversion "zeal."[84]

Two scenarios are possible if the two authors are the same: The most obvious one is that within less than a decade he had dramatically changed his convictions and repudiated his astrology by becoming a Christian. The alternative is that he embraced both at the same time: if so, in the two works, he is attempting to harness two different sources of influence in the world (the stars and God) and to explain how both influence the human species. In this approach he might be regarded as "a Christian Gnostic."[85]

The astrologer is known to have been a Roman senator hailing from Sicily. After a temporary career in law, he tired of the confrontations and heavy-handed tactics that were common and turned to the study of literary matters. After years of research, he provided his friend and former governor of Campania with his *Matheseos Libri Octo* (*Eight Books of Astrology*). Due to a reference to a recent eclipse, it appears that the work cannot be earlier than c. A.D. 330.[86]

Maternus' astrology was developed, he asserts, from Egyptian sources.[87] In actual fact, it appears (not unexpectedly) to be derived from Greek ones instead.[88] In his construction of astrology, there is a "Mundi Themea" ("Theme of the World") that was established for the future of the earth itself at the very moment of its origin. Against this primeval nexus individuals must strive to adjust their own astrological fates to that which was inherent for the world from its beginning. By reuniting their private destiny with that of the globe, the breach produced between the inanimate world and the human is resolved and reconciled. Furthermore, only by integrating the astrologically determined destinies of world and individual can one's complete fate be properly determined. However important this concept of an astrological destiny for the world was to him, it was rarely embraced by astrologers of later centuries.[89]

Although *The Error of the Pagan Religions* and *Eight Books of Astrology* may, indeed, be by the same person, it is extremely hard to reconcile the contents of the works if he was a Christian at the time of the latter's composition or if he retained the same astrological convictions after conversion. For example, his explanation for unjust events in life — the honorable being crushed and the disreputable victorious — is "the chance movement of the stars" rather than being due to a higher Divine purpose or response to human behavior.[90] Also he speaks of astrology as constituting, in effect, a religion,[91] hardly the kind of thinking one would have associated with most Christians.

On the other hand, for better or worse, there has always been a certain appeal to a segment of Christian opinion in astrological matters. Perhaps it is rooted, in part, in a creative interpretive interpolation into "the heavens declare the glory of God; and the firmament shows His handiwork" (Psalms 19:1, New King James Version). Interpreted this way, it could be taken as meaning to "declare" or "reveal" in a more literal sense, as a predictor of the future. Be that as it may, the work was preserved throughout the Middle Ages in certain monastic communities and enjoyed a wider breadth of popularity during the Renaissance.[92]

AURELIUS CLEMENS PRUDENTIUS (348–c. 413)
Spanish Poet

Very little is actually known about this man. He was born somewhere in Spain, a northern locale being preferred by most scholars though a minority hold out for the southern part of the country.[93] Although it is usually assumed that he was raised a Christian, what little is known of his early life gives no indication that it had a particularly major impact upon his adult behavior or actions.[94]

After an active life working as both a lawyer and then judge, he retired to devote himself to his spiritual interests. Only then did he turn to writing at least seven volumes of hymns and other works.[95]

Prudentius and others like him reshaped Latin literature to fit the new special interests of Christianity, just as quality earlier authors had reshaped the literature of their era in a similar manner.[96] He does not honor the normal categories of elegiac, epic, or lyric poetry but blends elements of all three together into his own formulation.[97] His work was read with considerable pleasure into the middle of the eighteenth century, when changing fashions and preferences caused him to go into eclipse.[98]

Prudentius has had an impact — either consciously or through the adoption of independently developed similar reasoning — on subjects surprisingly far removed from anything explicitly Christian, for example, the Orpheus work behavior psychological test which measures employee's likely behavior. Here the contrasting types of action are considered as rooted in the behavioral parallelisms pioneered by the ancient poet.[99] In the fictional realm of J. K. Rowling's "Harry Potter" it is argued that the author has metaphorized Prudentius' "battle of the soul" from his *Psychomachia* into Harry's life. Both in the traditional sense of the battle within that occurs during the years of teenage maturation as one adopts a permanent persona and in his dual consciousness with Voldermort.[100]

In love with poetic expression in general and with poetry that could be utilized for hymn singing in particular, he produced both types of work. Of the various examples of the first, we might point to his *Liber Peristephanon,* which was written after he had toured various martyr shrines in Spain and in Rome. Based upon the stories and paintings of the deaths that he found in these places, he used his pen to glorify their sacrifice for their religion.[101] He saw himself as preserving for future generations stories that the persecutors had often tried to suppress. According to him, on at least one occasion a Roman soldier had intentionally destroyed such records to assure that they were not available to those who wished to preserve accurate accounts of the events.[102]

These poems were especially influential because they raised the actions from mere narration of alleged past events to a symbolic level; the *act* of dying for one's faith became the core subject and not *who* was doing the dying.[103] He stressed the beneficialness of the act, not only to the salvation of the individual concerned but to the greater society. For example, the death of Eulalia, which had happened a century earlier, brought well-being to her city, "A powerful city, wealthy people, but made more prosperous by the blood of the virginal tomb."[104]

Composing hymns was a quite natural idea to him. He was convinced there was no higher privilege than to be able to express honor to God through one's singing: "What worthier service can the high-born soul, native of light and heaven, pay, than to chant the gifts she has received, singing of her Creator?"[105] Prudentius' hymn-poems are designed to be content orientated and express his highest literary quality. Their comprehensibility to the less educated audience and what they would sound like in actual singing were secondary concerns. In contrast, Ambrose's hymns come from approximately the same era yet state their points in more crystal clear language for the everyday individual who would be singing them.[106]

As an example of Prudentius' work, we might note these two stanzas from *Ades Pater Supreme*[107]:

> While daylight hours are passing,
> We live and work before Thee;
> Now, ere we rest in slumber,
> We gather to adore Thee.
> Our Christian name and calling
> Of our new birth remind us;
> The Spirit's gifts and sealing
> To firm obedience bind us.

> Begone, ye powers of evil
> With snares and wiles unholy!
> Disturb not with your temptings
> The spirits of the lowly.
> Depart! for Christ is present,
> Beside us, yea, within us;
> Away! His sign, ye know it,
> The victory shall win us.

The "sign" in the last stanza could simply be the cross as the abstract symbol for Jesus' death and triumph over it. However, in other places Prudentius refers to the making of the sign of the cross on one's body and it could be this that he has in mind, either in addition or as the dominant point of reference: "When sleep steals on and/ you retire to rest,/ See that the figure of the Cross/ marks brow and breast."[108]

However popular the poetic efforts of Prudentius became, they did not enjoy an immediate success among contemporary and near-time church leaders. Augustine, for example, does not mention these efforts at all.[109]

The tendency to ignore certain Christian poets likely originated in both theoretical and practical grounds. On the practical side, heretical groups had proved themselves all too capable of proselytizing and promoting their particular agendas through the sung word.[110] On the theoretical side, even those fond of such new works would have felt compelled to confess that the works of the Biblical Psalter surpassed that of any contemporary and could be quite adequate to meet their needs. Some were able to immediately overcome such potential obstacles either due to their personal prestige or the quality and clear usability of their material. For Prudentius, it took more time.

EPHRAEM (died 373)
Commentator and Poet

Although the city of Nisibis had found itself on both sides of the Roman-Persian border through the centuries due to recurring bouts of warfare and changing victors, it had reverted to Roman control in 298. Part of the treaty that did this made it the only legal gateway city for trade between the two rival powers, thereby increasing its economic importance.

When Bishop Jacob of Nisibis returned after the completion of the Nicaean Council he appointed Ephraem, a native of the city, to the post known as "interpreter" or "exegete." This title is unknown anywhere else and it is assumed it meant hymn and commentary writer and teacher of catechumens.[111]

When Julian the Apostate was killed in renewed fighting at the end of his reign, it was clear that Nisibis would again change hands. Ephraem's animosity toward the emperor had already begun to manifest itself in his *Hymns against Julian,* the first of which was finished before the ruler became a combat casualty. It speaks of the need for Christian perseverance under the trials imposed by the ruler's infidelity. The remainder of the collection continue that theme but also stress that God had proved His hostility to paganism by bringing death upon the apostate leader.[112] So though there were no tears over his death, there was profound sorrow because he and others like him had to move further west to stay within the boundaries of the Roman Empire.

Indeed, this was not optional; the peace agreement required the city to be handed over entirely empty of all residents. Ephraem chose to move to Edessa, where he remained till his death in 373. He appears to have continued a very active career of writing and teaching while there, as well as organizing choirs of young men and boys to sing his spiritual songs. This is typically viewed as an innovation carried out in response to the success of Bardesanes in promoting his "heretical" views through the means of hymns. Whether Ephraem utilized the cithara (a form of the lyre) as accompaniment has been more seriously questioned, however.[113]

He became recognized as the most important spiritual writer in Syriac in the ancient church.[114] His hymns, in particular, provided him a reputation that survived his death. The formidable barrier of language differences was overcome by enthusiastic translators who spread his work to Christian groups throughout the known world.[115] Jerome, for example, spoke of the power of his language even though he had the works only in translated form.[116]

Ephraem's hymns heavily emphasize various symbolisms within both testaments that might be interpreted to refer to the communion.[117] Indeed, he regarded the scriptures, the natural world, and the rituals of the church as three harps that God uses to symbolically convey spiritual truth of all types, and he conveys these insights through a heavy emphasis on visual imagery.[118]

Although Ephraem is most remembered for his poetic work, it remains true that he did not neglect prose. For example, in his *Refutations* (a term of convenience invented to lump together various antiheretical writings) there are attacks on the doctrines of men such as Bardaisan and Marcion. A few commentaries have survived that come from either him or disciples shortly thereafter. These include volumes on the Old Testament books of Genesis and Exodus and New Testament books such as Acts. Interestingly, in spite of the widespread inclination to dismiss the *Diatessaron* as heretical, he had sufficient respect for it to write a commentary on its contents.[119] This is clearly not something that would have been produced by someone who regarded it as so altering the gospels as to place it beyond usefulness.

Oddly enough there are two distinct Ephraem documentary traditions. The works he left in Syriac and which were preserved in that language are little found in other languages. In vivid contrast, works supposedly by him have survived in eight other languages, but they have no surviving Syriac originals.[120] The fact that a large body of pseudo-Ephraem material should have come into existence testifies, however, to the prestige his name could add to a work.

Epiphanius of Salamis (died 403)
Chronicler-Refuter of Heretical Movements

Born about 315 near Gaza in Palestine and raised in a Christian household there, Epiphanius, was sent to Egypt for an advanced education. While there he became a fervent supporter of monasticism, established his own monastery in Palestine when he was about twenty and supervised it for the following three decades. In 365 he moved to Cyprus and began the metropolitan of Constantia (the modern day Salamis).[121]

In his *Paranion* (*Medicine Chest*) he identified five parent heresies from which he claimed eighty had ultimately grown. In order to research this work, he sent out letters to church leaders requesting information on various heresies that had occurred in their regions. His enthusiasm for heresy hunting and his feared ability to sniff it out regardless of whether it was present, made the recipients cautious as to exactly what they said in response lest they become the target of his suspicions.[122] Even when locals wished to be fully and accurately responsive, the limitation of personal acquaintance with contemporary foes and the lack of interest in preserving records of heretics from the past limited the data they could provide even with the best of good will. Even so, he cast his net deep and wide and accumulated much data that would otherwise have vanished

Epiphanius deserves full credit for preserving this information as well as data on such earlier individuals as Hippolytus and Irenaeus, much of whose writings were scantily preserved. Unquestionably, considerable intellectual potential was present and can be seen in the fact that a variety of multilingual sources were open to him since, according to Jerome, he was able to work in five different languages.[123] Although lacking a training in philosophy and certainly below the ranks of the most astute theologians of his age, he still had a considerable mental agility leading, upon occasion, to perceptive critiques of religious theories he did not share and interesting use of scriptural texts that reveal a probing mind at work.[124]

Yet there were times when he clearly faltered. On some subjects he leaves the impression of futile verbal twisting about,[125] seemingly either not fully grasping his opponent's views or unable to quite come up with effective refutations. In such cases his prose can be, as Andrew Louth puts it, "tortuous and sometimes barely comprehensible."[126] Such failings are common enough that his reputation as a thinker has usually been cast in negative terms. William A. Jurgens describes him as a man "whose thought was too shallow ever to risk his falling into heresy...."[127] These are much harsher evaluations than the judgments of the time: Jerome speaks of how he was widely read by the well educated as well as the average Christians of his era; this was, he said, because of both his insight and his ability to express himself.[128]

Epiphanius regarded Origen as the premier heretic of the time. Due to maintaining his close connection with the monastery he had founded in Palestine, he was in an ideal position to stir up local discontent against him in spite of the physical distance separating the two parties.[129] Unable to convince Patriarch John of Jerusalem to act, Epiphanius excommunicated Origen on his own. In what was certainly a calculated insult of John, Epiphanius also ordained Paulinus, even though he ministered in the region under the authority of John.[130]

When Chrysostom of Constantinople generously received alleged Origenists into his city, this splintered the friendship with Epiphanius, and Chrysostom was added to his list of despised targets. Although the story of their final meeting is unlikely to be fully historical, it embodies so much of the two men's critical attitudes toward each other that it is impossible to dismiss the underlying attitudes being expressed, however much one might question the exact words: at its end Epiphanius provided the blessing-curse, "I hope you will not die — a bishop." To which Chrysostom quickly responded with his own pseudo-blessing, "To return home safely — do not expect."[131] Both men got their wishes: Epiphanius perished when his ship sank at sea a matter of days later; in slightly more than a year, Chrysostom was forced into permanent exile.

The heretic hunter was himself open to later challenge as shifting patterns of perceived orthodoxy cast some of his views beyond the pale of acceptance. For example, in spite of the growing popularity of image veneration he was a strong opponent of the practice. He wrote to John of Jerusalem of his revulsion[132]:

> When I came into a country church of Palestine, called Anablatha, I found a certain cloth hanging over the door, upon which there was a picture painted like that of our Savior or some saint, for I cannot certainly remember whose picture it was. However, seeing the figure of a man in the Church of Christ, contrary to the authority of the Holy Scriptures, I tore it, and gave orders to the church-wardens to wrap it around some corpse and bury it.

To him, it was all idle speculation, since no one had the foggiest idea of what Jesus really looked like: how could one possibly hope to produce an accurate and reliable result? Public resentment was so intense, however, that he soon had to back down and provide for the replacement of the destroyed image.[133] When the issue of images heated up at a later date, Epiphanius became an invaluable resource for those opposing the practice and one whose orthodoxy could not be questioned even by the most fervent proponent of the usage. The best proponents could come up with, however, was the unjustified accusation that the record of the embarrassing incident had been interpolated into his writings.[134]

Chapter 4

Biblical Translators and Textual Scholars

TATIAN (flourished c. post–150)
"Editor" of the Gospels

The exact time of Tatian's birth is unknown, with estimates typically ranging from c. A.D. 120 to 125. He was self-described as an "Assyrian." Some take this more or less at face value and interpret it as meaning he was from somewhere in Mesopotamia, while others attempt to pin it down more precisely as referring to either Adiabene or the northern part of Mesopotamia.

Tatian was provided a quality in-depth Greek-style education and had the opportunity to visit large sections of the civilized world of his day before proceeding to Rome.[1] The fact that Tatian came from a prosperous background can be seen in the fact that he had sufficient funds to carry out these travels.

The success of his educational endeavors was conceded even by his foes. Eusebius spoke of how he "was trained in the learning of the Greeks and gained no small repute in it."[2] His profession was that of teacher, even after he became a Christian. Irenaeus claimed that he was an egomaniac and speaks of how Tatian "exalted at the prospect of being a teacher, and puffed up as if he were superior to everyone else, he created a unique doctrine."[3] Perhaps; on the other hand, Irenaeus may simply be assuming that, since Tatian took pride in his educational skills, *excess* pride must have motivated his doctrinal innovations. The possibility that he could have been honest — but wrong — was a concept hard if not impossible for Irenaeus to accept.

In Rome, Tatian was converted about 160. A pupil and admirer of Justin Martyr, this close relationship may well have been the result of Justin having converted him.[4] Tatian himself became an active instructor within the Roman church around 165. He was a primary teacher of Rhodo, who became a major literary foe of Marcion.

After Justin's death Tatian's commitment to orthodoxy wavered and collapsed.[5] Doctrinally he was converted to a form of Gnosticism — the idea of there being a set of "secret" doctrines available only to the spiritual elite. The concept is concisely described in the introductory words of the *Gospel of Thomas*: "These are the *secret* words which the living Jesus spoke."[6] The idea of having access to wisdom given only to a narrow elite even *within* one's religion represented an enticing concept that created dissident groups in both Christianity and Judaism as well as in polytheism. Although a matter of much controversy, the view that Gnosticism sprang from a pre–Christian origin, quite likely Jewish, is the dominant view.[7]

Tatian's critics often implicitly argued that Tatian had adopted his new theology from Valentinus since they shared in common certain major beliefs — at least in the mind of their joint opponents.[8] Equally important would be differences in how the two men treated the same ideas. Unfortunately, the necessary volume of in-depth source material to conduct such an analysis of relative agreements and disagreements does not exist.[9]

The assumption that shared convictions must indicate a "borrowing" remains a standard tool for censuring doctrinal deviants even in our current century. This view is sometimes a quite accurate depiction of what has happened, but it is far from universally the case. Furthermore, it overlooks the fact that an individual may come to similar conclusions not because of "dependence" but because his thinking had already been moving in that direction or because of hearing views which stirred his own quite independent analysis. The same multiple paths of spiritual-intellectual development also existed in the second century.

Tatian as a Pioneer of Asceticism

Hand in hand with his doctrinal aberration went the adoption of a form of hyperspirituality that would have tested his acceptability even if he had retained his "orthodox" roots. This was called encraticism and involved asceticism far beyond what would have been considered acceptable even by those most sympathetic to the lifestyle.[10] So popular was asceticism in the East — even stringent forms — that some have questioned whether there ever was a distinct organized Encratic sect. In this view, the labeling of it as a distinct movement was an invention of hostile western "orthodox" critics. This served the practical purpose of allowing pointed criticism without seeming to impugn other individuals who were virtually identical in attitude and practice but not clearly aligned to Tatian's faction. Today, we would call this conscious or unconscious strategy one of "divide and conquer."[11]

Especially among those vigorously supporting celibate monasticism, the encratite movement was difficult to combat with doctrinal consistency. In a very real sense, it could be argued that it was simply a fuller working out of the principles that this larger group embraced, but which they refused to develop to its "logical" conclusion. In that scenario, the majority became the compromisers and the more rigidly one opposed all marriage and sexuality the more faithful one proved oneself to the apostolic ideal.[11]

Although not normally reckoned among the shapers of the ascetic movement in his home region, yet it seems inevitable that Tatian's converts would have played a significant (at least supporting) role in its rise.[12] After all, his *Diatessaron* (see below) was widely used and this popularity would have inevitably provided a psychological boost to those adopting part of his spiritual agenda as to behavior. On the other hand, his being under the accusation of "unorthodoxy" obviously made it inexpedient to cite him as a pioneer lest "orthodox" asceticism be suspect of similar doctrinal deviancy as well.

Be that as it may, moving back to the East he found a degree of receptivity to himself that was lacking in the West. In spite of the fact that the rigorous form of self-denial that he expected from converts obviously limited his potential for successful missionary efforts, he still managed to assemble a significant body of adherents who were willing to embrace it.

Virtually nothing is certain of his career after he left Rome except for the fact that he wrote two works that survived into the modern era (see next section) and several others that perished. Probably in 172 he established his own school of religious education for Christians in Mesopotamia. Nothing is known of the timing or nature of his death though its date has been placed in approximately 180.

The Diatessaron

Although his apologetic work *Oration to the Greeks* is of interest for its defense of Christianity, in the current context we are far more interested in his dedication to Biblical translation — albeit in a form that ultimately generated much controversy. We refer to the *Diatessaron,* which combined the four gospels into a single consecutive account of Jesus' life. No explanation was suggested by the ancients as to the motive behind this work. However, since such efforts were repeatedly produced by careful students of the scriptural text in both the nineteenth and twentieth centuries, it is quite possible that there is something inherently appealing on the psychological level in the effort to blend the diverse materials into one continuous account.

Furthermore, unlike today, when Biblical texts are readily available at very low cost, such was not the case in the second century. Then all books were handwritten and when one combined the cost of labor and writing materials, the cumulative cost for all four gospels had to be a significant one. In contrast, one combined text reduced costs significantly and enabled the material to be put in more peoples' hands than would otherwise have been possible.

Being an individual zealously wishing for the fundamentals of the life of the Jesus he preached to be widely shared, such factors surely played a role in Tatian's decision to produce the work. Other factors may well have been present as well, of course. As one scholar suggests, "If he was liturgically minded he may have hoped to produce something more suitable than the four separate gospels for regular Sunday readings in church. Or he may have felt that since there was only one Christian gospel (cf. Galatians 1:6–9), the literary records of its beginnings should also be one."[13]

Since a project of this length would have required much thought and a drawn out period of preparation, the speculation that he began it while still in Rome makes inherent sense.[14] Assuming he left Rome about 172 and that the likely release date of the work to public use was a few years later, about 173–175, a beginning date after his departure would have made it extremely difficult to complete his compilation in the time available.

Although it is not certain whether the *Diatessaron* was originally produced in Greek and then translated into Syriac rather than vice versa, scholars are inclined to a Greek original.[15] In either case, the most likely translator of the text was Tatian himself.[16]

Some have speculated that the *Diatessaron* rather than the four gospels were the source and inspiration for the *Gospel of Thomas*.[17] It was definitely the authoritative text for the Manichaean heresy.[18] Neither use would have encouraged its acceptability among the traditionally orthodox, of course.

Neither a Greek nor a Syriac full text has survived. On the other hand, an eleventh century Arabic translation from a Syriac manuscript at least two centuries younger is viewed as a reliable rendition of the text then available. Codex Fuldensis preserved a chronologically earlier Latin version, but in an adapted form in which Tatian's original choice and arrangement of passages is not fully maintained.[19]

Partial quotations were preserved in significant amount in the two fourth century Syriac speaking churchmen Aphraetes and Ephraem. Only Aphraetes' selections were preserved in the Syriac, though, while those of Ephraem are found in a third hand translation—a Latin text translated from the Armenian which had been based on the Syriac.[20]

Some suspect the Old Syrian New Testament form of the four gospels was produced first,[21] but the more common view seems to be that the *Diatessaron* preceded it.[22] The latter view hinges in large part upon the assumption that the *Diatessaron* was the dominant gospel text in the Syriac speaking region. Certainly it became such whether or not it was from the beginning.

There are several indications of the work's great popularity and how it was only squashed with determined and energetic effort. The *Doctrine of Addai,* which is best known for its fictional correspondence between Jesus and Edessa's king, must have been written no later than the early 200s, since it includes a prediction that Edessa would never be destroyed. Since the Romans did exactly that in A.D. 217, a composition at an earlier date is clearly required, at least for a significant part of the document.[23]

The *Doctrine* includes this important allusion: "Moreover much people day by day assembled and came together for prayer and for the reading of the Old Testament and the New, the *Diatessaron*."[24] In short, the New Testament is regarded as equivalent to the gospel as recorded in the *Diatessaron*. For this allusion to have made sense or to have been credible, it must at least have been the dominant "gospel" available in Syria and Armenia.[25] This, in turn, argues that the Old Syriac version with its four distinct gospels had either been generally displaced or had been more recently translated and not begun to make a major dent in the popularity of Tatian's compilation.

By the time of Eusebius' *Church History,* the work had gone into decline, at least in the regions Eusebius was most associated with. As he observes, "The former leader of the Encratites, Tatian, composed somehow a kind of combined and concurrent gospel and called it the *Diatessaron*, a work which is still circulated in some quarters."[26] Eusebius' derogatory reference to how Tatian "somehow" managed to compose the work reveals his contempt for the man's intellectual talents and likely springs out of abhorrence at his doctrinal views: since he had arrived at such outlandish and heretical extremes, how could one imagine he could have composed a work that could prove itself truly beneficial to believers in general? The most natural reading of his words would argue that Eusebius did not even have the work available to him. On the other hand, the clear contempt for Tatian's intellectual abilities likely indicates that he consciously avoided the assemblage regardless of whether he had access to it.[27]

In the early fifth century (A.D. 412–415), Bishop Rabbula of Edessa was actively propagating the circulation of the four gospels. He instructed, "Let the presbyters and deacons have a care that in all the churches there be provided and read a copy of the distinct Gospel."[28] The requirement does not explicitly call for the banning of Tatian's work but only for the making available of the traditional four gospels. The fact that these were to be "read" in the churches effectively relegated the *Diatessaron* to nonchurch settings and private usage. It was an effective way to edge the work out of congregational use without risking a major backlash by officially banning it. Writing in A.D. 453, Theodoret refers to his crusade to further crush the public usage of it[29]:

> He [Tatian] composed the so-called *Diatessaron* by cutting out the genealogies and whatever goes to prove the Lord to have been born of the seed of David according to the flesh. And this work was in use not only among his own party but even amongst those who follow the tradition of the Apostles, who used it somewhat too innocently as a compendium of the Gospels without recognizing the craftiness of its composition. I myself found more than 200 copies in reverential use in the churches of my diocese, all of which I removed, replacing them by the Gospels of the four Evangelists.

Criticizing the lengthy genealogies of Jesus for being omitted was an obvious target because of the amount of material involved and how it would be noted by even the most casual reader of the traditional four life accounts of Jesus. On the other hand, it represented a major omission that affected nothing of the readability or core message of the work. Quite likely the orthodox who were readers of the *Diatessaron* reasoned similarly. Only when the subject was shifted from the "usefulness" of such a compendium to its "orthodoxy"—the downplaying of the Jewish element in Jesus' life and teaching—would the omission shift from one of modest concern to one of major significance.

Since Theodoret had some 800 churches under his jurisdiction,[30] the 200 churches using the work represented a full quarter of the congregations answerable to him. His allusion to the popularity of the compilation among many orthodox argues that either the doctrinal significance of the changes were not so obvious to the rank and file or that they were not considered of great importance when compared with the ready usability of a combined four-in-one treatment: utilitarianism trumped orthodoxy. By removing the *Diatessaron* from its public worship use and thereby "delegitimizing" it, Theodoret had made a major step to undermine its credibility and acceptability throughout his diocese. This effort was ultimately successful but only after long, drawn-out effort.

ORIGEN (185–254)
Compiler of the Hebrew-Greek *Hexapla*

Origen's birth was about A.D. 185 and his parents were Christians, though some speculate the father may not have converted until shortly before his death. Regardless of whether this was so, his father died a martyr and Origen himself was prepared to turn himself into the authorities and die as well. His mother aborted this scheme by literally hiding all his clothes.[31] Origen was given a traditional education in the literature of the past and he apparently mastered it quite well since he supported himself as a teacher after his father was executed.[32]

Much later, Origen wrote against the kind of volunteering for death that had tempted him when young, presumably at least in part based upon a recognition of his own youthful folly. Cyprian and Clement of Alexandria, among others, took the same stance. Augustine also argued against such a course by stressing the difference between what amounted to suicide and genuine martyrdom.[33] Yet, such a high value was placed upon dying for one's faith by this time that many ignored such pleas both before Origen and after Augustine[34] and it is quite possible that as many people died in such needless sacrifices as were explicitly singled out for notice.[35]

During the persecution of the 230s, Origen was among those specifically targeted for arrest. To escape it, he fled and hid from his pursuers. When he wrote his *Exhortation to Martyrdom,* he praised the courage of those who had the misfortune to have been arrested. Yet there is no personal defensiveness about his own course of action, which goes totally unmentioned.[36] If there is an implicit point here it is likely that martyrdom is to be courageously endured if one must face it, but that there is no need to needlessly court it.

Origen as Religious Educator in Alexandria

Origen's intellect and maturity can be seen in the fact that, though he was barely eighteen or nineteen, he was chosen to head what we today would call the theological education school of the church as the replacement for Clement, his predecessor having fled persecution in Alexandria in A.D. 203. Although the opportunity was probably made possible because more mature individuals had perished in the repression, both friends and foes always conceded his great intelligence, so of those available he was no doubt the best remaining.

Origen's mind frame resulted in a distinct shift in the type of teaching being carried out. Clement of Alexandria happily used pagan poetry and literature to illustrate and make his spiritual points. In contrast, Origen avoided these as a matter of principle, except when he was writing for a non–Christian audience in his *Contra Celsum.*[37]

As he said in a sermon that used Psalms 36 as its jumping off point, "the poems of the poets, the fictions of the authors of comedy, the narratives (whether fictitious or horrifying) of the authors of tragedy, and the lengthy and varied volumes of histories" were of no value when compared to scripture and the religious insights provided by his predecessors in the church.[38]

He scorned even the subject of rhetoric, which provided an individual with the skills of speaking and public debate. The lack or neglect of the latter skills may well explain his complaint that church audiences tended to let their minds drift and not pay attention to his sermons.[39] A person may have tremendous insights to share but unless one also has the skill to present them clearly and appealingly inattentiveness is nearly always the result.

In the following years, he spent a goodly amount of time on the road, visiting Palestine, Greece, and Rome. Unfortunately for the sake of domestic peace in his Alexandrian home, Bishop Demetrius had fallen out with him. This was likely due to plain old-fashioned jealousy that a subordinate should be gaining a greater reputation than his leader, not to mention that he was also much smarter as well. As late as 216 Origen was still a mere layman and Demetrius was quite indignant that he had dared provide lectures to an audience of bishops while away from the city. On the way to Greece, Palestinian leaders happily ordained him to the priesthood so that he could escape any future charges of inappropriate behavior. Still dissatisfied, Demetrius claimed that Origen was self-castrated and that this invalidated any desire he might have to be a priest.

The denunciation did nothing to calm Demetrius' fury. Origen found himself put on trial, and excommunication came in 231. The death of the bishop occurred soon afterwards but after the successor kept the exclusion in place Origen moved to Palestine where he was greeted with open and enthusiastic arms.[40]

Origen as Religious Educator in Caesarea, Palestine

Caesarea Maritima had been founded by Herod the Great and contained the usual collection of facilities that marked a Roman city: an aqueduct system, a theater, an amphitheatre, and other marks of "civilized" living of the day. By the middle of the first century it had already gained a population of around 45,000.[41] It is quite likely that it had a civic library from its early days and the resident Jewish community surely must have had one of its own to provide for its special religious needs as well.[42]

At what point Christians began to compile an ad hoc library is unknown, but at least some type of archive or library seems certain to have begun when a sufficient volume of church correspondence accumulated. Likewise, one would anticipate copies of the scriptures being added. This is all speculation, though highly probable.

When Origen moved to Caesarea permanently about 232, he began to collect various manuscripts that would help him and his students in their study of the gospel and Torah. This was in connection with his service as director of the religious educational school at Caesarea. He served there going on twenty years and provided various classes on both philosophy and theology.[43]

His own extensive scholarly writings and biblical studies further enhanced the church's library. These grew rapidly as new material was composed and old material revised. Especially important in making their production and circulation widespread was the generous financial support of a former Gnostic he had converted by the name of Ambrose. He provided no less than seven shorthand specialists to take Origen's dictation in Alexandria and at least that many copyists. In Caesarea, one would assume that at least the same level of assistance was maintained, since Origen speaks of how Ambrose constantly kept encouraging him to ever greater literary efforts and studies.[44]

In 251 the anti–Christian programme of Decius caught him in its grip. Although he survived this, it has been speculated that injuries received at this time led to his death sometime during the next few years.[45]

The Theology of Origen

The bulk of his massive literary production — around 800 works in all — have long vanished. It is known that he wrote 574 sermons; 388 have perished. The percentage is even worse for his letters: Of a minimum one hundred letters that he wrote, no more than three have survived.[46]

This leaves us with a real problem as to what he believed. Some regarded him as a spiritual giant; others as a heretic; others as simply rhetorically obscure (at his worst) to the point of distraction; others a mixed bag of the highly inspiring yet also presenting arguments and language so disappointing it was best forgotten.[47]

The evidence concerning his convictions was clearly manipulated both in his lifetime and thereafter. He himself claimed that a debate he had held had been rewritten and was being distributed in altered form by his opponent.[48] Later, Rufinus provided a translation of one of Origen's works, but conceded he left much out because he regarded his source as suffering serious interpolations from hostile parties. On the other hand, Jerome brought out a rival translation of the same original source, putting *back in* the alleged heretical convictions that Rufinus had downplayed or omitted.[49] Assuming both were sincere, what were to be regarded as Origen's true convictions were already a subject of rival conclusions even at that early a date.

However mystically inclined Origen preferred to be (which probably contributed no small amount to the contradictory conclusions many reached concerning his orthodoxy), he could write well-reasoned analytical literature when he desired. In his *Against Celsus*, he dealt with a foe who had written significantly earlier, in approximately 175. Celsus was that rarity of his day or ours: one who knew the sacred texts of his opponent in detail and who knew exactly what passages to go to prove "contradictions" and what points those on the other side of the theological divide would encounter the most difficulty with.[50] Origen's refutation of these views is considered one of the classics of "apologetics"— as the defense of one's faith is called — and it is, perhaps, his ability to do so with a directness appealing to the modern mind that makes this his most interesting material to survive.[51]

The Hebrew-Greek Hexapla

On a verse-by-verse basis throughout the entire Old Testament, the first column of this compilation consisted of the Hebrew text. (The degree of Origen's knowledge of Hebrew is uncertain and some regard it as minimal.)[52] The second column consisted of a transliteration of the Hebrew into Greek letters.

The third column consisted of Aquila's translation, likely because it was the most literal of the versions Origen utilized.[53] This translation may have originated around A.D. 130 and strove so hard for literalness that one often needed to refer to the underlying Hebrew to grasp the point being made. It has been speculated that he was the same man as the one Jewish literature calls Onqelos and who composed a Pentateuch Targum.[54]

The fourth column contained the work of Symmachus, a Greek translation of the late second century. Epiphanius identifies him as a Samaritan convert to traditional Judaism. Jerome, though, thought he had embraced the Ebionite form of Judeo-Christianity.[55] Within the context of attempting to make a fully reliable translation, he still attempted to keep his Greek as "colloquial" as seemed consistent with that goal.[56]

It was said that he was an active propagandist against Christianity, taking time to compile a hostile critique of Matthew and passing it on to a Christian reader. This work ultimately landed in Origen's hands.[57] One would assume that he circulated other copies of the review as well in order to fully justify the time he had spent in working on it. Hence it is quite possible that it became one of the standard refutations circulating among traditionalist Jews.

The fifth column was the Septuagint, marked with all the necessary additions and subtractions required to bring its Greek into conformity with the Hebrew. This presupposes that there was a sufficiently widely used Hebrew form that would have been generally regarded as authoritative or the effort would have been inherently useless for him to undertake. Yet even Origen recognized that there were serious difficulties inherent in his project; he refers to the existence of significant textual differences even within the contemporary Hebrew manuscript tradition.[58]

Since Origen utilized the fifth column in his preaching, it is clear that he regarded his work not merely as a theological tool to further Christian-Jewish disputes about the text and its meaning, but as the jumping off point for his own exegesis before audiences already in agreement with him on these matters.[59]

Finally, the sixth column provided the translation traditionally ascribed to Theodotion. Assuming he did serious translation work (rather than just had the work of others incorrectly attributed to him), a range of A.D. 130–180 would seem required for the publication of his rendition.[60]

Originally, Origen intended the *Hexapla* to include additional translations as well. Eusebius speaks of how, in the original draft, Origen had used these in the early part of the Old Testament.[61] The additional volume of material may simply have become unmanageable when applied to the entire Torah and prophets. Alternatively, it may be that the supplementary versions covered only the Torah, just as in the twentieth century a number of New Testament translations went no further than the four gospels.

Because of the massive scope covered by the *Hexapla,* it is likely that no full copies were ever made of the entire work.[62] The largest single part of the multicolumn text that has survived consists of Psalms fragments and even *that* lacks the Hebrew. (In a church ever increasingly dominated by non–Hebrew speaking and reading Gentiles, this was the part of the work most vulnerable to disappearing due to lack of qualified copyists or interested parties.) These remains are called the "Milan Fragments," date from the ninth century at the earliest, and contain the text of only 150 verses. Oddly, the sixth column substitutes a different version for the work of Theodotion.[63]

Less often commented upon is Origen's companion work, the *Tetrapla*, which contained four Greek translations. Though most regard it as simply an abridgment of the larger work, it is, of course, possible that this was the preliminary draft that lay the foundation for his later expansion of the material into the *Hexapla*.[64] This early volume contained the widely respect LXX text as well as the translations of Aquila, Symmachus, and Theodotion.[65]

Ulfilas (c. 311–c. 381)
Bible Translator for the Goths

The ancestors of Ulfilas[66] were probably individuals captured in raids by the Western Goths during the 250s or 260s who were carried into the Danube region. Hence Ulfilas was a second or third generation Christian. The usual assumption is that his mother was Cappadocian and that his father was a Goth by ancestry, though there is no compelling reason why the reverse could not have been the case.[67]

He made his first visit to Constantinople no later than 337 if we accept the claim that he met Constantine before his death in that year. The other possibility places the journey in 338 or later, since it is claimed that Eusebius of Nicomedia ordained him and Eusebius became a bishop in that year.[68] Both sets of data could be explained if there was inadvertent confusion as to which emperor or bishop was involved in the appointment or if the decision had been tentatively made to appoint him under Constantine but not carried out till later.

By this point, Ulfilas' *official* position was the modest one of lector (scripture reader). His ability in his adult years to write papers in both Greek and Latin shows that he had become trilingual, and we would anticipate that some type of formal training had polished his writing skills by this point.[69] Furthermore, in his first visit to the imperial court, he was attached to an official Gothic delegation to discuss matters of mutual importance. As such, this argues that he was already recognized as a person of some significance regardless of the modesty of his ancestry or religious post: To send anyone of obscure status to the Roman emperor would have been viewed as a diplomatic insult.[70] Indeed, it may well be recognition of his de facto status that resulted in his being appointed bishop by the Romans in preference to any one else[71] and such a societal standing would have the potential for opening doors for Christianity that other Goths could not. Be that as it may, during this diplomatic visit he was consecrated to the post of bishop, in which he served for the next four decades.

A major priority of his was missionary work. There are two theories of how Ulfilas began this among his people. In one analysis, it was an outgrowth of his being a Bible "reader" within a circle of fellow Christians—which places it as beginning prior to his gaining major church office. In the other reconstruction, he was converted by Eusebius of Nicomedia in Constantinople and was appointed bishop with the explicit assignment of carrying the gospel to the Goths.[72] Although not impossible, the usual Roman contempt for the Goths (see Arianism below) makes anything more than a token admonishment in this direction to be unlikely. Even so, the number converted through Ulfilas' labor appears to have ultimately numbered in the thousands.[73]

From the standpoint of their societal well-being, however, the Goths regarded their local Christians as subversive allies of the Romans. Faced with a vigorous anti–Christian persecution, believing Goths sought a new and safer home under the leadership of their bishop. Indeed, some have speculated that the persecution and de facto expulsion was due to the success of the conversion efforts.[74]

The people settled in what is now Bulgaria in the region then known as Moesia, and Ulfilas continued to regard his mission to be one of converting those left behind. Because of his concern for these believers, it is likely that he discreetly encouraged them by both the written word and messengers. This would have been facilitated by the fact that Moesia, though Roman territory, was just fifty kilometers from the border.[75] The mind-frame of these refugees was distinctly unwarlike and (unlike the usual image assigned to Goths by the Romans) they were described by one ancient contemporary as the "numerous and unwarlike people of the Gothi minores."[76]

His Bible Translation

It is quite possible that Ulfilas was the first person to convert spoken Gothic—or any other Germanic language—into written form. He invented an alphabet using Greek letters as its foundation, but blending in borrowings from Latin and certain German runic symbols.[77]

In some cases he borrowed entire words from Greek or Latin to meet the limitations of Gothic speech. "Evangelia," for example, was borrowed to convey the word "gospel." In order to express the idea of "altar" he invented a compound word that, separately, meant "place" and "of sacrifice." Finally, he gave spoken Gothic words a new Christianized context: *galga,* which simply meant "pole," was used to describe the "cross" Jesus died on.[78]

The translation of the work began sometime after A.D. 350, perhaps as late as 360. His pivotal role in producing the translation does not rule out the possibility that he had assistance from others on the massive endeavor.[79]

The translator attempted to be very "literalistic," being zealous to conform it as closely as possible to the underlying Greek original. To a number of later critics this clearly compromised its readability and understandability, while others insist that it did full justice to contemporary Gothic idiom. Balancing "literalness" with maximum contemporary understandability has always been one of the greatest challenges to those working from this translation approach and if Ulfilas encountered difficulties it would be no more than expected.

Philostorgius wrote that Ulfilas had omitted the book of Kings from his Old Testament in an effort to discourage the war-making spirit so common among his ethnic group. In light of his insistence upon accurate translation, it would seem psychologically near impossible for him to have intentionally left out an entire book of the Old Testament even if the prospect tempted him. Hence it may be that the disappearance of Kings was caused by its loss in the manuscript transmission process.[80] It is also quite possible that, because of its war-centered subject matter, it was far less copied by later scribes and, therefore, never enjoyed more than limited circulation. Ulfilas certainly recognized that potential misunderstandings could grow out of the work in his militaristic culture: In other contexts, he clearly avoids a clear-cut literalistic translation of certain war related terms, which argues that he was sensitive to their possible repercussions and misuse.[81]

The only manuscripts surviving of the Bible translation come from the sixth century. Of the five partial copies, two have the Gothic on one side of the page and a Latin version on the other.[82] Interestingly, these provide evidence that certain Latin readings had crept into the Gothic version and certain Gothic preferences into Latin manuscripts as well, which argues that even among the users of Ulfilas' translation there was no perceived need for the original to be preserved when "improvements" could be incorporated.[83] As to contents, of the Old Testament the remains contain only Nehemiah. In the New Testament a quarter of the text has vanished.[84]

The Goths, Ulfilas, and Arianism

The initial Christians in Gothia were individuals who had been captured by raiding Goth forces and compelled to leave the boundaries of the Roman Empire by their captors. A significant number of these became respected in their new home because of specialized skills they brought with them. This was especially the case of those in the medical field, whose skill and knowledge level was far above that available locally. On a cultural level, the restrained Christian lifestyle made an impression upon many who did not see reason to adopt it themselves.[85]

However happy Roman Christians were to learn of the expansion of their faith among the "barbarian" Visigoths, it was carried out strictly on the basis of local initiative, even deep into the fourth century until the days of Ulfilas. Similarly, organizing their churches was strictly a matter of local initiative rather than outsider encouragement, as Goth Christians made the decision of whom to consecrate to church leadership independently of outside influence.[86]

The simple fact was that any zeal for new converts was overwhelmed by distaste for the culture they lived in and practiced—a very Roman snobbery for those they considered their inferiors. The *Opus Imperfectum* (an Arian work composed somewhere between 400 and 450) manifests this attitude extremely well. The author of this commentary on the gospel of Matthew criticizes even Gothic Christians as a lost cause because they were "unlearned, undisciplined, and barbarian peoples, who neither seek nor hear [God's word] with judgment and who have the name of Christians but the manners of pagans."[87] Even the names they chose rankled. As the same commentary argues, "The barbarian nations are in the habit of giving their sons names which recall the havoc caused by wild beasts or scavenging birds; they think it glorious to have such names, suitable for war and raging for blood."[88] This could not have endeared the author to the people being criticized nor to the many local admirers of Ulfilas: after all, his name meant "Little Wolf."[89]

The burst of numerical growth that began under Ulfilas and his disciples was likely carried out predominantly by Arian sympathizers, since the people themselves, when converted, were usually considered Arians. Of course this was not uniformly the pattern. Goths in the Crimean region embraced Nicene orthodoxy, though probably not with the doctrinal preciseness the more passionate Nicene advocates would have preferred. In contrast, Balkan Goths were considered Arian because of their insistence upon making a clear-cut distinction between Father and Son rather than blurring the difference, as Nicene tenets insisted upon.[90] Unquestionably, by the time large numbers of Goths began to pour into the Roman Empire, the bulk of them were Arians, though they were no more likely to have been sophisticated in the finer details of their theology than were those embracing the Nicene alternative.[91]

It has, from the days of Ambrose, commonly been assumed that the influx of Goths reintroduced Arianism into the Empire after Nicene supporters had effectively crushed and destroyed it. In both the Balkans and Italy there had always been a strong minority current of Arians, however, and what the arrival of outsiders did was to reinvigorate an already simmering movement.[92]

Ulfilas found himself in the most difficult position a leader can be in: he thought the Nicene definition of orthodoxy on the Godhead seriously overstated the unity of the trinity while the Arian view went too far in making a distinction. Hence he much preferred to speak of the "similar" rather than the Nicene "identical" nature of Father and Son, indeed, it was more a matter of "resemblance" than "essence" that marked their unity.[93]

To the orthodox, that made him guilty of implicit if not explicit Arianism[94] and his toleration for the more explicit forms of it made his "true" heretical intentions that much more transparent. Since this was the case, there were two derogatory positions taken about him: either he was an apostate Catholic (if one wished to denigrate his faith) or he was mentally incapable of grasping the nature of the trinity (if one wished to insult his intellect).[95]

Literally on his deathbed, he summed up his final convictions this way: "There is one eternal, unbegotten, and invisible God, who before time existed alone. Within time, he created the Son, the only-begotten God. He is the creator of all things, the Lord of the Holy Spirit whom the Father created through the Son before all things. The Holy Spirit is obedient and subject to the Son like the Son to the Father."[96] This was an odd statement to come while he was dying — where one's mind more naturally rests on one's mortality and meditation on what is to come — yet a very prudent one: it seems likely that he had no intention to permit the Nicene faction to claim he had changed or repudiated his convictions. They might denounce him, but he was not going to permit them to use his memory as a propaganda tool for their own interests.

JEROME (c. 340–420)
Translator of the Latin Vulgate

Jerome was born in Stridon (in modern Yugoslavia); family were both Christian and from the well-off stratum of local society. In his childhood, he wrote, he remembered spending much joyous time with his slave attendants in their quarters. (Slavery was still pervasive in that age and a mark of major economic accomplishment and social standing. Unlike the slavery that emerged beginning in the sixteenth to nineteenth centuries, this ancient slavery had no relationship with the race of those enslaved.)

At age six his formal elementary education began and continued till he was at least eleven. His parents desired first class advanced instruction and had the money to provide it. Hence he left home for Rome, where he was enrolled in the classes of Aelius Donatus, a widely respected and revered teacher of the time. He would have been about fifteen when he moved from classes under Donatus to training in rhetoric.[97] Judging from the quality of his adult work, he must have been an able student in all these years of his educational preparation. At what point in his life Christianity was transformed from being part of his societal-cultural background into being a core part of his own personal nature is unknown. He left no account of what changed him; we simply know that something did.[98]

After completing his education, Jerome began to visit various interesting parts of the world. During these travels he became intrigued by asceticism and was soon a fervent advocate of it. After stays in France, Syria, and Constantinople, he returned to Rome and served from 382 to 385 as a confidante of Bishop Damascus. He also became the spiritual adviser to various women of the upper class and began to pour out letters and essays. Hand in hand with this was an ever rising prestige in the eyes of emperor Theodosius, who found Jerome's commitment to militant "orthodoxy" meshing perfectly with his own similar agenda. Even so, Jerome thoroughly antagonized the local priests by his critiques of their behavior, who responded by noting the apparent incongruity of his close relations to leading women while claiming to be an ascetic. When Damascus died, they were able to get Jerome censured and he had no practical choice but to leave the city.[99]

He traveled for a while but chose Palestine in which to establish a monastery. This was financed by the wealthy Paula, who set up a similar facility for women in the same city. Palestine thereafter became the home for Jerome's many intellectual endeavors.

As can be seen from the wide variety of his works, he took his scholarship with dead seriousness. They required endless hours of mental sweat and effort; choosing between work and sleep, he often survived on the minimum of rest his body could tolerate. Like late twentieth century science fiction writers such as Isaac Asimov, Harry Turtledove, and David Webber (and the comparison is *not* meant derogatorily), Jerome was capable of grinding out reams of intense and impressive material on a schedule that would make normal individuals despair. In just two weeks he completed a *Commentary on Matthew* because Eusebius of Cremona was leaving and he wished to have it ready for him to take on his sea journey.[100] This kind of intellectual passion, combined with an abbreviated writing schedule, however, could produce errors that would otherwise have been caught, and could result in his placing heavy emphasis on very narrow subjects while letting other themes drift.[101] In spite of this proviso, the incredible thing is that he could repeatedly produce useful and credible works even in such a stringent time frame.

There was a nasty side to Jerome's rhetoric and personality that came out repeatedly. As we saw above, his rebukes of the Roman priesthood led to his de facto banishment when they got the upper hand. Those he disagreed with theologically were usually the recipients of sharp-tongued written rebukes. Although these can be fascinating to read, they created much unneeded animosity. It is only a mild exaggeration to say that if you were in continued disagreement with him he regarded you as little short of a fool.[102] This was a mentality that inflamed situations rather than providing a framework for their resolution.

Jerome's "Vulgate"

It is convenient to describe Jerome's translation as the "Vulgate" (i.e., "common," or the normally used translation), even though it did not generally become described as such until the 1500s.[103] He began his project about 390 and, with time out for commentary writing and religious controversies, the new project took until 406 to complete.

Three primary sources were blended together by Jerome in producing his Old Testament: the Hebrew, existing Greek translations, and Old Latin versions then available.[104] The Greek, oddly enough, represented the greatest difficulty in his work — not because he had difficulty in working with it but because so many regarded the Greek Septuagint Old Testament (LXX) as divinely inspired and were suspicious of any deviation from it even when it was well grounded in the Hebrew.

A major intellectual force on his work in regard to Greek sources was Origen. Regardless of his faults and alleged quasi-orthodox errors, Jerome was convinced that in regard to the text of the scriptures, Origen's scholarly endeavors and work pointed one in the right direction the bulk of the time. However much he repudiated the man's orthodoxy, he saw no reason to avoid using that material of his that he recognized as both orthodox and reliable.[105] Hence Origien's critical compilation of the *Hexapla* was doubtless utilized to the extent that all or part of it was available and, when that source failed, whatever sections of the Greek translations it utilized.

Of course the Hebrew itself could hardly be ignored, both because it was the mother language of the Torah and the prophets and because Jerome did not believe that the contemporary pro–LXX bias permitted its readings to be cavalierly set aside. Unlike his Greek capability, here he recognized his own serious limitations and set out to remedy them. There were few Christians of a scholarly disposition who worked in the language, so he was forced to utilize the assistance of a layman who had been converted from Judaism. Even with this help, he found the going difficult. As he wrote in one letter, "What labor I spent on this task, what difficulties I went through, how often I despaired and how often I gave up and in my eagerness to learn, started again."[106] He freely utilized the counsel and advice of contemporary Jewish scholars, though certainly with caution, since their religious conclusions in regard to potentially messianic texts could easily be 180 degrees contrary to his own.[107]

Finally, the Old Latin had great relevancy because Jerome was making a translation into that language and because there was a desire to preserve as much as practical of the existing version. The problem in evaluating the usefulness of the Old Latin version (both to him and to scholars of today) lies in whether it represents one translation that diverged into differing manuscript traditions (and readings) or whether there were several such similar Latin translations that were later altered and revised on an ad hoc basis.[108] Augustine refers to an "Itala" Latin version as well as others in that language, suggesting the latter as more likely.[109] Jerome's remark on wide variations in the existing Latin also seems far more compatible with the scenario of multiple Old Latin versions than in one basic text that had diverged in many directions: why would one treat a document regarded as divinely inspired in such a cavalier manner? Yet one would expect just such variations if independent Latin translations were being preserved. Judging from what has survived there was one basic African Old Latin tradition and a "European" one consisting of multiple sub-types.[110]

Jerome's remarks on the translation process reveal the tensions that are always at work between "literalism" and "paraphrasing" in the translation of the Bible or any other work. In a letter to Sunnia and Fretela, he speaks of the need for equivalency: from the sometimes untranslatable idiom of the original language (if one wishes the wording to make any sense) one has to use a phrase that carries the same basic connotation in one's own language. The same concept comes out in a letter to Pammachius: "From my youth up I have always aimed at rendering sense, not words.... A literal translation from one language to another obscures the sense."[111]

However, he also told Pammachius that a different translation approach was essential in regard to the scriptures because there "even the order of the words is a mystery," i.e., expresses the revelation of Divine truth rather merely humanly conceived ideas.[112] In actual fact, however, his work on the Vulgate invokes *both* approaches, a phenomenon probably best explained as due to a recognition that all mortal theories of translation must ultimately yield to the ultimate priority of meaningful communication; there comes a point where faithful maintenance of the minuscule aspects of the text will work to hinder its understanding in those approaching it through a different language.[113]

The major revisions of Jerome are found in the Old Testament section of his endeavor. In that of the New Testament, he mainly corrected the wording of the existing Old Latin rather than undertake a fully new rendering. The reason for this was that his papal commission was to *correct* the existing Latin text rather than provide a completely new one.[114]

How much of the New Testament Jerome personally translated beyond the four gospels has been a matter of great debate. In his own writings, he leaves the distinct impression that he completed that entire Testament.[115] What makes the issue more complicated is that in his own compositions he sometimes provides biblical renderings close to that of the Vulgate and at other times conspicuously different from it. The latter is true even in studies he wrote *after* the alleged completion of his Vulgate. The other side of the coin is that he also provided both types of translations of the gospels as well, which no one would question that he definitely completed.[116] The safest conclusion seems to be that he held to no rigid policy as to what translation he utilized.

Reaction to the Vulgate

In spite of the Vulgate's ultimately becoming the bastion of Catholic orthodoxy, Jerome's work was initially besieged by a sea of criticism. The opinion was widespread that the Greek Septuagint Old Testament had been inspired by God and he had dared to alter it to accord better with the "corrupted" Hebrew. Among such critics was Augustine, and he and similarly minded men were either ambivalent or outright hostile to the new translation.[117]

The translation unquestionably faltered on two points. The first was the translation of the Psalms. While still in Italy, Jerome had hurriedly prepared a minimally altered version now known as the Roman Psalter. In spite of the severe limitations on the degree of change permitted and despite the status the Vulgate ultimately gained, this version remained the one utilized in the mass in Rome even through the twentieth century. In Palestine he produced the Gallican Psalter with the help of the *Hexapla* of Origen. Such was the quality of this that it ultimately became the text of the Vulgate Psalter in spite of Jerome's having prepared a later translation for that work.[118]

The second place where the Vulgate was judged to stumble (at least later) was in regard to its canon of Old Testament books. In a move that would have branded him as an apostate or heretic centuries later, Jerome declined to translate the books of Maccabees, Sirach, Wisdom, and Baruch on grounds that they did not belong in the genuine canon of scripture. Hence these had to be added from the Old Latin in order to complete the Vulgate when these inter-testamental books were definitively accepted by the medieval papacy.[119]

Jerome rationalized including Tobit, in spite of not having a contemporary Hebrew manuscript of it, on the grounds that he could find it in the related language of Aramaic.[120] The result was a significantly shorter Tobit than the one normal in the then existing Latin version.[121]

Impact of the Vulgate on Theological Evolution

The Vulgate had a major impact on justifying Catholic theology for the current and future generations. This can be effectively illustrated by three examples that Erasmus, the Renaissance Catholic scholar, cited as weaknesses of the work. In Ephesians 5:21–23 the Vulgate speaks of the *sacramentum* of marriage, creating the precedent for marriage to be considered a "sacrament." Erasmus stressed that the underlying Greek actually means "mystery" instead.

Matthew 4:17 in the Vulgate spoke of the need to "do penance," a rendering that made the church and its hierarchy ever more vital to human redemption since the church's priests determined the terms of the "penance" that a person had to perform. Erasmus noted that the word properly meant "repent" (reform) instead.

When Mary is described in Luke 1:28 as "full of grace," that was gradually developed into a system in which she became a fount and major dispenser of divine grace. Erasmus properly argued that the Greek meant a "favored" person, shifting the emphasis to being a *beneficiary* of grace rather than a potential *giver* of it.[122] Jerome's effort to provide a more accurate translation had created intense controversy in his own age. Similarly, the effort of Erasmus and others to point out such mistakes a millennium later also engendered both anger and outrage.

Chapter 5

Defenders of Orthodoxy

CYPRIAN OF CARTHAGE (c. 200–258)
Opponent of Novatianism

Born in Carthage near A.D. 200, Cyprian's family came from the wealthier class of the city. Although he held Tertullian's writings in the highest esteem, it is likely Tertullian had died before Cyprian was converted. Cyprian's abhorrence of division makes it extraordinarily unlikely that he could have held Tertullian in such high regard while still alive and part of a "schismatic" faction outside the established church in Carthage.[1]

The theological similarities between the two men are great. Indeed, it has been argued that if one removes the Montanist element from Tertullian's writings one could mix them in with the compositions of Cyprian and be hard pressed to tell which works were written by which man.[2] Only in regard to allegoricalization — to which Cyprian is far more receptive — do we find a major difference. For example, in an analysis Tertullian would never have given, the "daily bread" that is to be prayed for in the Lord's Prayer is transformed from daily sustenance to the communion bread which is Christ's body.[3]

Cyprian converted to Christianity only two years before becoming a bishop in Carthage in about 248, and served in that position for a decade until his martyrdom in 258. His conversion was heavily influenced by repugnance at the excesses that he saw in his world: too many judges were all too bribable; torture, which was used to gain the "truth," all too often revealed no falsehood and left a permanently maimed innocent man; too many insurrections had been vainly attempted to rectify the existing order. These things left a bitter taste in his mouth and in Christianity he found offered an ethical substitute for the moral chaos and dishonor of existing society.[4]

The existing presbyters appear to have opposed his appointment — probably on the grounds of his having been a Christian for such a short period of time and because he lacked a track record of just what he stood for — but these concerns were overcome through heavy pressure from the membership at large.[5] There were practical concerns that encouraged such a choice as well: He had an in-depth training in rhetoric, which argued that he would be an effective preacher at their services.[6] He also brought wealth with him that could be used for the needy and sick. Furthermore, it was customary for the bishop (with the aid of the presbyters) to hear pleas for arbitration of financial and other disputes among the members. His secular experience and economic independence provided strong assurance that he would decide on the merits of the case rather than being compromised by self-interest and favoritism.[7]

Opposition to Novatianism's Ultra-Hard Line toward Apostates

In December 249 the Emperor Decius laid the groundwork for a systematic persecution of Christians. Although he did not require that a person *stop* being a Christian (or any other religious sect), he *did* require a token sacrifice to the Roman gods and that one eat of it. In January 250 the local commissioners in charge of enforcing the policy began to move against church officials throughout the empire. Bishop Fabian perished while imprisoned in Rome, Dionysius of Alexandria was tracked down, and Cyprian chose voluntary exile. The pressure was ratcheted up when in April both outright torture and systematic imprisonment without food began to be utilized to compel capitulation. Although apparently no one in Carthage was executed, the harsh treatment resulted in the death of a number, while others saw no choice but to undergo the obligatory ritual.[8]

Although Cyprian strongly stressed the importance of faithfulness even at the cost of martyrdom, he also emphasized that there was no obligation to needlessly volunteer for it either.[9] Steadfastness was not to be confused with recklessness.

As a result of the persecution of Decius, Cyprian faced a double edged challenge to preserving his authority. In Rome, Bishop Fabian had been executed and the presbyter Novatian took such a hard line toward reintegrating temporary apostates that he refused to recognize the legitimacy of Cornelius as Fabian's replacement, a leader who took a far more accommodating approach. Although Cyprian ultimately endorsed the validity of Cornelius' selection, he "pondered" the matter so long that he deeply angered both Cornelius (for the delay) and Novatian (for the endorsement).[10] Hence he managed to end up antagonizing both of the fractions in Rome as well as any local Carthaginians who either leader had an impact upon.

The other, overlapping challenge came locally from those favoring a more "forgiving" policy toward those who had compromised their faith under adversity. Felicissimus successfully gained control over the church in Carthage while Cyprian was in exile and permitted a return to active involvement on minimal terms. (See the chapter on Felicissimus.) In Rome the imprisoned supported the policy of church authorities, refusing to readmit these individuals to a place in the church until they went through a prolonged period of mourning for their lapse. In Carthage, however, the presbyters who were free were reluctant to take that severe a step. Furthermore, a number of those in prison prepared letters for the fallen in which they pledged to, after their death, intervene with God on their behalf.

One faction of presbyters readily accepted these letters after the individuals they came from had died, and considered them quite adequate for a full restoration of church membership rights and privileges. What made it even more controversial was that the language of some of the letters was so vague that it was questionable whether the individual martyrs knew much about its recipient. In other cases, survivors of imprisonment and abuse circulated letters on behalf of prisoners who had perished but who had allegedly wished any and all the lapsed to be treated mercifully.[11]

Cyprian provided only the most limited permission for the acceptance of such letters: only if a recipient were dying would the church accept its plea. Beyond that, any action about any of them was to be postponed until the persecution came to an end. This stance gained support from many of the leading individuals in the church. On the other hand, a large number insisted that, since they already had the pledge of the dying to have their sins forgiven, not even a bishop should arrogate to himself the right to forgive sins that the very blood of the martyrs had obtained.[12]

At this point the issue became not only a theological one but one of episcopate power as well: the bishop had been challenged. That was an unforgivable breach of faith since, to Cyprian, Christianity was defined as including the recognition of the power of the bishops as being at the heart of its institutional expression.[13] To deny that fact was to strike at the core of the system. In one of his letters he quotes Matthew 16:18–19 about the authority of Peter and the other apostles and how "from this source flows the appointment of bishops and the organization of the church, with bishop succeeding bishop down through the course of time, so that the church is founded upon the bishops, and every act of the Church is governed through these same appointed leaders." Hence he was outraged at receiving a letter purporting to come from the "church" since a true letter of that type could only have come with his approval or from his own hand.[14]

Since the New Testament presents the apostles as miracle workers and as supernaturally inspired as to what to speak, one would expect both aspects to have been claimed for their bishop-successors. In actual practice though, few bishops appear to have ever made such claims or had followers who made it for them; the idea of inspiration was regarded as a mark of Montanist heresy rather than orthodoxy. So apostolic authority was claimed without the auxiliary marks of it. Having *institutional* authority and a line of alleged succession to the past was deemed quite adequate, in Cyprian's mind, to definitively and permanently establish his prerogatives even when his decisions went diametrically opposite the wishes of the congregation. On the issue of lapsed membership he may well have been doing exactly that, depending on how one estimates the relative sectarian loyalty of his clique versus that of his rivals.

The Roman church sent a letter to the city backing Cyprian's decision, delaying action on the lapsed and implying that rebellious presbyters were behind the prior acceptance of the letters from the imprisoned and dead. So far as Rome was concerned, those who had written the letters had no right to grant absolution for the lapsed. Cyprian's effort to place new church officials in Carthage sparked an open rebellion, backed by five presbyters and many of the church members. If Cyprian could attempt to "bribe" his way to support through financial support given through his intermediaries to the needy, the local power holders could retaliate by denying communion to any who cooperated with the bishop's efforts to indirectly reassert his ultimate authority.[15]

Retaining control was far harder for the dissidents, however, when Cyprian reappeared on the scene. Returning from exile he drew sharp lines between the faithful (including those who had fled) and the lapsed, who had compromised their faith. He heavily stressed that anyone who refused to yield to his demand was guilty of the unforgivable sin of church schism.[16]

Apparently as part of his effort to rally support for a hard-line position at the forthcoming meeting of bishops, he circulated his essay *On the Lapsed*. The recent persecution was nothing less than God's retributive judgment on the church for its weaknesses and warts. (Granted that premise and a hard-line stance toward acceptance of the lapse was easily taken as not only justified but essential.) The portrait he paints of the apostate is so severe that Tertullian's conviction that the fallen could never be accepted back would have been a natural conclusion. Yet Cyprian backs off from that final and permanent breach: he concedes that if a demonstrated record of good works and other demonstrations of repentance were manifested for a sufficiently long time, then God will accept that person back—if the bishop does.[17] Effectively this permitted the bishop to have veto power over mercy that God would otherwise give, an approach that the unfriendly cynic might well regard as hierarchical arrogance of the first order. Doubtless Cyprian felt that divine providence was such a powerful factor that the bishop would be moved to do the right thing even if his personal inclinations were against it.

In the early months of 251 a regional meeting of African bishops met in Carthage and they embraced a more lenient policy than Cyprian demanded—but more restrictive than that of Cyprian's opponents as well. They held that if one had merely lied their way into government approval by obtaining a *false* certificate of compliance with the regal demands—and that could only have been obtained due to family relationships with the powerful or through outright bribery—they were to be immediately accepted back, though subject to a case-by-case review. Those who had actually sacrificed were required to carry out a series of acts to "prove" their repentance, and they would only be counted as fully reconciled at death.[18]

Cyprian also found himself partially undermined by the Roman church. In apparent retaliation for Cyprian's earlier refusal to recognize his own appointment, bishop Cornelius of Rome pointedly held meetings with Fortunatus, one of the presbyters opposed to Cyprian. These discussions concerned whether to recognize the validity of the church he had helped form in opposition to Cyprian,[19] an act which would effectively have branded Cyprian's faction as schismatic if not outright heretical. Although ultimately refusing to do so, Cyprian had been implicitly warned that his preference for ultra-hard line policies (and annoying the Roman bishop in the process) had to make room for at least some moderation or he ran the danger of being on the receiving end of Roman censure rather than praise.

Although the general African practice in the second century had been to base the validity of baptism upon the desire of the recipient to seek salvation, the growth of the power of the episcopate made it in the bishops' self-interest to additionally define valid baptism as requiring that one received it from the "true" church, of which they were leaders. Hence, in the past, even baptism from followers of Marcion and Montanus had been accepted as legitimate because it was the recipient's intent that was the pivotal factor.[20] The shift in thinking was manifest by the 230s, when an African church council insisted that the legitimacy of baptism rested on the authority of the person administering it and that in turn rested not merely on his intent in regard to the purpose of the baptism but on his being in fellowship with pure Christianity rather than a heretical faction.

Since those demanding a gentle policy toward the apostates in North Africa had formed their own congregations, the issue became revitalized — doctrinally the Cyprian group and the anti–Cyprian one held virtually identical convictions; only in regard to the treatment of the fallen were there unbridgeable differences. That was irrelevant so far as Cyprian was concerned. He began to demand that any individuals baptized by the rival party had to be "rebaptized" by those in allegiance with him and his group. No matter that they thought they were being baptized to receive God's forgiveness and those doing the baptism thought they were baptizing for that reason. The fact that heretics performed it meant the act was null and void as baptism, and only had the illusion of being one. Hence to them they were demanding a *first* baptism, since what had happened earlier was simply a vain imitation.[21]

A regional conference in Carthage in 256 embraced this policy.[22] Writing to the Roman bishop, it was stressed that this was strictly *their* policy and that they understood that other bishops might wish to follow a different approach. In response, bishop Stephen insisted that all that was needed was not rebaptism but a questioning of the individuals and their receipt into the true church by the laying on of hands. Upping the theological ante in the relationship between Rome and Carthage, Stephen insisted that this practice dated back to the very first century apostles.[23] If this were not enough, a delegation from Carthage was deliberately ignored and Stephen made a point of making derogatory remarks about Cyprian as well.[24]

Stephen was apparently willing to go even further: in one of his letters Cyprian challenges Stephen as to how he can possibly be honoring God when upholding the actions of heretics: "Does he give honor to God who, being a friend of heretics and the foe of Christians, considers that those priests who seek to protect the truth of Christ and the unity of the church deserve to be excommunicated?"[25] Hence Cyprian read in the Roman approach an implicit willingness to excommunicate — him. The potential for a major split was clearly present as Cyprian refused to back down.

A definitive rift with Rome was avoided in 257 because of Stephen's death and replacement by a new bishop who was on far more agreeable terms with the North Africans aligned with Cyprian. In addition, Cyprian himself was forced out of Carthage as a new persecution began: the proconsul had been informed of new orders to compel polytheist sacrifice, but he desired not to put Cyprian to death. Hence the proconsul was willing to settle for his exile in the countryside. The next proconsul was not so tolerant and ordered him to return to the city to either obey or face punishment.

Cyprian refused to sacrifice and in September 258 he was martyred. So great was his prestige among his faction of admirers that a crowd of supporters accompanied him to the execution, loudly demanding that they be given the opportunity to join him in death.[26] Stubborn, unyielding in so many ways, when the time came to choose between capitulation to polytheism and death he choose the same option he had expected others to follow — loyalty through self-sacrifice.

ATHANASIUS (296–373)
"Father of Orthodoxy"

Athanasius was born in the late 200s in Alexandria, Egypt, his "ancestral hearth," to use the words of Constantius.[27] Economically, Athanasius describes himself as coming from a poor family, a mild exaggeration if any.[28] His education was heavy on the scriptures and light on the Greek cultural heritage, no doubt in part due to the limited financial resources of his family. But this was certainly not the only factor. Gregory of Nazianzus described him as one who temperamentally saw no need for more than a minimal knowledge of such matters, just enough to keep himself from being accused of ignorance.[29]

The 10th century *History of the Patriarchs of Alexandria* claims that his mother met with a respected pagan "magician-philosopher" concerning how her son rejected all the marital matches she had suggested to him. He responded that marriage was an irrelevancy because he had already become a "Galilean" and would rise to greatness within "the church, who have destroyed the temples and demolished the statues."

Fearful of the reaction if she criticized her son for this secret change, she went to Bishop Alexander and told him the situation. Both parent and offspring were baptized as the result. Afterwards Alexander took him under his wing and "educated him with gentleness in every art. He memorized the gospels and the divine scriptures and when he was mature, Alexander ordained him a deacon and made him his scribe and he became like an interpreter of the father and a minister of the word which he wished to speak."[30]

The polytheist background is certainly consistent with the omissions of details of the persecution of 311–312 in Athanasius' *History of the Arians*, details which he would have been acquainted with if he had been of a Christian household.[31] The fact that Athanasius is presented to Alexander in the belief that it would open the door for his future greatness is not the type of claim — since it can easily be read as self-serving on his or his mother's part — that one would expect to be associated with his name by future generations that thought so highly of him. Hence it rings especially true. One could easily imagine Alexander being both amused and intrigued by the tale and encouraging the young boy in his education and, discovering talent and potential, edging him into a position of trust and responsibility as his scribe.

Although Athanasius was later described as playing a major role at the Council of Nicaea as a deacon, it is far more likely that he played the more modest role of writing preliminary drafts of his superior's ideas for his revision and correction.[32] The root of this exaggeration (or at least its ancient credibility) lay in the great influence of his later writings on the incarnation of Christ and his effective use of episcopate power to assure the victory of the Nicene Council definition of the Godhead.[33]

His reputation for strict orthodoxy made him a target of pious forgery: by putting his name on a work it not only assured a wider audience, it served as warranty of its unswerving reliability. It provided the opportunity for "Athanasius" to undercut new foes or old ones in a new manner and was likely rationalized by reasoning that this was the line of argument — or one similar to it — that the man would have taken if he were still alive. Hence one spoke for him, so to speak, what he no longer had opportunity to speak himself. The phenomenon was quite widespread. Of one list of 219 volumes once attributed to him, it appears that 139 are later fictions falsely attributed to him.[34]

Although the bulk of his work was targeted at fellow believers, he took time to write a more limited number that, theoretically, were for the benefit of outsiders. *Against the Pagans,* for example, is an apologetic work in the long tradition of defending Christianity from its polytheist foes. So far as he was concerned, such projects were more in the line of appropriate intellectual endeavors than anything of great significance: he describes Greek philosophy and religion as already disgraced and dying out. Unlike a century or two earlier, the "defense" had no need to convince; it basically reaffirmed the inevitability of the Christian triumph regardless of the polytheist reaction. Indeed the volume is addressed not to outsiders but to a friend who was already a Christian.[35]

The Potential Danger to His Episcopate Power: Monasticism

Athanasius faced both overt challenges to his authority (see below) but also some that were merely implicit or potential rather than an immediate danger. Increasingly, groups of male and female celibates joined together in the looser or tighter bounds of community to practice their more ascetic forms of life and worship. Some of these — like Pachomius and Antony — became very prominent in and of themselves. If the priests of Alexandria still looked upon themselves as only loosely under the control of their bishop, what was to be the relationship to these monastic movements that were even more removed from their direct supervision? They were operating quite nicely in their own independent manner and any direct challenge to their liberty could only be controversial and perhaps self-defeating.[36]

Athanasius' strategy (probably adopted not just for strategic but also out of deep and genuine affection) was to embrace such groups as his own, whether formal submissive admissions on their part were demanded or not. For example, in his *Life of Antony,* he expressed tremendous admiration for the hermit. Indeed, the text was often misread as indicating that Athanasius had lived in the desert with him.[37]

The bishop's most emotionally satisfying moments during his early years as bishop were spent among the monastic communities. In addition, during his third exile (356–361) he spent his time hiding among them. In light of the mutual affection and respect that developed, it is not surprising that he repeatedly chose from among these monks when he had important church posts to fill.[38] Who else could he trust more? Yet, by appointing them, he had simultaneously cemented the relationship of the bishop and the monks and undermined the capacity of any dissident movement to utilize them as a basis of opposition to his own ecclesiastical claims.

His First Front in His War for Episcopate Power: The Melitians and the Denial of His Right to His Post

Epiphanius in the fourth century insisted that Melitius of Lycopolis was responsible for the schism named after him due to his desire for an extremely strict treatment of those who lapsed during persecution.[39] Although this was involved in the conflict between the factions, there were clearly other important factors as well in creating both the breadth and intensity of dissidence.

The movement, at least initially, grew out of Bishop Peter in 304 being forced into hiding and being unable to carry out many of his administrative duties as bishop of Alexandria. In a burst of regional independence over the domination of Alexandria, Bishop Melitius of Lycopolis stepped into the breach by ordaining new clergy even in Alexandria itself. This deeply angered Peter, who refused to recognize the legitimacy of the new appointments and was ultimately able to have Melitius excommunicated. Supporters of southern regional rights refused to back down on the appointments issue and there came to be two distinct church systems throughout Egypt, one loyal to the Peter faction and one to that of Melitius and by the time the council met at Nicaea both sides were determined to dominate.[40]

Superimposed upon regional discontent was the issue of how strictly those who had compromised their faith during Roman persecution were to be treated. Supporters of Miletius were regarded as hard-liners on the subject and those following Peter's legacy were more accommodative. The orthodox/Peter/Athanasius camp then and later so stressed this aspect of the schism that it was only in the modern era that the geographic significance of the division has been recognized.[41]

When the Council of Nicaea was held in 325 it had decided in behalf of Bishop Alexander of Carthage and against his rival Melitius. It ordered the latter to play no further role in church government matters, but recognized the validity of his ordinations so long as they submitted themselves to Alexander. Although endorsing Alexander's supremacy, there remained the very real difficulty that many communities now had two rival and, theoretically, equally valid office-holding bishops — one appointed by Alexander and one by Miletius.[42] This was the unstable situation Athanasius faced when he gained the episcopate as Alexander's replacement in 328.

The new appointment brought swift and vehement protests that he was beneath the proper age to hold the post, which likely means that he was no more than in his very early 30s.[43] Furthermore, Athanasius' critics persistently insisted that he had manipulated the system in order to obtain office: in one version seven bishops met secretly and separately from the larger body that had assembled and made the appointment; in another, he locked the two bishops who performed the formal ordination in the church until they agreed to perform the rite upon him in exchange for being released.[44]

The fact that he was able to obtain the post at all — and maintain it in the face of his initial critics — argues that he already had a cadre of strong supporters. This in turn implies that he had already begun to have a major impact on the thinking of important elements inside the Alexandrian church.[45] Using these supporters as his base, he had to wage extended organizational and theological war in order to defeat the Melitians who continued to reject his authority.

The Second Front in His Effort to Hold Episcopate Power: The Arians

Under his predecessor Alexander's reign, Arius theology of the nature of the godhead had surfaced and gained many supporters. If the Melitians were *organizationally* dissenters to Athanasius' (and his predecessor's) hierarchical position, the Arians were *theological* opponents. (Indeed, the Melitians were not above playing one-upmanship on the subject, claiming that Melitius had opposed Arius before Alexander had gotten around to doing so! The fact that this was not true did not change its effectiveness as a taunt.)[46] Hence the second front of Athanasius' spiritual war involved combat with those opposed to his theology rather than his power.

In opposing Arianism, Athanasius soon discovered the usefulness of confusing the sources of opposition to his reign. He effectively utilized guilt by association to brand as "Arian" anyone with a dissident theology whom he wished to subjugate.[47]

There are two basic approaches to evaluating this strategy. One is that the vindication of his power-post was considered so vital that the legitimacy of his accusations were virtually irrelevant. In that case, victory had to be secured first to preserve, protect, and expand the prerogatives of the episcopate and only then could truth claims be calmly evaluated. If some temporary injustice were done, it was a sacrifice preferable to breaking the (actually nonexistent) unbroken chain of episcopate power that reached all the way back to the apostles.

The second approach in evaluating Athanasius' misbranding of foes is to attribute it to genuine paranoia about the extent of the dissident movements and their possible interlinks. After all, if they shared opposition to him, what else did they have in common that they were not as candid or open about? Perhaps the two factors of hierarchy and paranoia were so intertwined in his own mind that he could not have made a distinction between them if he had tried.[48]

In light of this strategy of blurring differences, it is not that surprising that the bulk of his work targets Arians and their sympathizers. Although he is clearly Nicene orientated, the *language* of Nicene is notably avoided, as if he is far more agreeable to its sentiment than to its specific wording.[49]

Arianism took on a life of its own after Arius' death, yet throughout Athanasius' many writings it remains Arius himself who is the target. This strange omission is true of Augustine as well, who targets the Arius of Egypt rather than the Arianism he himself faced.[50] This literary strategy served several purposes. It conveyed a not so subtle dismissal of any advocates who might present a varying case as being not worthy of consideration on their own merits and demerits. To the extent that it created an imaginary "definitive" Arianism, it also created a straw man that critics could joyously beat on who was long out of the picture and unable to personally respond.

His Five Exiles and Ultimate Death

Athansius held to his post tenaciously, but it was a stormy reign. He was compelled to leave the city five times over one dispute or another. The first occurrence was over the accusation of his responsibility for a murder. Although untrue, there were other cases where the evidence of his complicity in violence was far more credible. For example, four monks aligned to the Melitian faction nearly died as the result of a beating at the hands of his supporters, and his behavior afterwards strongly argues that he felt he was either morally or directly culpable for what had happened.[51]

However negative a view an unfriendly critic might have of Athanasius, no one can deny his persistence and the fact that he paid a high price in adversity in his attempt to get his way. (Praiseworthy if he is regarded as a spiritual hero; a lamentable indication of his self-centered theocratic arrogance if one believes he was too prone to winning by raw power those arguments he could not win with persuasion.) The Council of Tyre, called at Constantine's request, decided that Athanasius had encouraged violence against his opponents and deposed him from his post.

Athanasius secured a meeting with Constantine, who seemed to waver. When accusations that the bishop had wished to stop vital grain exports out of Egypt were brought forth, it was apparently a sufficiently credible charge for Constantine to decide that Athanasius was untrustworthy.[52] Hence Constantine sent him into exile in 335, where he remained till the emperor's death in 337. Riots in Alexandria demanding the bishops' return did nothing to secure a policy reversal[53] and may well have confirmed the emperor in his distrust of the bishop.

The bishop returned home to the exultation of the welcoming crowd and a hard-core body of opponents. The Council of Antioch was held and decided that the condemnation from the synod of Tyre was still in effect. Hence his occupation of the episcopate was inherently invalid since the decision had never been reversed. They also condemned him on new charges of violence by his enthusiastic supporters. Supporters seized on the fact that the foes had to select a bishop from outside Egypt and played up how this was blatant interference with the rights of the Egyptians, who already had a bishop and wished to keep him.[54] With government military support, the churches were turned over to the supervision of its new bishop, Gregory of Cappadocia. As a corollary to this, Athanasius went into exile from 339 to 346.

The emperor Constantius, who had been behind the banishment, began to reconsider his options when Gregory of Cappadocia died in 345. After (reluctantly) meeting with Constantius, Athanasius was restored to Alexandria, where he was again enthusiastically welcomed by his supporters and was able to settle down for a decade of residency.

Constantius was far from happy with the bishop's promotion of the Nicene scenario to explain the Godhead. In 351 the Council of Sirium was held, which explicitly rejected the Nicene decisions. Additional councils came to the same conclusion under the emperor's encouragement. The emperor sent Diogenes to arrest Athanasius but the degree of local support made this impractical. Now it moved into military hands. Near midnight on February 8, 356, armed forces surrounded the church so he could not leave without being captured. Even so, he was some how able to escape. He considered it a miracle.[55] The "miracle" did not extend to the consequence of his deposition: 356–362 were additional years of exile.

George of Cappadocia — yet another non–Egyptian — was brought in to be his replacement. Through heavy government pressure the churches were brought under George's authority and the suppression of Athanasius' supporters enthusiastically carried out. During this period of exile Athanasius hid in the desert among the monastics. This freed him from the administrative demands of the episcopate and he spent much of his time in writing. Over half his surviving writings date from these years.[56]

On the death of Constantius in 360, Julian took the reign of power. In 361 George of Cappadocia was murdered by a mob of Athanasius' supporters. George, however, had so antagonized local pagans that a rival version of the story claims that they lay behind the death.[57] Quite possibly both factions played a role, since the death was of great personal advantage to Athanasius, while to the polytheists it was a matter of revenge. The murder was the only form of "ecumenicalism" that Athansius' faction and the polytheists were ever likely to agree on.

In 362 Julian decreed that all exiled bishops could return. It took only months for Julian to realize that his generosity was not a wise one in regard to this particular church leader: the man simply had too much prestige in Egypt to be well regarded by someone seeking to restore ancient polytheism. (Of course, learning more details of his predecessors' conflicts with the man probably did not encourage him either.) Julian finally dismissed him as "that contemptible little fellow" and retroactively reinterpreted the meaning of his edict as referring to how bishops could go back to the *place* they lived rather than the *office* they had held.[58] Protests got nowhere. Athanasius had returned on February 21; he went into desert exile with the monks on October 23.

In late 363 he met with the new emperor, Jovian, who had been raised to that post as the result of the death of Julian in battle. Although Athanasius' opponents vigorously opposed his return to Alexandria and office, the emperor was more receptive and approved that of both him and the other Nicaean faction leaders.

Jovian wished a creedal statement from him. However such an effort exposed Athanasius to potential counterattack on virtually any subject he mentioned — if his critics thought there was the least fodder to work from — and the bishop prudently dodged the request. Instead he responded that holding to the Nicaean standard was fully adequate in and of itself. He did take the opportunity, however, to plead that he did not countenance any form of the Arian theology for, he said, the council "did not merely say that the Son is like (*homois*) the Father, so that it should be believed that he is merely like God instead of true God from true God. But they wrote '*homoousios*' which is what properly applies to a genuine and true Son, who belongs to the Father truly and by nature."[59]

Unfortunately for Athanasius, chance intervened against him yet again. When Jovian died in late February 364, Valens became regional emperor and, like his brother who appointed him (Valentinian), was friendly to the anti–Nicene movement. Valens revoked the return edict and ordered all previously banished bishops, including Athanasius, back into exile. Dragging his feet against obeying, the church where he was expected to be was raided by the military, but their target had fled ahead of them into his fifth period of banishment.

Politics now intervened in behalf of the patriarch: Valens was challenged for leadership on the battlefield. Three factors entered to make the bishop look more tolerable: the bishop had deep support in the region, the province could easily be destabilized if the religious polemics spilled over into the economic arena, and, in the worst case scenario, there was the possibility of rebellion in the province while Valens was being militarily challenged elsewhere. The easiest way to minimize this set of dangers was to — as he decided — permit Athanasius to return to office. From then until his death in 373, Athanasius remained in Alexandria. Not that efforts ceased to replace him: at one point, a substitute as bishop was sent from Antioch. The pro–Athanasius faction (clearly dominant and widespread) made it clear that the substitute would be assassinated if he remained and he was provided a military guard back home.[60]

We have traced the varied up-and-down career of Athanasius in more detail than most church leaders in order to illustrate how any church official was subject to dramatic reversals in fortune — sometimes in an extraordinarily short period of time. Athanasius was far from the only "orthodox" or "deviant" to face such dangerous cycles, but he was certainly one of those whose orthodox power was most perceived as deeply rooted in repeated bloodshed aimed at foes and challengers.

Evaluating Athanasius' Career

Evaluations of his career vary immensely. Those who think of him well depict him as a bold and courageous upholder of orthodoxy; those who think ill of him stress his violent streak and willingness to enthusiastically use government power and street violence to suppress his religious foes. On paper, he strongly rebuked the use of force against religious enemies.[61] The problem is that these rebukes come in the context of discussing the impropriety of his *foes* using violence against his *supporters*.[62] This still left the theoretical loophole for the use of coercion against others, since *he* had the "truth" (and "legitimate" church office) and *they* were in apostate "error." In addition to the concrete evidence pointing toward, at a minimum, his tolerance for such bloodshed, his foes vigorously stressed his willingness to use such tools against them, clearly perceiving him as vulnerable to the accusation.[63]

GREGORY OF NAZIANZUS (c. 325–389)
Reluctant Bishop, Extraordinary Preacher

Gregory's father may have held only a minor local office, but he had the kind of practical political intelligence that can lead one far: upon seeing how receptive the emperor Constantine was to Christianity at the Council of Nicaea, he promptly "converted" and soon found himself the local bishop.[64] Throughout the remainder of his father's long life, the son retained a great affection and respect for him that was repeatedly tested by his inclination to well-intended meddling in his grown son's affairs.[65]

Gregory and Basil the Great may have been born in the same year. They were certainly contemporaries and close friends and shared similar prosperous backgrounds. Their paths first intersected when they were both studying rhetoric in Athens and they would find their paths crossing several times later for periods of mutual study and encouragement.[66]

They were blessed with outstanding teachers who, in a type of relationship that did not always occur, held these particular students in high regard for their talents. As Gregory once wrote, "whoever knew of Athens knew of our teachers, and whoever knew of our teachers knew of us."[67]

The close relationship of Gregory and Basil began to break up during the rule of Julian the Apostate. Julian found no room for Christianity, since everything had to be rooted in Greek culture. An irate Gregory bluntly insisted that they both could and should be combined into a synthesis that advanced mankind's cultural and spiritual aspirations. In contrast, an increasingly disillusioned Basil began to believe that the educational background all three shared was merely a preliminary stage of life. Instead of opting for the Grecian heritage or combining it with Christianity, one could and should minimize the Greek influences as one maximized the Christian component of life.[68]

During the winter months of 361–362, Gregory was ordained priest at the insistence of his bishop. Since this bishop was his father and since he was personally strongly inclined toward a more ascetic and removed role as his spiritual calling, he resented the interference. "My father was well aware of my thinking," he explained, but refused to yield. Yet he recognized that it was not nepotism at work but "paternal love" that ultimately motivated the pressure.[69]

He fled the city after ordination, but returned in the spring and publicly admitted that the active priestly course now set before him was not the one he preferred. In a sermon he explained that he had reversed course because of his "longing" to be among them and the obligation to assure the well-being of his aging father. He conceded that many had joined in the pressure for him to become priest and now he would do his best to live up to their expectations.[70]

Gregory was a man of many talents. His 249 surviving letters are very personal ones in which his attitudes and feelings are preeminent. Useful as these are in fleshing out the picture of him as a human being, they do not provide the historical details and theological arguments that are so common in the writings of other church leaders of the time.[71]

Not only was he a letter writer, he also enjoyed poetry. The majority of his compositions that survived were apparently written after he was forced out of church office in the closing years of his life. These deal with everything from religious dogma to moral values to autobiography and are composed in a number of poetic formats that were popular in the ancient world.[72] The autobiographical poems are of special interest, as he attempts to interpret and, returning to the same events a second time at a later date, "better" interpret them and their significance.[73]

In his own life and throughout the Byzantine age, he was regarded as one of the preeminent theologians of Christian history, not to mention one of its greatest orators. The modern era, however, tends to view him as little more than an effective echo of the sentiments of others and as far from deserving the degree of prestige as a thinker that he was given.[74]

This devaluation of his talents does not, however, extend to his oratorical ability. In his sermons, he used his skill to turn a phrase, to come up with formulations that would make sense of ideas so abstract that the nonspecialist would otherwise tend to shrug them off as being as incomprehensible as the religious controversies that gave them birth.[75] To be recognized as authoritative did not require oratorical skill, only the holding of the right church office; to have people come to one's sermons on an ongoing basis, however, required that one polish those speaking skills to their finest edge. As he came to recognize in Constantinople, multitudes regarded preaching as simply another way to be entertained and if they didn't like the sermons, well, there was always, as he said, "race horses and the theater."[76]

At least in Constantinople he did not, at first, have to worry about administrative responsibilities and could concentrate on teaching. However, when Theodosius I deposed an Arian bishop in Constantinople and replaced him with Gregory, he was pushed to the center of the bitter theological controversy surrounding Arianism. At the 381 Council of Constantinople, the presiding officer died and a bitter fight erupted over making Gregory the replacement. He was already bishop of Sasima, quite possibly still of Nazianzus as well, and had been made new bishop of Constantinople. His opponents argued that holding simultaneous multiple episcopates was inherently wrong and that there was no authority for being considered "transferred" from one to the other. Under an intense fire of criticism—not to mention laboring under the burden of being physically ill and exhausted—he offered to resign.

Whether this was a tactical move or a sincere offer, the delegates to the council took him up on it. He returned to Nazianzus but was talked into retaining his episcopate position there. Still chased by stinging charges of illegal post holding and feeling the tiredness of advancing age, he ultimately resigned and retired, dying about A.D. 390.[77]

BASIL THE GREAT (c. 330–379)
Defender of Eastern Nicene Faith

Basil was born c. A.D. 330 in Pontus to a well-to-do Christian family. Gregory of Nazianzus later spoke of how his parents had demonstrated their faith through their behavior, referring to "their care of the poor, their hospitality toward strangers, their purity of soul achieved through austerity, the dedication of a portion of their goods to God."[78]

The parents had the finances to provide him a first-rate education in Caesarea, Constantinople, and Athens. After visiting Egypt and Syria (which easily could have involved excursions into other nearby regions), he returned home in anticipation of setting up a monastic style life with several individuals of a similar mind. He had observed it firsthand in the countries he visited and had been deeply impressed by its practitioners.[79] Circumstances led him, however, into a more overt leadership role than he had desired or anticipated.

He was ordained as priest in 357 and in 365 moved to Cappadocian Caesarea. Of his initial five years there as priest, before moving upwards to the episcopate, he wrote very little either then or afterwards. Some have thought he exercised this restraint lest he be viewed as usurping rights that belonged to the then serving bishop. In behalf of this scenario can be introduced Gregory of Nazianzus' description of the period as one when "He received the honor according to the law and order of spiritual advancement [and] recognized the laws of obedience."[80] Although the words can certainly be read in a self-effacing manner, the language can also be taken as implying significant disagreement with the current bishop on one or more matters and that he felt it inappropriate, both as a newcomer and of lower rank, to take issue with his superior. Once he moved up to that office, he utilized its powers freely and gained so many admirers that he was given the appellation "the Great" while he was still alive.

Opponent of Arianism

Although his letters are filled with defense of his beliefs, he produced only two doctrinal treatises specifically with that purpose in mind. In his *Against Aunomius* he defended the divinity of both Jesus and the Holy Spirit. *On the Holy Spirit* defends the premise that the Holy Spirit is as worthy of being worshipped as the Father or Son. Since this involved a heavy emphasis on defending a church doxology that linked the three together, in a very real way he was as much interested in defending the validity of church practice/ritual as in defending the deityship of the Spirit. The former justifies the latter.[81]

Basil carried out an intentional and effective campaign to establish his own authority, while simultaneously securing his region for Nicene orthodoxy. His primary tool in this campaign was the careful placing of trusted individuals in subordinate places of religious leadership throughout the area. By carrying out an unrelenting anti–Arian policy, he played a major role in setting the stage for "orthodoxy's" ultimate triumph in 381 at the Council of Constantinople.[82]

His position was made easier by divisions within the Arian ranks. On the other hand, some Arians who drifted back into Nicene loyalty eventually drifted away again. This second breach occurred not over the relationship of Father and Son but over whether the Holy Spirit could also be regarded as deity, and their denial that such was the case. These type views were quite popular in his area and the pure force of numerical superiority could not be brought to bear as effectively against this deviancy as against traditional Arianism.[83]

Basil's stance was not without its political risks: the eastern emperor from 364 to his death in battle in 378 was Valens and he was an energetic supporter of the Arian alternative. Indeed, Basil was one of the few significant pro–Nicene figures in the East who was able to retain his office against the opposition of the Arians. Dealing with the emperor, he shifted (according to circumstances) from a quiet refusal to yield to obeying his demands on selected matters to finding ways to circumvent the emperor's wishes.[84] The fact that Valens put up with this argues strongly for Basil's ability to appear flexible while astutely maneuvering to stay just short of actions that would force the emperor's hand.

Dedication to Monasticism

One of Basil's major secondary priorities was to create a more homogeneous form of monasticism in his region. Prior to him, there had been a number of types, some of them extreme even by stringent ascetic standards; others lapsed into questionable and even outright heretical theology. While crushing the last type, he prodded the redeemable back toward orthodoxy and pushed for a consensus of behavior that all would recognize as valid and acceptable.[85]

One of the extreme and heretical forms was that of Eustathius of Sebaste. Basil regarded him as essentially Arian in theology and in 373 repudiated him because of it, though his form of asceticism had had major influence on shaping Athanasius' own beliefs on the matter.[86] While forcing the issue, Basil not only brought the ascetics into a broader consensus of behavior, he simultaneously enhanced the power of the episcopate over the movements, as subject to its authority and ultimate decisions. Hence the establishment of orthodoxy and personal religious power went conveniently hand in hand, however well intentioned Basil's motives were.

His interest in asceticism can be found expressed in the "Longer and Shorter Rules" to govern such a life. Although more a question and answer collection than "rules" in the usual sense, they have customarily borne that title. Traditionally attributed to Basil (which, at the minimum, would indicate that they had his support and backing), the "rules" and their supporting auxiliary letters and sermons may have been, in large part, written or based on the work of the "heretic" Eustathius. The church historian Sozomen, for example, noted that the "ascetic treatises commonly attributed to Basil of Cappadocia" were assigned to Eustathius by a significant number of his contemporaries.[87] Since the two were later locked in vigorous dispute — with Eustathius dismissed by Basil as little different from an Arian[88] — neither Basil nor his supporters were likely to have looked kindly upon any mention of their rival's impact upon the preparation and circulation of the ascetic "rules." Hence the dissemination of the material as if his alone.

Churchman as Humanitarian

Although he was so deeply involved in the theological and monastic matters of his day, Basil did not neglect what he regarded as his more mundane humanitarian obligations. His so-called hospital (the *basileias*, as it was known even while he was alive; a double-duty facility for helping both the sick and lodging travelers) was established c. 372 and became the prototype for church sponsored institutions of a similar nature throughout the Roman East. Their primary health duty was to provide assistance to the despised leper class.

Gregory of Nazianzus, looking back on this, spoke of how it represented a major innovation in the social thinking of the time: "We have no longer to look on the fearful and pitiable sight of men like corpses before death, with the greater part of their limbs dead, driven from cities, from dwellings, from public places, from water-courses. Basil it was more than anyone who persuaded those who are men not to scorn men, nor to dishonor Christ the head of all by their inhumanity towards human beings."[89] So powerful was this concept of a major and direct benevolent role of organized religion that when Julian reverted to polytheism he encouraged the establishment of similar institutions by those who were non–Christians.[90]

AMBROSE (c. 340–397)
Temporary Bridge between Orthodoxy and Arianism

Only a century or so before the time of Ambrose, the major cities of the Empire were at their numerical and economic height. By his time they were in decline. Politically, the city of Rome was no longer the capital though it retained its mystique and historical-psychological connections. In the West, Ambrose's Milan had become far more important both officially and unofficially. In the East the dominant city was the young

Constantinople. In the final decades of the fourth century the Germanic "barbarians"—even those accepted peacefully within the Empire and partially acclimated—represented major security threats due to their lack of full assimilation and undivided political loyalty. Violence could erupt from them at any time and everyone knew it.

When Rome was sacked in 410 it was only a more blatant example of the danger that faced the entire Roman world. The Roman imperial authority itself had become unusually brittle. In 378 Valens died in battle; in 383 Gratian was assassinated; and in 392 Valentinian II probably suffered the same fate (some believe it was suicide).[91] It was within this context of European uncertainty that Ambrose arose and functioned.

His father died while apparently serving as praetorian prefect in Gaul. Returning to Rome, Ambrose was sent through the kind of intense, quality education that offered opportunity for entrée into his own positions of responsibility. During those years his mother adopted an ascetic style, and minor and important church officials were regular visitors to the household. Hence Ambrose had an insight into the changing religious tides of the day even before reaching his full maturity.[92]

Not being of the elite, he and his brother became lawyers functioning with Italy's praetorian prefect. Due to their highly capable performance they both received important governorships, with Ambrose being sent to pivotal Milan.

Ambrose was not all that much of a Christian in his youth in Rome. Yet he entertained, at least vaguely, the idea of rising in the church hierarchy, since he would joke about becoming a bishop one day.[93] Yet he was so determined to rise in the public ranks of the law profession that being publicly active in the church would be counterproductive because of the large remaining influence of polytheists. (The same was true of any other role that would be regarded as socially important.)[94] Public expectations required attendance at the ultra-violent gladiatorial competitions, not to mention strongly encouraged at least some participation in the pagan sacrifices of the day.

Hence many males attempted to create a kind of "halfway covenant" with God by being accepted as a catechumen and remaining such. This permitted one to be tutored in their purported new faith while not being expected to carry out the full break with polytheism that would be demanded of a baptized individual.[95] In Italy wives might be acceptable in fully expressing their monotheism, but husbands still would not be.[96] These obstacles, of course, could be overcome, but the less elevated one's family connections the greater was the perceived impediment to advancement. Hence the popularity of embracing Christianity—but not definitively compromising one's career prospects by become an outspoken stalwart of it.

Appointment to Bishop

Milan was an Arian stronghold, with the highly capable Auxentius serving as bishop. The emperor Valentian I supported him and even exiled Hilary of Poitiers for denying the legitimacy of the Auxentius episcopate. The Nicene clique maintained its identity by regular meetings in various homes and held larger outdoor conclaves in places such as cemeteries, where they would be more or less out of public view.[97]

When a meeting was held to choose Auxentius' replacement in 374, there was much unrest and nervousness throughout the city due to the high tensions between the two camps. A group of anti–Arians attended the meeting to select a replacement and pushed heavily for the appointment of someone favorable to their cause. There was no indication that anyone had turned to violence in this potentially inflammable situation, however.[98]

The fact that they even bothered to be there was itself an oddity: the normal means of assuring that the "right" bishop was selected was to assure that only members of one's own faction went to such a gathering. If one was already in process, one held one's own conference and, afterwards, the rival bishops would battle it out in the court of Christian opinion.[99] Due to the intensity of the rival commitments at this point in time, it was no small accomplishment that both sides could actually be peacefully in the same place at one time.

Officially Ambrose intervened with military force to assure that the meeting did not collapse into a threat to public order. The fact that he did not order anyone expelled provided de facto support for the presence of the rival partisans and of the involvement of both sides in selecting an episcopal replacement.[100]

Whether by prearrangement or pure coincidence, what came next proved that Ambrose was widely respected as a capable and honest governor and with a lifestyle at least reasonably tolerable to Christian standards. Somewhere in the vast assembly of onlookers a child hollered out, "Ambrose for bishop!" Quickly the consensus of the meeting — of those on both sides of the Nicene issue — embraced the plea.[101] Perhaps they recognized that all the individuals they would normally nominate would be a bone of contention and by going outside their ranks they could select a leader who would enjoy a broad base of support throughout all factions of the Christian community.[102]

Ambrose repeatedly begged off the request and acted in outrageous ways in the hope of temporarily inflaming opinion against himself. Then he fled the city, yet delegates pursued and brought him back to Milan. He appealed to the emperor but the emperor grasped the value of having a bishop that could unify the city and was not about to let the opportunity pass. Furthermore, from Ambrose's standpoint, having clear approval from the emperor meant that his hand would be immeasurably strengthened if he finally had to accept the post of bishop and face serious opposition.[103] With this background in mind, he finally yielded to the convocation's pleas.

Although there was likely a genuine predisposition to remain in secular service — he had proven himself quite good at it — he positioned himself from the very beginning to come down on the Nicene side. The contemporary Paulinus wrote that he "asked to be baptized by no one but a Catholic bishop, for he was wary of the treachery of the Arians."[104] This implies that he clearly knew enough of the rival claims to have determined which side he would ultimately promote.

Opponent of Arianism

It was not till 379 that Ambrose began to come out decisively against the Arians when Gratius took over as emperor. Meeting together in Milan, he convinced the emperor to take steps against them, quite possibly because opposition to his pro–Nicene stance had reached the point where he felt it imperative to crush it,[105] not to mention that he now felt he had sufficient support to make it a feasible undertaking.

The following spring when the emperor returned, Ambrose had finished the beginning of his *De fide* and its vigorous assault on the dissidents. He lumps them all together as taking the most extreme positions that any of them embraced. The politically astute element of his character carefully stressed the recent Roman defeat at Adrianople at the hands of the Goths: Adrianopole was overwhelmingly Arian; was not the defeat proof positive that God's wrath was on those favoring such an outrageous heresy? The implication, of course, was that if the emperor embraced Ambrose's Nicene-ism, not only would doctrinal "truth" triumph but so would Roman military power as well.[106]

In 381 the emperor ordered a church council to be held to deal with the issue. By convincing the ruler to send invitations only to Italians and, among them, only to those likely to embrace Ambrose's approach to the controversy, he had effectively "stacked" both the membership and the meeting's results. He assured that the convocation ultimately issued a plea that Nicene orthodoxy be enforced against the alleged church dividers and disturbers of the spiritual peace (i.e., the other side, the Arians). This course the emperor proceeded to adopt.[107]

In spite of his venomous preoccupation with anti–Arianism, Ambrose managed to find time to contribute to the development of church doctrine in other areas. He pioneered concepts that would later be elaborated on at length by more famous individuals: For example, what was the nature, results, and consequences of the "original sin" of Adam and Eve? Then there was the perpetual question inherent in Christian acceptance of carnal warfare: what is required for a war to be considered "just" and "moral?"[108]

In the more strictly Roman Catholic tradition, he argued that when the words of consecration are recited in the Eucharist, at that point the bread and wine are altered from their natural form into something transcending those limitations. He also so exuberantly praised the glories of Mary that he laid the groundwork for the outburst of her "veneration" that would develop afterwards.[109]

Confrontation with Imperial Power

On the one hand Ambrose was unquestionably devout and dedicated to his cause, but this was combined with quite worldly skills of inventing, on minimal notice, some stratagem or other to get him out of situations where his position was being dangerously challenged.[110] There was a touch of the daredevil who risks all to accomplish his task. As Ivor Davidson observes, "words like 'brinkmanship,' 'chutzpah,' and 'effrontery' might also be deployed. The shrewdness of the political operator, the theatricality of the demagogue, and the evocative powers of the image-maker all had a part in his make-up and contributed to his ultimate achievement."[111]

This especially comes out in his daring confrontations with more than one emperor. Much as he sought, pled for, and even demanded their backing for his anti–Arian crusade, he equally vigorously agitated that when they differed with him on church-state matter *they* must back-down, an astounding posture when the raw power seemed to be in their hands and not his.

To give only one example, when vigilante Christians burned down a synagogue, the emperor Theodosius demanded that the church pay for its rebuilding. Outraged, Ambrose compared himself to the Old Testament prophet Nathan rebuking David's adultery and announced that no more masses would be made until the emperor reversed himself. Oddly enough, he did just that,[112] though one can't help but wonder whether the ruler realized that he had established a precedent for the church to define orthodoxy totally independent of the emperor, not to mention the church leadership being able to enforce its will on the state when religious matters could be cited as the reason or excuse.

JOHN CHRYSOSTOM (c. 347–407)
Renowned Orator of Fourth Century Christianity

Coming from a well-off family in Antioch, Syria, John Chrysostom's father died while John was still a small child. John began his young adult life studying philosophy. At eighteen he was baptized and he shifted to the study of the Christian religion. After following this course in his hometown, he withdrew to the mountains outside the city and spent four years living with a respected spiritual hermit and then two further years living alone under severe conditions. He drove his body so relentlessly — striving, for example, to literally get by without any sleep at all — that his body ultimately rebelled and he returned home to seek physical treatment.[113]

Setting aside these extremes of self-denial, he became a deacon in 381 and moved upward to the post of priest five years later. He remained such from 386 to 397 and solidified his reputation as one of the most powerful preachers of the contemporary church. Indeed, the "Chrysostom" in his name comes from the appellation "golden-mouthed," given by contemporary Christians in recognition of these skills. Both in Antioch and then in Constantinople, he preached at least two or three times a week for almost two decades.[114]

The fact that he could attract an audience for such an extended period of time pays considerable tribute to his rhetorical skills and ability to maintain an interested listenership. Judging from passing references in his sermons, virtually every type of human being passed through his audiences: the poor to the rich, the blacksmith to the aristocrat, the humble to the government bureaucrat seeking to advance himself by well-announced church attendance. Even "whoremongers and effeminate become religious" in times of civic crisis and joined themselves to his congregational audience.[115]

In spite of his oratorical skills, he could occasionally be stymied in public discussion when up against an unusually able foe. Once he dueled with rival bishop Sisinius in Constantinople over the other's unorthodoxy. "Because you are a heretic, I will end your preaching!" Chrysostom vigorously threatened. Sisinius immediately fired back, "And I will thank you for relieving me of such a burden."[116]

To us the riposte was well deserved, regardless of which side we believe was in the right. The contemporary reaction was likely more muted. Although the orthodox would occasionally utilize levity, the quickest route to be considered a confirmed heretic was to be a church leader and have a generous sense of humor.[117] The audience might not be able to judge the rival theological claims with any great insight, but to treat a controversial religious subject with laughter seems to have been regarded as proof that one did not take Christianity seriously enough and, therefore, *must* be heretical.

Although it was a mark of honor to be offered the post of patriarch of Constantinople, in 397, he was apparently quite unwilling to take it and his ensuing mercurial relationships with the imperial rulers who made their residence in the city confirmed the wisdom of his reluctance. Eudoxia, wife of the emperor and the hand that moved the hand that ruled, went through periods of profound support and profound estrangement with him that both grated on his nerves and endangered his ability to remain in office.

In particular, she was known to drive him to distraction by her intervention on behalf of his subordinates she regarded as ill-treated at his hands. While away from Constantinople in 402, his representative had arrogated to himself the rights of Chrysostom's own post — at least in Chrysostom's view. Determined to abort the coming head-on collision, she brought her infant to church, put him in the arms of the patriarch, and demanded that he make a public oath to end the hostilities with his subordinate. Faced with this embarrassing situation, he grudgingly promised to do so.[118]

His fiery tongue and determination to oppose whatever he regarded as evil — even deposing bishops who had bought their office — alienated many of the powerful clerics and laymen of Constantinople. Even the clerics directly under his jurisdiction became increasingly estranged from him. Part of the opposition lay in his insistence on a stricter lifestyle than they were used to. Many of his actions represented reforms that were well needed but that did nothing to appease those now being forced to live up to the theoretical standards that had often been ignored.[119]

The ultimate result of his repeated conflicts was that in 404 he offended the empress once too often and was sent to Cucusus, Armenia, in exile. In two ancient accounts it is claimed that his climactic sermon began with the words, "Again Herodias raves, again she rages, again she dances, again she demands the head of John on a platter."[120] If "John" was John Chrysostom, it took no great imagination to determine who the contemporary "Herodias" was! Hence, whatever the actual words uttered in that sermon, there was no doubt who was the target, and this was one criticism too many.

This does not mean, of course, that he was without a hardy cadre of supporters among the clergy just as he had among the laypeople of the city. This is confirmed by the fact that several dozen bishops accompanied Chrysostom into exile,[121] an action that surely implied not merely organizational loyalty but personal respect as well. Even in exile, he was in regular contact with friends in Constantinople and it was arranged for him in 407 to be sent even further away, to the city of Pityus on the Black Sea. Whether even this would have severed his contacts is open to question but became irrelevant due to his death en route.

His reputation has been enhanced among admirers by the pure bulk of his writings that have survived. These include more than 240 letters and approaching 1,000 homilies.[122] Although most of the letters can clearly be dated to his years of exile, his sermons may date from either Antioch or Constantinople or, most likely, a combination of both.

Although he ended his life rejected and in exile, his reputation quickly soared after his passing. So great was this reaction that about thirty years later his bones were returned to the city and became objects of deep reverence by both his successors in the office of bishop and the emperor.[123]

HILARY OF POITIERS (died 368)
Opponent of Arianism and Advocate of Close Scriptural Interpretation

Hilary was born in Poitiers (then known as Limonum) at some point in the 310s and raised as a polytheist. The educational level presumed by his writing style, reasoning, and subjects discussed presuppose that he came from the kind of affluent background that could provide him with a quality education.[124] Where this was gained is unknown, but Bordeaux was the nearest community to offer that type of superior educational opportunity[125] and, barring having family or kin in some other place, it would be most natural to take advantage of it. He carried over from these years a lasting appreciating for Stoicism and the ways it could be welded into a Christian worldview.[126]

When he was appointed bishop is unknown. There is no indication that he played any significant role at the 353 synod of Aries and it follows that his appointment likely occurred either just as it was held or a short time afterwards.[127] In that year Constantius came to the throne and shifted imperial favor from the Nicene faction to the Arian. In 355, the emperor encouraged the synod of Milan to exclude and exile Nicene bishops. In agreement with various other pro–Nicene leaders in Gaul, Hilary refused to have anything to do with the measure. Nor was he pleased with the 356 synod of Beziers, which produced a censure of the Nicene Athanasius. Hilary was one of only two bishops present who opposed that move.

After only about six years' service, the emperor had had enough defiance and Hilary was sent into imperial exile. Traditionally it has been assumed that the regal purpose was retaliation for Hilary's support for Nicene Christianity but some suspect that the bishop's support for would-be monarch Silvanus played even a larger role in the decision to depose him.[128] Theological "disloyalty" was defiance; support for a replacement emperor toyed with outright political treason.

Hilary took advantage of his absence, however, to agitate for the purported "orthodox" faction at several church councils. During these years in the Roman East, he took the opportunity to examine in detail both sides of the arguments being utilized. Although this did not compromise the core of his convictions, he came to recognize that one could become so insistent upon *verbal* agreement that *real* or *underlying* concurrence might be easily overlooked.

In his *De synodis* (359) he put a pro–Nicene spin on decisions of Eastern Church synods that might be interpreted in either direction. He also attempted to show how certain creedal decisions that *appeared* pro–Arian might actually be given the opposite interpretation without undue abuse of the actual wording.[129]

He recognized that the divisiveness that was so common in his era was inherently self-destructive for all parties. As he wrote the emperor, "Every year, nay, every moon, we make new creeds to describe invisible Mysteries. We repent of what we have done, we defend those who repent, we anathematize those whom we defended. We condemn either the doctrine of others in ourselves or our own in that of others; and, reciprocally tearing one another to pieces, we have been the cause of each other's ruin."[130]

He thought that if one were to limit oneself to scriptural language and avoid the theologically charged newer vocabulary in which war was being waged the gap between factions might be bridged and removed. When such an effort was actually made by the emperor, however, he was far from convinced that the chosen wording was actually adequate to affirm the truth he believed needed to be expressed.[131]

Although such attitudes represented an extraordinarily accommodative stance for many of his faction, it did not diminish in the least his determination for the victory of the Nicene bloc. When he was denied in 360 the right to participate in a council at Constantinople and it proceeded to endorse an Arian stance, he responded with the venomous *In Constantium*, which branded the ruler as nothing less than Antichrist.

He returned that same year to Gaul to lobby for Nicene style orthodoxy. He expanded his efforts into Italy and unsuccessfully attempted to depose Auxentius in Milan for tolerance of Arian creedal statements. He continued his energetic stance until he died late in 367 or near the beginning of the following year.

Laying aside his preoccupation with the battle over Arianism, he made other significant contributions to the development of western spirituality. He was the first identifiable Latin hymn writer. Though others may have made such attempts earlier, their efforts disappeared in the mists of history. Unfortunately, even in regard to Hilary, only a partial text of three of his hymns have survived.[132] There must originally have been quite a few of them, however, because Jerome speaks of him as having prepared a full collection.[133]

Hilary was also the author of the earliest Latin language commentary on the gospel of Matthew that has survived. This work dates to before his A.D. 356 exile. He indulged the fanciful freedom that heavy allegorical and typological interpretation permitted him. After his return, he devoted considerable time to an analysis of at least a third of the Psalms and it is possible that significantly more were treated but that the material has vanished as has so much ancient literature.

In regard to religious doctrine, his *De Trinitate* was his most important effort. He began it during his years in exile and both that motivation and his presence in a region where the sentiments he despised were so popular doubtless contributed to the intensity of his effort to denounce the Arian approach to the godhead. The chronology as to when he completed the work (before or after his return from exile) is unclear. This and his various other religious works gained a ready audience and were widespread throughout the following centuries.[134]

AUGUSTINE OF HIPPO (354–430)
The Reluctant Believer

To us, Augustine appears as a larger-than-life figure, equal to if not towering defiantly over all his contemporaries. In his era, however, opinion was very much subdued and divided, and many people considered him an interesting but not overly significant figure.

This can be illustrated from an event in 421 when Augustine sent off his analysis of human sexuality—a subject that he had been considering for more than twenty years—to the bishop of Constantinople. In spite of all his earlier writing and service to the church, no reply came. After a lengthy wait, he finally wrote another letter suggesting an explanation that would save his own pride—perhaps the reason for the delay might be an erroneous report in Constantinople that he had died.[135] Hence, in the real world, Augustine was simply another well-meaning church leader whom more prestigious individuals could safely delay answering for however long they wished.

Augustine's father was named Patrick and was a moderately prosperous farmer. Monica was his mother and she seems to have been a shrewd woman, though lacking anything more than the most rudimentary education, if any. Their son was born in the town of Thagaste (in modern Algeria, at the border with Tunisia), in a valley known for its agricultural productivity.[136]

Patrick held the post of town councilor which, like all Roman civic appointments, was a double-edged sword: it provided considerable personal prestige, but it also required one to spend generously on various civic causes. It has been reasonably conjectured that such expenses may account for the family's inability to provide their son the education they wished and the need to seek assistance for it elsewhere.[137]

Although Augustine doubtless had many happy days as a youth, as he looked back upon his young years he conceded that it had been, overall, a period to be endured rather than relived: "Who is there who would not recoil in horror and choose death, if he was asked to choose between dying and going back to his childhood!"[138] The schooling of his early years was typical of that which anyone received in the Roman Empire of that day and assumed the worst of motives in explaining the behavior of the student and did little to encourage the thirst for knowledge. Inability to understand was automatically insubordination; when in doubt the child was punished. The teacher's cane was not only a symbolic token of authority, but one freely and energetically administered.[139]

The Pleasures of Carthage

Augustine's advanced education in Carthage was made possible by the financial support of a wealthy citizen of his hometown. He brought with him a woman from there and took her as his long-term concubine, and, in a decision which reveals considerable loyalty and affection on his part, remained faithful to her: "with her alone, since I kept faith with her bed," was the way he expressed it.[140] This has been appealed to as evidence that Augustine's moral excesses in these years were not as severe as usually thought. (Either that or the period of his extreme laxity was rationalized away due to its brevity or, perhaps, because it occurred during her pregnancy.) Oddly enough, he never mentions the woman's name: perhaps a sense of the potential embarrassment it might bring her or a sense of shame at never marrying her.

Shortly after he had reached Carthage the woman bore him a son. Augustine fully realized that the baby had been born because he had shown no interest in taking the contraceptive alternatives that could have avoided it. However, he had learned his lesson and though the two were partnered for fifteen years there were no more children.[141]

During this period he became deeply absorbed in philosophy, especially the ideas of Cicero. He turned to the scriptures and spent some time studying them but was disappointed: they were, he said, "unworthy by comparison with the dignity of Cicero."[142] Of course, part of the problem may have rested in his own linguistic restrictions: though educated in the great Latin literature, his knowledge of Greek was modest.[143] He would have had to rely on a Latin version, with the inherent problem that even the greatest literature tends to lose some of its power in translation.

The opportunities and cultural resources of Carthage thoroughly intrigued him. He took pleasure in the gladiatorial conflicts and the theater. His standing as an outstanding student gave him a personal ego boost as well. He was becoming a scholar-gentleman, the ancient equivalent of belonging to a prestigious educational establishment, with all its snobbishness and exclusiveness, and he loved it. As he sought to work out an adult religious consciousness he walked the tightrope of trying to find one that would do justice to his concept of truth while remaining acceptable to the intellectual-cultural elite whose embrace he cherished.[144]

Conversion in Milan

After completing his education, in 376, he himself became a teacher in Carthage. Having the desire to move up in the socio-bureaucratic ranks of Roman society, he recognized that a move to Italy would help him immensely. Close acquaintances of the Manichaean persuasion found him individuals who would finance his move and residence in Rome. He was 29 years old when he arrived there in 383. It was a rough year for him due to physical illness, though his talents and the impression he left on his new acquaintances did much to increase his reputation. In 384 he moved to Milan and became a teacher on the payroll of the city's prefect.

Due to his educational background, social popularity, and growing breadth of relationships with the important and influential, he was quite hopeful of eventually gaining an important post in government service. It was even possible that he might gain a secondary governorship somewhere in the empire. Although many friendly doors opened for him in the imperial capital of Milan, he was still held back by his own modest finances. If this were not bad enough, he also lacked the major resource most likely to enable him to work around that limitation: a well-connected spouse.

To us it seems like a callous act — setting aside the mistress he had lived with in apparent peace and contentment for so many years. Yet in the brutal calculus of financial and personal self-advancement it seemed quite natural; to remain with a lover would have been the unusual decision.[145] Sending her back home, he found for himself a potential match: true, she was still too young to marry, but he could afford to wait and she came from a family whose financial well-being could unquestionably further his ambitions.[146]

However "calmly" and "rationally" he seemed to take these actions, it is hard to avoid the suspicion that one of the key psychological impetuses to conversion was an undercurrent of guilt over how he had treated someone who had stayed loyal to him for so many years. Another factor involved in his conversion was the ever dissolving connection to Manicheanism (see below). Augustine was psychologically predisposed to seek something beyond himself, and when the prime alternative slowly dissolved in credibility that of its Christian alternative increased proportionately.

Finally there was the reality of old-fashioned friendship. He had begun to listen to the sermons of Ambrose and he found in him the kind of wide-based knowledge and first-class intellect that both the Manichean leader Faustus and the Christians he had known in Africa had lacked.[147] In addition, Ambrose began to poke further holes in the Manichean thought that Augustine had already begun to question.

At the same time, he grew fond of the man personally. As he described it, "And I began to love him, of course, not at the first as a teacher of the truth, for I had entirely despaired of finding that in the Church — but as a friendly man. And I studiously listened to him — though not with the right motive — as he preached to the people." Even though he was looking for the stylistic and rhetorical reasons for how and why Ambrose was such a powerful preacher, the contents were worming themselves deeper into Augustine's mind: "Yet I was drawing nearer, gradually and unconsciously."[148]

He became increasingly impressed (and preoccupied) by the stories of how earlier martyrs and intellectuals and others had been converted. Finally, on the most pivotal day of his life, in severe emotional torment about what to do, he heard a child cry in a chant, "Pick it up, read it; pick it up, read it!" He records what happened next[149]:

> Immediately I ceased weeping and began most earnestly to think whether it was usual for children in some kind of game to sing such a song, but I could not remember ever having heard the like. So, damming the torrent of my tears, I got to my feet, for I could not but think that this was a divine command to open the Bible and read the first passage I should light upon. For I had heard how Antony, accidentally coming into church while the gospel was being read, received the admonition as if what was read had been addressed to him: "Go and sell what you have and give it to the poor, and you shall have treasure in heaven; and come and follow me." By such an oracle he was forthwith converted to thee.
>
> So I quickly returned to the bench where Alypius was sitting, for there I had put down the apostle's book when I had left there. I snatched it up, opened it, and in silence read the paragraph on which my eyes first fell: "Not in rioting and drunkenness, not in chambering and wantonness, not in strife and envying, but put on the Lord Jesus Christ, and make no provision for the flesh to fulfill the lusts thereof." I wanted to read no further, nor did I need to. For instantly, as the sentence ended, there was infused in my heart something like the light of full certainty and all the gloom of doubt vanished away.

This was the turning point. He had made his decision to turn to the Christ he had scorned in the past. He had found a way out of his torments.

Having become convinced that the ideal way to serve God was through forming a monastery and using it as a base for further spiritual development, he and several friends decided to return to his hometown of Thagaste to fulfill that goal. There was also a matter of personal obligation: to oversee the family property so that it would be preserved and ready for his son to inherit.[150] His journey was interrupted at Ostia because Rome's seaport was being blockaded. While he tarried there, his mother took sick and died. He was 36.

Appointment to Bishop and Perpetual Accusations of Being a Covert Manichee

After his return to Africa he eventually traveled to Hippo, a port in Algeria, though he did not have any intention of staying there permanently. The bishop needed someone who spoke Latin fluently and he wished to utilize Augustine's obvious talents. At the bishop's encouragement, the moderate-size congregation[151] strong-armed Augustine into accepting the post of presbyter. With the acceptance of this post began his preoccupation with scriptural exegesis.[152]

Bishop Valerius was quite pleased at the young man's success and was convinced that he would be the ideal successor in his own post. To be sure of it, he arranged for his appointment prior to his own death. This violated the established custom and became the grounds for charging that Augustine's holding the office was automatically null and void. He never felt sufficiently guilty to surrender it, but he did feel sufficiently ambiguous about the procedure to gather support to prohibit it from being repeated in the future.[153] Interpreted friendly, he was trying to assure that no one else would ever have to face the distraction of such a controversy; interpreted hostilely, he was tacitly admitting that he had been in error and should have resigned.

There were more than a few suspicious of his free-wheeling amoral youth and his earlier enthusiasm for the Manichaean sect.[154] For that matter, it was argued, if he was really all that much changed, why had he remained a teacher of rhetoric after the alleged conversion rather than leaving it and its pagan connections fully behind?

His alleged hidden agenda was vigorously attacked by critics. The rumor was widespread that the monastic institutions he encouraged were actually orthodox only in superficial appearance; in reality they were created as institutional disguises in which Manichees could covertly flourish. Hence it was essential to prove his orthodoxy by continued anti–Manichee writings and denunciations of them in other works where they were not the primary subject.[155] A few paragraphs of further explanation on the movement would be useful to understand why the issue was regarded by both pro– and anti–Augustine elements as so pivotal.

The Manichees were an offshoot of Christianity and heavily emphasized the writings of Paul, though accompanied by a rejection of the Old Testament in a manner that would have horrified the apostle. To them the God of the Old Testament was an anthropomorphic creature totally at odds with the deity of the New Testament. The specific laws of that testament were barbaric, calling for the sacrifice of animals and even the mutilation of the body through circumcision.[156]

They targeted traditional beliefs of the Christian community as well: How could deity be born in human form in the first place? How could a God-man actually "die" by crucifixion? The gospel accounts were self-condemned as contaminated by vain Jewish myths.[157] Hence the Manichees represented a serious challenge to the doctrines of both testaments.

Its alternative to "orthodoxy" lay in a myth of the conflict of good and evil in its most literal form in both the physical universe and in the human soul. As T. Kermit Scott concisely sums up its purpose, "This myth seems to serve three basic purposes: (1) it literally identifies good and evil and the struggle between them with objects and processes of the physical universe; (2) it further identifies those objects and processes with the corresponding good and evil aspects of each human being; and (3) it provides both a mode of life that seeks to maximize one's identity with the good aspects of the universe and the optimistic hope that such an effort will result in final redemption."[158]

The two forces of good and evil are roughly balanced, unlike the Christian concept of the supremacy of God and the vain effort of Satan to undermine His power.[159] Scott suggests that the mythology had a significantly different appeal according to the background of the individual believer: to the minimally educated (though prosperous) person, it assured them that they were now united with the light/sun that "ruled" the universe and through that union had true peace with the supernatural. To the intellectual it was yet another (and not necessarily exclusive) tool by which one sought true wisdom.[160]

Augustine had been a Manichee for years. He had been respected among them. Combine these admitted facts with the reality that there were enough similarities with Christianity that one could, at least superficially, be both at the same time and the claim that Augustine had a covert agenda in that direction made more than a little sense to those hostile toward him. It was his Achilles' heel for those skeptical and challenging of his leadership and credentials. His preoccupation with repeatedly refuting it bears witness to how dangerous an accusation he regarded it.

Laboring against this ghost of convictions now past, he pursued many other studies as well and always found time to encourage the monastic ideal. The monastery he and his friends came back to Africa to jointly establish became a center of great importance for those in the church from modest backgrounds who wished an entrée into the leadership echelon of the church. Possidius later wrote that, "No fewer than ten men, known to us as holy and venerable, chaste and learned, were supplied by the most blessed Augustine to various churches in response to requests."[161] To use the language of a later age, it became something of a priestly placement agency and his monastery put them on the first step of advancement that sometimes could lead to much higher posts in the future.

In a very real sense his monastic-educational effort became a victim of its own success. In his last years he became aware that the new generation(s) he had succored often had far different centers of interest than those he himself had encouraged.[162] By early 427 he had shifted the burdens of administrative responsibility onto the backs of others, while he himself continued in the post of bishop primarily in name only. His explanation was his age, but the last few years had brought a series of disappointments in the behavior and attitudes of his subordinates that doubtless played no small role in his decision to let others carry the heaviest load of responsibility.[163]

His Writings

Augustine was a voluminous writer: the large part of it that has survived surpasses 5,000,000 words.[164] His writings cover a vast ground, including autobiography, theology, and philosophy.

He not only builds upon ancient philosophy, he introduces the individual personality—the "I"—into what had previously been an abstract study.[165] Through the interjection of a Christian viewpoint, he lays the foundation for what later became medieval philosophy. In theology he dealt with the leading religious controversies of his day and played a significant role in how they were perceived by what was the evolving orthodoxy of his time.

Yet he also considers the more practical (and potential embarrassing) issues of personal faith and behavior. For example, in one of his most important works, *The City of God,* he tackled the accusation of polytheists that the conversion of the empire to Christianity had directly led to the success of the barbarian invasions. This response was necessary not only as a matter of preserving the positive image of the church to outsiders but also to wrestle with a thorny and difficult correlation of events that could be introduced against Christianity. As he explained it, the history of the western world becomes, essentially a tale of two "cities": one is Jerusalem (more or less equivalent to the church) and the other Babylon (more or less the Roman Empire).[166] However certain he was that Christianity had nothing to do with the ill condition of the empire, it certainly did not help his frame of mind that when he was dying in 430 the Vandal invaders were then in North Africa and approaching the gates of his own city of Hippo.[167]

Augustine had little interest in the autobiographical. He refers to his conversion only in his *Confessions*, a work that may have been written as long as fifteen years after it occurred. (By then most of those who had known him well at the time had passed away and none of them left their own account of the events.) Nor did he see fit to describe the incidents surrounding his advancement in the church, limiting himself to the short time after his conversion. Even what he does include is padded through the weaving in of much material that has only the most marginal connection with his personal life or character: of what real relevance is a lengthy discussion of the creation of Genesis 1 in connection with his life or his embracing of Christianity?

Perhaps the unspoken linkage in Augustine's mind is that just as God had shaped the initial creation, God had also crafted the events of his life to lead him to conversion[168]: He was, after all, a devout believer in predestination. This is the belief that God chooses, disposes, and alters our individual destiny independently of our own desires and willingness to be at His service. To him, this was the Divine overriding that led to his conversion. (To the critic, the doctrine of predestination makes individuals little more than divine automatons, but to those friendly to the concept it traditionally has been oddly reassuring.)

Chapter 6

Proponents of "Heretical" Alternatives

MARCION (c. 90–160)

Marcion launched an extremely vibrant movement however much his opponents were horrified by it. In his own lifetime, it set down roots as least as far away as Gaul.[1] Congregations remained in existence for centuries. During the fifth century, one Syrian bishop was quite proud of how eight different villages had been converted from their Marcionite convictions, bringing thousands back into orthodoxy. Even as late as the tenth century, Arabic language writings make passing mention that such groups were still in scattered existence.[2]

Marcion was so notably successful in carving out a large cadre of supporters within the church that his contemporaries of the more traditional school felt compelled to present an explanation for both his doctrine and its popularity in order to explain it away to outsiders—and to themselves. Justin Martyr, for example, described it all as demonic[3]:

> And, as we said before, the devils put forward Marcion of Pontus, who is even now teaching men to deny that God is the maker of all things in heaven and on earth, and that the Christ predicted by the prophets is His Son, and preaches another god besides the Creator of all, and likewise another son. And this man many have believed, as if he alone knew the truth, and laugh at us, though they have no proof of what they say, but are carried away irrationally as lambs by a wolf, and become the prey of atheistical doctrines, and of devils.

Marcion's Life and Bid for Roman Support

Born in Sinope, Pontus, a port city on the Black Sea (located within the boundaries of modern Turkey), Marcion came from a wealthy family whose fortune was rooted in profitable shipbuilding. He was reported to have been the offspring of a bishop and some question this, but it would certainly help explain his deep interest in Christian spiritual matters.[4] His critics claimed that he left home after a split with the church leadership. If his father was still alive and in a position of authority, this would indicate not only a split with the congregation but within his own family as well.

The purported church schism in his hometown was later explained as growing out of his corruption of a "virgin." Marcion's own ascetic lifestyle makes that extremely unlikely unless one entertains the scenario that he reacted against his own excess by adopting an austere life afterwards. More likely, the original critics were utilizing the virgin-bride imagery of Paul in Ephesians and meant corrupting the church. Seeking to maximize the evil of the man, later foes could have easily "literalized" this into a charge of personal moral degradation.[5]

His evolving ideas found rejection at home, and his stays elsewhere in Asia Minor brought no greater short-term success.[6] Eusebius records a story from Irenaeus about the collision between Bishop Polycarp and Marcion. Marcion pled "recognize us," i.e., accept if not endorse. Polycarp responded sharply, "I recognize, I recognize the firstborn of Satan!"[7]

Arriving in Rome about A.D. 140, he gave the Roman church the quite impressive figure of 200,000 sesterces from the proceeds of the sale of the ship that had carried him to the West. This generosity doubtless built a debt of gratitude that made it that much more painful for both sides as Marcion's religious beliefs became so well known and manifestly different from that of the majority that they could no longer be ignored. From the standpoint of practical theo-politics it also likely delayed action against him and, on the positive side, created a readiness to hear him that would not have been granted to one who was unknown or with a less clear-cut record of supporting the congregation.

After he had spent several years advocating his theories, a council was held in A.D. 144 in which his ideas were formally presented to the Roman church — and rejected. This action was accompanied by his own expulsion. During the session with the presbytery, Marcion challenged them as to the meaning of Jesus' teaching about not putting new wine into old wineskins lest they both be destroyed.[8] In Biblical context, Jesus' point had been that one could not shoehorn His teaching into the confines of others of His day without destroying the usefulness of both. Apparently Marcion believed that the point went revolutionarily beyond this limited application and meant that *everything* in the church's Jewish roots had to be repudiated — a quite logical stance given his two-god theory and other theories that were incompatible with the validity of those roots. The Roman church was able to scrape together the equivalent of the money he had given and returned it to him,[9] no small indication of the intensity of feelings on their own side.

Although Marcion is normally regarded as a pioneering Gnostic, his behavior is significantly out of keeping with the norm of such individuals. As Antonia Tripolitis (who accepts the classification) concedes, "Unlike other Gnostic teachers, Marcion proceeded to found a church. In general, Gnostic groups organized as schools in which the teachings were transmitted, interpreted, and kept secret. Marcion was the first Gnostic to establish a church with an organization, liturgy, and Scripture that was very similar to the church at Rome."[10] His goal was clearly not to be head of a mere advocacy group but to transform it into *the* church, preempting and replacing the existing institution.

Although Marcion readily admitted that his teaching differed dramatically from that of others, he made no pretense to being a prophet with a new revelation. Rather, he insisted, he was *restoring* the apostolic truth in its purity.[11] This was essentially the *Pauline* truth, for all the other apostles had drifted away from it,[12] a daring proposition for those who regarded apostolic contradictory teaching as a priori impossible and unthinkable.

The Reasons for the Appeal of His Theology

The power of Marcion's theological stance was enhanced by the fact that similar views were already being aired by dissenters within the Roman congregation. There were those already advocating the scenario of two rival gods being in existence: First there was the vindictive, hateful God who created the physical world and its many beings and it was this god whose exploits and actions are chronicled in the Jewish Testament. The true and superior God was a God of love and it was He who sent Jesus to earth.[13] The challenge was whether the church within Rome was ready to move this scenario from the fringes into the heart of its belief system.

Another powerful force in popularizing his theories was its enthusiastic embracing of a "de–Judaized" Christianity. With an increasing proportion of Gentiles in the church and the seemingly irreversible determination of an overwhelming number of Jews to permanently reject Jesus as Messiah, Christianity became self-defined not merely as the "fulfillment" of Jewish aspirations in the now "Old" Testament, but their replacement as God's people as well.

With the shift in ethnic membership and scorn at the Jewish rejection of Jesus, it also became easy to reject anything that could be labeled "Jewish," including the Old Testament itself. It did not have to be that way and for many it was not; to others it became a nigh irresistible temptation to scorn the Jewish roots of Christianity as a means of elevating the claims of their new faith. Hence, though Marcion's views on the Old Testament and its God were unquestionably extreme, they represented one effective means of demeaning the old faith system while building up one's own, and both factors doubtlessly help explain at least some of his doctrine's appeal at the time.

Finally, he advocated an extreme ascetic doctrine which, a few centuries later and modesty loosened, would become a hallmark of purported orthodoxy. Since the physical world was inherently contemptible, it followed, in his thinking, that the sexual instinct was equally so. The thought of having children was abhorrent, for it brought yet more people into this base world. Tertullian says that the Marcionites went so far as to normally baptize only the unmarried; they expected strict celibacy thereafter. Baptism for all others was delayed until they were facing death.[14]

Hence it is initially hard to take seriously Hippolytus' censure of the movement for attracting those "of a sensual mode of life, inasmuch as he was one of lustful propensities."[15] Although this became an all too common tool to ostracize doctrinal deviants in the following centuries (whether the accusation was deserved or not)[16] it is not impossible that some supporters reversed Marcion's reasoning. His premise that one should *abstain* from human sexuality because it is part of the earth's corruption could easily be inverted to mean that one *should* engage in it because it is part of one's depraved human nature *until* one makes the radical break and becomes completely celibate. As to Marcion's actual conduct, if the accusation of personal "lustful propensities" has any historical basis at all, it far more likely refers to his admitting the power of fleshly temptation while calling for extreme sexual self-repression — two tenets that many later "orthodox" ascetics clearly felt themselves, if one may judge by the vigor and venom of their denunciation of human sexuality.

Marcion's asceticism, however, had a fatal flaw so far as the later "orthodox" approach: To them a hatred of fleshly sexuality drove them, for example, to the desert and to abhorrence of the body. Marcion took it one step further: *the very god who created the body must be evil.*[17] As he saw it, how can one consistently have contempt for the body and its desires without having contempt for the creator of the body as well?

Revising Christianity to Fit Marcion's Theology

If Marcion's theology offered the appeal of demeaning traditional Judaism, it also posed major problems for Christianity as well and it was this aspect of his beliefs that guaranteed a collision with those who refused to accept his premises. First of all, he separated the creator God from the God-Father of Jesus. Marcion popularized the still common antithesis of the "punitive" God of the Old Testament versus the "loving" one of the New.[18] Although today that alleged discrepancy — which carefully overlooks the presence of both streams of thought in both testaments — is typically used as evidence of the irreconcilable fundamental difference of the two covenants. In contrast, Marcion took it a step further and argued, in effect, that two different supernatural beings must have been involved.

Marcion's interpretative scenario denouncing the Old Testament presented obvious difficulties, since even the four gospels repeatedly portray Jesus as an observant Jew in a Jewish environment. He is presented as discussing the meaning of the Torah and its application to His own age — rejecting the popular and traditional glosses that permitted its intent to be ignored or reversed. This was an approach clearly built upon the belief that it was authoritative, honorable, and praiseworthy.

Marcion tried to resolve this difficulty by relying on the only Gentile composed gospel, that of Luke. Since even that had clear-cut Jewish aspects, he went about purging it of such elements.[19] To him, any sympathetic "Jewish" aspects were the result of early Christian misunderstanding of the true intent and purpose of Jesus.[20] Since the kindly words *had* to be Judaizing additions (else they would not have been there in the first place) he did not feel like he was tampering with the text by removing such supposed unjustified additions.[21]

Although little of his revised text has survived, he appears to have avoided *adding* anything to the text, however; what differences that occurred in that regard appear to have been no more than the usual variants that happen in the copying of any manuscript by hand.[22] Ultimately, the pivotal issue with Marcion was not the true canon of the New Testament, but its theology. This was what motivated his limiting himself to Luke and his pruning of its contents to better fit his theology.

If Marcion's creed drastically redefined Christianity by repudiating its Jewish elements, it also required a drastic revision in the assumptions about Jesus himself. In light of his contempt for the physical creation, it was quite natural for Marcion to deny not only the fact but the very possibility that Jesus could have undergone a physical birth. Instead, He suddenly appeared in Galilee to teach and preach.[23] Marcion's view of Jesus' body might well be called a form of "consubstantiation"—it *appeared* to be flesh and blood but was *really* a spiritual entity that could not undergo death and decay. Hence the "resurrection" body was not a miraculously altered body but the same one He had before His apparent physical death.[24] If a far later age could speak of the "imitation of Christ," Marcion advocated the opposite, that Christ was, if you will, an imitation of the human.

If having thoroughly revised the "orthodox" understanding of Jesus' nature were not enough, he also rewrote the theology of the believers' future. To Marcion, an individual's existence ended with death, even among those no longer under the control of the evil creator deity. Hence even for them that was no promise of a bodily resurrection.[25] There was to be one life, one time, and nothing beyond it except oblivion.

TERTULLIAN (born c. 160)
Apologist for Both Orthodoxy and Dissidence

Very little is actually known of Tertullian's life. One of the few facts that can be established with certainty is that he was brought up a polytheist, since he himself refers to it. The time of his birth and death are pure guesswork, unfortunately. His writings contain references indicating his works were composed approximately in the range of A.D. 196 to 220, with his turn to the Montanist theology being no later than 205 to 207.[26]

There is no indication that his polytheist youth was any different than that of most young men of his age: amphitheatre events fascinated him, and his sexual misadventures seem to have been not particularly grandiose by the standards of the day.[27] He was converted perhaps in the 170s or 180s, since by the middle 190s he was writing in detail on religious matters. What individual(s) played the greatest influence in his conversion is unknown. References in his writings to both exorcisms and the bravery of Christians facing death could indicate that these indirect influences played a major role in challenging his own religious background, but he himself does not say anything directly linking either phenomenon with his religious change.[28]

Coming from a wealthy background in Carthage, he may well have been a lawyer before turning to religious discourse, though there is nothing in his writings that explicitly requires that conclusion.[29] Two major lines of evidence can be introduced to overcome that lack of direct mention. One is that a Roman lawyer of the same name—but without data as to his life and actions—practiced his profession in the same time period. Evidence linking the two together, however, is lacking beyond this minimum of a shared name.

A second line of evidence can be found in the abundant legal terminology he introduces in his writing,[30] but that need not imply anything more than that he was a well read and knowledgeable individual. For him to have used "a number of basic notions of Roman Law,"[31] for example, only testifies to his general knowledge, not to his legal background. Furthermore, such terminology would be appropriate to his religious agenda: believers were to be law abiders in the spiritual realm just as they should be in the temporal.

Jerome says that after his conversion Tertullian became a presbyter in Carthage, and he may well have been, but there are those who vigorously question the reliability of even this piece of data.[32] He wrote at least as late as 212, and he may well have lived on many years beyond that but no account of his passing has survived to provide us any detail. Jerome can speak only vaguely of how "he is said to have lived to a decrepit old age."[33]

Attitude toward Heresy — Both "Orthodox" and "Heretical"

Tertullian could make his point crystal clear: one either respects his argument or recoils from it. He is not one who can be ignored due to his obscurity.[34] At least in his orthodox days he saw proof of who was a heretic, not only in their doctrinal stances but in their behavior; they were nonhierarchical and freely permitted one and all to share in mutual teaching of each other and outsiders[35]:

> I must not omit an account of the conduct also of the heretics — how frivolous it is, how worldly, how merely human, without seriousness, without authority, without discipline, as suits their creed. To begin with, it is doubtful who is a catechumen, and who a believer; they have all access alike, they hear alike, they pray alike — even heathens, if any such happen to come among them. "That which is holy they will cast to the dogs, and their pearls," although (to be sure) they are not real ones, "they will fling to the swine".... All are puffed up, all offer you knowledge. Their catechumens are perfect [acceptable to play a role in public worship] before they are full-taught.
>
> The very women of these heretics, how wanton they are! For they are bold enough to teach, to dispute, to enact exorcisms, to undertake cures — it may be even to baptize. Their ordinations are carelessly administered, capricious, changeable. At one time they put novices in office; at another time, men who are bound to some secular employment; at another, persons who have apostatized from us, to bind them by vainglory, since they cannot by the truth. Nowhere is promotion easier than in the camp of rebels, where the mere fact of being there is a foremost service. And so it comes to pass that today one man is their bishop, tomorrow another; today he is a deacon who tomorrow is a reader; today he is a presbyter who tomorrow is a layman. For even on laymen do they impose the functions of priesthood.

To those opposed to these movements this was heavy damnation, indeed. To the accused heretics these elements represented key strengths and the lack of them revealed the spiritual hallowness of would-be orthodoxy. When he himself turned to Montanism, with its own heavily nonhierarchical component, that did not slow him down in the least. As a Montanist, he vigorously assailed the Roman bishops and his sympathizers with equal zeal and passion, assaulting their doctrine, behavior, and character with the same determination he had used against others.[36] Heretics still existed, but in significant part their identities were now reversed.

His Contributions to "Orthodoxy"

Tertullian's two major apologetic works were *To the Nations* and the *Apology*. Both contain similar arguments and it has been suspected that the former was a preliminary version of the latter.³⁷ *Nations* was addressed to individuals at large and *Apology* is addressed to rulers. One targets the unconverted masses, the other the rulers who will determine what is tolerated and encouraged.

Against Marcion is Tertullian's most exhaustive publication and delves in detail into the weakness he finds in Marcion's theories. Since it would have been easy for Marcion to dismiss as irrelevant many passages of scripture — which he had expunged — Tertullian relies upon those books that even Marcion accepted. Tertullian drove home with passion the theme that even his censored New Testament made no sense unless one accepted the validity, legitimacy, and honorableness of the ancient Jewish texts and practices they refer to.³⁸

Even when he embraced the Montanist agenda, it was nearly impossible to totally dismiss the "orthodox" contributions of his earlier years. Indeed, he pioneered the rhetoric of the Godhead that would become the fulcrum of future orthodoxy in its disputes with Arianism and other dissident movements. As Gerald O'Collins notes, "In writing of one substance (*substantia*) in three persons, Tertullian was the first Christian writer to exploit the term 'person' in theology, the first to apply 'Trinity' (*Trinitas*) to God, and the first to develop the formula of 'one substance in three persons.'"³⁹

In regard to the slowly developing exaltation of asceticism and the underlying rejection of the honorableness of even married sexuality, he did his part to further such agendas while in the orthodox camp. Although still married, he terminated sexual relations with his spouse and wrote her a public letter urging her to develop the fine art of celibacy. Sexual relations he wrote, at a different time, were incompatible with Christian faith. To repudiate marriage entirely as the Montanists did was but the logical next step.⁴⁰ Those who remained within the "orthodox" faction refused to take that step, while a significant percentage of its leaders in the next two centuries promoted asceticism with a passion only marginally short of that extreme.

After his shift to the Monanist movement, Tertullian became even more venomous in regard to second marriages. If being married was repugnant, being married a second time was obscene. God absolutely prohibited such, he insisted. The only excuse was the human sexual drive and that was condemnation enough for undertaking such marriages. If anything, this stance bred a reaction among many which bestowed at least limited approval upon such second marriages — in significant part in order to make plain a clear-cut differentiation between Tertullian style views and the self-designated true "orthodoxy."⁴¹

The Montanist Years

Tertullian became a Montanist around 205 and some have speculated that he led a splinter group called the "Tertullianists," since such a group bearing his name is known to have existed over a century and a half later. Of course, the nickname may have been adopted by his followers after his death, either out of respect for him or out of reservations about the actions or spiritual evolution of Montanists in other regions.

As to Tertullian himself, some have even argued that Tertullian never *became* a Montanist at all; rather, the system represented conclusions so similar or identical to ones he had *always* held that any transition date is only arbitrary.[42] Furthermore, that he was *not* regarded as heretical locally is argued by the fact that his writings have survived uncensored, complete with their references to Montanist ideas and concepts.[43] This survival was assisted, of course, by the fact that he did not come under official censure in Rome until 494 and by then his reputation had become too deeply established to be seriously injured by views that a latter generation might regard as sad aberrations.[44]

Laying aside the question of whether there was ever a clear-cut "break" point between his orthodox and heretical years, that leaves the issue of why he drifted in a pro–Montanist direction in the first place. Tertullian felt that his generation of Christians had become too complacent, too tolerant of moral excess, and too comfortable in a world that was not really their home. Hence, Peter Brown argues, the Montanist movement provided the solution to the problem of compromise with the world: through the new, direct instruction of the Holy Spirit the comfortable would be made uncomfortable and the loose-living would be rebuked into a more godly lifestyle. Christianity would be born again.[45]

In the Montanist church, the idealized leadership would be in the hands of those who combined the guidance of the divine spirit with a physical and emotional maturity derived from having raised children and seeing a spouse die. Even these middle-aged to aging individuals still needed emotional bonds, however. Hence, in his *Exhortation to Chastity,* Tertullian urges one widower to take a mature female coreligionist into his household to act as housekeeper and nonsexual companion, apparently convinced that either the power of the spirit or their mature years would nullify any danger of the relationship turning into a sexual one.[46]

One way God spoke was through dreams and Tertullian cited Joel 2:28 as verification, though conceding that other dreams were demonically inspired.[47] So important were dreams as a means of grasping the divine will that he insisted, "just about the majority of people get their knowledge of God from dreams."[48] In those dreams a person stands as naked as a gladiator who has been stripped of his weapons and forced to undergo a battle — but it all happens in the mind as one wrestles and fights with the forces and influences that spell out the story he sees within his head.[49] God speaks through this means, Tertullian was convinced, and, if one is prudent, one derives the necessary lesson from what has been observed.

VALENTINUS (flourished 120–160)
Advocate of Gnosticism

Valentinus, the most important identifiable second-century Gnostic Christian,[50] was born and educated in Egypt. He established schools both on Cyprus and in Egypt to educate individuals in his way of thinking and these survived for at least two centuries after his death. Only after creating these educational establishments did he make his way to Rome, where he once again established a school as the forum for propagating his teaching. He remained in the city as a teacher from the mid–130s through the mid–140s at the earliest and c. A.D. 160 at the latest. Even then, the school he established continued to be a center of agitation for his doctrines for at least a century after his death.[51]

Tertullian conceded that the man was a very effective speaker. According to Tertullian's denunciation, Valentinus pushed his doctrines to the point of division only after he unsuccessfully was a candidate to become the next bishop of Rome.[52] The first statement, at least, was unlikely to have been made unless he actually was eloquent, since it was a tacit concession of his skills and abilities that Tertullian would naturally have preferred not to make of any heretic.

The chronological division as to when his distinctive doctrines became the center of his agenda is unclear and Tertullian's chronological reference may, indeed, be true. Yet their existence prior to his bid for power is virtually certain as well, since dramatic shifts in belief rarely spring up overnight. That raises the far more difficult question of why a man of such skills lost his bid for Rome's highest church office. Were his supporters too few or his opponent more agile at episcopate electioneering? Was his opponent simply considered the better qualified on his merits alone? Or were Valentinus' views so savaged by a more able (or desperate) opposing faction that he then lashed out in open schism since he had nothing more to lose?

These questions are impossible to answer. The sad fact is that even those we may regard as having the "truth" on a religiously controversial matter may regard their victory as so essential that the tools of smear and misrepresentation are rationalized away. They fuel, in reaction, a far more bitter adversary than they would have otherwise ever had.

In spite of what we can determine about the fate of Valentinus' movement (see below), little is known of what the man himself did in the remainder of his life. Epiphanius asserted that Valentinus later was shipwrecked on Cyprus and went insane, which sounds more like the retelling of a juicy tall tale than anything historical, since it cast an effective slur on a heretic: what more deserved fate could he have?[53] On the other hand, the fact that Clement of Alexandria makes repeated use of his material could well argue that Valentinus spent some time in that city,[54] though that impact could have been via writings rather than through personal contact.

Although Valentinus' views were apparently formally rejected by the Roman church, Ismo Dunderberg notes that there is no record of a formal excommunication of the man himself either then or later,[55] which suggests that his element remained so strong that at least some restraint was exercised. To the extent that his supporters formed separate congregations (or worked within the confines of a "house church" setting), they existed on the edge of attention of the more organized orthodox church. Indeed, it was possible for at least some Valentinians to operate even within the traditional church structure itself. As late as Bishop Victor (A.D. 189–199), one of his subordinate presbyters was named Florinus and had embraced this theology. Irenaeus wrote to Victor to plead with him to examine what Florinus had written and to remove him,[56] an admonition that makes sense only if there was considerably more toleration for Valentinian thought in Rome than in certain other areas.

Groups of Valentinians set down roots throughout the Empire. They soon were in various places throughout Italy, in Gaul to the west and in Syria and Egypt to the east. So far as Egypt and modern Turkey these groups remained in existence at least two hundred years later.[57] The movement was a very viable one, surviving in places into the eighth century.[58]

The Valentinians avoided forming a separate church, being generally content to remain within the orthodox movement. This drove Irenaeus to distraction, probably because it is far easier to successfully demonize an exterior movement that one has little contact with rather than one composed of individuals who one rubs shoulders with at every worship service. Irenaeus speaks of their indignation at being labeled heretics and how they insisted that they taught "the same doctrine" as the orthodox. They spoke of honoring "God the Father" and "our Lord Jesus Christ," as if the terms had the same meaning and connotation for them as for everyone else.[59]

Irenaeus criticized them for permitting participation in pagan civic celebrations and of consuming meat that had been sacrificed to idols. They even attended the bloody and violent gladiator events, he reports.[60] Since one or more of these behaviors were likely found among an embarrassing number of the orthodox as well, he threw in the accusation of sexual misconduct. That he is engaged in considerable exaggeration can be seen in the fact that even he had to concede that many Valentinians lived a morally upstanding life. (These, oddly enough, he dismissed as victims of arrogance.)[61]

Valentinus' Theology

Although the Egyptian *Evangelium Veritatis (Gospel of Truth)* has no explicitly claimed authorship, some are convinced that it came from his pen.[62] If not, it certainly reflects the type of thinking common in the circle within which he moved.[63]

Valentinus became a firm rejecter of the Genesis tradition of God as creator of the physical universe. To him, it was the aeon Sophia acting independently of God and in subversion of the divine purpose that performed the creative work. As the result of this colossal error, the supernatural element within individuals became trapped in a mere physical, material body.[64] (In relevant mythology, aeons are embodiments of various divine attributes; in Christian theology one might think of them roughly as wise and powerful archangels, with an explicit divinity as part of their nature.)

Those who walked in the Valentinian tradition thought that the human race could be divided into three types. The phylic and psychic humans were destitute of any element of inner spirituality. Only those who were part of the pneumatic race of humans enjoyed some modest access to the divine essence. The pneumatic alone were certain of ultimate redemption in eternity. More liberal thinking advocates among them were willing to concede that a limited number of psychics might share in that blessing. As for the lowest level — the phylic humans — they were totally beyond any hope.[65]

This approach collided vigorously with that of the New Testament. The idea that only a small percentage could be saved — not because of their behavior but their inner essence — stood in vivid contrast to the idea that human redemption, at least potentially, is available to the entire human species. Furthermore, viewing the human body as a prison, even for the spiritual elite, carried such an extreme negative evaluation of the flesh that it had the quite natural result of repudiating the Pauline idea of a bodily resurrection.[66] After all, if the flesh is despicable and a curse, how could God possibly compel us to remain within such abhorrent limitations in the afterlife, even if it be a rejuvenated and miraculously altered flesh?

Another issue that Valentinus wrestled with was how to reconcile Jesus' supernaturalness with His having a human body at all. (The radical denigration of the flesh came perilously close to making the two approaches irreconcilable.) One means of explaining the situation was to assert that the physical body was a phantasm for the benefit of others; this option was ultimately rejected as heretical. Another was that of Clement of Alexandria, who argued that Jesus was kept alive by the power of the Holy Spirit and did not need fleshly nourishment at all; He ate simply to disprove any future delusion that He did not have a real body.[67]

Valentinus' approach was surprisingly close to that of Clement: "He was continent, enduring all things. Jesus practiced divinity; he ate and drank in a special way, without excreting his solids. He had such a great capacity for continence that the nourishment within him was not corrupted, for he did not experience corruption."[68] It is useful to note that the heretic Valentinus conceded that Jesus' body required nourishment (it simply was processed in a different manner), while the orthodox Clement denied it was required at all, which put the orthodox Clement closer to doceticism's conception of the nontemporal body of Jesus than did Valentinus.[69]

Of course, the admission that Jesus was divine while within a physical body did not explain how it was possible, since the physical body was viewed by Valentinus as so inherently destructive of spiritual nature. It has been speculated that Valentinus attempted to resolve this tension by arguing that, though Jesus' body existed, it was not *material* flesh and blood but a visible embodiment of the "heavenly" nature, thereby maintaining the distinction between His body and that of other men.[70] Mortals had a depraved physical body; Jesus had a different style body not subject to that corruption.

FELICISSIMUS (flourished c. 250)
Defender of Presbyterial Authority against That of the Episcopate

Although Felicissimus was briefly discussed in the context of Cyprian's controversial leadership of the church in Carthage, here we shift perspective and examine the controversies of that period through the prism of Felicissimus' attitudes and actions. Although Cyprian enjoyed major support from the Carthaginian church members at large, the situation was considerably shakier in regard to clergy. In fact, a clear majority of the presbyters opposed his selection. Unable to convince his opponents, Cyprian quickly took the "brass knuckles" approach of the application of brute power: he replaced a number of people with men fully loyal to himself.[71] From the standpoint of power politics and maximizing his own authority, this represented the most prudent policy. It also amounted to a declaration of war upon those who refused to capitulate.

Five presbyters in the church of Carthage so vigorously opposed the selection of Cyprian as new bishop that one of their number, Novatus, appointed Felicissimus to the post of deacon. In turn, leadership of those refusing to yield presbyterial authority to the bishop became concentrated in the new deacon.[72]

How shall we describe the issue of power that was at the core of this conflict?

Certainly the question of presbyterial authority was one of its central aspects. Cyprian was a clear-cut case of a man who believed in a monarchical episcopate: in its crudest formulation, he had the power by divine right, and both clergy and laity had only the "right" to obey. By his very "legitimate" selection, the issue had been settled. The dissenting majority of clergy insisted that the distribution of power remain more collegial and that their views and interests play a major role in shaping and even modifying the bishop's own policies and decisions.[73]

Another power issue involved who had the right to select new bishops. Some see the situation as one in which Cyprian was stoutly in defense of the people's right to choose, while the presbyters were determined to see that it remained exclusively their own.[74] Yet, once appointed bishop, Cyprian saw his power as, effectively, absolute.[75] Whatever power the mass of Christians had possessed initially, vanished when the bishop gained power and however theoretically they had the right to reject a flagrantly sinful leader[76] the odds of them successfully securing his deposition — except in the rarest of cases — ranged from slim to nonexistent. As fellow clergy, the presbyters represented the only realistic hope for at least a partial check on the bishop's authority and behavior.

So long as Cyprian visibly held the office of bishop and remained in the city, the psychological upper hand was his. When Decius launched his massive persecution in 250, Cyprian, however, had to flee for his life and this provided the opportunity for Felicissimus and those similarly minded to increase their own power. At this point the new issue of how to treat temporarily apostate Christians was stirred into the brew, with Felicissimus and his compatriots arguing for more lenient treatment and supporters of Cyprian demanding a far harsher one.

At this point Cyprian tried to intervene by sending three bishops along with two priests to the city to assist those who had remained steadfast and suffered financially from the oppression.[77] Felicissimus, now a presbyter, regarded the delegation as improperly undercutting his own legitimate authority. None of the bishops were local men; they were blatantly outsiders and clearly the knowing and willing agents of a bishop (Cyprian) who was not even in the city itself.[78]

Church relief was normally carried out locally and the resident clergy were in charge of its distribution. Instead, those seeking relief had to meet with the new commission and be verified by them as both needful and deserving of help,[79] effectively cutting the local clergy out of their traditional role.

Felicissimus threatened his own ecclesiastical rejection of any who accepted this largesse, presumably regarding it as, in effect, an effort by Cyprian to "bribe" himself back into influence. There seems no way to avoid the conclusion that the perception was fundamentally sound.[80] No doubt Cyprian justified his unconventional procedure of managing the money on the grounds that much of it came out of his personal resources[81] and the fact that whoever was bishop, he was convinced, had the inherent right to arrange for relief assistance in whatever form he deemed best regardless of the wishes of the subordinate priests.

Cyprian took advantage of the rejection of this theoretically humanitarian financial help as rationale for his own excommunication of Felicissimus and those church leaders most openly associated with him. He declined to act immediately against the lapsed questionably restored to fellowship by them. Perhaps, in a test of wills, he reckoned that he simply did not have sufficient support to make the latter action credible and a failed attempt would add to the prestige of Felicissimus and undermine his own.

Felicissimus convinced four former bishops to obtain Fortanus to the post of bishop of Carthage.[82] This had several advantages. It provided a bishop actually in Carthage (rather than in hiding elsewhere) who could make a claim to having been selected by the presbyters rather than in defiance of them. It also provided a public spokesman whose agenda duplicated that of the various dissenters. There was no doubt that Felicissimus remained de facto leader of the group, even if the attempt had been made to provide the cover of de jure authority via a replacement for Cyprian.

Cyprian's return was temporarily blocked by the threat of civil unrest if he did so, a danger he was convinced originated from this clique.[83] Felicissimus sent the presbyter Novatius to Rome to lobby support just as Cyprian was using pen and ink to do the same. When he was finally able to return, Cyprian held a synod that formally expelled Felicissimus and his allies. The influence of the dissidents was fatally undermined, however, only when Cyprian was able to gain the reluctant support of the Roman Church (whose foot dragging on the matter had been blatantly obvious)[84] and when a compromise on handling apostates was dragged from *him*.

The confrontation effectively reveals that religious controversies often move on multiple levels: whatever the initial cause of disruption, they became merged with additional religious grievances, creating a synthesis far more challenging than that which originally existed. Only when the passion could be bled out of the later grievances was it possible for the power of the bishop to be effectively restored.

ARIUS (c. 250–336)
Founder of the Arian Alternative to Orthodoxy

Where Arianism and "Orthodoxy" Parted Paths

Arius and his successors struck at the fundamental question of the relationship of Father, Son, and Holy Spirit—their nature, their relationship to each other, and the question of where their "oneness" ended and began. To Arius, to consider the Logos of John 1 (Son of God, Jesus) as uncreated and eternal would imply the existence of multiple gods. Yet the Son was clearly more than a mere mortal: that is what the expression "only-begotten" meant in regard to Him, Arius insisted. He was the first of God's creation, unique, and through Him the creator of everything else. He existed before the earth and, hence, "time" as we know it, but not for all eternity.[85]

In contrast, the orthodox doctrine became, in effect, one in which Father, Son, and Holy Spirit are virtually synonyms yet simultaneously distinct and "separate" individuals. They became, if you will, different aspects of the same Being. Athanasius later explained the idea with such analogies as the difference between sunlight and the sun: distinct and yet so tightly linked as to have an unbreakable bond that transcended the distinguishing language that made them different.[86]

In the Old Testament, Arius and those who came later found especially appealing Proverbs 8:22, "The Lord created me at the beginning of his work, the first of his acts of old" (Revised Standard Version). The term *created* is found in such other English translations as Today's English Version and the Jewish Publication Society 1917 Bible. Most translations go with the vaguer "possessed me." In the New Testament, a key text was Colossians 1:15, which describes Jesus, in nearly all translations, as "the first-born of all creation" (Revised Standard Version, for example).[87] Arian advocates could also introduce various remarks made by Origen and other writers which could be interpreted in a manner to indicate that Christ originated at some point in time rather than being without beginning as the Father Himself is.[88]

But the key emphasis of the Arian-inclined was that they were using the language of the Bible itself to describe the relationship. In light of the traditional reverence for the authority of scripture and acceptance of its divine origin, why then should they abandon "scriptural language" for creedal expressions totally alien to Scripture? Their core premise was that supposedly scriptural doctrines should be expressed in scriptural terms, not humanly invented ones that might take on completely different connotations and implications.[89]

Arius and His Conflict with Clerical Superiors

However unorthodox Arius was later considered, he was still the first to lay out a key assertion that later became pervasive: when God created the heavens and the earth he did so *ex nihilo*, out of nothing.[90] But this, of course, was not what gained him the contemporary ire, but his rejection of what became known as "trinitarianism."

For a long while various presbyters in Alexandria had been upset with Arius' teaching along this line and had been unsuccessfully encouraging Bishop Alexander of their city to act against him. Arius had been a respected and admired preacher for many years[91] and this fact assured that his views received a receptive hearing and even acceptance among many. Finally the Bishop came down on the side of the anti–Arian faction and decided it was desirable to quash Arius and his interpretation of the divine nature.

At this stage Arius was not the leader of a vast movement, but little more than a single priest in vigorous dissent from the convictions of the bishop to whom he was hierarchically answerable. Recognizing the degree of disagreement and the intensity of Alexander's opposition, Arius sent a series of letters to recipients throughout the East informing them of his convictions, his reasoning, and what he regarded as the weakness of the approach of his bishop.

Alexander called a council to condemn the dissident and after they acted the bishop himself began to circulate letters to fellow bishops in his own effort to discredit his opponent. Although the exact chronology of events surrounding the dispute is uncertain,[92] it was the distribution of this series of letters by the two sides that transformed the issue from a local controversy into one of widespread interest and debate.[93]

The basis of Alexander's censure was twofold: the first was that Arius' theology of the relationship of the heavenly Father and Son was fatally flawed. When that was not enough to resolve the split, Alexander invoked the power of the episcopate: I am bishop and you are a mere presbyter and, therefore, you must yield on the matter to me.[94] However one judged the merits of the theology, the clergy of Alexandria had historically expected and exercised considerable leeway in their religious teaching and speculation, a stance fully in accord with the city's Roman tradition as a center of free-wheeling learning and debate.[95]

Furthermore, however much all Alexandrian clergy were willing to accept the superiority of their bishop over priests throughout the region, *within* the city they had traditionally selected who would be bishop and viewed him as "first among his equals" rather than an authoritative superior who could apply his authority unilaterally upon them without their consent and concurrence.[96] Hence his effort to "pull rank" to settle the issue rather than to do so through the power of his argumentation and creating a consensus among the local clergy endangered traditional arrangements and assured far greater sympathy for Arius than would otherwise have been the case.

Nicene Council and the Drawing of Schism Lines

At the suggestion of Emperor Constantine, the Council of Nicaea declared in A.D. 325 that *homoousios* ("consubstantial," "one in being") described the relationship of Father and Son, thereby repudiating Arius' approach. Beyond having the ruler's endorsement, virtually none of the participants wrote of why the term had been selected nor did any provide then or later a written analysis of what it was intended to include or exclude. The one exception was Eusebius of Caesarea and he conspicuously avoided spinning out the kind of detailed anti–Arian meaning of the term that later theologians embraced as being required by its use.[97] Furthermore, in the Eastern Church during the 340s and 350s, bishops tacitly accepted the designation but manifested an extreme reluctance to use it. Instead they usually preferred formulations of their own that expressed, essentially, the same idea.[98]

Since Arius had already gone on the record as explicitly rejecting the validity of describing the Father-Son relationship by *homoousios*, it is quite probable that the Council participants were using it far more as a means of *rejecting* Arius' views than of spelling out their own alternative.[99] To do the latter might well have created divisions within their own camp and an inability to arrive at a formulation that would be generally acceptable. Of course, it should be noted that there is also no reason to believe that those who were essentially on Arius' side of the controversy were any more united. Agreeing with the general concept of his, they did not necessarily agree with every nuance of it or prefer expressing their convictions in exactly the same manner.[100]

In spite of the official façade of unity that came out of the Council of Nicaea, in many ways it represented a superficial papering over of continuing conflicts. By October 325 Constantine realized things were not working out as he wished. He deposed Eusebius of Nicomedia and one Theognis of Nicaea for their sympathetic treatment of pro–Arian elements in the church.

He denounced both the character and actions of the two men in strong terms: "I had some Alexandrian heretics sent here because the flames of discord had been stirred up by their efforts. But these fine bishops, whom once the truth of the synod had preserved for repentance, not only received them and kept them safe in their houses, but also shared in their wickedness. For this reason I decided thus concerning these ingrates: I ordered them taken off to exile as far away as possible."[101] (Later, Constantine's annoyance at Eusebius was considerably mollified.) One of these tolerated individuals may have been Arius himself,[102] and such direct involvement in shielding the man would go far to explain why the emperor would actively pursue these particular bishops while passing over in benign neglect more passive supporters of Arianism whose public actions were more discrete.

Some accounts claim that Arius ultimately accepted, under oath, the *homoousios* creedal statement and was readmitted to the "orthodox" communion, though that would not necessarily exclude his own unorthodox interpretive spin upon the word. The hopes aroused by such a "reconciliation" would certainly explain Constantine coming down hard on Athanasius for refusing to admit repenting Arians back into the fold, since it was in defiance of Constantine's own preference for reuniting all the disputants.

If the doctrinal reversal is true, Arius' interpretation of the language must have remained very close to his earlier beliefs, since ultimately Constantine came down hard in a written rebuke to him arguing that his current theological convictions on the Godhead were still dangerously erroneous. This was apparently written in response to Arius' request to be permitted to form his own church in Alexandria, since Athanasius had refused to readmit him.[103]

Arius was a fading light, though his doctrine was not. By the time of the Nicene meeting Arius was already around seventy.[104] His years left were few but the doctrinal interpretation he put on the relationship of Father and Son gained an audience and support far wider and larger than he could possibly have guessed at, even if he did not live to enjoy it.

Indeed, the movement took on a life of its own, often with no tangible direct connection between "Arians" and the Arius who brought their shared ideas to public attention.[105] In the western empire especially, bishops such as Auxentius, Palladius, and Secundianus explicitly denied having met Arius or read his writings, but their doctrines were sufficiently similar that their foes branded them with the epithet "Arian."[106] Even after Arianism was widely suppressed within the Empire (at least in above-ground manifestations), it retained major support among Christians outside it.[107]

The Tools for Defeating Arianism

A variety of tools were ultimately utilized to turn back the very real danger of Arianism triumphing and becoming the "orthodoxy" of the world rather than its Nicene alternative. At the top of the list was government suppression of the movement. The danger here was that of an emperor coming to power who believed the *Arians* were the truly orthodox, and the example of Constantius showed that basing religious triumph on government coercion was to utilize a tool that could be used against oneself.

Even with the power of intimidation behind it, the triumph did not always come easily. In the East, for decades Arianism clearly had more adherents than Roman style orthodoxy. Constantinople was rocked by riotous protesters and Gregory Nazianzus could be installed as Patriarch in that city only through the force of military intervention; otherwise the Arians were simply too numerous to permit it to have occurred.[108]

Also high on the list of techniques used to undermine Arianism was the demonizing of it as a barbarian theology — literally so, turning the major source of numerical strength for Arianism among outsiders into a method to discredit the truthfulness of the shared theology. Skillful propaganda from Ambrose and others stressed that the dangerous Gothic invaders imperiling the empire held the same beliefs as the Arians.[109] Bishop Sidonius Apollinaris in Gaul wrote of how, "I must confess that, formidable as the mighty Goth may be, I dread him less as the assailant of our walls than as the subverter of our Christian laws."[110]

Just as reliance on imperial power held the danger that it might shift its allegiance to the other side, demonizing the barbarians also had the potential for creating a dangerously explosive reaction. First of all, the outsiders were hardly likely to take kindly to having their religion viciously demeaned. Furthermore, many of the "barbarians" had been recruited into the Roman army and constituted its largest single source of personnel. Indeed, Arianism prospered within the army and remained common even as the movement was losing popular support elsewhere. Because of their military importance, army personnel were permitted to practice Arianism at the same time it was being repressed outside their camps — and it was inevitable that, through their encouragement, the local population would be influenced in that direction regardless of official government hostility.[111]

Others treated the subject as it should have been treated — as a battle of ideas to be waged on an intellectual level. Some felt comfortable enough to go beyond the one-sided broadsides denouncing the foe (which often could be little more than hostile caricature and not real argument) to engage in actual public debate. Unfortunately this sometimes involved a bit of trickery to leave the other side unprepared: on more than one occasion Arians were invited to a religious gathering and found it turned into an unannounced disputation.[112] A debate takes considerably longer to prepare for than an informal meeting and the result of being blindsided into an unexpected one usually results in your case looking considerably weaker than it would have with preparation.

There was also the quite important tool of ostracism. Since Arianism was becoming equivalent to being a barbarian foreigner, contacts with its advocates was shunned. If you had dealings with such a person your own spiritual credentials were questioned. Sometimes priests were excommunicated for simply eating with Arians. If you married one you had disowned your church. Fulgentius of Ruspe was simply developing this line of extremism when he argued that believers must "never enter their churches to pray,"[113] not to listen to a sermon that might target your convictions, but merely to pray. If you are not permitted to have dealings with someone, if all your information must come from one side, if most or all efforts at intellectual competition are shunted aside, then obviously it is much easier to prove the "orthodoxy" of your own beliefs — no matter what they may be.

Finally, there was the control of a hierarchy. The Arians were usually joined together by shared creedal fundamentals, not by organization. What organization they had was looser run and less controlled from "above." Nor did they go in for monasticism, which became a major pillar of orthodox support.[114] In competition with the proudly hierarchical "orthodox" all this placed them at a disadvantage.

On the other hand, it created a potential vulnerability. If the "orthodox" rightly represent the situation, it was common for the population to accept the legitimacy of *whoever* was bishop.[115] This was the potentially fatal downside to a power structure where power and control flows from the top downward: if orthodoxy becomes, effectively, vindicated due to its acceptance by the "true" episcopate and you control that episcopate system then you have *become* the orthodox by default. By being able to hold onto the hierarchy and regain it when lost, the evolving Catholicism was able to avoid this danger—but such was only the ultimate outcome and never the guaranteed one.

Montanus, Maximilla, and Priscilla (c. 150–200)
Montanism and the New Prophetic Movement (Second Half of the Second Century)

The Movement

Although the term "Montanism" was only first used during the fourth century by Cyril of Jerusalem, it has become the overall descriptive term for a movement that contemporary foes called both the "Caraphrygian heresy" and the "Phrygian heresy," after its place of origin in the 150s and 160s.[116] It persevered against stringent opposition for centuries. Two of its most prominent centers of influence were Rome and Carthage, though there were significant differences within the movement between the two places and their surrounding regions.[117] Though it had been successfully repressed and discredited in the Western Empire by the sixth century, the movement evaporated in the Eastern Empire only in the twelfth century.[118]

Its adherents described their system as "the New Prophecy," a term embraced by Tertullian in defending it.[119] The self-description is itself intriguing and subject to different interpretations. Christine Trevett takes the "new" to refer to its advocates claiming to walk in the New Testament rather than Old Testament tradition of prophecy.[120] But (except for the obvious role of Jesus being honored) one is hard pressed to see how one would distinguish between the two forms of prophecy.

Instead, it may represent a repudiation as inadequate of whatever remnants of alleged supernatural revelation still existed. All of Perpetua's visions and at least some of Hermas' are clearly *dream*-visions. In contrast, Montanism manifested apparently conscious "revelations" and not necessarily in "vision" form at all. In comparison, orthodoxy's "dreams" surely paled in comparison.

Furthermore, Eusebius makes the provocative remark that the credibility of the Montanist revelations were increased by "the many other miracles that, through the gift of God, were still wrought in the different churches [which] caused their prophesying to be readily credited by many."[121] He leaves annoyingly vague just what those "miracles" were: healings? "impossible" salvation from martyrdom? simply astounding acts for which there seemed no natural explanation? Whatever they were, they gave credibility to the claims of the movement: if these could be granted as genuine why, they clearly reasoned, was it so extreme to accept the credibility of God miraculously speaking His message through them?

At least in part, Montanism was designed to be a definitive rejection of much (perhaps all) of Gnosticism, but backed up not by textual exegesis but on the basis of the new revelations in which its prophets "confirmed" the traditional understanding on contested matters. These oracles spoke of Jesus as being a complete human being rather than some type of semi- or superhuman of questionable physical corporality. Jesus did not merely seem to die, He *did* die and was physically resurrected. Salvation extended to all Christians and not merely the spiritual/Gnostic elite. The relationship of Jesus to the Father in the Godhead was the "Trinitarian" one, yet another effort to confirm the validity of "orthodoxy."[122]

In spite of such strict traditionalism in opposing Gnostic concepts, Montanism was commonly considered another brand of the same phenomenon.[123] The fact that Montanists were supposedly receiving new revelations made them open to the charge of being spiritual elitists who were somehow "guided," just as the Gnostics, into a deviant form of Christianity. The label also permitted guilt by association: the correlation of the two movements made it quite natural for an individual to take the *worst* or most *extreme* form of Gnosticism he or she was acquainted with and assume *that* was what the Montanists also advocated.

In addition to its anti–Gnostic elements, there were significant points where Montanists took orthodoxy a step further than was common and insisted on a more stringent form of it. They demanded more fasting. They embraced the ascetic inclination by strongly discouraging remarriage after a spouse had died. They permitted a marriage to be ended in order to free a person to greater religious service. The most notable example of the last is Montanus' approval of Maximilla and Priscilla leaving their spouses for a life of prophecy.[124] Stuart G. Hall points to their "tightening discipline over marriage, fasting, veiling, flight in persecution, and, above all, over the treatment of moral and religious lapse."[125] Hence we may see in it a precursor to Donatism in regard to church discipline. An unwise approach, perhaps, but, if anything an effort to be super-correct and undeviatingly loyal to their faith even when it cost members.

The problem Montanism faced in the Christian mainstream was twofold. First of all, mainstream orthodoxy was not yet that inclined toward such super rigor and, secondly, the basis for their demands lay not in interpretation of scripture or reliance on alleged tradition, but upon the authority inherent in receiving new revelation. If they could successfully assert the authority of those revelations in such matters, might they not also challenge fundamental premises of orthodoxy in a similar manner at some later date?

And they certainly *did* make significant changes upon occasion. Montanus appointed apostles and other religious leaders, each of whom was paid a wage for his labor.[126] Since there was a long-established cultural tradition of higher ranking individuals donating time and services in the public interest, accepting the legitimacy of paid spiritual work opened the door for those of lower societal rank to rise to positions of importance, and this rankled the pride of those who did not need such financial assistance.[127]

If that rattling of the rank conscious societal religious order were not enough, they went even further by being far more receptive to the idea of women in open positions of church leadership. Depending upon which ancient source describes their views (and actual practice may well have varied) there were both female deacons and bishops.[128] A male power structure—growing increasingly enticed by the idea of centralized episcopate power—was hardly likely to be enchanted.

This leads to the question of whether Montanism was compatible at all with a hierarchical structure, especially a increasingly centralized one. Tertullian insisted that it did not require the rejection of either scripture or the hierarchical structure of the church,[129] yet it inevitably created tensions that could easily escalate. How *could* a person claiming personal prophetic ability cede to such a bishop or presbyter the right of command when he or she had been "told" by personal revelation of God that they were in error?

In Tertullian's Montanist phase, on one occasion he reinforces his own reasoning by quoting a female prophet's words as establishing the definitive certainty of the issue.[130] Hence if a Montanist dominated church had been possible, there would have had to be a de facto balancing of command authority between hierarchy and ongoing "revelation," one in which bishops could not have demanded the kind of unconditional allegiance that became the norm.

Some have heavily stressed that the early criticisms of the movement conspicuously omit any claim of *doctrinal* deviancy—except, of course, for the question of whether they were engaging in true versus delusionary prophecy. The movement is criticized for allegedly breeding both moral laxity and extreme asceticism. The members are criticized for pride. They are criticized for the ecstatic nature of their revelations. But peculiar doctrinal deviancies are conspicuously omitted.[131] Even the rejection of the claim that the new Jerusalem would appear in Phrygia is far more a question of the timing and location of the appearance (and even its true nature) than that of the coming of the New Jerusalem itself.[132] Although "error" was clearly viewed as involved, the earliest critics seem to have been far more concerned with their excesses of zeal than with the content of their doctrine.

As time went by, it was not unexpected that different sets of followers altered the practices they had inherited. Here we are concerned not with these differences but with generally shared sentiments and the views of the three prominent founders of the movement: Montanus, Maximilla, and Priscilla. Although the movement continued to grow and prosper afterwards, no prophet/ess of their prestige arose to take their place.[133]

Only scattered isolated quotations survive from the three, though there is evidence that at one time considerable collections of their material existed. Hippolytus speaks of how those in one region were "in possession of an infinite number of their books." He speaks of how a "majority of their books are silly," a fascinating implied concession that not all of them were such. Then he insists that "their attempts at reasoning [are] weak, and worthy of no consideration. But it is not necessary for those who possess a sound mind to pay attention" to the arguments which they present—which, of course, made it far easier to refute them if one were not to hear their side of the argument.[134]

Their collective worship took on certain peculiarities of their own due to the reputed prophetic gift being exercised among them. Hippolytus speaks of how "They introduce, however, the novelties of fasts [novelties because deviating from the orthodox mainstream], and feasts, and meals of parched food, and repasts of radishes, alleging that they have been instructed by women" prophets to do so.[135]

Montanus

Montanus, Maximilla, and Priscilla were all described (by their foes, at least) as acting as if they were (demonically?) possessed when giving prophecies, speaking in an odd manner and words, and moving in a crazed style as if overpowered by some external force.[136] A standard rebuttal of their practice was that true prophecy could not be ecstatic and if a legitimate element of such were to be conceded at all, it had to be an extremely *controlled* ecstasy in which the emotions were still subject to mental and bodily restraint.[137]

An early critic described Montanus as drifting into his practices soon after conversion.[138] Even if the time between conversion and adopting a new theology was actually much longer, what religious system had he left behind? If one accepts Jerome's much later accusation that Montanus had been castrated, he might well have been a follower of Cybele. A different later critic spoke of him as having been a follower of Apollo, however.[139]

Montanus put a positive spin on the criticism he and others were receiving. He reasoned that one must receive disparagement from his or her contemporary or face rebuke from God. They should not be embarrassed, but proud of what they were undergoing: "You are exposed to public infamy; so much the better for you! He who is not exposed to so before men, is exposed before God. Do not blush. It is your righteousness which has brought you forth into the midst of it all. Why do you blush when you are accepting glory? Your power is born in the same moment when the gaze of mankind is fixed on you."[140]

Although the number of quotations attributed to him (and the two female prophetesses discussed next) are all limited, the fascinating fact is that there is so much compatible with the evolving orthodoxy of the time. Hence some of his quoted teachings speak of principles even the orthodox would have had no difficulty with. In regard to death he implored, "Do not wish to die in your bed, in failure or in languishing fevers, but rather in martyrdom, in order that he may be glorified who suffered for you."[141]

For those seeking to maximize the power of the institutional church, he was perhaps a bit ahead of orthodoxy when he spoke of how "The church has the power to remit sin; but I will not do so for fear that others will sin."[142] The first part of the statement represented the gradually growing sentiment of the church as having inherent spiritual authority over deciding such matters, while the second half holds up the warning that one may have to suffer the lack of forgiveness so that others will not inadvertently be encouraged to use that forgiveness as an excuse for their own evil.

His claimed oracles presented a picture of the trinity that could be invoked in the direction of traditional thinking as well. In potential favor of Trinitarian orthodoxy was the revelation, "It is I who am the Father and the Son and the Paraclete,"[143] making them three expressions of the same divine being. (The "unitarian" reading obliterating the distinction seems less likely.) In describing the specific nature of Jesus' incarnation the wording stresses that it had always been the same and repudiates Gnostic-style distinctions: "Christ has a single nature, a single energy both before the flesh and with the flesh, in order that he does not become different by doing actions dissimilar and different."[144]

Maximilla

The exact relationship between Montanus and Maximilla and Priscilla has been much discussed. The tradition has been that Montanus originated the movement, but some feminist interpreters have argued that male bias gave birth to this claim and that actually his role centered in being the *defender* of *their* teaching.[145] Certainly most surviving "prophecies" that carry specific names attached came from these or other women and they were certainly as important as he was to the development of the movement.[146] On the other hand, no one questions the major role of women in shaping the movement, so one is reduced to the unanswerable question of the relative *degree* of each individual's contribution.

As to Maximilla, in particular, in order to fully carry out her claimed religious responsibilities she opted for celibacy after leaving her husband behind.[147] She outlived Montanus and Priscilla, dying c. 180.[148]

The sense of frustration about strong hostility from within the mainstream church manifests itself in some of her revelations: "I am pursued as a wolf far from the sheep. I am not a wolf; I am the Word, Spirit and Power."[149] Followers were doubtlessly sympathetic with that evaluation, but not outsiders.

In another of the revelations attributed to her, she speaks of how divine knowledge came to her independent of her own choice and, indeed, in defiance of it; "The Lord sent me as a partisan of this labor, a revealer of this covenant, an interpreter of this promise, forced, whether I will or not, to learn the knowledge of God."[150] She disavowed any truly personal authority; she was but a spokeswoman for Someone great; "Do not listen to me, but listen to Christ."[151]

Even though she was a leader of a prophetic movement, even she confessed that the gift would soon vanish from the human race; "After me there will no longer be any prophetess. It will be the end of all."[152] Her judgment proved erroneous. Judging from the notices of their critics, several other prophetesses and prophets arose at later dates.[153]

This was not the only incorrect prediction she gave. She spoke forcefully of the coming wars that would plague the world. A critic, writing perhaps thirteen years after her passing, pointed out that the world had been free of such catastrophes and happily cited this as evidence of her being a false prophetess.[154]

Priscilla

Priscilla also made the decision to leave her husband in order to be celibate and devote herself fully to her religious responsibilities. As one of her revelations claimed, "continence makes harmony reign."[155] Perhaps reflecting her own attitudes, another revelation speaks of how "They are flesh and they hate the flesh."[156]

Some cynics suspect that the real-world situation was the reverse of what was claimed: rather than divorcing her husband (as did Maximilla) both had been on the receiving end of a divorce by their highly annoyed spouses because of their embracing of the new religious system.[157] Although this is purely conjectural, if they attempted to live their celibacy preferences *within* marriage, one could easily imagine their annoyed husbands washing their hands of them, which would have permitted others to put the onus for the divorce on whichever individual they preferred.

In Priscilla's visions, the true gender of the speaker might be disguised. In an endtime oracle she speaks of how, "Under the appearance of a woman, clothed in a shining robe, Christ came to me and said that this place [in Asia Minor] is sacred and that it is here that Jerusalem will descend from heaven."[158] It didn't and it hasn't and neither fact helped enhance her prophetic reputation.

DONATUS (c. 311–c. 355)
The Donatist Schism over Apostate Christians

The practical (rather than theological issue) which motivated the Donatist schism grew out of whether to obey the imperial edict in the early 300s that Christians hand over their copies of the scriptures to the government and offer sacrifice. Those who regarded the acts as unforgivable were the Donatists and those who took the more forgiving stance ultimately won and became considered the orthodox.

In Rome, Bishop Marcellinus obeyed the edict. After his death in 304 his post remained vacant for at least two years due to the difficulties of imperial repression making it impractical to arrange for a replacement. After Marcellus was selected, he quickly branded Marcellinus as nothing less than an apostate and demanded ultra caution and the passing of an extended period of time for readmitting the lapsed. The demands were so heavy that a large part of the church actively opposed the policy as intolerably excessive and they were more than a little pleased when the emperor ultimately forced him into exile, thereby neutralizing at least temporarily the application of his approach. His post remained vacant for several years because it was impossible to find a consensus replacement who could bridge the gap between the two factions.[159]

A rigid stringency was regarded as "orthodox," however misguided, when the bishop of Rome insisted upon it, but escalated into "heresy" when Donatus in Africa took the hard line even further and refused to back down under pressure from more charitable local and Roman bishops.

When Caecilian was ordained in 311 to the post of bishop in Carthage, a key participant in the ceremony was erroneously alleged to have been among those who surrendered their copies of the scriptures. This invalidated the appointment in the eyes of the stringent faction since the consecrator had effectively repudiated the faith and lost all valid claim to either holding church office or appointing others to it. Decisions had to be made immediately. Waiting for verification of the accusations was not regarded as practical — not to mention that it would give Caecillian time to cement his hold in office if he was in the wrong. Hence the stringent side selected a different individual to the post of "true" bishop and, in turn, it soon passed to Donatus. Caecilian refused to abandon his position and from this collision the Donatist controversy and schism grew.[160]

Church councils held both at Rome (in 313) and in Arles (in 314) backed the Caecilian side. These decisions were inadequate to convince the hard-liners. A commission investigated and ultimately endorsed Caecilian. Furthermore, a church council that examined the evidence that scriptures had been destroyed due to his consecrator surrendering them decided that the event had not happened.

By now it was November 316 and what had originated seemingly as an intra-church squabble in North Africa had taken on a life of its own. It became, from the Donatist view, a squabble between the firm upholders of true Christianity and those who would risk or tolerate compromise of an absolute loyalty to its traditions and accept back — as if any longer worthy of anything more than the most grudging toleration (if that) — those who had compromised their faithfulness during times of persecution and adversity. If the person were a church official it was even worse if he had lapsed. Because they were no longer Christians in good standing — much less priests in good standing — any baptism they performed was inherently null, void, and empty of any redemptive power.

Donatus had a magnetic personality and his strict stand echoed throughout the region. The Donatists became the dominant Christianity, with their own priests, hierarchy, and religious edifices. Even after Donatus himself had died, his successors maintained the popularity of their movement into the 380s.[161] In 393 approximately a quarter of the Donatists embraced what was called the Maximianist theology, thereby cutting the Donatist edge from an overwhelming one to near parity.[162]

When Augustine rose to the post of bishop in 395 he launched a vigorous intellectual assault on the Donatist ideology. This was not out of mere intellectual conviction, but because Hippo was a town in which the Donatists clearly had the majority and the relations between them and the "orthodox" minority were tenuous and reeked of mutual animosity.[163] Invoking the power of sympathizers in the government, laws were enacted that made the Donatists heretical criminals. In 411 Augustine was able to maneuver his foes into a meeting before a government committee in Carthage which, not surprisingly, supported Augustine's faction. More legislation was enacted to repress Donatism. Even then the victory was neither quick nor decisive. Just as violence was utilized against the Donatists, the systematic use of violence against those who had seized their churches or supported the "orthodox" takeover was also quite common in North Africa as well.[164] Significant numbers of Donatists still remained in functional congregations even into the eighth century.[165]

Technically speaking, the Donatists were not heretics; with perhaps minor exceptions where their theology was amenable to a potential Arian interpretation, they were as strictly "orthodox" as anyone. They were, however, "schismatics," since they had organizationally split off from the control of orthodoxy.

To bring them under imperial antiheresy laws, Augustine argued that prolonged schism created a kind of de facto heresy and thereby made those laws applicable to them as well.[166] The Donatists used similar "schismatic" accusation language to describe the purported orthodox.[167] Unfortunately for them, however, the bottom line was that the government was far more amenable to the Augustinian approach than to that of the hardliners. As S.L. Greenslade rightly sums it up, "Donatism was defeated less by argument than by coercion."[168]

JOVINIANUS (flourished 390s)
Opponent of Asceticism[169]

Jovinian boldly repudiated the ever growing popularity of asceticism, which had grown from being *an* option to manifest advanced spirituality to being *the* manifestation of superior faith for a large fraction of the church. The fact that many were still attracted to a form of spirituality that put normal marital life on a par with celibacy thoroughly angered Jerome. In refuting Jovinian, he quotes four key assertions for particular censure[170]:

> He says that "virgins, widows, and married women, who have been once passed through the layer of Christ, if they are on a par in other respects, are of equal merit."
>
> He endeavors to show that "they who with full assurance of faith have been born again in baptism, cannot be overthrown by the devil."
>
> His third point is "that there is no difference between abstinence from food, and its reception with thanksgiving."
>
> The fourth and last is "that there is one reward in the kingdom of heaven for all who have kept their baptismal vow."

Although there is more than a little interest to students of the evolution of religious systems in Jovinian's second point—which, in Jerome's presentation, is clearly Calvinism's impossibility of apostasy, more popularly known as "once saved always saved"—it was the teaching on virginity that raised the anger of Jerome the most.

According to Jovinian, virginity was fine, but not as an ego trip of spiritual self-glorification. As he had cautioned those women embracing perpetual virginity, "Be not proud, you are members of the same church as the married."[171] The same logic, of course, applied to those who became nuns or monks as well since it involved a similarly sexually abstinent lifestyle. Hence marriage was the moral equivalent of celibacy to Jovinian—neither absolutely better than the other[172]—and that was an intolerable doctrine for Jerome. Jerome devotes his entire first book on Jovinian's teaching to this matter and deals with all the other repudiated errors in the second epistle, which starkly reveals the relative importance of the issues to him.

To Jerome the matter was clearly not just an abstract issue of right and wrong, but the passionate need to exalt the particular path to holiness through virginity and celibacy that he himself had embraced. In short, it was profoundly personal. Any challenge was viewed as little less than undermining his entire rationale for spiritual existence.

A useful contrast can be found in comparing 1 Corinthians 7, the theoretical basis for Jerome's view, with his rhetoric: Paul goes out of his way to assert the honorableness of marriage while expressing his profound personal preference for celibacy. In Jerome, however, it is hard to see any respectability granted marriage except for the rhetorical minimum to keep himself from being accused of heresy.

At times he seems so determined to throw every usable objection imaginable against his opponent that separate arguments move in contradictory directions to each other.[173] Indeed, so intense and vigorously anti-marriage is the undercurrent in his writing that Augustine is usually interpreted as having Jerome in mind when he spoke of how celibacy advocates were accused of promoting their abstinence by demeaning marriage.[174] Although

Augustine wrote to Jerome in 415 praising the anti–Jovinian efforts, he conspicuously singles out certain *other* issues for praise rather than the treatment of marriage.[175]

Jovinian insisted that a sexual relationship between Adam and Eve was part of their married life in Eden.[176] This argument clearly was regarded as a powerful one against perpetual virginity — it invoked, if you will, the "Edenic pattern" from the time of the creation of man and woman and marriage. If it were part of the "perfect" and "idealic" life in the Garden of Eden, who should dare demean it in his own world?

How could the ascetic lobby react to the challenge? Ambrose's earlier writings promoting the superiority of virginity had never introduced the subject of Eve. Yet when he turned again to the theme in a sermon entitled, "On the consecration of a virgin and the perpetual virginity of Mary" at some point prior to Jovinian's formal censure by the bishop of Rome in 392, he suddenly inserts the claim that while in Eden she had remained a virgin.[177] Jerome dealt with the matter differently. He argued that the marriage occurred *after* the fall into sin and expulsion from Eden.[178] Yes, there was sex, but only after their fall into sin rather than before.

Although some regard Jovinian as a former monk,[179] the more common judgment is that he remained one while attempting to broaden the borders of permissible monastic behavior.[180] To most, the idea of a monk was of one whose attire, dietary habits, and general behavior was visibly different from that of the typical believer. To allow monks who — except for a more intense spiritual interest and time invested in it — become basically indistinguishable from everyone else was a challenge to the very definition of the ascetic pursuit as envisioned by its zealous advocates.

Jerome denounced Jovinian as the "Epicurus of the Christians."[181] This could be taken as a slur at the man's character, i.e., that he was a person given to abundant excess, and it seems clearly intended as such.[182] Of course, Jerome (not permitting consistency of argument to get in the way of a good insult) also describes Epicurus as advocating vegetarianism and warning that those who are wise seldom marry![183]

Jovinian was formally condemned and excommunicated both in Rome (389) and in Milan (390). Ultimately he faced a beating and was forced into exile for his views.

It has been reasonably speculated that it was Pammachius, a Roman senator, who represented the major force pushing for Jovinian's condemnation in Rome.[184] (Jerome had first grown close to him through his friendship with Pammachius' mother-in-law, Paula.) Having gained from Jerome the desired vehement denunciation in 392 to use as a literary weapon to destroy the credibility of Jovinian's arguments, he was so horrified at the rhetoric being interpreted as an insult to the character of every married man that he did everything he could to withdraw the material from circulation. There was the severest danger that a backfire would be lit that would rehabilitate the "heretic's" credibility and destroy Pammachius' and Jerome's own.[185]

When Jerome found himself being called upon to circulate an apology for the rhetorical and doctrinal excess, he replied that the request was really one in which "Manichaeus stabs me in the back."[186] He refused to back down. It was hardly reassuring to those made uneasy by his language to find him writing of a critic, "He must hear at least the echo of my cry 'I do not condemn marriage.' Indeed — and this I say to make my meaning quite clear to him — I should like every one to take a wife who, because he gets frightened at night, cannot manage to sleep alone."[187] Such could hardly have convinced his critics that he either appreciated or honored marriage!

BONOSUS (flourished 390s)
Opponent of the Doctrine of Mary's Perpetual Virginity

Bonosus was not simply a minor dissident, he had actually risen to the post of bishop and served as such in the city of Naissus in Sardicia. He denied the need to uphold the doctrine that Mary remained a virgin throughout her life, a stance that permitted the "brothers" of Jesus referred to in the canonical gospels to be literally such rather than a more distant relationship. Bonosus himself took this interpretive step and insisted that these "brethren" were literally children borne by Mary and Joseph from their own sexual, marital relationship.[188]

Others who held this view included Jovinian (who could be dismissed as a heretic) and Tertullian (who was harder to dismiss out of hand). Clement of Alexandria and Epiphanius held that they were half brothers, the children of Joseph by a first marriage. Jerome and Augustine held for an even more distant relationship, that they were mere cousins, children of Mary's sister (which assumes she had a sister).[189]

Bonosus embraced several other doctrinal stances that made him stand out from his contemporaries as well. In particular, his followers believed that the Word of the gospel of John (chapter 1) *became* divine due to "adoption" as God's Son rather than by virtue of being inherently and perpetually such.[190] According to Gregory I of Rome, baptism among them was not in the tri-fold names of Father, Son, and Holy Ghost/Spirit,[191] though some expect this was a later doctrinal evolution within the movement.[192]

A council was held in 389 at Capae to condemn him, but it concluded without doing so. The council specifically passed the task to review and censure to the bishops in his own region. In 390 a synod at Thessalonica condemned him but confirmed the validity of the men he had ordained, quite possibly a move to splinter his supporters off from him, implicitly recognizing their spiritual standing while condemning his. In 390 a synod was also held at Milan and came out strongly against him.[193]

Bishop Siricus of Rome (died 399) was the first individual to make the regular use of "decretals" (doctrinal epistles) to take the lead in shaping and defining the faith of the church. In these he both laid out what doctrinal stances he expected the bishops to adhere to and vigorously defended his authority to make such demands on the grounds that he was Peter's successor and had the authority to make final definitive judgments on such issues. In doing so he made one of the major leaps forward in Roman claims to organizational supremacy and, ultimately, authority over the church universal. Among his various decretal targets were both Jovinian and Bonosus for denying that Mary was a perpetual virgin.[194]

Bonosus remained a theological "bogeyman" long afterwards. Colombanus' *Penitentials* of Ireland (died A.D. 615) incorporated the presumably much earlier ban on communication with Bonosus' heretical followers as a precedent to be imitated in regard to such individuals of his own day, which presupposes that his supporters, even if not a formal movement, still existed: "If any layman in ignorance has communicated with the followers of Bonosus or other heretics, let him rank among the catechumens, that is, separated from other Christians for forty days, and for two other forty-day periods in the lowest rank of Christians, that is among the penitents....." If he had entered into discussion with these men after being instructed not to, then "let him do penance for a full year" more and then for two years more abstain from "wine and meat" and only then receive "the imposition of hands by a Catholic bishop [to] let him be restored to the altar."[195] Then, as today, it is far easier to assure doctrinal or ideological "purity" if one is forbidden all contact with the sources of argument that might convince one that the error is really one's own.

The concept of Mary's perpetual virginity was not the only doctrine concerning her that bloomed in the latter fourth century. To give but one other — one that would not evolve to its full development till centuries later — the manner of her demise brought forth scattered opinions.

Ambrose wrote against theories that she perished a martyr. His own suspicion was that "she may have remained alive, for God is not incapable of doing whatever he wills."[196] The "remained alive" reference is so ambiguous that it could refer to her bodily assumption (a view not documented explicitly until the following century)[197] or to her remaining on earth while never dying (a theory that has been applied to the apostle John by Mormons in the modern era).

The bitter controversialist Epiphanius refers to theories that Mary died a natural death (apparently the dominant view). Yet, ever so desirous to throw the accusation of heresy about with the abandon with which others offer casual opinions, even he could not summon up the will to be contentious: "No one knows her end."[198] It was an open and unresolved question.

If a firestorm of controversy could not yet be raised about the manner of her passing, the growing antisexual skepticism of asceticism had made it common to claim that, unlike other married women, she never had sexual relationships with her husband at all, even after the birth of Jesus. Indeed, that (in spite of the act of birthing a child) she had even remained a physically "intact" virgin.

Chapter 7

Alternative Routes to Holiness

ANTONY (c. 250–c. 350)
Founder of Christian Monasticism

The Background and Purposes of Monasticism:
Holiness through Separate Communities

Although monasticism existed before the Roman persecutions came to an end, prior to that event the greater proportion of individual believers saw their ideal end as one of dying for their faith. With that option generally eliminated by legalization of their religion, the monastic model of asceticism became viewed as the greatest embodiment of the full and complete spiritual life.[1] Although traditionally viewed as arising in the fourth century in Egypt, monasticism's earlier roots are actually Syrian.[2] So powerful was the idealization of asceticism in that region in the fourth century that some appear to have demanded a commitment to it prior to baptism: to be baptized one had to pledge that afterwards the sexual relationship within marriage was to cease entirely.[3]

The peculiar geographic conditions of Egypt, however, especially encouraged monasticism's development. Life was preserved by the power of the Nile River. In most segments of its length, a good walk took one to the edge of the desert itself and the maximum distance at which village life could still prosper. Hence it was peculiarly easy for those ascetically inclined to erect communities either adjoining those borderline villages or slightly further out into the desert itself. This way they had contact with the "solitude" of the barren wilderness but, if personal or institutional customs encouraged it, also ready contact with at least the fringes of civilization.

This worked in their behalf as well; even isolationist groups need food. By typically locating themselves on or near this fringe line between the empty wild and civilization, they gained an accessible market for any products they created and places where they could engage in occasional work to provide an individual or group income.[4]

Although developed for the purpose of the spiritual growth of its residents and as their refuge from the world, monasteries also came to serve other purposes as well. Some were more utilitarian than spiritual. For example, for travelers they became a place where they could rest on their journeys and pilgrimages free from the prostitution and corruption that remained easily available in the bulk of inns. Indeed, if an influential figure lived at a specific monastic site, then that provided further incentive to utilize its particular facilities. An excellent example of this can be found in Jerome's monastery in Palestine: virtually every major figure in Christianity in the late 300s seems to have passed through it.[5]

If monasteries existed to be (more or less) "free from the world," they simultaneously had a wider impact upon the church "in the world." Among these influences, it notably served as the seedbed for the development of psalmody as a pivotal element in contemporary worship. In a letter to Gregory of Nazianzus, Basil the Great spoke fervently of a recent stay in a monastery: "What is more blessed than to imitate the chorus of angels here on earth; to arise for prayer at the very break of day and honor the Creator with hymns and songs?"[6]

During the post-legalization of Christianity, the custom arose of having twice daily services in which selected examples of the Psalms (found in the biblical book of that name) were incorporated into the general worship. The universally favorable experience of men like Basil would have encouraged existing inclinations in that direction. Indeed, as their talents became available due to a location in an urban (rather than ultra-rural or isolated) setting, the monks and nuns themselves were often brought into the services as a kind of chorus to perform singing or chanting for the spiritual edification of those in attendance.[7]

As with modern choral practice in which a practiced and talented choir often becomes more "entertainment" than strictly "worship" to those in the audience, the same problem existed in these years as well. Augustine felt compelled to urge his readers to concentrate on the message being conveyed rather than the talent and quality of the singers. Yet even that concerned theologian conceded that the quality and magnificence of their voices had powerfully moved him.[8]

In spite of their contributions to the wider spiritual development of contemporary Christianity, monasteries and hermits represented a potentially subversive element in a growingly hierarchical church. Because such communities were begun independently of formal church control and, initially, on the decision of one or a very few individuals, it was unusually resistant to such supervision.[9] Likewise, the special bond of such movements made their prime loyalty to each other rather than to a "superior" external church leader outside their number.

The more isolated the more they were removed from the hierarchical "levers" that could be utilized to gain control. In particular, isolation would kept them from receiving communion from the clergy[10] and the right to deny or admit one to that service was becoming one of the major tools for compelling submission by dissenters.

If "heresy" became deeply engrained among them or if they supported a different faction within the church, the bishop could face challenge from a pillar of local spirituality. Hence, bishops generally regarded any monasteries that existed within the boundaries of their jurisdiction as automatically being under their authority and acted to assure that their practices and doctrines were in accordance with those the bishop regarded as orthodox.[11] According to the prestige of the local monastic leadership, they might decide to proceed gingerly, but tacitly and implicitly they created a tradition of the right to intervene on behalf of the institutional church.[12] The wisest bishops went out of their way to cultivate the monastic leaders not only to co-opt potential opposition but also because they represented a considerable reservoir of talent that it was unwise to ignore.

Antony: Youth and Monastic Efforts

Antony was the man who brought monastic life to its first widespread public attention. In spite of his Greek name, he sprung from the ranks of the Coptic farm community — in this case that of a prosperous family. Indeed, the bulk of his followers — and of monks in general in Egypt — came from a similar cultural-ethnic background. In marked contrast, however, either Jewish-Christian or Greek individuals dominated the post of bishop in the urban centers of Egypt.[13] Although monks from this lower class could speak Greek, it was for them their second tongue rather than the one they were raised in and where they felt most comfortable thinking and writing.[14] This would have reinforced the tendency to view the organized hierarchy and their particular monastic movement as parallel and somewhat "opposite" institutions that might not necessarily have the same overarching agenda shared in common.

Antony became an orphan at age 18. In an effort to imitate the apostolic "ideal" of leaving behind families and possessions to follow Christ, he then arranged for his younger sister to be cared for and put himself under the tutelage of an established ascetic. The period of transition from a "worldly" life to a "spiritual" one was difficult, and he tried himself even more by seeking periods of isolation in tombs in the desert.

To the modern eye it may well sound like he was seeking redemption through the cultivation of self-imposed spiritual and psychological torment. The location — a barren and depressing environment such as tombs — was one that could easily feed his worst inner nightmares rather than remove them — which it did. We see this grim cause and effect relationship peaking out from behind the pious rhetoric of Athanasius' myth-establishing *Life of Antony*. In the interest of brevity, we confine ourselves to this one narrative from Antony's early years.[15]

> But the devil, who hates and envies what is good, could not endure to see such a resolution in a youth, but endeavored to carry out against him what he had been wont to effect against others. First of all he tried to lead him away from the discipline, whispering to him the remembrance of his wealth, care for his sister, claims of kindred, love of money, love of glory, the various pleasures of the table and the other relaxations of life, and at last the difficulty of virtue and the labor of it; he suggested also the infirmity of the body and the length of the time. In a word, he raised in his mind a great dust of debate, wishing to debar him from his settled purpose.
>
> But when the enemy saw himself to be too weak for Antony's determination, and that he rather was conquered by the other's firmness, overthrown by his great faith and falling through his constant prayers, then at length putting his trust in the weapons which are "in the navel of his belly" and boasting in them — for they are his first snare for the young — he

attacked the young man, disturbing him by night and harassing him by day, so that even the onlookers saw the struggle which was going on between them. The one would suggest foul thoughts and the other counter them with prayers: the one fire him with lust, the other, as one who seemed to blush, fortify his body with faith, prayers, and fasting.

And the devil ... one night even took upon him the shape of a woman and imitated all her acts simply to beguile Antony. But he, his mind filled with Christ and the nobility inspired by Him, and considering the spirituality of the soul, quenched the coal of the other's deceit. Again the enemy suggested the ease of pleasure. But he, like a man filled with rage and grief, turned his thoughts to the threatened fire and the gnawing worm, and, setting these in array against his adversary, passed through the temptation unscathed.

Antony's attire was goatskin and he literally never took a bath. He engaged in extended periods of prayer, especially at night. He committed to memory many segments of scripture. To gain money both for his own minimal necessities and to help the destitute he made rope to sell. The ascetic life practiced and encouraged by him involved periods of extended fasting and, normally, only one meal a day, which centered on bread and vegetables. Wine was shunned (probably as a luxury, "worldly," and in imitation of the Nazarite vow of the Old Testament).

He spent two decades alone in a long-neglected fortress in the desert. Although there were those who brought him food (reportedly every six months), he shunned even seeing them and spoke to them through a closed door. After the initial two decades of ultra-isolation, he did begin to relent a bit. He began to visit and counsel monks who had settled nearby and to act similarly toward others in various towns and communities. Of course he made this change only after his admirers "encouraged" him by busting down the door to his lodgings! Apparently he gave no indication of anger at their intervention,[16] which argues that either he was inclined to suspect that it was time to make such a change or that he regarded the intervention, if you will, as the "hand of God" moving him to do what he should.

To return to the isolationist roots of his asceticism, he eventually discovered a well-watered site that was far deeper in the desert and which he made his permanent residence. He called this the "Inner Mountain" and the fortress location at Pispir his "Outer Mountain." As the community founded there grew he would take sporadic trips to the town of Pispir to teach and provide advice. He clearly loved this life of being a desert monk rather than an urban (or even rural) one, visiting the metropolis of Alexandria, it appears, only twice. Only a few visited him at his "Inner Mountain" due to the great distance involved, and this test of their faith must have made it easier for him to decide whether receiving them was desirable.[17]

The psychological toll his years of self-denial inflicted did nothing to fatally undermine his physical stamina. In spite of them, he lived to over a hundred and his disciples then buried him at a never identified site.

His Thought and Heritage

Two key concepts dominated Antony's approach to the spiritual life. One was a daily rededication to the monastic ideals, presumably out of an astute recognition that the physical limitations of the regimen could easily lead one to drift back into the desire for a less rigorous spiritual routine. Accompanying this rededication was a careful self-examination of his own thoughts, actions, and motives: the cultivation of internal self-honesty and candor permitted one to catch any tendency to wander from the goal before it took dangerous root and undermined the devotee's dedication to the cause. The recommitment aspect of his teaching stands out in his surviving letters and it is accompanied by the kind of "Gnostic" style reasoning and terminology that could easily be taken in a very unorthodox direction. Probably it is for this reason that Athanasius speaks of "paying heed to the self" rather than utilizing the actual language preferred by Antony himself.[18]

Even in death Antony continued to have an impact. When Athanasius of Alexandria took up his pen to write the *Life of Antony* he did so less than a year after his hero's passing. In it he magnifies Antony by minimizing his education while inflating his moral statue by attributing to him various miracles.[19] To the extent to which Antony's battles with demons had any objective root, the cynical modern nonascetic would be tempted to see them as visions produced by psychological maladjustment and the inability to come to terms with his inner drives and desires. To the monastics, isolation and stringent diets seemed methods to overcome sexual temptation;[20] to us the separation and inability to admit an honorable way to fulfill fundamental underlying desires seem far more likely to have magnified their intensity rather than removed their appeal.

In his volume Athanasius consciously reshaped the historical Antony to provide a Christian equivalent of contemporary works about respected "philosopher-heroes." In doing so, he created what quickly became the ancient and medieval standard format in which to discuss the lives of such individuals.[21] Yet Athanasius had a more self-serving agenda as well: he wished to invoke asceticism on behalf of Nicene orthodoxy and against the Arian dissidents. Since Antony wrote in one of his letters concerning how Arius had created "an un-healable wound" in the church, his opposition is clearly a well-founded fact,[22] though that does not necessarily make the opposition as central to Antony's life as it was to that of Athanasius.

In addition to the provisos that must be placed on specific aspects of Athanasius' treatment, the question of his overall reliability has been much discussed. A good part of the problem lies in the fact that any author will emphasize certain matters and deemphasize others, while a different author might make a significantly different choice as to what items fell in each category. For example, as a non-monastic, it is not that surprising that Athanasius emphasized Antony's relationship with outsiders.

Yet he omits matters that were regarded as important by others. Approximately seventy years later Palladius wrote his *Lausiac History,* a shorter account of Antony's life. In spite of coming from almost three-quarters a century later, the monk-author had access to additional sources of information and he emphasizes the man's sometimes stern relationship with subordinates, while this goes unmentioned by Athanasius.[23] Of course, in real life a leader is going to have to have such an element of steel in his character (as well as affability) if he is going to get his job done and not have his time wasted away by well-meaning subordinates and friends. Hence both very different emphases ring true.

Oddly enough, only a few of Antony's letters have survived, though it is clear that he wrote quite a few. These contain no biographical data and, as already noted, some of the expressions used are amenable to a nonorthodox interpretation. Both factors, and especially the second, may explain the willingness to let such valuable firsthand evidence fall into disuse.[24]

PACHOMIUS (c. 275–346)
Holiness through Cenobitic Monastic Life

Forced into the army to meet manpower needs in spite of his well-to-do family background, this traumatic event ultimately transformed Pachomius' life by bringing him into his first contact with Christians. He and other recruits were put up temporarily in a prison in Thebes and those in charge had made no great effort to provide food for them. Some local Christians arrived with supplies which the recruits gratefully received. Intrigued by their generosity, he inquired who they were and their charitable behavior so impressed him that he vowed to become a Christian at the first opportunity. This he defined to himself as when he left the military, which happened not many months later when the army was disbanded. He made his way back to the town where he met the Christians and began to study and indoctrinate himself in their faith, receiving baptism as the result.

Practices of His Movement

Placing himself under the tutelage of a veteran ascetic by the name of Palamon, he learned from him the basic standards that needed to be met in such a lifestyle. Palamon was candid as to how strenuous the young man's life would be: "I eat nothing but bread and salt," he warned him. Furthermore, "I never touch wine and I watch [meditation and prayer] half the night."[25] Pachomius responded that he felt confident that Christ would give him the strength and stamina to duplicate this regimen.[26]

After serving under Palamon's tutelage for seven years, he received a vision while in the abandoned village of Tabennisis in which a voice ordered him to construct a residence there. This would grow into a community of monks, the vision assured him.[27] This was a departure from the then accepted tradition of more or less separate existence in separate residences, with only the loosest of ties among the monks. Here there would be a true *community* of men with similar goals and aspirations, working in close proximity and interacting on a daily basis. By doing this, Pachomius became the individual most associated with the creation of the "cenobitic" (communal) monastery system.[28]

The selected location changed existing Egyptian monastic behavior in other ways as well. In the past, the more isolated the better for monastic groups. In this case the site was in a well-developed agrarian area near the Nile River. The community lived in groups of up to forty in separate buildings, sometimes in individual cells and sometimes sharing them. It had separate buildings for the sick, for visitors, and for collective worship, all enclosed within the boundaries of a wall to literally mark the line between their group and the surrounding world.[29] (This wall also provided protection against becoming the victims of slave dealing raiders who periodically regarded vulnerable monks as fodder for their trade.)[30]

Pachomius' initial efforts to create such a community failed badly. Over time he crystallized his thinking and convinced an increasing number of adherents to adopt his guidelines. These included a sharing of all the individuals' possessions for the common good as well as recognizing the ultimate authority of the "superior" of the group.[31]

None of the monasteries were named after their founder, Pachomius. Instead they adopted the name of the place where they were located. Daily scripture reading by the lector at communal services of the membership represented a key element of each location's routine. During his lifetime Pachomius took this responsibility upon himself.[32] This would be followed by a lesson by him on the lessons they could learn from the text.[33]

At least once a week a local priest would visit to provide the Eucharist. It was, however, de facto systematic policy to exclude priests from actual membership. It was feared that to do otherwise would open the door to the danger of them attempting to exercise authority over the monk community due to their priestly credentials.[34]

Before being permitted preliminary admission into the monastery, an individual had to recite from memory two of the apostle Paul's New Testament letters, though there was the option to choose from the shorter ones. From the Old Testament, an individual had to be able to repeat at least twenty of the Psalms.[35] Afterwards followed a trial period to assure that one would find the monastic life and its special requirements compatible with one's temperament and aspirations on an ongoing basis. Enthusiasm was one thing; the ability to *sustain* that commitment was what needed to be tested. If one passed this test as well, an appropriate ceremony was performed and he was given his monastic robes.[36]

The individual "dormitories" (to use a modern expression) received individuals, wherever possible, based upon the incomer's prior trade. By putting together butchers and scribes in separate places, for example, the groups could then pool their shared talents in order to best ply their trade. This way the monastery's various needs could be met internally[37] and income generated to meet their collective maintenance expenses.[38] (This did not, of course, preclude the monks being called upon, when needed, for some additional task, such as field work.)[39] A supervising monk led each dormitory to assure that everything got done and that all the residents were fulfilling their spiritual and temporal responsibilities. He, in turn, answered to the chief monk of the monastery.[40]

They viewed their primary relationship with the outside world as one of being servants — helping the destitute and sick, encouraging the downcast, and seeing for the well-being of orphans.[41] Charitableness and spiritual self-development were to march hand in hand.

Relationship of Pachomius to Notables of His Day

On a visit to Pachomius' monastery, Athanasius was urged by an accompanying fellow bishop to promptly ordain Pachomius to the priesthood. Pachomius literally vanished into the surrounding crowd to avoid the honor. Monks of this period were typically uneasy about accepting any formal church office and, when convinced or effectively compelled to assume it, avoided the exercise of any of the rights (such as offering communion) that came with it. To them, there seemed something inherently threatening to salvation in assuming such a post of authority over others while claiming to be simple monks.[42]

Whether Antony felt that way at the beginning of their relationship or not — human nature would have encouraged him to have felt at least a bit uneasy at the attention granted his efforts — there can be no question that he came to deeply admire him. When word reached him of Pachomius' death, he responded, "It was a good ministry he undertook in bringing together so many brothers."[43] When one of those who brought word insisted that it was Antony who deserved the overwhelming credit for the monastic movement, Antony firmly demurred: Pachomius deserved every bit of recognition he was giving him.[44] Clearly he had come to recognize Pachomius as a compatriot in a shared cause rather than in any sense a rival.

Pachomius had an ever growing literary reputation after his death; unfortunately, much of it was not by him: If Jerome is any guide, there were far fewer works circulating in his day under the names of Pachomius, Theodore, and Horsiesios (see below on these latter leaders) than there were at a later date.[45] The genuine materials that survived tend to be "minimalist": direct, to the point, unadorned with eloquence or lengthy prose.[46] In short, just as these men scorned the world, they seem to have applied the same logic to their personal writings and wished to maintain it in a simple form "uncontaminated" by the flourishes that marked external religious and secular literature.

The Movement after His Death

No one was expecting Pachomius' demise when he perished during a plague in 346. At this time there were eleven monasteries (with about 3,000 individuals) under his rule. Nine were for males and two for women.[47] The influence of the movement was significantly larger than its direct membership since certain monasteries are known to have adopted the rules embraced by Pachomius even though they were not organizationally tied to him.[48]

By most standards Theodore should have been the ideal replacement for Pachomius. However, a backlash had occurred against him two years earlier. At that time Pachomius seemed at death's door and the subordinate officials had selected Theodore as their next leader. Unexpectedly recovering, Pachomius was angered at what had happened and stripped him of all his power. Although he relented somewhat as time passed, he was never reconciled to being succeeded by the man.

While dying in 346 he appointed as his successor Petronios, a well-to-do convert. Having passed over many individuals with greater "seniority" of service in the movement, this likely rankled a goodly number. The problem soon worked itself out in a tragic manner as Petronios perished in the same plague that had killed his predecessor.[49]

Before dying he, in turn, selected Horsiesios as his replacement. Coming from a different monastery than the one that Pachomius had directly led, he was an outsider to the locals. Faced with the open rejection of at least one of the affiliated monasteries and facing massive resistance to his authority everywhere, after about a year he surrendered authority to Theodore, the original preferred choice for the succession. Due to this and his earlier ties to Pachomius, he was able to quell the unrest and reunify the movement.[50]

Under Pachomius there had been an arms length type of relationship with the Bishop. This was probably not caused by disagreement with his theology or his policies but by the conviction that the monastic movement was better served developing its spirituality as independently as possible of the ecclesiastical struggles and disputes that preoccupied the hierarchy.[51] In contrast, under Theodore there was a clear-cut alignment with Athanasius' pro–Nicene faction in Alexandria that further enhanced the movement's reputation in the eyes of Athanasius himself.[52] For the first time, Athanasius began to be able to openly and directly exercise at least a limited degree of authority over the monastic community, an authority that later was expanded further.[53]

If one accepts the Nag Hammadi codices, with their many Gnostic works, as springing out of the days of Pachomius and his successors — and it remains a much debated issue with the number of scholars embracing a monastic origin growing — then the speculative issues they discuss enjoyed a quite acceptable place among them, even if the works were not regarded as definitively authoritative. It is as if the movement as a whole still found the materials thought provoking and intriguing even as it increasingly took a pro-"orthodoxy" stance.[54]

After Theodore's death, oddly enough, Horsiesios returned to leadership in 368 and retained the position till his own death twelve years later. The movement struggled on until Justinian I ruled as emperor (A.D. 527–565), at which point it finally disintegrated. Details of these final decades are few and far between.[55]

Associated Female Institutions

Mary,[56] the sister of Pachomius, formed her own *Koinonia* (as the groups were known to Pachomius and his adherents) that provided a similar spiritual outlet for women. It was located on the opposite side of the river from that of Pachomius. The guidelines for behavior were those her brother had prepared for his own group as it evolved. These rules covered all aspects of life, from the spiritual exercises to be utilized to the practical governing of the group so it could remain functional and effective.[57]

The group was initially placed under the control of a selected male monk who carefully instructed them in the rules they were expected to follow. Judging Mary to be adequately prepared to take charge of the women's monastery, authority was passed into her hands. When a second women's group was established, it also was initially placed under the authority of a male. When a respected older woman was later recognized as capable of taking over, the reins of authority were transferred into her hands as well.[58]

When female units were established, they were always near the male one. Though the two women's groups had a degree of autonomy and their own female head, both were ultimately supervised by a single abbot who was in charge of the entire movement.[59]

After coming under their own female head, each women's group perpetuated rigid gender segregation from their male counterparts. As the ancient Palladius noted in his *Lausiac History,* "So when a virgin dies, the other virgins, having prepared her body for burial, act as bearers and lay it on the riverbank. But the brethren, having crossed in a ferry boat, with palm leaves and olive branches, take the body across, singing psalms the while, and bury it in their own cemetery. But apart from the priest and the deacon no man goes across to the women's monastery, and they only on Sunday."[60]

MARCELLINA (died c. 398)
Holiness through Perpetual Virginity

Marcellina is a useful example of the popular fourth century custom of women taking vows of perpetual virginity, both independent of entering nunneries and as an element of entering such. In the late twentieth century a significant element of women took the principle that "my body is my own" as a justification for sexual relationships with whomever they pleased and repeated abortions. In this earlier context, women were, in effect, asserting much the same claim but in the *opposite* direction, vowing neither to marry nor to have sexual relations with *any* other person. At the minimum, this "liberated" them from the need to submit to male authority in the sense that they would need to if married and with children.[61]

The inhibitions of their culture — especially in the East — further limited their functioning in society. Chrysostom admitted amazement at how Rebecca in the Old Testament could move about outside her home — even going to the well for water unescorted — without anyone reading into the account a criticism of her moral rectitude. In his own time, he admitted, such actions would never be taken as innocent.[62] Even in the book of Acts and the Pauline epistles, women are pictured as going about everyday life with a freedom of action totally unacceptable in his own time, he admitted. His explanation was that his age had become far more debased and the behavior of women in particular.[63] (Doubtless this would have come as quite a surprise to those of the first century who had been all too aware of the often freewheeling sexual libertinism of that earlier age!)

Most of the young women who opted for an independent life through individual or collective celibacy appear to have been daughters in households where the father had died. This death permitted effective familial power to be exercised by the mother,[64] who might well be far more tolerant of such a choice than the father. Ambrose once wrote of the inclination of husbands to oppose such an action. He described a young woman who rushed forward during church services and pled for the right. An indignant relative hollered out, "Do you think if your father was alive, he would have allowed you to remain unmarried?" She defiantly responded, "Maybe he died so that no one should stand in my way."[65]

From a societal standpoint, however, the issue had a direct impact upon the empire's very ability to survive. By the nature of the situation — limited data caused by all the vagaries of preservation and destruction — only a tentative picture can be projected, yet that is an alarming one. If we begin with a reasonably "low" estimate of life-expectancy in the fourth century, then one begins with an average lifespan of just twenty-five years, with a mere one-quarter of the male population surviving to fifty. Working against that backdrop a woman — every woman — would need to have five children in order to overcome infant mortality and early death.⁶⁶ Hence every consecrated virgin meant a blow to the maintenance of the empire's population and, on a more personal basis, to a *family's* ongoing survival. Hence it is no wonder that many were antagonistic to the phenomena of female asceticism and celibacy! However moderately "upward" one adjusts the lifespan figures, one only dilutes the societal dilemma rather than eliminating it.

The bulk of individuals who chose the permanent virginity option are unknown by name and, if that is available, usually by name alone. In contrast, more data is available on Marcellina because she was the sister of the influential churchman Ambrose of Milan (see chapter on his life).

Due to their mutual family connection she came from a prestigious family of the time. Her father had served in Gaul as praetorian prefect and at his death the surviving family members moved to Rome.

While still a youth, Ambrose's sister appeared before Bishop Liberius at the Basilica of St. Peter in Rome. There she formally underwent a public ritual to "wear the veil" and become a recognized consecrated virgin.⁶⁷ This is the first recorded case of public vows being made to ratify a woman's private decision on the matter.⁶⁸

The sermon Liberius preached in her honor that day was heavily Nicene-orientated, with the language and rhetoric of those stringently advocating that creedal approach. This made her action one of "orthodoxy" and implicitly challenged that of any who might question the wisdom or propriety of what she had done. His going out of the way to endorse her actions publicly may also argue that there was a close social and theological bond already in existence between the family and the bishop.⁶⁹ Of course the desire to encourage such actions by other socially prominent individuals probably played no small role as well.⁷⁰

In the directly relevant context of her future, Liberius heavily stressed Marcellina's obligation to be faithful to her duties. He cited as example the story of a page attending a polytheist rite in Alexandria who was so dedicated that even the drippings of hot wax did not cause him to move. It scarred his hands to the bone, but he did not depart from his duty. Neither should she.⁷¹

This was not a step she took without very careful consideration. Pivotal in her decision was the example, from the anti–Christian program of Diocletian, of how Sotheris had undergone death while dedicated to God as a continual virgin.⁷² Marcellina might not die for her faith like Sotheris, but she could make her goal to live with that same lifestyle and dedication. Her motivation was further enhanced by the fact that Sotheris was her ancestor.⁷³

A three party triangle of women lived in the house, devoted to acts of piety and good works. This group consisted of one outsider, Marcellina herself, and her mother After her mother's death, Marcellina moved into the nunnery that Marcella had formed — her residence, converted to this purpose — and her involvement added additional luster to its reputation. Marcella had been the first prominent woman matron of Rome to commit herself to a monastic existence and her action had marked the critical step in transforming the popular image of such a life from one only for the despised lower classes to one acceptable for women of all social standing.⁷⁴

Whether he fully expected it or not, the impact of Marcellina on her brother was considerable. Ambrose gradually became so impressed by the concept of virginity that after being ordained he wrote four essays advocating it and applied the principle to himself by never marrying. The personal bond with Marcellina continued throughout his life and the only record we have of several of his dramatic collisions with the emperor at his Milan court are due to letters he wrote his sister. In none of his correspondence does he "talk down" to her, but treats her as perceptive and worthy of intellectual respect.[75] One of his works, entitled *On Virginity*, was written specifically in response to her request.

One must wonder how she reacted to some of his criticism of the problems of the world being caused by the female gender, however. In refusing to grant the royal demand that he yield a basilica in Milan to the Arians, he wrote to her of his sermon defying the order. In it he repeatedly cites the examples of women stirring up trouble for the male — marching through the Bible from Eve to Job's wife, to Jezebel, to Herodias having John the Baptist beheaded. It is all the fault of women that he is threatened with a loss of a basilica to Nicene orthodoxy: "Each man seems to suffer from this or that woman; for me, in proportion as my merits are less, my trials are heavier. My strength is weaker, but I have more danger. Women succeed each other, their hatreds are interchanged, their falsehoods are varied, the elders are gathered together, the plea of wrong to the Emperor is put forward."[76] Seemingly, if the women would just leave him alone the church's problems would simply disappear!

Although we are clearly dealing with sermonic hyperbole, to the extent that one takes such reasoning seriously one would seemingly be faced with women being the ultimate root of all the church's difficulties and heresies — of which precious few (if any) are attributed to them by the critics of ancient quasi-orthodoxy. Might one see here yet another reason why Ambrose (in spite of his clear affection for his sister) would be a mighty promoter of female celibacy — that it would rid the world of a new generation of heresy encouragers and facilitators?

He intensely felt his ongoing familial responsibilities toward his sister. After he was ordained he set apart adequate resources to provide for her the rest of her life and gave the remainder to both the poor and the Church he served. Ambrose died in 397 and Marcellina passed away an unknown number of years afterwards.

So many took Ambrose's advice in rejecting marriage — and at so early an age — that he endured vigorous criticisms on both matters. So intense was the contrary sentiment in some places that one council (Saragossa, Spain, 380) prohibited any woman from taking the step until she was at least forty.[77]

Paula (347–404)
Pioneer of Female Monasticism

Paula came from a Roman senatorial family which, according to Jerome, had multiple prestigious ancestors on both sides of the family. This assertion, however, has been challenged on the grounds that the actual example he provides on the father's side came from deep in the past and he conspicuously omits any reference to officeholders of more recent times. The claim for prestige on her mother's side appears better rooted, however.[78]

Even discounting Jerome's excessive hyperbole, to be from a senatorial background of *any* perceived rank was nothing to scoff at.

Jerome had lived in the desert for a while as a hermit, though those who came in contact with him were inclined to view him at that stage as of questionable doctrinal orthodoxy. Part of this evaluation likely lay in the fact that Origen had a clear-cut influence on him[79] and Origen's orthodoxy itself had come under challenge: "the friend of the enemy is my enemy" would express the root suspicion in a modern idiom.

Paula, along with Marcella and the lady friends of both women, turned to Jerome after his arrival in Rome seeking extremely detailed spiritual guidance. He spent many a night working late to provide the answers to the questions that such women were regularly sending his way.[80]

He did not have a high opinion of women who were married: they had unwisely and imprudently lost the opportunity for maximizing their spirituality by both marrying and enjoying the pleasures of the flesh that warred against the development of the soul. On the other hand, by virtue of losing their spouse, they had regained the opportunity to practice virginity and become, as they should be, centered on matters of the spirit to the full exclusion of matters of the flesh.[81] Hence his encouragement of women like Paula. Of the various wealthy widows he came in contact with, she was the one he most stood in awe of. As he later wrote, "Of all the ladies in Rome, but one had power to subdue me, and that one was Paula."[82]

He vigorously propagandized for the celibate lifestyle for women as well as passionately arguing it should be the male ideal as well. Jerome's written denunciations of those opposed to his asceticism sent shivers of delight through (of all people) pagan opponents of the faith who enthusiastically followed his denunciations and exhibited them as evidence of the lunacy of the Christian movement.[83] To traditional Christians he had become an embarrassment by his rhetorical self-indulgence and proclamation of bitterly controversial views on the glories of celibacy that were so intense that the implicit debasement of marriage seemed inescapable.

Paula had a daughter named Blessila. After the death of her husband, Blessila had successfully survived a potentially lethal illness and had enthusiastically adopted the ascetic lifestyle, encouraged by her mother and the tutelage of Jerome. Her fasting and self-imposed restrictions wore down her health so drastically that she died in a matter of months. Then at the funeral her mother passed out. Jerome was given the blame for both the death and the collapse of the mother.

Soon bishop Damascus died and Jerome's pivotal supporter was no longer there to protect his flanks from critics. Jerome had already been considering leaving Rome, and when accusations were made against him (perhaps related to Blessila's death) he decided to yield to the strong request that he depart for somewhere else.[84] He chose the Near East.

It is uncertain whether Paula had also endured criticism (and blame) for the death of her daughter[85] but her own encouragement of Blessila's close relationship with Jerome makes that a reasonable conjecture. Certainly her own family was indignant at the idea of her leaving the city and devoting her life to holy celibacy. Her son and other daughter argued vigorously against the decision but she refused to listen.[86]

Paula crossed paths with Jerome again in Antioch or on Cyprus and they became a traveling pair who visited important sites in Palestine before continuing on to Egypt. She visited the major monastic figures of the land and may have wished to remain there to open a convent for female ascetics. Certainly it was only with the encouragement of Jerome that she decided to alter course and settle in Palestine.[87]

Her contemporaries Melania and Rufinus had already created adjoining monasteries not many years earlier on the Mount of Olives. After staying for a while with them, she and Jerome continued to Bethlehem and established their own monastic institutions in A.D. 385.[88] Paula's effort, both because of its success and her friendship with the far more important Jerome, has led to much more attention being devoted to her effort as female monastic pioneer in Palestine than to Melania.

Lifestyle in Her Monastic Community

Paula had made a basic change in her attitude toward the world as the result of her spiritual meditations during the preceding years: She was in the world but not of the world, an admirable sentiment but not one requiring the degree of repudiation of even the innocent luxuries of life that she (and others like her) engaged in. She had taken Psalms 39:12 as her lodestar and it represented the guiding principle of her life: "For I am a stranger with thee, and a sojourner, as all my fathers were."[89]

Within her community the discipline was quite strict. The plain attire was not unexpected. On the other hand, she discouraged the kind of cleanliness that we would take as routine because she dismissed it as vanity and betraying weakness of the flesh. The rigor of Paula's asceticism did not relinquish with age. Even at an advanced age and visiting in Egypt, she rebuked a fellow traveler for not living up to the strict rigor she had long observed[90]:

> Be sure of this, be sure of it, that I am in the sixtieth year of my life and except for the tips of my fingers neither my feet nor my face nor any of my limbs have touched water, although I am a victim to various ailments and the doctors try to force me. I have not consented to make the customary concessions to the flesh; never in my travels have I rested on a bed or used a litter.

No individual possessions were permitted within the nunnery. The members met for collective worship through the singing of psalms six times a day.[91] Isolation from males was the order to the day. Routine leaving of the grounds was permitted only for Sunday worship—and that was to a church facility nearby.[92] Males were banned from the premise as servants—even eunuchs (a seemingly unthreatening presence because of their physical limitations) were forbidden in the nunnery.[93]

Though such attitudes could be presented by the cynic as "straightlaced" and even "Victorian" in its excess, hand in hand with it went the potential for spiritual ecstaticism that occasionally broke out in a form that could almost be described as a "spiritual" form of physical orgasm: Jerome describes how during a visit to Jerusalem's Church of the Holy Sepulcher Paula was so overcome that she felt compelled to fall to the floor and kiss the large stone that had supposedly once blocked entrance to Jesus' tomb. Then "she even licked with the mouth the very spot on which the Lord's body had lain, like one athirst for the river which he had longed for."[94] Egeria visited the tomb not far distant in time from Paula's and commented that quite a few individuals had a similar reaction.[95]

If one was tempted by sexual desires, the solution was not a candid admission that one was not cut out for the ascetic and celibate lifestyle but additional fasts beyond the normally required ones. These, it was believed, would either crush the desires or empower one to overcome them.[96]

Leaders were expected to take their fair share of the drudge work just like anyone else. For example, when it came to the dull "housekeeping" chores of everyday life and of preparing the food and tables for their joint meals, Paula was just as involved as any other group member.[97]

There was, however, a threefold division of the convent members and it has been speculated that this was based upon the social class of the member, which would nearly inevitably involve monetary resources since it was the dominant part of how one was perceived on the social totem pole of the day.[98] The highest rank category was permitted to have a helper. Since they ate as a separate group, this may suggest a better quality of food being served them as well. Be that as it may, everything else was communal, with no distinctions in the ranks.[99]

Paula saw herself and her group as obligated to provide social welfare services for the pilgrims and sick in the Bethlehem area. She created several hospices and not only managed them but also involved herself in the nitty-gritty of everyday operations. Jerome spoke of how "She was often by them that were sick, and she laid their pillows aright; and ... she rubbed their feet and boiled water to wash them. And it seemed to her that the less she did to the sick in service, so much the less service she did to God."[100] (Note the contrast with her own aversion to personal cleanliness described above.)

Paula and Her Financial Largesse

Although the women no longer technically had property of their own, the possessions remained theirs to dispose so long as it was for nonpersonal benefit. These funds were spent on such things as helping the needy, assisting other less financially blessed monastic groups, and those they were in theological agreement with.[101] When Paula died in 404, Jerome's own monastery underwent a serious financial crunch due to her personal resources no longer being available to assist him.[102]

Although her generosity proved so beneficial, her intellectual demands proved extremely taxing. She always wanted to know more and expected her friend to lead in meeting that thirst for knowledge. Jerome candidly confessed that to answer the probing questions of Paula and her daughter was one of the major motivations for certain of his major commentary efforts.[103] She lit a fire under him on other projects as well. For example, she wished to have him translate Origen's sermons on Luke so that her nuns could be benefited by it.[104] She was also discontented with the Psalter their group was using and implored Jerome to provide a more reliable translation.[105]

If she and her associates pressured him to ever more intellectual endeavor, he responded that he needed their help in regard to it as well. In particular, he needed additional copies of his works to be produced so they could be more widely distributed. They responded by making a personal commitment to be responsible for providing them.[106] They got access to his intellectual labors; he received copies to share with a broader audience.

As can be seen from these representative examples of her intellectual interests, Paula never lost her zeal for greater knowledge. Jerome had to confess that in at least one area she clearly surpassed his own such talents: "While I myself beginning as a young man have with much toil and effort partially acquired the Hebrew tongue and study it now unceasingly lest if I leave it, it also may leave me; Paula, on making up her mind that she too would learn it, succeeded so well that she could chant the psalms in Hebrew and could speak the language without a trace of the pronunciation peculiar to Latin."[107]

Her financial generosity to Jerome cost Paula considerable money. Although her lavish generosity on both intellectual and humanitarian causes was obviously well intended — and even those with anti-monastic biases would have to admit that a significant proportion of it was laudworthy in helping the poor and encouraging Jerome's intellectual pursuits — it was not always *her* money that was actually given away. She appears to have borrowed significantly and those debts were passed, upon her death, to the shoulders of her children to pay off.[108]

Paula's Death

By the time of her passing, Paula had gained widespread recognition and respect. Her passing was treated by large numbers as seriously as if close kin had passed away. Jerome describes the reaction at length[109]:

> Then her breath failed her and she gasped for death; yet even when her soul was eager to break free, she turned the death-rattle (which comes at last to all) into the praise of the Lord. The bishop of Jerusalem and some from other cities were present, also a great number of the inferior clergy.... No weeping or lamentation followed her death, such as are the custom of the world; but all present united in chanting the psalms in their several tongues. The bishops lifted up the dead woman with their own hands, placed her upon a bier, and carrying her on their shoulders to the church in the cave of the Savior, laid her down in the centre of it. Other bishops meantime carried torches and tapers in the procession, and yet others led the singing of the choirs.
>
> The whole population of the cities of Palestine came to her funeral. Not a single monk lurked in the desert or lingered in his cell. Not a single virgin remained shut up in the seclusion of her chamber. To each and all it would have seemed sacrilege to have withheld the last tokens of respect from a woman so saintly.... Strange to say, the paleness of death had not altered her expression; only a certain solemnity and seriousness had overspread her features. You would have thought her not dead but asleep.
>
> One after another they chanted the Psalms, now in Greek, now in Latin, now in Syriac; and this not merely for the three days which elapsed before she was buried beneath the church and close to the cave of the Lord, but throughout the remainder of the week.

Paula had died, but the memory of her benevolence and dedication had burned into the collective memory of her followers.

Chapter Notes

Chapter 1

1. John W. Rogerson, "The First Christian Writings," in *First Christian Theologians*, edited by G.R. Evans (Oxford: Blackwell Publishing, 2004), 21.
2. W.C. van Unnik, "Studies on the So-Called First Epistle of Clement: The Literary Genre," in *Encounters with Hellenism: Studies on the First Letter of Clement*, edited by Cilliers Breytenbach and Laurence L. Welborn (Leiden: Brill, 2004), 119.
3. Carolyn Osiek, "Apostolic Fathers," in *The Early Christian World*, 1:n.4, 522.
4. L. L. Welborn, "The Preface to 1 Clement: The Rhetorical Situation and the traditional Date," in *Encounters with Hellenism: Studies on the First Letter of Clement*, edited by Cilliers Breytenbach and Laurence L. Welborn (Leiden: Brill, 2004), 196–197.
5. Osiek, "Fathers," 1:508.
6. van Unnik, 119.
7. W. Jaeger, Early Christianity and the Greek Paideia: 1 Clement," in *Encounters with Hellenism: Studies on the First Letter of Clement*, edited by Cilliers Breytenbach and Laurence L. Welborn (Leiden: Brill, 2004), 108.
8. Garry Wills, *Why I Am a Catholic* (New York: Houghton Mifflin Company/Mariner Books edition, 2003), 79.
9. Cf. Burton L. Mack, *Who Wrote the New Testament?: The Making of the Christian Myth* (New York: HarperCollins, 1995), 244.
10. As quoted by Welborn, 202.
11. *Ibid.*, 216.
12. *Ibid.*, 202–205.
13. XLIV.2–4, as quoted by Paige Patterson, "The Meaning of Authority in the Local Church," in *Recovering Biblical Manhood and Womanhood: A Response to Evangelical Feminism*, ed. John Piper and Wayne Grudem (Wheaton, IL: Crossway, 1991), 250–251.
14. *Ibid.*, 250.
15. Louis W. Countryman, *Living on the Border of the Holy: Renewing the Priesthood of All* (Harrisburg, PA: Morehouse, 1999), 131.
16. Mack, 244, calls it "ideological controversy."
17. Simon Tugwell, *The Apostolic Fathers* (New York: Continuum, 1989), 91–92.
18. Osiek, "Fathers," 1:511–512.
19. As quoted from Clement, *Second Clement*, translated by J. B. Lightfoot in *Apostolic Fathers* (1885), http://www.earlychristianwritings.com/text/2clement-hoole.html (accessed February 2006). Unless other sources are identified, all quotes come from this source.
20. Osiek, "Fathers," 1:511.
21. Old, Hughes O. *The Reading and Preaching of the Scriptures in the Worship of the Christian Church* (Grand Rapids, MI: Wm. B. Eerdmans, 1998), 280, 283, 284.
22. Joseph T. Lienhard, *The Bible, the Church, and Authority: The Canon of the Christian Bible in History and Theology* (Collegeville, MN: Michael Glazier/Liturgical, 1995), 31.
23. *Ibid.*, 32.
24. On a variant form of this statement which Clement of Alexandria attributes to the *Gospel of the Egyptians*, see *ibid.*, n. 20, 32–33.
25. *Ibid.*, 33.
26. For the reasoning, see Eugene A. LaVerdiere, *The Eucharist in the New Testament and in the Early Church* (Collegeville, MN: Liturgical Press, 1996), 148–149, and attached notes.
27. *Ibid.*, 164.
28. For example, Francis A. Sullivan, *From Apostles to Bishops: The Development of the Episcopacy in the Early Church* (Mahwah, NJ: Newman Press/Paulist Press), 115.
29. *Ibid.*
30. *Ibid.*
31. *Ibid.*, 117.
32. *Ibid.*, 118.
33. *Ibid.*, 118; raises the possibility as a question but does not explicitly embrace it.
34. *Ibid.*, 105.
35. William A. Jurgens, *The Faith of the Early Fathers* (Collegeville, MN: Liturgical Press, 1970), 1:17.
36. Osiek, "Fathers," 1:516, and Sullivan, 105. There remains a minority opinion highly skeptical of all forms of the epistles. See the lengthy analysis of Bernard D. Muller, "The Epistles of Ignatius: Are They All Forgeries?" http://www.geocities.com/b_d_muller/ignatius.html (accessed February 2006), and Hermann Detering, "1 Clement and the Ignatiana in Dutch Radical Criticism," translated by Frans-Joris Fabri, http://www.hermann-detering.de/clem_engl.htm (accessed February 2006).
37. For three translations of the three forms of the letters, see Ignatius of Antioch, *Ignatius of Antioch*, http://www.earlychristianwritings.com/ignatius.html (accessed February 2006).
38. LaVerdiere, n. 15, 165.
39. *Ibid.*, and Raymond E. Brown, *Antioch and Rome: New Testament Cradles of Catholic Christianity* (Mahwah, NJ: Paulist Press, 1983, 2004), n. 82, 35.

40. Sullivan, 119.
41. *Ibid.*, 120.
42. Cf. *ibid.*
43. *Ibid.*, 125.
44. Both quoted by L. Russ Bush, ed., *Classical Readings in Christian Apologetics, A.D. 100–1800: A.D. 100–1800* (Grand Rapids, MI: Zondervan, 1983), 1.
45. Eric Osborn, "The Apologists," in *The Early Christian World*, 1:527.
46. Emily J. Hunt, *Christianity in the Second Century: The Case of Tatian* (London: Routledge, 2003), 56–57.
47. David Dunn-Wilson, *A Mirror for the Church: Preaching in the First Five Centuries* (Grand Rapids, MI: Wm. B. Eerdmans), 36.
48. Bush, xiv.
49. For quotations see Osborn, "Apologists," 1:528.
50. For a survey of the divergent theories about him, see T.J. Horner, *Listening to Trypho: Justin Martyr's Dialogue With Trypho Reconsidered* (Leuven, Belgium: Peeters, 2001), 15–32. The dominant view grants only a minimum genuine historical element in the account, viewing it as a literary fiction with an unrealistically weak defense of Judaism (27).
51. For the points in this paragraph, see *ibid.*, 12, 20–21, 24. Horner's own view is that any incongruities in the document can be accounted for on the thesis that the original account was written soon after the event and that two decades later Justin came back to it and expanded it greatly (32).
52. Cf. Graham N. Stanton, "The Spirit in the Writings of Justin Martyr," in *The Holy Spirit and Christian Origins: Essays in Honor of James D.G. Dunn*, ed. Graham N, Stanton, Stephen C. Barton, Bruce W. Longenecker (Grand Rapids, MI: Wm. B. Eerdmans, 2004), 325.
53. Marvin R. Wilson, *Our Father Abraham: Jewish Roots of the Christian Faith* (Grand Rapids, MI: Wm. B. Eerdmans, 1989), 83.
54. Cf. *ibid.*, n. 23, 83. For the iron curtain coming into existence on the conventional Jewish side, see H. Wayne House, "The Church's Appropriation of Israel's Blessings," in *Israel: The Land and the People*, ed. H. Wayne House (Grand Rapids, MI: Kregel, 1998), 86–87. On that minority of Jews who attempted to be more tolerant in spite of their personal abhorrence of the Christian views, see n. 90, 109.
55. Wilson, n. 22, 83.
56. *Ibid.*, 91–92.
57. *Ibid.*, 89.
58. House, 99.
59. Jeremy Cohen, *Living Letters of the Law* (Berkeley: University of California Press, 1999), 12.
60. Wilson, 93.
61. Brevard S. Childs, *The Struggle To Understand Isaiah as Christian Scripture* (Grand Rapids, MI: Wm. B. Eerdmans, 2004), 32.
62. *Ibid.*, 34.
63. *Ibid.*, 37.
64. Cf. House, 97–98.
65. For a detailed argument in this behalf, see Tugwell, 63–64.
66. G.R.S. Mead, *Thrice Greatest Hermes: Studies in Hellenistic Theosophy and Gnosis* (1992; new edition, York Beach, ME: Weiser, 2001), 257–258.
67. Larry W. Hurtado, *Lord Jesus Christ: Devotion to Jesus in Earliest Christianity* (Grand Rapids, MI: Wm. B. Eerdmans, 2003), n. 112, 602.
68. L. Michael White, *From Jesus to Christianity: How Four Generations of Visionaries & Storytellers Created the New Testament and Christian Faith* (New York: HarperCollins Publishers, 2004), 341.
69. *In Rome*, 16:14, as quoted by Brown and Meier, 204.
70. *Against Heresies*, 4.20.2, as cited by *ibid.*, 204.
71. Eusebius, *Church History*, 3.3.6, as cited by *ibid.*, 203.
72. Brown and Meier, 203. For examples of how Hermas' Christology can be read in varying ways, see Roger E. Olson and Christopher A. Hall, *The Trinity* (Grand Rapids, MI: Wm. B. Eerdmans, 2002), 18.
73. Alistair Stewart-Sykes, "Hermas the Prophet and Hippolytus the Preacher: the Roman Homily and Its Social Context," in *Preacher and Audience: Studies in Early Christian and Byzantine Homiletics*, edited by Marry B. Cunningham and Pauline Allen (Leiden, Netherlands: Brill, 1998), 43.
74. *Ibid.*, 43–44, cites *Vision* 2, in regard to his farming success, and *Vision* 3.6.7, and *Mandate* 3.5, in regard to his financial loses.
75. *Ibid.*, 44.
76. Of 3.6.6: Osiek, "Fathers," 1:510.
77. Unless otherwise indicated, all quotations come from Hermas, *The Pastor of Hermas*, in *Ante-Nicene Fathers* (Buffalo, Christian Literature Publishing, 1885.), vol. 2, http://www.ccel.org/fathers2/ANF-02/anf02-04.htm#TopOfPage (accessed March 2006).
78. Patricia Miller, *Dreams in Late Antiquity: Studies in the Imagination of a Culture* (Princeton, NJ: Princeton University Press, 1994), 35.
79. *Ibid.*; cf. page 139.
80. Charles A. Gieschen, *Angelomorphic Christology: Antecedents and Early Evidence* (Leiden, Netherlands: Brill, 1998), 215, cites various textual references to show that the figure is used as being synonymous with the church, yet providing the instruction to go and build a tower that is itself presented as synonymous with the church, and as equivalent to the Holy Spirit as well.
81. Miller, 63, 131.
82. *Ibid.*, 63.
83. *Ibid.*
84. For examples, see Gieschen, 215–216.
85. For citations see Carolyn Osiek, *Rich and Poor in the "Shepherd of Hermas:" An Exegetical-Social Investigation* (Washington, DC: Catholic Biblical Association of America, 1983), 12–13.
86. For a compilation of texts, see *ibid.*, 40–44.
87. Tugwell, 59.
88. David Instone-Brewer, *Divorce and Remarriage in the Bible: The Social and Literary Context* (Grand Rapids, MI: Wm. B. Eerdmans, 2002), 240.
89. *Ibid.*, 241.
90. James Dallen, *The Reconciling Community: The Rite of Penance* (Collegeville, MN: Liturgical Press, 1991), 48; cf. 32.
91. Allen Brent, *Hippolytus and the Roman Church in the Third Century: Communities in Tension Before the Emergence of a Monarch-Bishop* (Leiden, Netherlands: Brill, 1995), 292–293.
92. Sherman E. Johnson, "Asia Minor and Early Christianity," in *Christianity, Judaism, and Other Greco-Roman Cults: Studies for Morton Smith at Sixty*, part 2:

Early Christianity (Leiden, Netherlands: Brill, 1975), 109.
   93. C. Clifton Black, *Mark: Images of an Apostolic Interpreter* (Columbia: University of South Carolina Press, 1994), 82.
   94. D.A. Carson, *Gospel According to John* (Grand Rapids, MI: Wm. B. Eerdmans, 1991), 334.
   95. Black, 83–84.
   96. Andrew Chester, "The Parting of the Ways: Eschatology and Messianic Hope," in *Jews and Christians: The Parting of the Ways, A.D. 70 to 135*, ed. James D. G. Dunn (1992; new edition with additional English translations, Grand Rapids, MI: Wm. B. Eerdmans, 1999), 263.
   97. *Against Heresies,* V.33–34, as quoted by *ibid.,* 263–264.
   98. *Ibid.,* 264.
   99. Jurgens, 1:38.
   100. *Ibid.,* n. 85, 104.
   101. House, 101.
   102. *Ibid.*
   103. *Ibid.*
   104. Kenneth Berding, *Polycarp and Paul: An Analysis of Their Literary and Theological Relationship in Light of Polycarp's Use of Biblical and Extra-Biblical Literature* (Leiden, Netherlands: Brill, 2002), 9, and n. 39, 9.
   105. Paul Hartog, *Polycarp and the New Testament: The Occasion, Rhetoric, Theme, and Unity of the Epistle to the Philippians and Its Allusions to New Testament Literature* (Tubingen, Germany: Mohr Siebeck, 2002), 33–34.
   106. Irenaeus, *Against Heresies*, 3.3.4, as quoted by L. Michael White, 324.
   107. See the discussion in Berding, n. 40, 9.
   108. For a discussion of the evidence, see *ibid.*, n. 51, 11.
   109. For text see Hartog, 37.
   110. *Ibid.*, 37–38.
   111. Berding, n. 48, 10.
   112. *Ibid.*, 10–11, and accompanying notes.
   113. Osiek, "Fathers," 1:n. 17, 523.
   114. Sullivan, 121.
   115. Cf. Sullivan, 126–127.
   116. As quoted by *ibid.*, 127; cf. 15, 107.
   117. Cf. *ibid.*, 130.
   118. On the evidence for rival dates, see J.W. van Henten and Friedrich Avemarie, *Martyrdom and Noble Death: Selected Texts from Graeco-Roman, Jewish and Christian Antiquity* (London: Routledge, 2002), n. 30, 94.
   119. Osiek, "Fathers, 1:519–520.
   120. Ben C. Johnson, *The God Who Speaks: Learning the Language of God* (Grand Rapids, MI: Wm. B. Eerdmans, 2004), 53–55.
   121. Quotations from K. Waaijman, *Spirituality: Forms, Foundations, Methods,* translated by John Vriend (Leuven, Belgium: Peeters, 2002), 284.
   122. Alistair Stewart-Sykes, *The Lamb's High Feast: Melito, Peri Pascha and the Quartodeciman Paschal Liturgy at Sardis* (Leiden, Netherlands: Brill, 1998), 1, 2.
   123. Sherman E. Johnson, 36. Cf. Stewart-Sykes, *High Feast*, 2, 4. See 4–5 for a discussion of those who deny that Eusebius was correct in his calling Melito such.
   124. Miriam S. Taylor, *Anti-Judaism and Early Christian Identity: A Critique of the Scholarly Consensus* (Leiden, Netherlands: Brill, 1995), 60.
   125. As quoted by Martin C. Albl, *And Scripture Cannot Be Broken: The Form and Function of the Early Christian Testimonia Collections* (Leiden, Netherlands: Brill, 1999), 110–111.
   126. *Ibid.*, 111.
   127. *Ibid.*
   128. *Ibid.*
   129. Sherman E. Johnson, 136, and Eric Werner, *The Sacred Bridge: The Interdependence of Liturgy and Music in Synagogue and Church During the First Millennium* (New York: KTAV Publishing, 1989), 146–147.
   130. Taylor, 52, 55.
   131. Both quotes from Werner, 144.
   132. *Ibid.,* 147.
   133. Taylor, 52–53, and Mary C. Boys, *Has God Only One Blessing?: Judaism as a Source of Christian Self-Understanding* (Mahwah, NJ, Paulist Press, 2000), 52.
   134. Taylor, 60, 62–63.
   135. Cf. *ibid.*, 58–59, who rejects this scenario.
   136. Jurgens, 1:82.
   137. Thomas T. Talley, *The Origins of the Liturgical Year* (Collegeville, MN: Liturgical Press, 1986, 1991), 17.
   138. Jurgens, 1:82–84. Cf. Mark Edwards, "The Development of Office in the Early Church," in *The Early Christian World*, 1:320.
   139. Talley, 13.
   140. For text, see *ibid.*, 20–21.
   141. Edward Scobie, "African Popes," in *African Presence in Early Europe*, ed. Ivan Van Sertima (New Brunswick, NJ: Transaction, 1985), 100.
   142. Cf. Walter Bauer, *Orthodoxy and Heresy in Earliest Christianity,* translated from the 1934 2nd German edition (Philadelphia: Fortress, 1971), 97.
   143. The view, among others, of Joseph Dahmus, *A History of the Middle Ages* (New York: Barnes and Noble, 1968), 52–53.
   144. Leo D. Davis, *The First Seven Ecumenical Councils: Their History & Theology* (Collegeville, MN: Liturgical Press, 1983), 22.
   145. For an effective presentation of this approach see Talley, 22–24.
   146. Sullivan, 153.
   147. Edwards, 320.
   148. Denis Minns, *Irenaeus* (Washington, DC: Georgetown University Press, 1994), 1. Minns (6) argues that his denial of having any background in rhetoric is repudiated by the literary techniques he clearly utilizes.
   149. *Ibid.*, 2.
   150. Richard A. Norris, Jr., "Irenaeus of Lyon," in *The Cambridge History of Early Christian Literature*, eds. Frances Young, Lewis Ayres, Andrew Louth, Augustine Casiday (Cambridge: Cambridge University Press, 2004), 46.
   151. Minns, 2, and Eric Osborn, *Irenaeus of Lyons* (Cambridge: Cambridge University Press, 2001), 2.
   152. Cf. Minns, 4.
   153. Gerald Bray, "The Early Theologians," in *The Early Christian World*, 1:554.
   154. Gerd Ludemann, *Heretics: The Other Side of Early Christianity*, translated by John Bowden (Louisville, Kentucky: Westminster John Knox Press, 1996), 15.
   155. Lienhard, 27.

156. Bray, 1:553.
157. Richard A. Norris, Jr., "Irenaeus," 47, and Ludemann, 16.
158. Ludemann, 16, sees him as heavily dependent upon prior individuals. For a theoretical reconstruction of one case of possible reliance on earlier authorities, see 19.
159. *Ibid.*, 18–20.
160. *Ibid.*, 19.
161. Ross S. Kraemer and Shira L. Lander, "Perpetua and Felicitas," in *The Early Christian World*, 2:1048.
162. Rosemary Rader, "Introduction to Perpetua," in *A Lost Tradition: Women Writers of the Early Churchu*, ed. Patricia Wilson-Kastner (Washington, DC: University Press of America, 1981), 1.
163. Peter Dronke, *Women Writers of the Middle Ages: A Critical Study of Texts from Perpetua (Died 203) to Marguerite Porete (Died 1310)* (Cambridge: Cambridge: University Press, 1984), 6–7.
164. For an analysis of the imagery from this polytheist background, see *ibid.*, 7–15.
165. *De natura et origine animae*, 4.10.12, as quoted by Kraemer and Lander, 2:1056.
166. *Ibid.*, 1058. These authors are quite skeptical of any great reliance being put in that claim, however: see their analysis, 1051–1057.
167. Thomas M. Finn, "Mission and Expansion, in *The Early Christian World*, 2:301.
168. For a good concise summary of these factors, see *ibid.*
169. Maureen A. Tilley, "The Passion of Perpetua and Felicity," in *Searching the Scriptures: A Feminist Commentary* (New York: Crossroad, 1994), 2:831.
170. Finn, 303. W.H.C. Frend, "Martyrdom and Political Oppression," in *The Early Christian World*, 2:826, leaves open the question of whether the arrest and death was the direct result of the emperor's decree or was based on other legal precedents.
171. *Ibid.*
172. For a concise summary of them, see Kraemer and Lander, 2:1049–1050.
173. Perpetua, *The Passion of Saints Perpetua and Felicity*, translated by W.H. Shrewring (London: 1931), *Medieval Source Book*, http://www.fordham.edu/HALSALL/source/perpetua.html (accessed April 2006). All quotes from this version unless otherwise noted.
174. Carlin Barton, "Honor and Sacredness in the Roman and Christian Worlds," in *Sacrificing the Self: Perspectives on Martyrdom and Religion*, ed. Margaret Cormack (New York: Oxford University Press, 2002), n. 25, 35–36.
175. *Ibid.*, 31. Cf. Rader, 9.
176. Rader, 11.
177. Cf. Rader, 2, and Susan Elm, "Montanist Oracles," in *Searching the Scriptures: A Feminist Commentary* (New York: Crossroad, 1994), 2:132. For the argument that the prophesying depicted differs significantly from that practiced by Montanists, see Tilley, 2:834–835.
178. Rader, 11.
179. Tilley, 2:832.
180. Denise K. Buell, *Making Christians: Clement of Alexandria and the Rhetoric of Legitimacy* (Princeton, NJ: Princeton University Press, 1999), 10, and n. 21, 10.

181. *Paed.*, 1.1.2, as cited by Peter Karavites, *Evil, Freedom, and the Road to Perfection in Clement of Alexandria* (Leiden, Netherlands: Brill, 1999), 4.
182. *Ibid.*, 4–5.
183. *Ibid.*, 5.
184. *Ibid.*, 2.
185. Bray, 1:559.
186. Buell, 12.
187. For the complete list, see *ibid.*, n. 25, 10.
188. Bray, 1:558.
189. *Ibid.*
190. Cf. Buell, 70–73.
191. Karavites, 3.
192. *Stromata* 7.18, as quoted by Scott Hahn and Mike Aquilina, *Living the Mysteries: A Guide for Unfinished Christians* (Huntington, IN: Our Sunday Visitor Publishing, 2003), 24. For others who thought similarly and the underlying rationale, see 24–25.
193. Bray, 1:559.
194. Alan J. Hauser and Duane F. Watson, "Introduction and Overview," in *A History of Biblical Interpretation*, ed. Alan J. Hauser and Duane F Watson (Grand Rapids, MI: Wm. B. Eerdmans, 2003), 43.
195. *Ibid.*
196. *Stromata* 5.32.2, as quoted by Peter Borgen, "Philo of Alexandria as Exegete," in *A History of Biblical Interpretation*, ed. Alan J. Hauser and Duane F Watson (Grand Rapids, MI: Wm. B. Eerdmans, 2003), 137.
197. *Ibid.*, 5.39.2.

Chapter 2

1. Bill Leadbetter, "Constantine," in *The Early Christian World*, 2:1075.
2. Leadbetter, "From Constantine to Theodosius (and Beyond)," in *The Early Christian World*,1:264–265.
3. Michael Grant, *Constantine the Great: The Man and His Times* (New York: Barnes & Noble, 1993), 138–143; quote from 140.
4. T.G. Elliott, *The Christianity of Constantine the Great* (Scranton, PA: University of Scranton Press, 1996), 71.
5. Michael Grant, *Constantine*, 142–143.
6. "Constantine the Great," *Catholic Encyclopedia,* http://www.newadvent.org/cathen/04295c.htm (accessed September 2005). Second usage of all non-attributed articles from the *Catholic Encyclopedia* in this volume are abbreviated *C.E.* to identify the source.
7. Tertullian, *First Apology*. 21, in *Nicene and Post-Nicene Fathers*, ed. Philip Schaff (New York: Christian Literature Publishing, 1892), vol. 3, http://www.ccel.org/fathers2/ANF-03/anf03-05.htm (accessed March 2006).
8. Leadbetter, "Constantine," 2:1077.
9. Leadbetter, "Theodosius," 1:262.
10. Eusebius, *Life of Constantine*, 2.45, as cited by Leadbetter, "Constantine," 2:1077.
11. *Ibid.*
12. Charles M. Odahl, *Constantine and the Christian Empire* (London: Routledge, 2004), 172–173.
13. J.E. Merdinger, *Rome and the African Church in the Time of Augustine* (New Haven: Yale University Press, 1997), 18.
14. *Ibid.*, 19.
15. *Ibid.*

16. Quotes from Odahl, 196–197.
17. Merdinger, 19.
18. Trevor Hart, "Creeds, Councils and Doctrinal Development," in *The Early Christian World*, 1:652.
19. Maxwell E. Johnson, "Worship, Practice and Belief," in *The Early Christian World*, 1:489.
20. Leadbetter, "Theodosius,: 1:267.
21. Bruce J. Malina, "Social Levels, Morals and Daily Life," in *The Early Christian World*, 1:386.
22. A.H.M. Jones, "The Social Background of the Struggle between Paganism and Christianity," in *The Conflict between Paganism and Christianity in the Fourth Century*, ed. Arnaldo Momigliano (Oxford: Clarendon Press, 1963), 31.
23. Malina, 381.
24. Finn, 295–296.
25. Michael DiMaio, Jr., and Robert Frakes, "Constantius II (A.D. 337–361)," *Online Encyclopedia of Roman Rulers*, http://www.roman-emperors.org/constaii.htm (accessed February 2006).
26. *Ibid.*
27. Diana Bowder, *The Age of Constantine and Julian* (New York: Barnes & Noble, 1978), 76.
28. Ammianus, as quoted by Michael Grant, *The Ancient Historians* (New York: Barnes & Noble Publishing, 1970), 372.
29. *Ibid.*
30. *Contra Constantium imperatorem*, no attribution, "Flavius Julius Constantius," *Catholic Encyclopedia*, http://www.newadvent.org/cathen/16027c.htm (accessed August 2005).
31. Bowder, 78–79.
32. *Ibid.*, 99.
33. No attribution, "Julian the Apostate," *Catholic Encyclopedia*, http://www.newadvent.org/cathen/08558b.htm (accessed September 2005).
34. Dahmus, 33.
35. Michael B. Simmons, "Julian the Apostate," in *The Early Christian World*, 2:1252.
36. Clifford Ando, *Imperial Ideology and Provincial Loyalty in the Roman Empire* (Berkeley: University of California Press, 2000), 195–196.
37. *Ibid.*, 196.
38. "Julian," *C.E.*
39. Leadbetter, "Theodosius," 1:277–278.
40. *Ibid.*, 1:278.
41. Simmons, 2:1253.
42. See the more detailed discussion in my book *Messiahs and Messianic Movements through 1899* (Jefferson, North Carolina: McFarland, 2005), 50–51.
43. Simmons, 2:1253.
44. *Ibid.*
45. Bowder, 100.
46. *Ibid.*
47. *Ibid.*, 101.
48. Simmons, 2:1260–1262.
49. Bowder, 54.
50. John W. Wand, *History of the Early Church to A.D. 500* (London: Routledge, 1937; reprint, 1994), 53.
51. Dio Cassius, *Roman History* (LXXII), http://www.penelope.uchicago.edu/Thayer/E/Roman/Texts/Cassius_Dio/72*.html (accessed April 2006).
52. G. Williamson, *Eusebius: From Christ to Constantine*, revised edition (London: Penguin, 1989), 423.
53. *Ibid.*, 424, and Wand, 54.
54. Richard Smith, "Introduction to the Coptic Book of Ritual Power from Leiden," in *Ancient Christian Magic: Coptic Texts of Ritual Power*, ed. Marvin W. Meyer and Richard Smith (Princeton, NJ: Princeton University Press, 1999), 312.
55. See the discussion of length of military service in my volume *The Seven Cities of the Apocalypse & Roman Culture* (Mahwah, NJ: Paulist Press, 1999), 7, 19–20, n. 20, 148–149.
56. Ronald G. Musto, *The Catholic Peace Tradition* (New York: Orbis, 1986), 41.
57. *Ibid.*
58. Richard Fletcher, *The Barbarian Conversion: From Paganism to Christianity* (1998; reprint, Berkeley: University of California Press, 1999), 37.
59. Musto, 42.
60. Johannes Quasten, "Introduction" to Nola Paulinus," *Letters of Saint Paulinus of Nola* (Ramsey, NJ: Paulist Press, 1966), 6.
61. Charles Moreschini, "Jerome and His Learned Lady Disciples," *The City and the Book*, International Congresses in Florence's *Certosa*, 30–31 May, 1 June 2001, http://www.translate.google.com/translate?hl=en&sl=it&u=http://www.florin.ms/aleph2.html&prev=/search%3Fq%3DPammachius%26start%3D60%26hl%3Den%261r%3D%26sa%3DN (Google translation of the Italian) (accessed December 2005).
62. Edward L. Cutts, *History of Early Christian Art* (1893; reprint, [n.p.]: Kessinger, 2004), 143.
63. Catherine Conybeare, *Paulinus Noster: Self and Symbols in the Letters of Paulinus of Nola* (Oxford: Oxford University Press, 2000), 46.
64. Alfred W. Wishart, *A Short History of Monks and Monasteries* (n.d.), 30, http://www.historion.net/a.w.-wishart-short-history-monks-monasteries/page-30.html (accessed December 2005).
65. John Curran, *Pagan City and Christian Capital: Rome in the Fourth Century* (Oxford: Oxford University Press, 2000 John), 315.
66. Maribel Dietz, *Wandering Monks, Virgins, and Pilgrims: Ascetic Travel in the Mediterranean World, 300–800* (University Park, PA: Pennsylvania State University, 2005), 1.
67. No attribution, "Ostia." *Ostia—The Harbor District: Ostia*, http://www.ostia-antica.org/portus/remainsn.htm (accessed December 2005). The exact chronology is contested. Alvin J. Schmidt, *How Christianity Changed the World* (Grand Rapids, MI: Zondervan, 2004), 156, argues that it was actually the second, the first having been built about eight years earlier in Rome itself. Vivian Nutton, *Ancient Medicine* (London: Routledge, 2004), 307, puts the Roman hospital at c. 397 and that of Ostia as being established not long afterwards.
68. Schmidt, 155, 157, and Dan Graves, *Doctors Who Followed Christ: 32 Biographies of Historic Physicians and Their Christian Faith* (Grand Rapids, MI: Kregel, 1999), 28–29.
69. Edmund H. Oliver, *The Social Achievements of the Christian Church* (1930; reprinted, Vancouver, British Columbia: Regent College Publishing, 2004), 62. Cf. Vicki Leon, *Uppity Women of Ancient Times* (Boston, Massachusetts: Conari Press, 2000), 228–229.
70. No attribution, "Saint Pammachius," *Catholic Encyclopedia*, http://www.newadvent.org/cathen/11436a.htm (accessed December 2005).
71. Fletcher, 39.

72. Curran, 295, and Rowa A. Greer, *The Fear of Freedom: A Study of Miracles in the Roman Imperial Church* (University Park, PA: Penn State University Press, 1989), 140.
73. Carolinne White, *Christian Friendship in the Fourth Century* (Cambridge: Cambridge University Press, 1992; paperback edition, 2002), 7, 129.
74. Marcia Colish, *Stoic Tradition from Antiquity to the Early Middle Ages* (Leiden, Netherlands: Brill, 1990), 87.
75. Carolinne White, *Friendship,* 133.
76. Curran, 295.
77. Katharina M. Wilson and Elizabeth M. Makowski, *Wykked Wyves and the Woes of Marriage: Misogamous Literature from Juvenal to Chaucer* (Albany: State University of New York Press, 1990), 47.
78. Henry Chadwick, *The Church in Ancient Society: From Galilee to Gregory the Great* (Oxford: Oxford University Press, 2001), 440.
79. *Ibid.*
80. No attribution, "Saint Pammachius," *Catholic Online Saints,* http://www.catholic.org/saints/saint.php?saint_id=807 (accessed December 2005).

Chapter 3

1. James R. Partington, *A History of Greek Fire and Gunpowder* (Cambridge: W. Heffer & Sons, 1960; reprinted, Baltimore, MD: Johns Hopkins Press, 1999), 6–7.
2. Both quotes from Peter Richardson, *Herod: King of the Jews and Friend of the Romans* (Columbia: University of South Carolina Press, 1996), 52–53. Richardson tries to dilute the antagonism that seems clearly reflected in the description.
3. Albretch Dihle, *Greek and Latin Literature of the Roman Empire: From Augustus to Justinian,* English translation (London: Routledge, 1994), 334.
4. Partington, 7.
5. As quoted by Brent, *Third Century,* 86. Those who take as a reference to his being an architect include Brent (90), and Chadwick, *Ancient Society,* 130.
6. Hans D. Betz, ed., *The Greek Magical Papyri in Translation: Including the Demotic Spells* (Chicago: University of Chicago Press, 1992; paperback edition, 1996), n. 18, 263. In a similar vein, Dihle, 334, and Raoul Mortley, *The Idea of Universal History from Hellenistic Philosophy to Early Christian Historiography* (Lewiston, NY: Edwin Mellen Press, 1996), 134.
7. Allen Kent, *Encyclopedia of Library and Information Science* (New York: Marcel Dekker, 1979), 25–26.
8. *Ibid.,* 26.
9. Chadwick, *Ancient Society,* 130, believes there was such a statue. Brent, *Third Century,* reviews the alleged evidence and ultimately rejects the possibility (100).
10. Brent, *Third Century,* 101.
11. Chadwick, *Ancient Society,* 131.
12. *Ibid.*
13. *Ibid.*
14. Brent, *Third Century,* 88, and Lawrence Besserman, "The Challenge of Periodization: Old Paradigms and New Perspectives," in *The Challenge of Periodization: Old Paradigms and New Perspectives,* ed. Lawrence Besserman ([n.p.]: Routledge, 1996), 7.

15. Cf. Brent, *Third Century,* 88.
16. Besserman, 7.
17. Stephen Toumlin and June Goodfield, *The Discovery of Time* (Chicago: University of Chicago Press, 1965), 61.
18. Robert Browning, "History," in *The Later Principate: The Cambridge History of Classical Literature,* ed. E.J. Kenney and W.V. Clausen (Cambridge: University of Cambridge Press, 1983), 52.
19. *Ibid.*
20. Arnaldo Momigliano, "Pagan and Christian Historiography in the Fourth Century A.D.," in *The Conflict between Paganism and Christianity in the Fourth Century,* ed. Arnaldo Momigliano (Oxford: Clarendon Press, 1963), 85.
21. Williamson, xxii.
22. Mark Golden, *Sport and Society in Ancient Greece* (Cambridge: Cambridge University Press, 1998; reprint, 2003), 61.
23. Gerald P. Verbrugghe and John M Wickersham, *Berossos and Manetho, Introduced and Translated: Native Traditions in Ancient Mesopotamia and Egypt* (Ann Arbor: University of Michigan Press, 1996), 29.
24. Dihle, 334.
25. Betz, 264.
26. Richard Kieckhefer, *Magic in the Middle Ages* (Cambridge: Cambridge University Press, 1989, 2000), 40.
27. Fletcher, 34.
28. Raymond van Dam, *Families and Friends in Late Roman Cappadocia* (Philadelphia, Pennsylvania: University of Pennsylvania Press, 2003), 40.
29. Fergus Millar, *Rome, the Greek World, and the East;* Volume 2: *Government, Society, and Culture in the Roman Empire* ([n.p.]: University of North Carolina Press, 2004), 461–462.
30. Fletcher, 35.
31. Stephen Mitchell, "The Life and *Lives* of Gregory Thaumaturgus," in *Portraits of Spiritual Authority: Religious Power in Early Christianity, Byzantium and the Christian Orient,* edited by Jan W. Drijvers and John W. Watt (Leiden, Netherlands: Brill, 1999). 106.
32. For the reasoning, see Mitchell, 104–105.
33. Cf. *ibid.,* 105.
34. Raymond van Dam, *Becoming Christian: The Conversion of Roman Cappadocia* (Philadelphia: PA: University of Pennsylvania Press, 2003), 73.
35. See Mitchell, 109–110.
36. Herbert W. Bateman, *Authentic Worship: Scripture's Voice, Applying Its Truth* (Grand Rapids, MI: Kregel, 2002), 156–157.
37. Fletcher, 36.
38. *Ibid.*
39. For an examination of the arguments against literalization, see Andrew J. Carriker, *The Library of Eusebius of Caesarea* (Leiden, Netherlands: Brill, 2003), 19–20.
40. Andrew Louth, "Eusebius and the Birth of Church History," in *The Cambridge History of Early Christian Literature,* ed. Frances Young, Lewis Ayres, Andrew Louth, and Augustine Casiday (Cambridge: Cambridge University Press, 2004), 266.
41. Robert M. Grant, *Eusebius as Church Historian* (Oxford: Clarendon Press, 1980), 165.
42. Louth, "Eusebius," 267–268.
43. *Ibid.,* 268.

Notes — Chapter 3

44. Quotes from Grant, *Historian,* 166.
45. For a brief survey, see David Rankin, "Arianism," in *The Early Christian World,* 2:977–978.
46. *Ibid.*
47. Odahl, 197.
48. *Ibid.*
49. *Ibid.,* 199.
50. Momigliano, "Historiography," 89.
51. *Ibid.,* 89–90.
52. Louth, "Eusebius," 271.
53. Grant, *Historian,* 13–14.
54. William Adler, "Eusebius' *Chronicle* and Its Legacy," in *Eusebius, Christianity, and Judaism,* ed. Harold W. Attridge and Gohel Hata (Leiden, Netherlands: Brill, 1992), 478.
55. Louth, "Eusebius," 270.
56. Antonio Arbea, *Carmen Sacrum of Faltonia Betitia Proba, the First Christian Poetess,* http://www.translate.google.com/translate?hl=en&sl=es&u=http://www.conocereisdeverdad.org/website/index.php%3Fid%3D2591&prev=/search%3Fq%3DFaltonia%2BProba%26start%3D80%26hl%3Den%26lr%3D%26sa%3DN (Google translation of the Spanish) (accessed December 2005).
57. For a discussion, see G. Ronald Kastner and Ann Millin, "Introduction to Proba," in *A Lost Tradition: Women Writers of the Early Church,* ed. Patricia Wilson-Kastner (Washington, DC: University Press of America, 1981), 33–35.
58. *Ibid.,* 33.
59. For example, *ibid.*
60. *Ibid.*
61. Dorothy Disse, "Proba /Faltonia Betitia Proba (c.322–c.370)," *Other Women's Voices: Translations of Women Writing before 1700,* http://www.home.infionline.net/~ddisse/proba.html (accessed December 2005).
62. David Noy, "Women in Latin Love Poetry," http://www.lamp.ac.uk/~noy/roman5.htm (accessed December 2005).
63. Anita Obermeier, *The History and Anatomy of Auctorial Self-Criticism in the European Middle Ages* (Amsterdam, Netherlands: Editions Rodopi B.V., 1999), 51.
64. Carl P.E. Springer, "Jerome and the *Cento* of Proba," in *Studia Patristica,* vol. 28: *Papers Presented at the Eleventh International Conference on Patristic Studies Held in Oxford, 1991,* ed. Elizabeth A. Livingstone (Louvain, Belgium: Peeter, 1993), 96.
65. *Ibid.,* 96, 98.
66. Kastner and Millin, 37.
67. Disse, "Proba /Faltonia Betitia Proba" (Internet).
68. Kastner and Millin, 36. For a translation of the work, see Proba, Falconia [aka Faltonia], "Cento," translated by Jeremy Reedy, in *A Lost Tradition: Women Writers of the Early Church,* ed. Patricia Wilson-Kastner, 45–69 (Washington, DC: University Press of America, 1981), 45–69.
69. Susan A. Harvey, "Women and Words: Texts by and about Women," in *The Cambridge History of Early Christian Literature,* ed. Frances Young, Lewis Ayres, Andrew Louth, and Augustine Casiday, 382–390 (Cambridge: Cambridge University Press, 2004), 382.
70. Arbea, *Carmen Sacrum* (Internet).
71. Gillian Cloke, *This Female Man of God: Women and Spiritual Power in the Patristic Age, A.D. 350–450* (London: Routledge, 1995), 13–14.
72. Elizabeth A. Clark, "Jesus the Hero in the Vergilian *Cento* of Faltonia Betitia Proba," abstract of a paper presented at the Sixth Annual Byzantine Studies Conference, October 24–26, 1980, at Oberlin College and the College of Wooster, Oberlin, Ohio, http://www.byzconf.org/1980abstracts.html (accessed December 2005).
73. *Ibid.*
74. David Noy, "Women in Latin Love Poetry" (Internet).
75. Mary J. Carruthers, *The Craft of Thought: Meditation, Rhetoric, and the Making of Images, 400–1200* (Cambridge: Cambridge University Press, 1998), 59, implies the analogy.
76. *Ibid.,* 59.
77. No attribution, "Firmicus Maternus," http://www.newadvent.org/cathen/06080a.htm (accessed December 2005).
78. Marvin W. Meyer, *The Ancient Mysteries: A Sourcebook of Sacred Texts* (Philadelphia, PA: University of Pennsylvania Press, 1987), 207, and Robert Browning, "Minor Figures," in *Cambridge History of Classical Literature,* ed. P.E. Easterling and R. J. Kenney (Cambridge: Cambridge University Press, 1982; 1996 reprint), 771.
79. Robert Turcan, *The Cults of the Roman Empire,* translated by Antonia Nevill (Oxford, England: Blackwell, 1996; 2001 reprint), 8.
80. James Megivern, *The Death Penalty: An Historical and Theological Survey* (Mahwah, NJ: Paulist Press, 1997), 28.
81. *Ibid.*
82. David Pingree, "Astrology," in *The Dictionary of the History of Ideas,* http://www.etext.lib.virginia.edu/cgi-local/DHI/dhi.cgi?id=dv1-20 (accessed December 2005), puts the date of his writing at c. 335. Nick Campion, "The Concept of Destiny in Islamic Astrology and Its Impact on Medieval European Thought," reprinted from *Aram: The Journal for Syro-Mesopotamian Culture* 1:2 (Summer 1989): 281–289, http://www.nickcampion.com/nc/history/articles/islamic.htm (accessed December 2005), suggests c. 334. Matthew Dickie, *Magic and Magicians in the Greco-Roman World* (London, England: Routledge, 2001, 2003), 284, suggests the range of 334–337.
83. Lynn Thorndike, *History of Magic & Experimental Science* (New York: Columbia University Press, 1923), 525.
84. Browning, "Minor Figures," 771.
85. The view of Liz Green, *Astrology of Fate* (Boston: Red Wheel/Weiser, 1984), 143.
86. David McCann, "Julius Firmicus Maternus: Profile of a Roman Astrologer," *The Traditional Astrologer* (Autumn 1994), http://www.skyscript.co.uk/firmicus.html (accessed December 2005).
87. R. Blackhurst, "Astrology, Autochony and Salvation," copyright 2003–2004, http://www.religioperennis.org/documents/blacks/Astrology.pdf (accessed December 2005).
88. Bernadette J. Brooten, *Love Between Women: Early Christian Responses to Female Homoeroticism* (Chicago, Illinois: University of Chicago Press, 1996), 132.
89. R. Blackhurst. "Astrology" (Internet).
90. *Mathesis,* 1.7.37, as quoted by Michael A. Williams, *The Immoveable Race: A Gnostic Designation*

and the Theme of Stability in Late Antiquity (Leiden, Netherlands: Brill, 1985), n. 41, 134. On the same theme, also see Liz Green, 145–146.

91. Brooten, 132.
92. *Ibid.*
93. No attribution, "Prudentius, Aurelius Clemens, 348-c. 413," *Evangelical Lutheran Hymnary Handbook: Biographies and Sources, P-Z,* http://www.blc.edu/comm/gargy/gargy1/ELH.biographies.P ... Z.html (accessed December 2005).
94. Karl P. Harrington, *Medieval Latin,* 2nd edition, revised by Joseph M. Pucci ([n.p.]: University of Chicago Press, 1997), 103.
95. For names, see no attribution, "Aurelius Clemens Prudentius, 348–c. 413," part of the *Cyber Hymnal,* Website which includes biographies of hymn writers and recordings of their music, http://www.cyberhymnal.org/bio/p/r/prudentius_ac.htm (accessed December 2005).
96. Dihle, 584, and Harrington, 68.
97. Harrington, 103.
98. Laurance Wider, "Review of *Hymns of Prudentius,*" *First Things* 74 (June-July, 1997), available: http://www.firstthings.com/ftissues/ft9706/reviews/wieder.html (accessed December 2005).
99. John Rust, "Validation of the Orpheus Minor Scales in a Working Population," *Social Behavior and Personality* (1998), http://www.looksmartweightloss.com/p/articles/mi_qa3852/is_199801/ai_n8797744 (accessed December 2005).
100. "Lady Alchima" [pseudonym], "The Battle for the Soul," http://www.mugglenet.com/editorials/editorials/edit-ladyalchymia01.shtml (accessed December, 2005).
101. Dietz, 158–159.
102. G. W. Bowersock, *Martyrdom and Rome* (Cambridge: Cambridge University Press, 1995; 2002 paperback edition), 23, 24.
103. Cf. Joyce E. Salisbury, *Blood of Martyrs: The Impact and Memory of Ancient Violence* (London: Routledge, 2004), 5.
104. *Ibid.,* 140. For older roots of the connection between blood and fertility, see 140–141.
105. *Cath.* 3.31–35, as quoted in prose translation by W. Evenepol, "The Place of Poetry in Latin Christianity," in *Early Christian Poetry: A Collection of Essays,* eds. J. den Boef and A. Hillhorst (Leiden, Netherlands: Brill, 1993), 46.
106. Harrington, 287.
107. As translated into English under the title "Father, Most High, Be with Us" and published as part of *Hymns Ancient and Modern* (1889), No Attribution, *Cyber Hymnal* (Internet). For the entire Latin and English translation of Prudentius' *Cathemerinon Liber* ("Hymns for the Christian Day") see Prudentius, *The Hymns of Prudentius,* translated by Martin R. Pope. London: J. M. Dent and Company MDCCCV, http://www.gutenberg.org/files/14959/14959-h/14959-h.htm (accessed December 2005).
108. *Cathemerinon* (along with other references as far back as Tertullian, c. A.D. 225 [the citation from "Barnabas" being of unknown but earlier date], in No attribution, "The Sign of the Cross," http://www.latin-mass-society.org/2005/signofthecross.html [accessed December 2005]).
109. Evenepol, 56, and n. 77, 56.
110. *Ibid.,* 56.
111. Kathleen E. McVey, "Ephrem the Syrian," in *The Early Christian World,* 2:1229.
112. *Ibid.,* 2:1244.
113. James W. McKinnon, *Music in Early Christian Literature* (Cambridge: Cambridge University Press, 1987; 1993 reprint), 92.
114. McVey, 1228–1229.
115. *Ibid.,* 2:1231.
116. *Ibid.*
117. For examples see Sidney H. Griffith, "'Spirit in the Bread; Fire in the Wine': The Eucharist as 'Living Medicine' in the thought of Ephraem the Syrian," in *Catholicism and Catholicity,* eds. Sarah Beckwith, James Buckley, Gregory Jones (Oxford: Blackwell, 1999), 118–119.
118. Sidney H. Griffith, "The Image of the Image Maker in St. Ephraem the Syrian," in *Studia Patristica 25: Biblica et Apocrypha, Orientalia, Ascetica,* ed. Elizabeth A. Livingtstone (Louvain, Belgium: Peeter, 1993), 259, 261.
119. Sebastian P. Brock, "Ephrem and the Syriac Tradition," in *The Cambridge History of Early Christian Literature,* eds. Frances Young, Lewis Ayres, Andrew Louth, and Augustine Casiday (Cambridge: Cambridge University Press, 2004), 365–366.
120. McVey, 2:1231.
121. Andrew Louth, "Palestine: Cyril of Jerusalem and Epiphanius," in The *Cambridge History of Early Christian Literature,* eds. Frances Young, Lewis Ayres, Andrew Louth, and Augustine Casiday (Cambridge: Cambridge University Press, 2004), 286, and Karen Rae Keck, "Epiphanius of Salamis (Cyprus)," *Ecole Initiative* website, http://www.2.evansville.edu/ecoleweb/glossary/salamis.html (accessed December 2005).
122. For the example of Basil, see the discussion of van Dam, *Christian,* 43–44.
123. Jurgens, 1:67.
124. Frank Williams, "Introduction, *The Panarion of Epiphanius of Salamis* (Books II and III) (Leiden, Netherlands: Brill, 1994), xii.
125. *Ibid.*
126. Louth, "Palestine," 286.
127. Jurgens, 1:68.
128. *Ibid.,* 1:67.
129. Louth, "Palestine," 286.
130. Keck, "Epiphanius" (Internet).
131. Jurgens, 1:67–68.
132. Dave Armstrong, "Exposition on the Christian Veneration of Images," available: http://www.bringyou.to/apologetics/a121.htm (accessed December 2005).
133. *Ibid.*
134. Glenn Peers, *Subtle Bodies: Representing Angels in Byzantium* (Berkeley: University of California Press, 2001), 64–65.

Chapter 4

1. Hunt, 1.
2. Eusebius, *Church History* 4.16.7, as quoted by William L. Petersen, "Tatian the Assyrian," in *A Companion to Second-Century Christian "Heretics,"* edited by Anti Marjanen and Petri Luomanen (Leiden, Netherlands: Brill, 2005), 132–133.
3. *Against Heresies,* 1.28.1, as quoted by *ibid.,* 132.

Petersen believes that the claimed egocentric aspect of Tatian's character is well-grounded (134–136, 151).

4. Hunt, 1. Although it is common to assume that the heretic Valentinus had the dominant impact on Tatian's convictions after Justin died, Hunt, (52–73, especially 52, 73) argues that Justin's impact remained the dominant influence on Tatian's thinking even after his mentor's death.

5. Osborn, "Apologists," 1:537.

6. Jeffrey S. Siker, "Christianity in the Second and Third Centuries," in *The Early Christian World,*1:249.

7. Hunt, 18.

8. For a summary of the evidence, see *ibid.*, 20–21.

9. For an examination of apparent non–Valentinus concepts in Tatian's thinking, see *ibid.*, 45–51.

10. Cf. W. Stewart McCullough, *A Short History of Syriac Christianity to the Rise of Islam* (Chico, California: Scholars Press, 1987), 31. For a basically skeptical evaluation of alleged encratic readings found in some Diatessaron texts, see Hunt, 146–150.

11. On the problem of retaining respect for marriage while promoting celibacy during these centuries, see Teresa M. Shaw, "Sex and Sexual Renunciation," in *The Early Christian World,* 1:415.

12. McCullough, 31.

13. *Ibid.*, 31–32.

14. Philip Rousseau, *The Early Christian Centuries* (London: Longman, 2002), 68.

15. Ira Price, William A. Irwin, and Allen P. Wikgren, *The Ancestry of our English Bible*, 3rd revised edition (New York: Harper & Brothers, 1956), 190. Specific examples include McCullough, 31, Rousseau, 68, and Herbert G. May, *Our English Bible in the Making* (Philadelphia: published for the Cooperative Publication Association by Westminster Press, 1962), 12.

16. Rousseau, 68.

17. For a brief advocacy of this approach, see Han J. W. Drjivers, *East of Antioch: Studies in Eastern Christianity* (London: Variorum Reprints, 1984), 172–175, and the book length analysis of Nicholas Perrin, *Thomas and Tatian: The Relationship between the "Gospel of Thomas" and the "Diatessaron"* (Atlanta: Society of Biblical Literature, 2002).

18. Drjivers, 174.

19. A. Augustus Hobson, *The Diatessaron of Tatian and the Synoptic Problem* (Chicago: University of Chicago Press, 1904), 9–10.

20. *Ibid.*, 9. For a survey of other surviving sources, see Price, 189–190, and Perrin, n. 54, 15.

21. Rousseau, 68.

22. For example, Price, 189.

23. For a translation of the prediction, see Harris, 10.

24. 35:15–16, as quoted by *ibid.*, 9.

25. McCullough, 31, and David G. K. Tayler, "Christian Regional Diversity," in *The Early Christian World,*1:338.

26. Harris, 10.

27. For related views, see *ibid.*, 11.

28. *Ibid.*, 12.

29. *De fab haer.*, as quoted by *ibid.*, 13.

30. Theodret, *Epistle 113*, as cited by *ibid.*

31. Fred Norris, "Origen," in *The Early Christian World*, 2:1008.

32. Robert M. Grant, "Theological Education at Alexandria," in *The Roots of Egyptian Christianity*, ed. Birger A. Pearson and James E. Goehring (Philadelphia, PA: Fortress Press, 1986), 186.

33. Carole Straw, "'A Very Special Death:' Christian Martyrdom in Its Classical Contex," in *Sacrificing the Self: Perspectives on Martyrdom and Religion*, ed. Margaret Cormack (New York: Oxford University Press, 2002), 42, and n. 13, 52.

34. Cf. John Q. McGuckin, "Martyr Devotion in the Alexandrian School: Origen to Athanasius," in *Martyrs and Martyrologies,* ed. Diana Wood (Oxford: Blackwell, 1993), 38.

35. Henk Bakker, "Potamiaena: Some Observations about Martyrdom and Gender in Ancient Alexandria," in *The Wisdom of Egypt: Jewish, Early Christian, and Gnostic Essays in Honor of Gerald P. Luttikhuizen*, eds. Anthony Hilhorst and George H. van Kooten (Leiden, Netherlands: Brill, 2005), 331.

36. McGuckin, 38.

37. Robert M. Grant, "Alexandria," 186.

38. *Ibid.*, 185.

39. *Ibid.*

40. Bray, 1:560.

41. Carriker, 1–2.

42. *Ibid.*, 2.

43. *Ibid.*, 7.

44. *Ibid.*, 4–5.

45. Bray, 1:560.

46. *Ibid.*, and Fred Norris, 2:1005.

47. For a summary of the varying views the ancients had of his work, see Fred Norris, 2:1005–1007.

48. *Ibid.*, 2:1005.

49. *Ibid.*, 2:1007.

50. Bray, 1:561–562.

51. Cf. *ibid.*

52. Cf. William McKane, *Selected Christian Hebraists* (Cambridge: Cambridge University Press, 1989), 1.

53. Ernst Wurthwein, *The Text of the Old Testament: An Introduction to the Biblia Hebraica,* English translation of 5th German edition (Grand Rapids, MI: Wm. B. Eerdmans, 1995), 57.

54. Timothy R. McLay, *The Use of the Septuagint in New Testament Research* (Grand Rapids, MI: Wm. B. Eerdmans, 2003), 130.

55. *Ibid.*

56. *Ibid.*

57. Williamson, 418.

58. See quotations in McKane, 28.

59. *Ibid.*, 27; cf. 197.

60. McLay, n. 53, 128.

61. Wurthwein, 130.

62. Fred Norris, 2:1010.

63. McLay, 24, and Wurthwein, 58.

64. Wurthwein, 59.

65. Williamson, 194.

66. Also/known/as Wulfila.

67. Herwig Wolfram, *History of the Goths* (Berkeley: University of California Press. 1988; paperback edition, 1990), 52, 75–76.

68. *Ibid.*, 75, 77.

69. Herwig Wolfram, *The Roman Empire and Its Germanic Peoples* (Berkeley: University of California Press, 1997), 75–76.

70. See *ibid.*, , for a discussion of how the Goths would have perceived Ulfilas' status in their society.

71. *Ibid.*, 75.

72. Of the two possibilities, the latter is favored as

more probable by Michael Hines, "Barbarian Breakthrough," http://www.christianchronicler.com/history1/barbarian_breakthrough.html (accessed January 2006).
73. *Ibid.*, and cf. Philip W. Comfort, *Essential Guide to Bible Versions* ([n.p.]: Tyndale, 2000), 130.
74. Patrick J. Geary, *Myth of Nations: The Medieval Origins of Europe* (Princeton, NJ: Princeton University Press, 2002), 88.
75. Wolfram, *Goths*, 63, 78, and Noel Lenski, *Failure of Empire: Valens and the Roman State in the Fourth Century* (Berkeley: University of California Press, 2002), 119, 125.
76. Wolfram, *Goths*, 63.
77. Wolfram, *Germanic*, 77, David Ewert, *General Introduction to the Bible: From Ancient Tablets to Modern Translations* (Grand Rapids, MI: Zondervan, 1990), 181, and Matthias Huning, "The Gothic Bible Translation," http://www.ned.univie.ac.at/publicaties/taalgeschiedenis/en/gotbibel.htm (accessed January 2006).
78. For a detailed account of his adaptation of traditional Gothic to a Christianized usage, see Wolfram, *Goths*, 106–114, especially 113–114. Cf. Huning, "Gothic" (Internet).
79. Wolfram, *Goths*, 75, and Wolfram, *Germanic*, 16, 17, 70, who accepts there having been such assistance.
80. Wolfram, *Goths*, 75.
81. *Ibid.*
82. Huning, "Gothic" (Internet), and Patrick Amory, *People and Identity in Ostrogothic Italy, 489–554* (Cambridge: Cambridge University Press, 1997; paperback edition, 2003), 240.
83. Cf. Amory, 240–241.
84. Huning, "Gothic" (internet).
85. E.A. Thompson, "Christianity and the Northern Barbarians, in *The Conflict between Paganism and Christianity in the Fourth Century*, ed. Arnaldo Momigliano (Oxford: Clarendon Press, 1963), 18.
86. *Ibid.*, 64.
87. *Ibid.*, 69.
88. Thompson, 69.
89. *Ibid.*
90. Wolfram, *Goths*, 79.
91. Cf. Harry R. Boer, *A Short History of the Early Church* (Grand Rapids, MI: Wm. B. Eerdmans, 1976), 126.
92. Amory, 237–238.
93. Wolfram, *Germanic*, 78–79.
94. Wolfram, *Goths*, 79, and Geary, 88–89.
95. Wolfram, *Goths*, 79.
96. As quoted by Wolfram, *Goths*, 84–85.
97. Dennis Brown, "Jerome." in *The Early Christian World*, 2:1151.
98. Stefan Rebenich, *Jerome* (London: Routledge, 2002), 7.
99. *Ibid.*, 24–25, and Ivor Davidson, "Later Theologians of the West," in *The Early Christian World*, 1: 616.
100. Dennis Brown, 2:1172.
101. *Ibid.*
102. Davidson, "Theologians," 1:618–619.
103. Alister E. McGrath, *Historical Theology: An Introduction to the History of Christian Thought* (Oxford: Blackwell, 1998), 146.
104. *Ibid.*
105. Rebenich, 54–55.
106. *Epistle* 125.12, Dennis Brown, 2:1158.
107. Rebenich, 55.
108. Wurthwein, 91–92.
109. *Ibid.*
110. *Ibid.*, 92.
111. Bruce M. Metzger, "Theories of the Translation Process," *Bibliotheca Sacra* 150:598 (1993): 140–150, http://www.biblicalstudies.org.uk/article_trans_metzger2.html (accessed December, 2005).
112. *Ibid.*
113. Cf. *ibid.*
114. Dennis Brown, 2:1162, and John Thorley, *Documents in Medieval Latin* (Ann Arbor: University of Michigan Press, 1998), 12.
115. Dennis Brown, 2:1162.
116. *Ibid.*, 2:1162–1163.
117. Wurthwein, 96.
118. *Ibid.*, 95, 96.
119. *Ibid.*, n. 15, 99.
120. Joseph A. Fitzmyer, *The Dead Sea Scrolls and Christian Origins* (Grand Rapids, MI: Wm. B. Eerdmans, 2000), 136–137.
121. *Ibid.*, 134, 162.
122. McGrath, *Historical*, 122–123; cf. 149–150.

Chapter 5

1. Bray, 1:572–573.
2. Cf. *ibid.* 1:573.
3. *Ibid.*
4. Chadwick, *Ancient Society*, 145–146.
5. J. Patout Burns, Jr., *Cyprian the Bishop* (London: Routledge, 2002), 1.
6. Chadwick, *Ancient Society*, 147.
7. *Ibid.*
8. Burns, Jr., 2.
9. Chadwick, *Ancient Society*, 67.
10. Ronald E. Heine, "Cyprian and Novatian," in *The Cambridge History of Early Christian Literature*, eds. Frances Young, Lewis Ayres, Andrew Louth, and Augustine Casiday (Cambridge: Cambridge University Press, 2004), 154–155.
11. Burns, Jr., 2–3.
12. *Ibid.*, 3–4.
13. Heine, 156.
14. Letter 33, in Sullivan, 193–194.
15. Burns, Jr., 4.
16. *Ibid.*, 5.
17. Stuart G. Hall, *Doctrine and Practice in the Early Church* (Grand Rapids, MI: Wm. B. Eerdmans, 1991), 87–88.
18. Burns, Jr., 5.
19. *Ibid.*, 7.
20. *Ibid.*, 9.
21. Hall, *Church*, 92.
22. J. Patout Burns, Jr., 9.
23. *Ibid.*, 10.
24. *Ibid.*
25. Letter 74 in Sullivan, 214.
26. Bowersock, 43.
27. Timothy D. Barnes, *Athanasius and Constantinius* (Cambridge, MA: Harvard University Press, 1993), 11.
28. Athanasius, *Apol. c. Ar.*, 9.4, as cited by *ibid.*, 11.

29. Barnes, *ibid.*, 11, who proceeds to argue in detail how the supposed grounding of Athanasius in Greek culture and tradition has been drastically overstated in the past.
30. Khaled Anatolios, *Athanasius* (London: Routledge, 2004), 3–4.
31. *Ibid.*, 4.
32. David Brakke, "Athanasius," in *The Early Christian World*, 2:1103, and Charles Kannengiesser, "Athanasius of Alexandria vs. Arius: The Alexandrian Crisis," in *The Roots of Egyptian Christianity*, eds. Birger A. Pearson and James E. Goehring (Philadelphia, PA: Fortress, 1986), 207.
33. Andrew Louth, "Later Theologians of the Greek East," in *The Early Christian World*, 2:583.
34. *Ibid.*, "The Fourth-Century Alexandrians: Athanasius and Didymus," in *The Cambridge History of Early Christian Literature*, eds. Frances Young, Lewis Ayres, Andrew Louth, and Augustine Casiday (Cambridge: Cambridge University Press, 2004), 276.
35. Barnes, 12.
36. Cf. Brakke, 2:1107.
37. Kannengiesser, "Athanasius," 211.
38. *Ibid.*
39. Anatolios, 5.
40. Brakke, 2:1104.
41. *Ibid.*
42. *Ibid.*, 2:1106.
43. Louth, "Later Theologians," 1:583.
44. Anatolios, 5.
45. Maurice Wiles, "Attitudes to Arius in the Arian Controversy," in *Arianism after Arius: Essays on the Development of the Fourth Century Trinitarian Conflicts*, eds. Michel R. Barnes and Daniel H. Williams (Edinburgh: T & T Clark, 1993), 32.
46. Brakke, 2:1104–1105.
47. Wiles, 43.
48. Cf. Rebecca Lyman, "A Topography of Heresy: Mapping the Rhetorical Creation of Arianism," in *Arianism after Arius: Essays on the Development of the Fourth Century Trinitarian Conflicts*, 54–55, who sees in Athanasius a leader who considered the legitimacy of his episcopate as proof positive that his views must represent the genuine spiritual truth as well.
49. Andrew Louth, "Alexandrians," in 278.
50. *Ibid.* Louth notes that the same occurs in regard to criticism of the Arian Asterius, who died long before Athanasius.
51. Most scholars consider this incident the decisive evidence in behalf of his willingness to either use or tolerate intimidation in behalf of establishing his power: Brakke, 2:1109.
52. Anatolios, 13.
53. *Ibid.*
54. *Ibid.*, 16.
55. For his account of the event see *ibid.*, 26–27.
56. *Ibid.*, 30.
57. For a discussion of the evidence, see Richard Alston, *The City in Roman and Byzantine Egypt* (London: Routledge, 2002), 286. For a chart of religious violence in the fourth and fifth centuries in the city see 287.
58. Anatolios, 31.
59. *Ibid.*, 32.
60. *Ibid.*, 32–33.
61. For a collection of these remarks, see Duane W-H. Arnold, *The Early Episcopal Career of Athanasius of Alexandria* (Notre Dame, Indiana: University of Notre Dame Press, 1991), 87.
62. *Ibid.*, 87–88.
63. For an evaluation of whether he endorsed or tacitly permitted such violence, see Arnold, 70–89, who is reluctant to concede the point.
64. van Dam, *Friends*, 1.
65. *Ibid.*, 6, 13.
66. Andrew Louth, "The Cappadocians," in *The Cambridge History of Early Christian Literature*, eds. Frances Young, Lewis Ayres, Andrew Louth, and Augustine Casiday (Cambridge: Cambridge University Press, 2004), 289.
67. van Dam, *Friends*, 25.
68. Raymond van Dam, *Kingdom of Snow: Roman Rule and Greek Culture in Cappadocia* (Philadelphia: University of Pennsylvania Press, 2002), 5.
69. *Ibid.*
70. van Dam, *Friends*, 45–46.
71. Louth, "Cappadocians," 295.
72. *Ibid.*, 297.
73. van Dam, *Christian*, 5.
74. Louth, "Cappadocians," 295.
75. Cf. *ibid.*, 297.
76. van Dam, *Christian* 9.
77. Morwenna Ludlow, The Cappadocians, in *First Christian Theologians*, ed. G. R. Evans (Oxford: Blackwell, 2004), 173.
78. Philip Rousseau, *Basil of Caesarea* (Berkeley: University of California Press, 1994), 4.
79. *Ibid.*, 1, and Marilyn Dunn, *The Emergence of Monasticism: From the Desert Fathers to the Early Middle Ages* (Oxford: Blackwel, 2000), 35.
80. Rousseau, *Basil*, 135.
81. Cf. Louth, "Cappadocians," 293–294.
82. *Ibid.*, 290, and Rousseau, *Basil*, 2.
83. William A. Jurgens, *The Faith of the Early Fathers* (Collegeville, MN: Liturgical Press, 1979), 2:2.
84. *Ibid.*, 2:3, and Rousseau, *Basil*, 2.
85. Dunn, *Monasticism*, 34.
86. *Ibid.*, 35–36.
87. Louth, 292.
88. *Ibid.*
89. *Oration 20*, as quoted by Daniel W. Amundsen and Gary B. Ferngren, "Philanthropy in Medicine: Some Historical Perspectives," in *Beneficence and Health Care*, ed. Earl E. Shelp (Dordrecht, Holland: D. Reidel, 1982), 15. For a detailed discussion of the institution, see Andrew T. Crislip, *From Monastery to Hospital: Christian Monasticism and the Transformation of Health Care in Late Antiquity* ([n.p.]: University of Michigan Press, 2005), 104–110.
90. Amundsen and Ferngren, 15.
91. Boniface Ramsey, *Ambrose* (London: Routledge, 1997), 11, 13.
92. Ivor Davidson, "Ambrose," in *The Early Christian World*, 2:1177, 1178.
93. Craig A. Satterlee, *Ambrose of Milan's Method of Mystagogical Preaching* (Collegeville, MN: Liturgical Press, 2002), n. 12, 34.
94. Peter Brown, *The Body and Society: Men, Women, and Sexual Renunciation in Early Christianity* (New York: Columbia University Press, 1988), 34.
95. *Ibid.*, 341–342, and Satterlee, 35.
96. Peter Brown, 342.

97. Davidson, "Ambrose," 2:1179.
98. *Ibid.*
99. Neil B. McLynn, *Ambrose of Milan: Church and State in a Christian Capital* (Berkeley: University of California Press, 1994), 9–10.
100. Davidson, "Ambrose," 2:1179.
101. *Ibid.*
102. For various scenarios to explain this willingness of both factions to unite behind the same candidate, see McLynn, 4–5.
103. Davidson, "Ambrose," 2:1180.
104. Satterlee, 36.
105. Davidson, "Ambrose," 2:1186.
106. *Ibid.*, 2:1186–1187.
107. Ramsey, *Ambrose*, 25.
108. Ivor Davidson, "Theologians," 1:614.
109. *Ibid.*
110. Davidson, "Ambrose," 2:1176.
111. *Ibid.*
112. Leadbetter, 1:285.
113. Jurgens, 2:84.
114. Andrew Louth, "John Chrysostom and the Antiochene School to Theodoret of Cyrrhus," in *The Cambridge History of Early Christian Literature*, eds. Frances Young, Lewis Ayres, Andrew Louth, and Augustine Casiday (Cambridge: Cambridge University Press, 2004), 345.
115. Dunn-Wilson, 102.
116. van Dam, *Christian*, 12.
117. *Ibid.*
118. Pauline Allen and Wendy Mayer, "John Chrysostom," in *The Early Christian World*, 2:1134.
119. *Ibid.*, 2:1138 and Jurgens, 2:85.
120. Jurgens, 2:85.
121. Allen and Mayer, 2:1138.
122. *Ibid.*, 2:1131.
123. Louth, "Chrysostom," 344.
124. G.W. Newlands, *Hilary of Poitiers: A Study in Theological Method* (Bern, Germany: Peter Lang, 1978), 7.
125. *Ibid.*
126. On how the areas in which he made the application differed from that of contemporary Christians, see Colish, 123–125.
127. Newlands, 7.
128. David G. Hunter, "Fourth-Century Latin Writers: Hilary, Victorinus, Ambrosiaster, Ambrose," in *The Cambridge History of Early Christian Literature*, 302.
129. *Ibid.*, 304.
130. *Hilarius and Constantium*, as quoted by Joan O'Grady, *Heresy: Heretical Truth or Orthodox Error? A Study of Early Christian Heresies* (Longmead, [Britain]: Element, 1985), 89.
131. Chadwick, *Ancient Society*, 290–291.
132. Davidson, "Theologians," 1:611.
133. Hunter, "Writers," 305.
134. Smulders, 1.
135. Conrad Leyser, *Authority and Asceticism from Augustine to Gregory the Great* (Oxford: Clarendon Press, 2000), 3.
136. Andrew Knowles and Pachomios Penkett, *Augustine and His World* (Downers Grove, IL: InterVarsity Press, 2004), 18, 28.
137. *Ibid.*, 29.
138. Rebenich, 5.
139. *Ibid.*
140. Gary Wills, *Saint Augustine's Childhood* (New York: Viking, 2001), 3–4.
141. *Ibid.*, 4.
142. Gareth B. Matthews, *Augustine* (Oxford: Blackwel, 2005), 9.
143. T. Kermit Scott, *Augustine: His Thought in Context* (Mahwah, NJ: Paulist Press, 1995), 71.
144. *Ibid.*, 71, 73.
145. Knowles and Penkett, 45.
146. Henry Chadwick, "Augustine," in *The Cambridge History of Early Christian Literature*, 329.
147. Matthews, 10.
148. Augustine, *Confessions*, 5.13.23, translated by Albert C. Outler, *Nicene and Post-Nicene Fathers* (New York: Christian Literature Publishing Company, 1892), series 2, vol. 4, http://www.ccel.org/a/augustine/confessions/confessions.html (accessed March 2006). All quotations from the *Confessions* are from this source unless otherwise noted.
149. *Ibid.*, 8.12.29 (Internet).
150. Wills, *Childhood*, 127.
151. *Ibid.*, 5.
152. Chadwick, "Augustine," 330.
153. Karl F. Morrison, *Conversion and Text: The Cases of Augustine of Hippo, Herman-Judah, and Constantine Tsatos* (Charlottesville: University Press of Virginia, 1992), 9.
154. Chadwick, "Augustine," 331.
155. *Ibid.*
156. For citations of the sources for their critical beliefs in regard to the Old Testament, see Scott, 75–76.
157. For citations of sources, see *ibid.*, 76.
158. *Ibid.*, 77. For a concise summary of the myth, see 78–80.
159. Knowles and Penkett, 52.
160. Scott, 80.
161. Leyser, 22.
162. See the analysis in *ibid.*, 22–23.
163. *Ibid.*, 24.
164. Davidson, "Theologians," 1:622.
165. Matthews, 8.
166. Chadwick, "Augustine," 337.
167. Matthews, 8.
168. Cf. Morrison, 10.

Chapter 6

1. Bauer, 172.
2. Heikki Raisanen, "Marcion," in *A Companion to Second-Century Christian "Heretics,"* eds. Anti Marjanen and Petri Luomanen (Leiden, Netherlands: Brill, 2005), 101.
3. Justin Martyr, *First Apology*, LVIII, in *Ante-Nicene Fathers* (Buffalo, Christian Literature Publishin, 1885), vol. 2, http://www.ccel.org/ccel/schaff/anf01.viii.ii.html (accessed March 2006).
4. Ludemann, 159, and Antonia Tripolitis, *Religions of the Hellenistic-Roman Age* (Grand Rapids, MI: Wm. B. Eerdmans, 2002), 128.
5. Ludemann, 159.
6. David E. Smith, *The Canonical Function of Acts: A Comparative Analysis* (Collegeville, MN: Michael Glazier/Liturgical Press, 2002), 44.
7. Ludemann, 160.
8. *Ibid.*, 161.

9. David E. Smith, 44.
10. Tripolitis, 128.
11. Hurtado, 491.
12. *Ibid.*
13. Paul J. Achtemeier, Joel B. Green, and Marianne M. Thompson, *Introducing the New Testament: Its Literature and Theology* (Grand Rapids, MI: Wm. B. Eerdmans, 2001), 593.
14. Rodney Stark, *For the Glory of God: How Monotheism Led to Reformations, Science, Witch-Hunts, and the End of Slavery* (Princeton, NJ: Princeton University Press, 2003), 27–28.
15. *Ibid.*, 28.
16. *Ibid.*
17. Ludemann, 165.
18. Cf. Siker, 1:237.
19. Hunt, 16.
20. Siker, 1:237.
21. Raisanen, 113–114.
22. *Ibid.*, 114.
23. Hurtado, 555–556.
24. *Ibid.*, 557.
25. *Ibid.*, 491.
26. Ludemann, 22.
27. David Wright, "Tertullian," in *The Early Christian World*:1027.
28. *Ibid.*
29. Bray, 1:565.
30. Cf. Wright, 2:1027, 1031.
31. J. H. Waszink, "Tertullian's Principles and Methods of Exegesis," in *Early Christian Literature and the Classical Intellectual Tradition,* eds. William R. Schoedel and Robert L. Wilken (Paris: Editions Beauchesne, 1979), 18–19.
32. Ludemann, 22.
33. Jerome, *Famous Men* 53, as quoted by Wright, 2:1027.
34. Bray, 1:565.
35. Tertullian, *Prescription Against Heretics,* in *Ante-Nicene Fathers* (Buffalo, Christian Literature Publishin, 1885), vol. 3, http://www.ccel.org/fathers2/ANF-03/anf03-24.htm#P3679_1237903 (accessed August 2005).
36. Ludemann, 24.
37. Bray, 1:566–567.
38. *Ibid.*, 1:569.
39. Gerald O'Collins, *The Tripersonal God: Understanding and Interpreting the Trinity* (Mahway, NJ: Paulist Press, 1999), 105.
40. James A. Brundage, *Law, Sex, and Christian Society in Medieval Europe* (Chicago: University of Chicago Press, 1987), 64.
41. *Ibid.*, 68–69.
42. Bray, 1:566.
43. *Ibid.*
44. *Ibid.*
45. Peter Brown, 76.
46. *Ibid.*, 79.
47. Miller, 69.
48. *Ibid.*, 67.
49. *Ibid.*, 68.
50. O'Grady, 27.
51. *Ibid.*
52. Bauer, 129.
53. Cf. Ismo Dunderberg, "The School of Valentinus," in *A Companion to Second-Century Christian "Heretics,"* 73.
54. *Ibid.*
55. *Ibid.*, 95.
56. *Ibid.*
57. Bauer, 172.
58. Alastair H. B. Logan, "Gnosticism," in *The Early Christian World,* 2:922.
59. Irenaus, *Against Heresies,* 3.15.2, as quoted by Dunderberg, 64.
60. Dunderberg, 69.
61. *Ibid.*, 69–70.
62. O'Grady, 27.
63. Fred Norris, 2:1015.
64. Hunt, 45–46.
65. *Ibid.*, 47–48.
66. *Ibid.*, 48.
67. Dunderberg, 74.
68. *Ibid.*
69. *Ibid.*
70. O'Grady, 32.
71. Karen Jo Torjesen, "The Episcopacy—Sacredotal or Monarchical? The Appeal to Old Testament Institutions by Cyrpian and the *Didascalia*," in *Studia Patristica*, vol. 36: *Papers Presented at the Eleventh International Conference on Patristic Studies Held in Oxford, 1999*, eds. M.F. Wiles and E.J. Yarnold (Louvain, Belgium: Peeters, 2001), 395.
72. [Unattributed authorship], "Felicissimus," *Catholic Encyclopedia,* http://www.newadvent.org/cathen/06027c.htm (accessed December 2005).
73. Cf. Torjesen, "Episcopacy," 397.
74. For example, Karen Jo Torjesen, "Social and Historical Setting: Christianity as Culture Critique," in *The Cambridge History of Early Christian Literature*, 189, who quotes Cyprian himself on how his rise to power had been secured through a base of popular support.
75. In regard to treatment of subordinates and the unlimited right to excommunicate solely on his own authority, see *ibid.*, "Episcopacy," 395–396.
76. *Ibid.*, "Christianity," 189.
77. G.W. Clarke, *Letters of St. Cyprian of Carthage* (Ramsey, NJ: Paulist Press, 1984), 10.
78. Torjesen, "Episcopacy," 396.
79. *Ibid.*
80. *Ibid.*, "Christianity," 189.
81. *Ibid.*, "Episcopacy," 396.
82. J. Vernon Bartlet, *Early Church History: A Sketch of the First Four Centuries* (reprint, [n.p.]: Kessinge, 2004), 120.
83. Clarke, 11.
84. *Ibid.*, 17.
85. Louth, "Later Theologians," 1:582–583, and Rankin, 2:977.
86. Louth, "Later Theologians," 1:585.
87. On their Biblical proof texts, see S.L. Greenslade, "Heresy and Schism in the Later Roman Empire," in *Schism, Heresy and Religious Protest,* ed. Derek Baker (Cambridge: At the University Press, 1972), 11.
88. *Ibid.*
89. *Ibid.*
90. Louth, "Later Theologians," 1:582.
91. Leadbetter, 2:1080.
92. Rankin, 2:976.
93. Leyerle Blake, "Communication and Travel," in *The Early Christian World,* 1:470.
94. Leadbetter, "Constantine," 2:1080.
95. Brakke, 2:1105.

96. *Ibid.*, 2:1104.
97. Louth, "Later Theologians," 1:583.
98. A.I.C. Heron, "Homoousios with the Father," in *The Incarnation: Ecumenical Studies in the Nicene-Constantinopolitan Creed, A.D. 381*, ed. Thomas F. Torrance (Edinburgh: Handrel Press, 1981), 65.
99. Heron, 63, and Louth, "Later Theologians," 1:583.
100. Cf. Davidson, "Theologians," 1:609.
101. Elliott, 231.
102. *Ibid.* 231.
103. *Ibid.*, 241, 242, 277, 278–283.
104. Kannengiesser, "Athanasius," 209.
105. Michael R. Barnes and Daniel H. Williams, "Introduction," in *Arianism after Arius: Essays on the Development of the Fourth Century Trinitarian Conflicts*, eds. Michel R. Barnes and Daniel H. Williams (Edinburgh: T & T Clark, 1993), xiv. 106. Wiles, 40–41.
107. A. Momigliano, "Christianity and the Decline of the Roman Empire," in *The Conflict between Paganism and Christianity in the Fourth Century*, ed. Arnaldo Momigliano (Oxford: Clarendon Press, 1963), 10.
108. Leadbetter, "Theodosius," 1:284.
109. Davidson, "Theologians," 1:610.
110. William A. Sumruled, *Augustine and the Arians: The Bishop of Hippo's Encounters with Ulfilan Arianism* (Selinsgrove: Susquehanna University Press, 1994), 28.
111. *Ibid.*, 28–29.
112. *Ibid.*, 30–31.
113. *Ibid.*, 31.
114. *Ibid.*, 158–159.
115. *Ibid.*, 31.
116. Elm, 132.
117. Christine Trevett, "Montanism," in *The Early Christian World*, 2:929. For a description of the development in these two regions see 941–945.
118. Elm, 132.
119. Trevett, 2:929.
120. *Ibid.*, 2:930.
121. Eusebius, *Church History*, v.3.4, in *Nicene and Post-Nicene Fathers* (New York: Christian Literature Publishing Company, 1892), series 2, vol. 2, http://www.ccel.org/fathers2/NPNF2-01/Npnf2-01-10.htm#P2729_1313445 (accessed March 2006).
122. Sheila E. McGinn, "Internal Renewal and Dissent in the Early Christian World," in *The Early Christian World*, 2:903–904.
123. *Ibid.*, 2:904.
124. Trevett, 2:930.
125. Stuart G. Hall, "Women among the Early Martyrs," in *Martyrs and Martyrologies*, ed. Diana Wood (Oxford: Blackwel, 1993), 14.
126. Edwards, 1:319.
127. Trevett, 2:930.
128. *Ibid.*, 2:932.
129. Greenslade, 5.
130. Hall, "Martyrs," 20.
131. Elaine C. Hubert, *Women and the Authority of Inspiration: A Reexamination of Two Prophetic Movements From a Contemporary Feminist Perspective* (Lanham, MD: University Press of America, 1985), 40.
132. Cf. *ibid.*, 37.
133. Trevett, 2:931.
134. Hippolytus, *Refutation of all Heresies*, VIII.12, in *Ante-Nicene Fathers* (Buffalo, Christian Literature Publishing, 1885), vol. 2, http://www.ccel.org/fathers2/ANF-05/anf05-12.htm#P2023_625620 (accessed March 2006).
135. *Ibid.*
136. Trevett, 2:939.
137. For citations, see Antti Marjanen, "Montanism: Egalitarian Ecstatic 'New Prophecy,'" in *A Companion to Second-Century Christian "Heretics,"* 197–198.
138. Trevett, 2:939.
139. *Ibid.*
140. Hubert, 219.
141. *Ibid.*, 219–220.
142. *Ibid.*, 140.
143. *Ibid.*, 218.
144. *Ibid.*, 220.
145. Trevett, 2:937, among others, finds this reconstruction unconvincing.
146. *Ibid.*
147. McGinn, 2:904.
148. Trevett, 2:934.
149. Hubert, 221.
150. *Ibid.*
151. *Ibid.*
152. *Ibid.*, 220.
153. See the citations in Marjanen, 197–198.
154. Trevett, 2:941.
155. Hubert, 221.
156. *Ibid.*
157. Marjanen, 189.
158. Hubert, 222.
159. Leadbetter, "Theodosius," 1:259.
160. Davidson, "Theologians," 1:606.
161. *Ibid.*, 1:607.
162. James Alexander, "Donatism," in *The Early Christian World*, 2:952–953.
163. Cf. Davidson, "Theologians," 1:607.
164. For a description, see Alexander, 2:958–962.
165. Davidson, "Theologians," 1:608.
166. *Ibid.*
167. Alexander, 2:962.
168. Greenslade, 10.
169. Also known as Jovianus.
170. Jerome, "Against Jovinianus," in *Nicene and Post-Nicene Fathers* (New York: Christian Literature Publishin, 1892), series 2, vol. 6, http://www.ccel.org/fathers2/NPNF2-06/Npnf2-06-09.htm#TopOfPage (accessed December 2005).
171. R. A. Markus, *End of Ancient Christianity* (Cambridge: Cambridge University Press, 1990), 40.
172. Matthew Kuefler, *The Manly Eunuch: Masculinity, Gender Ambiguity, and Christian Ideology in Late Antiquity* (Chicago: University of Chicago Press, 2001), 185.
173. Warren S. Smith, "Satiric Advice: Serious or Not?" in *Satiric Advice on Women and Marriage: From Plautus to Chaucer*, edited by Warren S. Smith (Ann Arbor: University of Michigan Press, 2005), 18–19.
174. David D. Hunter, "Sex, Sin, and Salvation: What Augustine Really Said," lecture at the Washington Theological Union, http://www.wtu.edu/news/lectures/Augustine_Lec1_text.htm (accessed December 2005).
175. Markus, *Ancient*, 45.
176. Kim E. Power, "The Rehablitation of Eve," originally appeared in *Religion in the Ancient World: New Themes and Approaches*, ed. M. Dillon (Amster-

dam: Hakkert, [n.d.]), http://www.womenpriests.org/theology/power3.asp (accessed December 2005).

177. *Ibid.*
178. Wilson and Makowski, 48.
179. Jordan Aumann, "Monasticism in the West," chapter 4 of his *Christian Spirituality in the Catholic Tradition,* http://www.op.org/domcentral/study/aumann/cs/cs04.htm (accessed December 2005).
180. For example, Markus, *Ancient,* 39. Markus argues (n. 49, 76) that the assault on Jovinian for a more "permissive" monastic lifestyle only makes sense if Jovinian continued to count himself as one.
181. Markus, *Ancient,* 39.
182. For detailed argumentation, see Karl O. Sandnes, *Belly and Body in the Pauline Epistles* (Cambridge: Cambridge University Press, 2002), 240.
183. Elizabeth A. Clark, "Dissuading from Marriage: Jerome and the Ascetization of Satire," in *Satiric Advice on Women and Marriage: From Plautus to Chaucer,* ed. Warren S. Smith (Ann Arbor: University of Michigan Press, 2005), 162. Some do not see any inconsistency in these two lines of argument (Sandnes, 240), though that seems a difficult proposition to uphold.
184. Greer, 140.
185. Cloke, 40–41, and Elizabeth A. Clark, Elizabeth, *Women in the Early Church* (Collegeville, MN: Michael Glazier/Liturgical Press, 1983), 126.
186. Wilson and Makowski, 54.
187. *Ibid.*
188. Chadwick, *Ancient Society,* 357.
189. Ben Witherington, *The Gospel of Mark: A Socio-Rhetorical Commentary* (Grand Rapids, MI: Wm. B. Eerdmans, 2001), 193–194.
190. John H. Blunt, *Dictionary of Sects, Heresies, Ecclesiastical Parties, and Schools of Religious Thought* (London: Rivingtons, 1874), 7, and George H. Tavard, *The Thousand Faces of the Virgin Mary* (Collegeville, MN: Liturgical Press, 1996), 64.
191. Tavard, 64.
192. Blunt, 76.
193. *Ibid.*, 32.
194. John J. Pasquini, *True Christianity: The Catholic Way* ([n.p.]: iUniverse, [n.d.]), 371.
195. As quoted by J.N. Hillgarth, ed., *Christianity and Paganism, 350–750: The Conversion of Western Europe,* revised edition ([n.p.]: University of Pennsylvania Press, 1986), 136.
196. Stephen J. Shoemaker, *The Ancient Traditions of the Virgin Mary's Dormition and Assumption* (Oxford: Oxford University Press, 2002), 14.
197. *Ibid.*, 26.
198. *Ibid.*, 14.

Chapter 7

1. Monika Pesthy, " 'Mulier est Instrumentum Diaboli': Women and the Desert Fathers," in *The Wisdom of Egypt: Jewish, Early Christian, and Gnostic Essays in Honor of Gerald P. Luttikhuizen,* eds. Hilhorst and George H. van Kooten (Leiden, Netherlands: Brill, 2005), 360, who provides examples of the shift from Clement of Alexandria and the pseudo-Chrysostom homily describing the martyrdom of Thecla.
2. Columba Stuart, "Monasticism," in *The Early Christian World,*1:346–347.
3. For the inferential evidence see *ibid.*, 1:347.
4. *Ibid.*, 1:349.
5. Blake, 1:464.
6. *Epistle* 2.2, as quoted by James W. McKinnon, "Music," in *The Early Christian World,* 2:784–785.
7. *Ibid.*, 2:785.
8. For quotations, see *ibid.*, 2:786–787.
9. Momigliano, "Decline," 11.
10. W.H.C. Frend, "Town and Countryside in Early Christianity," in *The Church in Town and Countryside,* ed. Derek Baker (Oxford: Basil Blackwell, 1979), 28.
11. Edwards, 1:327.
12. Cf. Frend, "Town," 28.
13. *Ibid.*, 27.
14. *Ibid.*
15. Athanasius, *Life of Antony,* Chapter 5, in *Nicene and Post-Nicene Fathers;* series 2, vol. 4, *Medieval Sourcebook,* http://www.fordham.edu/Halsall/basis-/vita-antony.html (accessed March 2006).
16. Leadbetter, "Constantine," 1:1099.
17. Columba Stuart, "Antony of the Desert," in *The Early Christian World,* 2:1092, 1095.
18. Leadbetter, 1:1096–1097.
19. Dunn, *Monasticism,* 10.
20. See the discussion in *ibid.*, 16–17.
21. Stuart, "Antony," 2:1088.
22. Dunn, *Monasticism,* 9–10.
23. Stuart, "Antony," 2:1090.
24. *Ibid.*, 2:1091.
25. Holly Roberts, *Vegetarian Christian Saints: Mystics, Ascetics & Monks* (Washington: Anjeli Press, 2004), 27.
26. *Ibid.*
27. Martha A. Kirk, *Women of Bible Lands: A Pilgrimage to Compassion and Wisdom* (Collegeville, MN: Liturgical Press, 2004), 232.
28. Stuart, "Monasticism," 1:351.
29. Carolinne White, "General Introduction," in *Early Christian Lives,* ed. Caroline White (London: Penguin, 1998), xx.
30. Chadwick, *Ancient Society,* 401.
31. Stuart, "Monasticism," 1:352.
32. Comfort, 69. For ancient Bible manuscripts that were likely either copies by his monks or preserved in their first monastery, see 68–70.
33. William A. Graham, *Beyond the Written Word: Oral Aspects of Scripture in the History of Religion* (Cambridge: Cambridge University Press, 1987; paperback edition, 1993), 138.
34. Chadwick, *Ancient Society,* 404, and Jill Kamil, *Christianity in the Land of the Pharaohs: The Coptic Orthodox Church* (London: Routledge, 2002), 125.
35. Clifford R. Backman, *The Worlds of Medieval Europe* (New York: Oxford University Press, 2003), 71.
36. Kamil, 126.
37. Backman, 71.
38. Chadwick, *Ancient Society,* 402.
39. Cf. the comments of Graham, n. 67, 231.
40. Backman, 71.
41. Kamil, 125.
42. Leslie M. Bernard, "Athanasius and the Pachomians," in *Studia Patristica 32, Athanasius and His Opponents, Cappadocian Fathers, Other Greek Writers after Nicaea,* ed. Elizabeth A. Livingstone (Leuven, Belgium: Peeters, 1997), 4–5.
43. Carolinne White, "General Introduction," xxi.

44. *Ibid.*, xxii.
45. For a survey of the literature attributed, sometimes falsely, to these men, see Tito Orlandi, "Coptic Literature," in *The Roots of Egyptian Christianity,* eds. Birger A. Pearson and James E. Goehring (Philadelphia: Fortress, 1986), 60–63.
46. *Ibid.*, 63.
47. Nicholas Sagovsky, *Ecumenism, Christian Origins and the Practice of Communion* (Cambridge: Cambridge University Press, 2000), 151.
48. Armand Veilleux, "Monasticism and Gnosis in Egypt," in *The Roots of Egyptian Christianity,* ed. Birger A. Pearson and James E. Goehring (Philadelphia: Fortress Press, 1986), 276.
49. James E. Goehring, New Frontiers in Pachomian Studies," in *The Roots of Egyptian Christianity,* eds. Birger A. Pearson and James E. Goehring (Philadelphia: Fortress, 1986), 236, 242.
50. *Ibid.*, 243–244.
51. *Ibid.*, 246.
52. *Ibid.*, 244–245.
53. Bernard, 7, 11.
54. For a consideration of the pros and cons of a monastic tie in to explain the origin of the discovered works see Goehring, 247–252.
55. *Ibid.*, 237, 252–253.
56. Also known as Maria.
57. Pieternella van Doorn-Harder, *Contemporary Coptic Nuns* (Columbia: University of South Carolina Press, 1995), 52, and Terry G. Wilfong, " 'Friendship and Physical Desire': The Discourse of Female Homoeroticism in Fifth Century C.E. Egypt," in *Among Women: From the Homosocial to the Homoerotic in the Ancient World,* eds. Nancy Sorkin Rabinowitz and Lisa Auanger (Austin: University of Texas Press, 2002), 307.
58. Wilfong, 307.
59. *Ibid.*, 30, 308, and Edwards, 1:327.
60. Palladius, *Lausiac History,* chapter 33, *Medieval Source Book,* translated by W.K.L. Clark (New York: Macmillan, 1918), http://www.fordham.edu/halsall/basis/palladius-lausiac.html#CHAPTER%20XXXII:%20PACHOMIUS%20AND%20THE%20TABENNESIOTS (accessed April 2006).
61. Kirk, 52.
62. Elizabeth A. Clark, *Jerome, Chrysostom, and Friends: Essays and Translations* (New York: Edwin Mellen Press, 1979), n. 153, 34.
63. *Ibid.*, 20.
64. Peter Brown, 344.
65. *Ibid.*, 343–344.
66. Kirk, 52.
67. Satterlee, 34. For the controversy over exactly when in the year this happened, see Edmund K. Chambers, *The Mediaeval Stage* (London: Oxford University Press, 1903; reprint, Toronto, Canada: General Publishing, 1996), n. 3, 239.
68. Jurgens, 2:171.
69. Satterlee, 35–36.
70. Curran, 274.
71. Omer Englebert, *The Lives of the Saints* (1951; reprint, Barnes & Noble, 1994), 275.
72. Satterlee, 8.
73. Boniface Ramsey, "Ambrose," in *First Christian Theologians,* edited by G.R. Evans (Oxford: Blackwell, 2004), 230.
74. Patricia Ranft, *Women and the Religious Life in Premodern Europe* (1996; reprint, New York: Palgrave Macmillan, 1998), 4–5.
75. Patricia Ranft, *Woman's Way: The Forgotten History of Women Spiritual Directors* (New York: Palgrave, 2000), 39.
76. Ambrose, Letter 20, *The Letters of Saint Ambrose of Milan,* translated by E.B.P. (Oxford: James Parker, 1881), http://www.tertullian.org/fathers/ambrose_letters_00_intro.htm (accessed April 2006).
77. David G. Hunter, "Clerical Celibacy and the Veiling of Virgins: New Boundaries in Late Ancient Christianity," in *The Limits of Ancient Christianity: Essays on Late Antique Thought and Culture,* eds. William E Klingshirn and Mark Vessey (Ann Arbor: University of Michigan Press, 1999), 143.
78. Anne E. Hickey, *Women of the Roman Aristocracy as Christian Monastics* (Ann Arbor: University of Michigan Research Press, 1987), 22.
79. Dunn, *Monasticism,* 48.
80. *Ibid.*
81. Marilyn R. Dunn, "Spiritual Philanthropists: Women as Convent Patrons in Seicento Rome," in *Women and Art in Early Modern Europe: Patrons, Collectors, and Connoisseurs,* ed. Cynthia Lawrence (University Park, PA: University of Pennsylvania Press, 1997), 181.
82. Ranft, *Directors,* 40.
83. Dunn, *Monasticism,* 48.
84. *Ibid.*, 49; cf. 61.
85. Dunn, 49.
86. Dietz, 126.
87. Dunn, *Monasticism,* 49.
88. *Ibid.*, 49, 57.
89. Jerome's version of the text, as quoted by Dietz, 127, though attributing it to Psalms 38:18.
90. Dunn, *Monasticism,* 50.
91. *Ibid.*
92. *Ibid.*, 57.
93. *Ibid.*
94. Dietz, 128.
95. *Ibid.*
96. Cf. Dunn, *Monasticism,* 50.
97. *Ibid.*
98. *Ibid.*, 50, sees Jerome as implying the division on the basis of class. Hickey, 31, notes that the text is actually ambiguous as to the basis of the division but concedes that the class consciousness of the Roman mind makes any other basis unlikely.
99. Hickey, 31.
100. Mary E. O'Brien, *Spirituality in Nursing: Standing on Holy Ground,* 2nd edition (Sudbury, MA: Jones and Bartlett, 2003), 27.
101. Cf. Dunn, *Monasticism,* 50.
102. *Ibid.*, 51, 69.
103. Ranft, *Premodern,* 6.
104. *Ibid.*
105. *Ibid.*
106. *Ibid.*
107. Jerome, Letter 108.27, in *Nicene and Post-Nicene Fathers* (New York: Christian Literature Publishing, 1892), series 2, vol. 6, http://www.ccel.org/fathers2/NPNF2-06/Npnf2-06-03.htm#TopOfPage (accessed April 2006).
108. Hickey, 24.
109. Jerome, Letter 108.29–31, in *Nicene and Post-Nicene Fathers.*

Bibliography

PRIMARY SOURCES

Ambrose. *The Letters of Saint Ambrose of Milan.* Translated by E.B.P. Oxford: James Parker, 1881. Available online at http://www.tertullian.org/fathers/ambrose_letters_00_intro.htm (accessed April 2006).

Athanasius. *Life of Antony.* In *Nicene and Post-Nicene Fathers,* series 2, vol. 4. Available online at *Medieval Source Book,* http://www.fordham.edu/Halsall/basis/vita-antony.html (accessed March 2006).

Augustine. *Confessions.* Translated by Albert C. Outler. Philadelphia: Westminster Press, 1955. (Library of Christian Classics, v. 7). Available online at http://www.ccel.org/a/augustine/confessions/confessions.html (accessed March 2006).

Cassius, Dio. *Roman History* (Book LXXII). Available online at http://www.penelope.uchicago.edu/Thayer/E/Roman/Texts/Cassius_Dio/72*.html (accessed April 2006).

Clement. *Second Clement.* Translated by J. B. Lightfoot. In *Apostolic Fathers* (1885). Available online at http://www.earlychristianwritings.com/text/2clement-hoole.html (accessed February 2006).

Eusebius. *Church History.* In *Nicene and Post-Nicene Fathers,* series 2, vol. 2. New York: Christian Literature Publishing Company, 1892. Available online at http://www.ccel.org/fathers2/NPNF2-01/Npnf2-01-10.htm#P2729_1313445 (accessed March 2006).

Hermas. *The Pastor of Hermas.* In *Ante-Nicene Fathers,* vol. 2. Buffalo, Christian Literature Publishing Company, 1885. Available online at http://www.ccel.org/fathers2/ANF-02/anf02-04.htm#TopOfPage (accessed March 2006).

Hippolytus. *Refutation of all Heresies.* In *Ante-Nicene Fathers,* vol. 2. Buffalo, Christian Literature Publishing Company, 1885. Available online at http://www.ccel.org/fathers2/ANF-05/anf05-12.htm#P2023_625620 (accessed March 2006).

Ignatius of Antioch. *Ignatius of Antioch.* Three translations. Available online at http://www.earlychristianwritings.com/ignatius.html (accessed February 2006).

Jerome. "Against Jovinianus." In *Nicene and Post-Nicene Fathers,* series 2, vol. 6. New York: Christian Literature Publishing Company, 1892. Available online at http://www.ccel.org/fathers2/NPNF2-06/Npnf2-06-09.htm#TopOfPage (accessed December 2005).

_____. "Letters." In *Nicene and Post-Nicene Fathers,* series 2, vol. 6. New York: Christian Literature Publishing, 1892. Available online at http://www.ccel.org/fathers2/NPNF2-06/Npnf2-06-03.htm#TopOfPage (accessed April 2006).

Justin Martyr. *First Apology,* LVIII. In *Ante-Nicene Fathers,* vol. 2. Buffalo, Christian Literature Publishing, 1885). Available online at http://www.ccel.org/ccel/schaff/anf01.viii.ii.html (accessed March 2006).

Palladius. *Lausiac History.* Translated by W.K.L. Clark. New York: Macmillan, 1918. Available online at *Medieval Source Book,* http://www.fordham.edu/halsall/basis/palladius-lausiac.html#CHAPTER%20XXXII:%20PACHOMIUS%20AND%20THE%20TABENNESIOTS (accessed April 2006).

Perpetua. *The Passion of Saints Perpetua and Felicity.* Translated by W.H. Shrewring. London: 1931. Available online at *Medieval Source Book,* http://www.fordham.edu/HALSALL/source/perpetua.html (accessed April 2006).

Proba, Falconia (aka Faltonia). "Cento." Translated by Jeremy Reedy. In *A Lost Tradition: Women Writers of the Early Church* (45–69), edited by Patricia Wilson-Kastner. Washington, DC: University Press of America, 1981.

Prudentius. *The Hymns of Prudentius.* Translated by Martin R. Pope. London: J.M. Dent, 1805. Available online at http://www.gutenberg.org/files/14959/14959-h/14959-h.htm (accessed December 2005).

Tertullian. *First Apology.* In *Ante-Nicene Fathers,* vol. 3. Buffalo, Christian Literature Publishing, 1885). Available online at http://www.ccel.org/fathers2/ANF-03/anf03-05.htm (accessed March 2006).

_____. *Prescription Against Heretics.* In *Ante-Nicene Fathers,* vol. 3. Buffalo, Christian Literature Publishing, 1885). Available online at http://www.ccel.org/fathers2/ANF-03/anf03-24.htm#P3679_1237903 (accessed August 2005).

SECONDARY SOURCES

Achtemeier, Paul J., Joel B. Green, and Marianne M. Thompson. *Introducing the New Testament: Its Literature and Theology.* Grand Rapids, MI: Wm. B. Eerdmans, 2001.

Adler, William. "Eusebius' *Chronicle* and Its Legacy." In *Eusebius, Christianity, and Judaism* (467–491), edited by Harold W. Attridge and Gohel Hata. Leiden, Netherlands: Brill, 1992.

Albl, Martin C. *And Scripture Cannot Be Broken: The Form and Function of the Early Christian Testimonia Collections.* Leiden, Netherlands: Brill, 1999

Alexander, James. "Donatism." In *The Early Christian World* (2:952-974), edited by Philip K. Esler. London: Routledge, 2000.

Allen, Pauline, and Wendy Mayer. "John Chrysostom." In *The Early Christian World* (2:1128-1150), edited by Philip K. Esler. London: Routledge, 2000.

Amory, Patrick. *People and Identity in Ostrogothic Italy,* 489–554. Cambridge: Cambridge University Press, 1997; paperback edition, 2003.

Amundsen, Daniel W., and Gary B. Ferngren. "Philanthropy in Medicine: Some Historical Perspectives." In *Beneficence and Health Care* (1–32), edited by Earl E. Shelp. Dordrecht, Holland: D. Reidel, 1982.

Anatolios, Khaled. *Athanasius.* London: Routledge, 2004.

Ando, Clifford. *Imperial Ideology and Provincial Loyalty in the Roman Empire.* Berkeley: University of California Press, 2000.

Arnold, Duane Wade-Hampton. *The Early Episcopal Career of Athanasius of Alexandria.* Notre Dame, IN: University of Notre Dame Press, 1991.

Backman, Clifford R. *The Worlds of Medieval Europe.* New York: Oxford University Press, 2003.

Bakker, Henk. "Potamiaena: Some Observations about Martyrdom and Gender in Ancient Alexandria." In *The Wisdom of Egypt: Jewish, Early Christian, and Gnostic Essays in Honor of Gerald P. Luttikhuizen* (331-350), edited by Anthony Hilhorst and George H. van Kooten. Leiden, Netherlands: Brill, 2005.

Barnes, Michel R., and Daniel H. Williams. "Introduction." In *Arianism after Arius: Essays on the Development of the Fourth Century Trinitarian Conflicts* (xiii-xvii), edited by Michel R. Barnes and Daniel H. Williams. Edinburgh: T & T Clark, 1993.

Barnes, Timothy D. *Athanasius and Constantinius.* Cambridge, MA: Harvard University Press, 1993.

Bartlet, J. Vernon. *Early Church History: A Sketch of the First Four Centuries.* Reprint, [N.p.]: Kessinger, 2004.

Barton, Carlin. "Honor and Sacredness in the Roman and Christian Worlds." In *Sacrificing the Self: Perspectives on Martyrdom and Religion* (23-38), edited by Margaret Cormack. New York: Oxford University Press, 2002.

Bateman, Herbert W. *Authentic Worship: Scripture's Voice, Applying Its Truth.* Grand Rapids, MI: Kregel, 2002.

Bauer, Walter. *Orthodoxy and Heresy in Earliest Christianity.* Translated from the 1934 2nd German ed. Philadelphia: Fortress, 1971.

Berding, Kenneth. *Polycarp and Paul: An Analysis of Their Literary and Theological Relationship in Light of Polycarp's Use of Biblical and Extra-Biblical Literature.* Leiden, Netherlands: Brill, 2002.

Bernard, Leslie M. "Athanasius and the Pachomians." In *Studia Patristica.* Vol. 32, *Athanasius and His Opponents, Cappadocian Fathers, Other Greek Writers after Nicaea,* edited by Elizabeth A. Livingstone, 3–11. Leuven, Belgium: Peeters Publishers, 1997.

Besserman, Lawrence. "The Challenge of Periodization: Old Paradigms and New Perspectives." In *The Challenge of Periodization: Old Paradigms and New Perspectives* (3–28), edited by Lawrence Besserman. New York: Garland, 1996.

Betz, Hans D., ed. *The Greek Magical Papyri in Translation: Including the Demotic Spells.* Chicago: University of Chicago Press, 1992; paperback edition, 1996.

Black, C. Clifton. *Mark: Images of an Apostolic Interpreter.* Columbia: University of South Carolina Press, 1994.

Blake, Layerle. "Communication and Travel." In *The Early Christian World* (vol. 1:452-474), edited by Philip K. Esler. London: Routledge, 2000.

Blunt, John H. *Dictionary of Sects, Heresies, Ecclesiastical Parties, and Schools of Religious Thought.* London: Rivingtons, 1874.

Boer, Harry R. *A Short History of the Early Church.* Grand Rapids, MI: Wm. B. Eerdmans, 1976.

Borgen, Peter. "Philo of Alexandria as Exegete." In *A History of Biblical Interpretation* (114–143), edited by Alan J. Hauser and Duane F Watson. Grand Rapids, MI: Wm. B. Eerdmans, 2003.

Bowder, Diana. *The Age of Constantine and Julian.* New York: Barnes & Noble, 1978.

Bowersock, G. W. *Martyrdom and Rome.* Cambridge: Cambridge University Press, 1995; 2002, paperback edition.

Boys, Mary C. *Has God Only One Blessing?: Judaism as a Source of Christian Self-Understanding.* Mahwah, NJ: Paulist Press, 2000.

Brakke, David. "Athanasius." In *The Early Christian World* (2:1102-1127), edited by Philip K. Esler. London: Routledge, 2000.

Bray, Gerald. "The Early Theologians." In *The Early Christian World* (vol. 1: 553–579), edited by Philip K. Esler. London: Routledge, 2000.

Brent, Allen. *Hippolytus and the Roman Church in the Third Century: Communities in Tension Before the*

Emergence of a Monarch-Bishop. Leiden, Netherlands: Brill, 1995.

Brock, Sebastian P. "Ephrem and the Syriac Tradition." In *The Cambridge History of Early Christian Literature* (362–374), edited by Frances Young, Lewis Ayres, Andrew Louth, and Augustine Casiday. Cambridge: Cambridge University Press, 2004.

Brooten, Bernadette J. *Love Between Women: Early Christian Responses to Female Homoeroticism*. Chicago, IL: University of Chicago Press, 1996.

Brown, Dennis. "Jerome." In *The Early Christian World* (vol. 2: 1151–1174), edited by Philip K. Esler. London: Routledge, 2000.

Brown, Peter. *The Body and Society: Men, Women, and Sexual Renunciation in Early Christianity*. New York: Columbia University Press, 1988.

Brown, Raymond E., and John P Meier. *Antioch and Rome: New Testament Cradles of Catholic Christianity*. Mahwah, NJ: Paulist Press, 1983, 2004.

Browning, Robert. "History." In *The Later Principate: The Cambridge History of Classical Literature* (50–72), edited by E. J. Kenney and W. V. Clausen. Cambridge: University of Cambridge Press, 1983.

———. "Minor Figures." In *Cambridge History of Classical Literature* (770–773), edited by P.E. Easterling and R.J. Kenney. Cambridge: Cambridge University Press, 1982; 1996 reprint.

Brundage, James A. *Law, Sex, and Christian Society in Medieval Europe*. Chicago, IL: University of Chicago Press, 1987.

Buell, Denise K. *Making Christians: Clement of Alexandria and the Rhetoric of Legitimacy*. Princeton, NJ: Princeton University Press, 1999.

Burns, J. Patout. *Cyprian the Bishop*. London: Routledge, 2002.

Bush, L. Russ, ed. *Classical Readings in Christian Apologetics, A.D. 100–1800: A. D. 100–1800*. Grand Rapids, MI: Zondervan, 1983.

Carriker, Andrew. *The Library of Eusebius of Caesarea*. Leiden, Netherlands: Brill, 2003.

Carruthers, Mary J. *The Craft of Thought: Meditation, Rhetoric, and the Making of Images, 400–1200*. Cambridge: Cambridge University Press, 1998.

Carson, D.A. *Gospel According to John*. Grand Rapids, MI: Wm. B. Eerdmans, 1991.

Chadwick, Henry. "Augustine." In *The Cambridge History of Early Christian Literature* (328–341), edited by Frances Young, Lewis Ayres, Andrew Louth, and Augustine Casiday. Cambridge: Cambridge University Press, 2004.

———. *The Church in Ancient Society: From Galilee to Gregory the Great*. Oxford: Oxford University Press, 2001.

Chambers, Edmund K. *The Mediaeval Stage*. London: Oxford University Press, 1903; reprint, Toronto, Canada: General Publishing, 1996.

Chester, Andrew. "The Parting of the Ways: Eschatology and Messianic Hope." In *Jews and Christians: The Parting of the Ways, A.D. 70 to 135* (239–314), edited by James D.G. Dunn. 1992; new edition with additional English translations, Grand Rapids, MI: Wm. B. Eerdmans, 1999.

Childs, Brevard S. *The Struggle to Understand Isaiah as Christian Scripture*. Grand Rapids, MI: Wm. B. Eerdmans, 2004.

Clark, Elizabeth A. "Dissuading from Marriage: Jerome and the Ascetization of Satire." In *Satiric Advice on Women and Marriage: From Plautus to Chaucer* (154–181), edited by Warren S. Smith. Ann Arbor, MI: University of Michigan Press, 2005.

———. *Jerome, Chrysostom, and Friends: Essays and Translations*. New York: Edwin Mellen, 1979.

———. *Women in the Early Church*. Collegeville, MN: Michael Glazier/Liturgical Press, 1983.

Clarke, G.W. *Letters of St. Cyprian of Carthage*. Ramsey, NJ: Paulist Press, 1984.

Cloke, Gillian. *This Female Man of God: Women and Spiritual Power in the Patristic Age, AD 350–450*. London: Routledge, 1995.

Cohen, Jeremy *Living Letters of the Law*. Berkeley: University of California Press, 1999.

Colish, Marcia. *Stoic Tradition from Antiquity to the Early Middle Ages*. Leiden, Netherlands: Brill, 1990.

Comfort, Philip W. *Essential Guide to Bible Versions*. [N.p.]: Tyndale, 2000.

Conybeare, Catherine. *Paulinus Noster: Self and Symbols in the Letters of Paulinus of Nola*. Oxford: Oxford University Press, 2000.

Countryman, Louis W. *Living on the Border of the Holy: Renewing the Priesthood of All*. Harrisburg, PA: Morehouse, 1999.

Crislip, Andrew T. *From Monastery to Hospital: Christian Monasticism and the Transformation of Health Care in Late Antiquity*. [N.p.]: University of Michigan Press, 2005.

Curran, John. *Pagan City and Christian Capital: Rome in the Fourth Century*. Oxford: Oxford University Press, 2000.

Cutts, Edward L. *History of Early Christian Art*. 1893. Reprint, [N.p.]: Kessinger, 2004.

Dahmus, Joseph. *A History of the Middle Ages*. New York: Barnes and Noble, 1968.

Dallen, James. *The Reconciling Community: The Rite of Penance*. Collegeville, MN: Liturgical Press, 1991.

Davidson, Ivor. "Ambrose." In *The Early Christian World* (vol. 2: 1175–1204), edited by Philip K. Esler. London: Routledge, 2000.

———. "Later Theologians of the West." In *The Early Christian World*, (vol. 1: 602–635), edited by Philip K. Esler. London: Routledge, 2000.

Davis, Leo D. *The First Seven Ecumenical Councils: Their History & Theology*. Collegeville, MN: Liturgical Press, 1983.

Dickie, Matthew. *Magic and Magicians in the*

Greco-Roman World. London, England: Routledge, 2001, 2003.

Dietz, Maribel. *Wandering Monks, Virgins, and Pilgrims: Ascetic Travel in the Mediterranean World, 300–800*. University Park, PA: Pennsylvania State University, 2005.

Dihle, Albretch. *Greek and Latin Literature of the Roman Empire: From Augustus to Justinian*. English translation. London: Routledge, 1994.

Drjivers, Han J. W. *East of Antioch: Studies in Eastern Christianity*. London: Varioum Reprints, 1984.

Dronke, Peter. *Women Writers of the Middle Ages: A Critical Study of Texts from Perpetua (Died 203) to Marguerite Porete (Died 1310)*. Cambridge: Cambridge: University Press, 1984.

Dunderberg, Ismo. "The School of Valentinus." In *A Companion to Second-Century Christian "Heretics"* (64–99), edited by Antti Marjanen and Petri Luomanen. Leiden, Netherlands: Brill, 2005.

Dunn, Marilyn. *The Emergence of Monasticism: From the Desert Fathers to the Early Middle Ages*. Oxford: Blackwell Publishing, 2000.

———. "Spiritual Philanthropists: Women as Convent Patrons in Seicento Rome." In *Women and Art in Early Modern Europe: Patrons, Collectors, and Connoisseurs*, (154–188), edited by Cynthia Lawrence. University Park, PA: University of Pennsylvania Press, 1997.

Dunn-Wilson, David. *A Mirror for the Church: Preaching in the First Five Centuries*. Grand Rapids, MI: Wm. B. Eerdmans, 2005.

Edwards, Mark. "The Development of Office in the Early Church." In *The Early Christian World* (vol. 1:316–329), edited by Philip K. Esler. London: Routledge, 2000.

Elliott, T.G. *The Christianity of Constantine the Great*. Scranton, PA: University of Scranton Press, 1996.

Elm, Susanna. "Montanist Oracles." In *Searching the Scriptures: A Feminist Commentary* (vol. 2:131–138). New York: Crossroad, 1994.

Englebert, Omer. *The Lives of the Saints*. 1951; reprint, Barnes & Noble, 1994.

Evenepol, W. "The Place of Poetry in Latin Christianity." In *Early Christian Poetry: A Collection of Essays* (35–60), edited by J. den Boef and A. Hillhorst. Leiden, Netherlands: Brill, 1993.

Ewert, David. *General Introduction to the Bible: From Ancient Tablets to Modern Translations*. Grand Rapids, MI: Zondervan, 1990.

Finn, Thomas M. "Mission and Expansion." In *The Early Christian World* (vol. 1: 295–315), edited by Philip K. Esler. London: Routledge, 2000.

Fitzmyer, Joseph A. *The Dead Sea Scrolls and Christian Origins*. Grand Rapids, MI: Wm. B. Eerdmans, 2000.

Fletcher, Richard. *The Barbarian Conversion: From Paganism to Christianity*. New York: Henry Holt & Co., 1998; reprint, Berkeley: University of California Press, 1999.

Frend, W.H.C. "Martyrdom and Political Oppression." In *The Early Christian World* (vol. 2: 815–839), edited by Philip K. Esler. London: Routledge, 2000.

———. "Town and Countryside in Early Christianity." In *The Church in Town and Countryside* (25–42), edited by Derek Baker. Oxford: Basil Blackwell, 1979.

Gieschen, Charles A. *Angelomorphic Christology: Antecedents and Early Evidence*. Leiden, Netherlands: Brill, 1998.

Goehring, James E. "New Frontiers in Pachomian Studies." In *The Roots of Egyptian Christianity* (236–257), edited by Birger A. Pearson and James E. Goehring. Philadelphia, PA: Fortress, 1986.

Golden, Mark. *Sport and Society in Ancient Greece*. Cambridge: Cambridge University Press, 1998; reprint, 2003.

Graham, William A. *Beyond the Written Word: Oral Aspects of Scripture in the History of Religion*. Cambridge: Cambridge University Press, 1987; paperback edition, 1993.

Grant, Michael. *Constantine the Great: The Man and His Times*. New York: Barnes & Noble, 1993.

———. *The Ancient Historians*. New York: Barnes & Noble, 1970.

Grant, Robert M. *Eusebius as Church Historian*. Oxford: Clarendon Press, 1980.

———. "Theological Education at Alexandria." In *The Roots of Egyptian Christianity* (178–189), edited by Birger A. Pearson and James E. Goehring. Philadelphia, PA: Fortress, 1986.

Graves, Dan. *Doctors Who Followed Christ: 32 Biographies of Historic Physicians and Their Christian Faith*. Grand Rapids, MI: Kregel, 1999.

Greary, Patrick J. *Myth of Nations: The Medieval Origins of Europe*. Princeton, NJ: Princeton University Press, 2002.

Green, Liz. *Astrology of Fate*. Boston, MA: Red Wheel/Weiser, 1984.

Greenslade, S.L. "Heresy and Schism in the Later Roman Empire." In *Schism, Heresy and Religious Protest* (1–20), edited by Derek Baker. Cambridge: At the University Press, 1972.

Greer, Richard A. *The Fear of Freedom: A Study of Miracles in the Roman Imperial Church*. University Park, PA: Penn State University Press, 1989.

Griffith, Sidney H. "'Spirit in the Bread; Fire in the Wine:' The Eucharist as 'Living Medicine' in the Thought of Ephraem the Syrian." In *Catholicism and Catholicity* (113–134), edited by Sarah Beckwith, James Buckley, and Gregory Jones. Oxford: Blackwell, 1999.

———. "The Image of the Image Maker in St. Ephraem the Syrian." In *Studia Patristica*. Vol. 25, *Biblica et Apocrypha, Orientalia, Ascetica* (258–269), edited by Elizabeth A. Livingtstone. Louvain, Belgium: Peeters, 1993.

Hahn, Scott, and Mike Aquilina. *Living the Myster-*

ies: A Guide for Unfinished Christians. Huntington, IN: Our Sunday Visitor, 2003.

Hall, Stuart G. *Doctrine and Practice in the Early Church.* Grand Rapids, MI: Wm. B. Eerdmans, 1991.

———. "Women among the Early Martyrs." In *Martyrs and Martyrologies (1–22),* edited by Diana Wood. Oxford: Blackwell Publishers, 1993.

Harrington, Karl P. *Medieval Latin.* 2nd ed. Revised by Joseph M. Pucci. [N.p.]: University of Chicago Press, 1997.

Hart, Trevor. "Creeds, Councils and Doctrinal Development." In *The Early Christian World* (vol. 1: 636–659), edited by Philip K. Esler. London: Routledge, 2000.

Hartog, Paul. *Polycarp and the New Testament: The Occasion, Rhetoric, Theme, and Unity of the Epistle to the Phillipians and Its Allusions to New Testament Literature.* Tubingen, Germany: Mohr Siebeck, 2002.

Harvey, Susan A. "Women and Words: Texts by and About Women." In *The Cambridge History of Early Christian Literature* (382–390), edited by Frances Young, Lewis Ayres, Andrew Louth, and Augustine Casiday. Cambridge: Cambridge University Press, 2004.

Hauser, Alan J., and Duane F. Watson. "Introduction and Overview." In *A History of Biblical Interpretation* (1–54), edited by Alan J. Hauser and Duane F Watson. Grand Rapids, MI: Wm. B. Eerdmans, 2003.

Heine, Ronald E. "Cyprian and Novatian." In *The Cambridge History of Early Christian Literature* (152–160), edited by Frances Young, Lewis Ayres, Andrew Louth, and Augustine Casiday. Cambridge: Cambridge University Press, 2004.

Heron, A.I.C. "Homoousios with the Father." In *The Incarnation: Ecumenical Studies in the Nicene-Constantinopolitan Creed, A.D. 381,* edited by Thomas F. Torrance. Edinburgh: Handrel Press, 1981.

Hickey, Anne E. *Women of the Roman Aristocracy as Christian Monastics.* Ann Arbor, MI: UMI Research Press, 1987.

Hillgarth, J.N., ed. *Christianity and Paganism, 350–750: The Conversion of Western Europe.* Revised ed. Philadelphia: University of Pennsylvania Press, 1986

Hobson, A. Augustus. *The Diatessaron of Tatian and the Synoptic Problem.* Chicago: University of Chicago Press, 1904.

Horner, T.J. *Listening to Trypho: Justin Martyr's Dialogue With Trypho Reconsidered.* Leuven, Belgium: Peeters, 2001.

House, H. Wayne. "The Church's Appropriation of Israel's Blessings." In *Israel: The Land and the People* (77–112), edited by H. Wayne House. Grand Rapids, MI: Kregel, 1998.

Hubert, Elaine C. *Women and the Authority of Inspiration: A Reexamination of Two Prophetic Movements From a Contemporary Feminist Perspective.* Lanham, MD: University Press of America, 1985.

Hunt, Emily J. *Christianity in the Second Century: The Case of Tatian.* London: Routledge, 2003.

Hunter, David G. "Clerical Celibacy and the Veiling of Virgins: New Boundaries in Late Ancient Christianity." In *The Limits of Ancient Christianity: Essays on Late Antique Thought and Culture* (139–152), edited by William E Klingshirn and Mark Vessey. Ann Arbor, MI: University of Michigan Press, 1999.

———. "Fourth-Century Latin Writers: Hilary, Victorinus, Ambrosiaster, Ambrose." In *The Cambridge History of Early Christian Literature* (302–317), edited by Frances Young, Lewis Ayres, Andrew Louth, and Augustine Casiday. Cambridge: Cambridge University Press, 2004.

Hurtado, Larry W. *Lord Jesus Christ: Devotion to Jesus in Earliest Christianity.* Grand Rapids, MI: Wm. B. Eerdmans, 2003.

Instone-Brewer, David. *Divorce and Remarriage in the Bible: The Social and Literary Context.* Grand Rapids, MI: Wm. B. Eerdmans, 2002.

Jaeger, W. "Early Christianity and the Greek Paideia: 1 Clement." In *Encounters with Hellenism: Studies on the First Letter of Clement (104–114),* edited by Cilliers Breytenbach and Laurence L. Welborn. Leiden: Brill, 2004.

Johnson, Ben C. *The God Who Speaks: Learning the Language of God.* Grand Rapids, MI: Wm. B. Eerdmans, 2004.

Johnson, Maxwell E. "Worship, Practice and Belief." In *The Early Christian World* (vol. 1: 475–499), edited by Philip K. Esler. London: Routledge, 2000.

Johnson, Sherman E. "Asia Minor and Early Christianity." In *Christianity, Judaism, and Other Greco-Roman Cults: Studies for Morton Smith at Sixty.* Part 2, *Early Christianity,* 77–145. Leiden, Netherlands: Brill, 1975.

Jones, A.H.M. "The Social Background of the Struggle between Paganism and Christianity." In *The Conflict between Paganism and Christianity in the Fourth Century (17–37),* edited by Arnaldo Momigliano. Oxford: Clarendon Press, 1963.

Jurgens, William A. *The Faith of the Early Fathers,* vol. 1. Collegeville, MN: Liturgical Press, 1970.

———. *The Faith of the Early Fathers,* vol. 2. Collegeville, MN: Liturgical Press, 1979.

Kamil, Jill. *Christianity in the Land of the Pharaohs: The Coptic Orthodox Church.* London: Routledge, 2002.

Kannengiesser, Charles. "Athanasius of Alexandria vs. Arius: The Alexandrian Crisis." In *The Roots of Egyptian Christianity* (204–215), edited by Birger A. Pearson and James E. Goehring. Philadelphia, PA: Fortress, 1986.

Karavites, Peter. *Evil, Freedom, and the Road to Perfection in Clement of Alexandria.* Leiden, Netherlands: Brill, 1999.

Kastner, G. Ronald, and Ann Millin, "Introduction to Proba." In *A Lost Tradition: Women Writers of the Early Church* (33–45), edited by Patricia Wilson-Kastner. Washington, DC: University Press of America, 1981.

Kent, Allen. *Encyclopedia of Library and Information Science*. New York: Marcel Dekker, 1979.

Kieckhefer, Richard. *Magic in the Middle Ages*. Cambridge: Cambridge University Press, 1989, 2000.

Kirk, Martha A. *Women of Bible Lands: A Pilgrimage to Compassion and Wisdom*. Collegeville, MN: Liturgical Press, 2004.

Knowles, Andrew, and Pachomios Penkett. *Augustine and His World*. Downers Grove, IL: InterVarsity, 2004.

Kraemer, Ross S., and Shira L. Lander. "Perpetua and Felicitas." In *The Early Christian World* (vol, 2: 1048–1068), edited by Philip K. Esler. London: Routledge, 2000.

Kuefler, Matthew. *The Manly Eunuch: Masculinity, Gender Ambiguity, and Christian Ideology in Late Antiquity*. Chicago: University of Chicago Press, 2001.

LaVerdiere, Eugene A. *The Eucharist in the New Testament and in the Early Church*. Collegeville, MN: Liturgical Press, 1996.

Leadbetter, Bill. "*Constantine*." In *The Early Christian World* (vol. 2: 1069–1087), edited by Philip K. Esler. London: Routledge, 2000.

———. "From Constantine to Theodosius (and Beyond)." In *The Early Christian World*, (vol. 1: 258–292), edited by Philip K. Esler. London: Routledge, 2000.

Lenski, Noel. *Failure of Empire: Valens and the Roman State in the Fourth*. Berkeley: University of California Press, 2002.

Leon, Vicki. *Uppity Women of Ancient Times*. Boston, Massachusetts: Conari, 2000.

Leyser, Conrad. *Authority and Asceticism from Augustine to Gregory the Great*. Oxford: Clarendon, 2000.

Lienhard, Joseph T. *The Bible, the Church, and Authority: The Canon of the Christian Bible in History and Theology*. Collegeville, MN: Michael Glazier/Liturgical Press, 1995.

Logan, Alastair H.B. "Gnosticism." In *The Early Christian World*, (vol. 2: 907–928), edited by Philip K. Esler. London: Routledge, 2000.

Louth, Andrew. "Eusebius and the Birth of Church History." In *The Cambridge History of Early Christian Literature* (266–274), edited by Frances Young, Lewis Ayres, Andrew Louth, and Augustine Casiday. Cambridge: Cambridge University Press, 2004.

———. "John Chrysostom and the Antiochene School to Theodoret of Cyrrhus." In *The Cambridge History of Early Christian Literature* (342–352), edited by Frances Young, Lewis Ayres, Andrew Louth, and Augustine Casiday. Cambridge: Cambridge University Press, 2004.

———. "Later Theologians of the Greek East." In *The Early Christian World* (vol. 1: 580–601), edited by Philip K. Esler. London: Routledge, 2000.

———. "Palestine: Cyril of Jerusalem and Epiphanius." In *The Cambridge History of Early Christian Literature* (283–289), edited by Frances Young, Lewis Ayres, Andrew Louth, Augustine Casiday. Cambridge: Cambridge University Press, 2004.

———. "The Cappadocians." In *The Cambridge History of Early Christian Literature* (289–301), edited by Frances Young, Lewis Ayres, Andrew Louth, and Augustine Casiday. Cambridge: Cambridge University Press, 2004.

———. "The Fourth-Century Alexandrians: Athanasius and Didymus." In *The Cambridge History of Early Christian Literature* (275–282), edited by Frances Young, Lewis Ayres, Andrew Louth, and Augustine Casiday. Cambridge: Cambridge University Press, 2004.

Ludemann, Gerd. *Heretics: The Other Side of Early Christianity*. Translated by John Bowden. Louisville, Kentucky: Westminster John Knox Press, 1996.

Ludlow, Morwenna. "The Cappadocians." In *First Christian Theologians* (168–185), edited by G. R. Evans. Oxford: Blackwell, 2004.

Lyman, Rebecca. "A Topography of Heresy: Mapping the Rhetorical Creation of Arianism." In *Arianism after Arius: Essays on the Development of the Fourth Century Trinitarian Conflicts* (45–62), edited by Michel R. Barnes and Daniel H. Williams. Edinburgh: T & T Clark, 1993.

Mack, Burton L. *Who Wrote the New Testament? The Making of the Christian Myth*. New York: HarperCollins, 1995.

Malina, Bruce J. "Social Levels, Morals and Daily Life." In *The Early Christian World* (vol. 1: 369–400), edited by Philip K. Esler. London: Routledge, 2000.

Marjanen, Antti. "Montanism: Egalitarian Ecstatic 'New Prophecy.'" In *A Companion to Second-Century Christian "Heretics"* (185–212), edited by Antti Marjanen and Petri Luomanen. Leiden, Netherlands: Brill, 2005.

Markus, R.A. *End of Ancient Christianity*. Cambridge: Cambridge University Press, 1990.

Matthews, Gareth B. *Augustine*. Oxford: Blackwell, 2005.

May, Herbert G. *Our English Bible in the Making*. Philadelphia: published for the Cooperative Publication Association by Westminster Press, 1952.

McCullough, W. Stuart. *A Short History of Syriac Christianity to the Rise of Islam*. Chico, California: Scholars Press, 1987.

McGinn, Sheila E. "Internal Renewal and Dissent in the Early Christian World." In *The Early Christian World* (vol. 2: 893–906), edited by Philip K. Esler. London: Routledge, 2000.

McGrath, Alister E. *Historical Theology: An Intro-*

duction to the History of Christian Thought. Oxford: Blackwell Publishing, 1998.

McGuckin, John A. "Martyr Devotion in the Alexandrian School: Origen to Athanasius." In *Martyrs and Martyrologies* (35–46), edited by Diana Wood. Oxford: Blackwell, 1993.

McKane, William. *Selected Christian Hebraists.* Cambridge: Cambridge University Press, 1989.

McKinnon, James W. "Music." In *The Early Christian World* (vol. 2: 773–790), edited by Philip K. Esler. London: Routledge, 2000.

———. *Music in Early Christian Literature.* Cambridge: Cambridge University Press, 1987; 1993 reprint.

McLay, R. Timothy. *The Use of the Septuagint in New Testament Research.* Grand Rapids, MI: Wm. B. Eerdmans, 2003.

McLynn, Neil B. *Ambrose of Milan: Church and State in a Christian Capital.* Berkeley: University of California Press, 1994.

McVey, Kathleen E. "Ephrem the Syrian." In *The Early Christian World* (vol. 2: 1228–1250), edited by Philip K. Esler. London: Routledge, 2000.

Mead, G.R.S. *Thrice Greatest Hermes: Studies in Hellenistic Theosophy and Gnosis.* 1992; new edition, York Beach, ME: Weiser, 2001.

Megivern, James. *The Death Penalty: An Historical and Theological Survey.* Mahwah, NJ: Paulist Press, 1997.

Merdinger, J.E. *Rome and the African Church in the Time of Augustine.* New Haven: Yale University Press, 1997.

Meyer, Marvin W., ed. *The Ancient Mysteries: A Sourcebook of Sacred Texts.* Philadelphia: University of Pennsylvania Press, 1987.

Millar, Fergus. *Rome, the Greek World, and the East.* Vol. 2, *Government, Society, and Culture in the Roman Empire.* Chapel Hill: University of North Carolina Press, 2004.

Miller, Patricia C. *Dreams in Late Antiquity: Studies in the Imagination of a Culture.* Princeton, NJ: Princeton University Press, 1994.

Minns, Denis. *Irenaeus.* Washington, DC: Georgetown University Press, 1994.

Mitchell, Stephen. "The Life and *Lives* of Gregory Thaumaturgus." In *Portraits of Spiritual Authority: Religious Power in Early Christianity, Byzantium and the Christian Orient* (99–138), edited by Jan W. Drijvers and John W. Watt. Leiden, Netherlands: Brill, 1999.

Momigliano, Arnaldo. "Christianity and the Decline of the Roman Empire." In *The Conflict between Paganism and Christianity in the Fourth Century* (1–15), edited by Arnaldo Momigliano. Oxford: Clarendon Press, 1963.

———. "Pagan and Christian Historiography in the Fourth Century A.D." In *The Conflict between Paganism and Christianity in the Fourth Century* (79–99), edited by Arnaldo Momigliano. Oxford: Clarendon Press, 1963.

Morrison, Karl F. *Conversion and Text: The Cases of Augustine of Hippo, Herman-Judah, and Constantine Tsatos.* Charlottesville: University Press of Virginia, 1992.

Mortley, Raoul. *The Idea of Universal History from Hellenistic Philosophy to Early Christian Historiography.* Lewiston, NY: Edwin Mellen, 1996.

Musto, Ronald G. *The Catholic Peace Tradition.* New York: Orbis, 1986.

Newlands, G.M. *Hilary of Poitiers: A Study in Theological Method.* Bern, Germany: Peter Lang, 1978.

Norris, Fred. "Origen." In *The Early Christian World* (vol. 2: 1005–1026), edited by Philip K. Esler. London: Routledge, 2000.

Norris, Richard A., Jr. "Irenaeus of Lyon." In *The Cambridge History of Early Christian Literature* (45–54), edited by Frances Young, Lewis Ayres, Andrew Louth, and Augustine Casiday. Cambridge: Cambridge University Press, 2004.

Nutton, Vivian. *Ancient Medicine.* London: Routledge, 2004.

Obermeier, Anita. *The History and Anatomy of Auctorial Self-Criticism in the European Middle Ages.* Amsterdam, Netherlands: Editions Rodopi B.V., 1999.

O'Brien, Mary E. *Spirituality in Nursing: Standing on Holy Ground.* 2nd ed. Sudbury, MA: Jones and Bartlett, 2003.

O'Collins, Gerald. *The Tripersonal God: Understanding and Interpreting the Trinity.* Mahway, NJ: Paulist Press, 1999.

Odahl, Charles M. *Constantine and the Christian Empire.* London: Routledge, 2004.

O'Grady, Joan. *Heresy: Heretical Truth or Orthodox Error? A Study of Early Christian Heresies.* Longmead, UK: Element, 1985.

Old, Hughes O. *The Reading and Preaching of the Scriptures in the Worship of the Christian Church.* Grand Rapids, MI: Wm. B. Eerdmans, 1998.

Oliver, Edmund H. *The Social Achievements of the Christian Church.* 1930; reprinted, Vancouver, British Columbia: Regent College Publishing, 2004.

Olson, Roger E., and Christopher A. Hall. *The Trinity.* Grand Rapids, MI: Wm. B. Eerdmans, 2002.

Orlandi, Tito. "Coptic Literature." In *The Roots of Egyptian Christianity* (51–81), edited by Birger A. Pearson and James E. Goehring. Philadelphia, PA: Fortress, 1986.

Osborn, Eric. *Irenaeus of Lyons.* Cambridge: Cambridge University Press, 2001.

———. "The Apologists." In *The Early Christian World* (vol 1:525–552), edited by Philip K. Esler. London: Routledge, 2000.

Osiek, Carolyn. *Rich and Poor in the "Shepherd of Hermas": An Exegetical-Social Investigation.* Washington, DC: Catholic Biblical Association of America, 1983.

———. "The Apostolic Fathers." In *The Early Chris-*

tian World (vol. 1: 503–524), edited by Philip K. Esler. London: Routledge, 2000.

Partington, James R. *A History of Greek Fire and Gunpowder.* Cambridge: W. Heffer & Sons, 1960; reprinted, Baltimore, MD: Johns Hopkins Press, 1999.

Pasquini, John J. *True Christianity: The Catholic Way.* New York: iUniverse, 2003.

Patterson, Paige. "The Meaning of Authority in the Local Church." In *Recovering Biblical Manhood and Womanhood: A Response to Evangelical Feminism* (248–261), edited by John Piper and Wayne Grudem. Wheaton, IL: Crossway, 1991.

Peers, Glenn. *Subtle Bodies: Representing Angels in Byzantium.* Berkeley: University of California Press, 2001.

Perrin, Nicholas. *Thomas and Tatian: The Relationship between the "Gospel of Thomas" and the "Diatessaron."* Atlanta: Society of Biblical Literature, 2002.

Pesthy, Monika. "'Mulier est Instrumentum Diaboli': Women and the Desert Fathers." In *The Wisdom of Egypt: Jewish, Early Christian, and Gnostic Essays in Honor of Gerald P. Luttikhuizen* (351–362), edited by Anthony Hilhorst and George H. van Kooten. Leiden, Netherlands: Brill, 2005.

Petersen, William L. "Tatian the Assyrian." In *A Companion to Second-Century Christian "Heretics"* (125–158), edited by Antti Marjanen and Petri Luomanen. Leiden, Netherlands: Brill, 2005.

Price, Ira, William A. Irwin, and Allen P. Wikgren. *The Ancestry of our English Bible.* 3rd revised ed. New York: Harper & Brothers, 1956.

Quasten, Johannes, "Introduction to Nola Paulinus," *Letters of Saint Paulinus of Nola.* Ramsey, NJ: Paulist Press, 1966.

Rader, Rosemary. "Introduction to Perpetua." In *A Lost Tradition: Women Writers of the Early Church* (1–18), edited by Patricia Wilson-Kastner. Washington, DC: University Press of America, 1981.

Raisanen, Heikki. "Marcion." In *A Companion to Second-Century Christian "Heretics"* (100–124), edited by Antti Marjanen and Petri Luomanen. Leiden, Netherlands: Brill, 2005.

Ramsey, Boniface. *Ambrose.* London: Routledge, 1997.

———. "Ambrose." In *First Christian Theologians* (225–233), edited by G. R. Evans. Oxford: Blackwell, 2004.

Ranft, Patricia. *A Woman's Way: The Forgotten History of Women Spiritual Directors.* New York: Palgrave, 2000.

———. *Women and the Religious Life in Premodern Europe.* New York: PalgraveMacmillan, 1996.

Rankin, David. "Arianism." In *The Early Christian World* (vol. 2: 975–1001), edited by Philip K. Esler. London: Routledge, 2000.

Rebenich, Stefan. *Jerome.* London: Routledge, 2002.

Richardson, Peter. *Herod: King of the Jews and Friend of the Romans.* Columbia: University of South Carolina Press, 1996.

Roberts, Holly. *Vegetarian Christian Saints: Mystics, Ascetics & Monks.* Washington: Anjeli, 2004.

Rogerson, John W. "The First Christian Writings." In *First Christian Theologians* (15–23), edited by G. R. Evans. Oxford: Blackwell, 2004.

Rousseau, Philip. *Basil of Caesarea.* Berkeley: University of California Press, 1994.

———. *The Early Christian Centuries.* London: Longman, 2002.

Sagovsky, Nicholas. *Ecumenism, Christian Origins and the Practice of Communion.* Cambridge: Cambridge University Press, 2000.

Salisbury, Joyce E. *Blood of Martyrs: The Impact and Memory of Ancient Violence.* London: Routledge, 2004.

Sandnes, Karl O. *Belly and Body in the Pauline Epistles.* Cambridge: Cambridge University Press, 2002.

Satterlee, Craig A. *Ambrose of Milan's Method of Mystagogical Preaching.* Collegeville, MN: Liturgical Press, 2002.

Schmidt, Alvin J. *How Christianity Changed the World.* Grand Rapids, MI: Zondervan, 2004.

Scobie, Edward. "African Popes." In *African Presence in Early Europe* (96–107), edited by Ivan Van Sertima. New Brunswick, NJ: Transaction, 1985.

Scott, T. Kermit. *Augustine: His Thought in Context.* Mahwah, NJ: Paulist Press, 1995.

Shaw, Teresa M. "Sex and Sexual Renunciation." In *The Early Christian World* (vol. 1: 401–421), edited by Philip K. Esler. London: Routledge, 2000.

Shoemaker, Stephen J. *The Ancient Traditions of the Virgin Mary's Dormition and Assumption.* Oxford: Oxford University Press, 2002.

Siker, Jeffrey S. "Christianity in the Second and Third Centuries." In *The Early Christian World* (vol. 1: 231–257), edited by Philip K. Esler. London: Routledge, 2000.

Smith, David E. *The Canonical Function of Acts: A Comparative Analysis.* Collegeville, MN: Michael Glazier/Liturgical Press, 2002.

Smith, Richard. "Introduction to the Coptic Book of Ritual Power from Leiden." In *Ancient Christian Magic: Coptic Texts of Ritual Power* (311–313), edited by Marvin W. Meyer and Richard Smith. Princeton, NJ: Princeton University Press, 1999.

Smith, Warren S. "Satiric Advice: Serious or Not?" In *Satiric Advice on Women and Marriage: From Plautus to Chaucer* (1–25), edited by Warren S. Smith. Ann Arbor: University of Michigan Press, 2005.

Smulders, P. *Hilary of Poitiers' Preface to His "Opus Historicum:" Translation and Commentary.* Leiden, Netherlands: Brill, 1995.

Springer, Carl P.E. "Jerome and the *Cento of Proba.*" In *Studia Patristica.* Vol. 28, *Papers Presented at the Eleventh International Conference on Patristic Studies Held in Oxford, 1991* (87–96) edited by

Elizabeth A. Livingstone. Louvain, Belgium: Peeters, 1993.

Stanton, Graham N. "The Spirit in the Writings of Justin Martyr." In *The Holy Spirit and Christian Origins: Essays in Honor of James D.G. Dunn* (321–334), edited by Graham N, Stanton, Stephen C. Barton, Bruce W. Longenecker. Grand Rapids, MI: Wm. B. Eerdmans, 2004.

Stark, Rodney. *For the Glory of God: How Monotheism Led to Reformations, Science, Witch-Hunts, and the End of Slavery.* Princeton, NJ: Princeton University Press, 2003.

Stewart-Sykes, Alistair. "Hermas the Prophet and Hippolytus the Preacher: the Roman Homily and Its Social Context." In *Preacher and Audience: Studies in Early Christian and Byzantine Homiletics* (33–64), edited by Mary B. Cunningham and Pauline Allen. Leiden, Netherlands: Brill, 1998.

_____. *The Lamb's High Feast: Melito, Peri Pascha and the Quartodeciman Paschal Liturgy at Sardis.* Leiden, Netherlands: Brill, 1998.

Straw, Carole. "'A Very Special Death': Christian Martyrdom in Its Classical Context." In *Sacrificing the Self: Perspectives on Martyrdom and Religion* (39–54), edited by Margaret Cormack. New York: Oxford University Press, 2002.

Stuart, Columba. "Anthony of the Desert." In *The Early Christian World* (2:1088–1101), edited by Philip K. Esler. London: Routledge, 2000.

_____. "Monasticism." In *The Early Christian World* (1:344–366), edited by Philip K. Esler. London: Routledge, 2000.

Sullivan, Francis A. *From Apostles to Bishops: The Development of the Episcopacy in the Early Church.* Mahwah, NJ: Newman Press/Paulist Press, 2001.

Sumruled, William A. *Augustine and the Arians: The Bishop of Hippo's Encounters with Ulfilan Arianism.* Selinsgrove: Susquehanna University Press, 1994.

Talley, Thomas T. *The Origins of the Liturgical Year.* Collegeville, MN: Liturgical Press, 1986, 1991.

Tavard, George H. *The Thousand Faces of the Virgin Mary.* Collegeville, MN: Liturgical Press, 1996.

Tayler, David G. K. "Christian Regional Diversity." In *The Early Christian World* (1:330–343), edited by Philip K. Esler. London: Routledge, 2000.

Taylor, Miriam S. *Anti-Judaism and Early Christian Identity: A Critique of the Scholarly Consensus.* Leiden, Netherlands: Brill, 1995.

Thompson, E. A. "Christianity and the Northern Barbarians." In *The Conflict between Paganism and Christianity in the Fourth Century* (56–78), edited by Arnaldo Momigliano. Oxford: Clarendon Press, 1963.

Thorley, John. *Documents in Medieval Latin.* Ann Arbor, MI: University of Michigan Press, 1998.

Thorndike, Lynn. *History of Magic & Experimental Science.* New York: Columbia University Press, 1923.

Tilley, Maureen A. "The Passion of Perpetua and Felicity." In *Searching the Scriptures: A Feminist Commentary* (829–858). New York: Crossroad, 1994.

Torjesen, Karen Jo. "Social and Historical Setting: Christianity as Culture Critique." In *The Cambridge History of Early Christian Literature* (181–199), edited by Frances Young, Lewis Ayres, Andrew Louth, and Augustine Casiday. Cambridge: Cambridge University Press, 2004.

_____. "The Episcopacy — Sacredotal or Monarchical? The Appeal to Old Testament Institutions by Cyprian and the *Didascalia*." In *Studia Patristica*. Vol. 36, *Papers Presented at the Eleventh International Conference on Patristic Studies Held in Oxford, 1999* (387–408), edited by M.F. Wiles and E.J. Yarnold. Louvain, Belgium: Peeters, 2001.

Toumlin, Stephen and June Goodfield. *The Discovery of Time.* Chicago: University of Chicago Press, 1965.

Trevett, Christine. "Montanism." In *The Early Christian World*, (2:929–952), edited by Philip K. Esler. London: Routledge, 2000.

Tripolitis, Antonia. *Religions of the Hellenistic-Roman Age.* Grand Rapids, MI: Wm. B. Eerdmans, 2002.

Tugwell, Simon. *The Apostolic Fathers.* New York: Continuum, 1989.

Turcan, Robert. *The Cults of the Roman Empire.* Translated by Antonia Nevill. Oxford, England: Blackwell, 1996; 2001 reprint.

van Dam, Raymond. *Becoming Christian: The Conversion of Roman Cappadocia.* Philadelphia: University of Pennsylvania Press, 2003.

_____. *Families and Friends in Late Roman Cappadocia.* Philadelphia: University of Pennsylvania Press, 2003.

_____. *Kingdom of Snow: Roman Rule and Greek Culture in Cappadocia.* Philadelphia: University of Pennsylvania Press, 2002.

van Doorn-Harder, Pieternella. *Contemporary Coptic Nuns.* Columbia: University of South Carolina Press, 1995.

van Henten, J.W., and Friedrich Avemarie. *Martyrdom and Noble Death: Selected Texts from Graeco-Roman, Jewish and Christian Antiquity.* London: Routledge, 2002.

van Unnik, W.C. "Studies on the So-called First Epistle of Clement: The Literary Genre." In *Encounters with Hellenism: Studies on the First Letter of Clement* (115–181), edited by Cilliers Breytenbach and Laurence L. Welborn. Leiden: Brill, 2004.

Veilleux, Armand. "Monasticism and Gnosis in Egypt." In *The Roots of Egyptian Christianity* (273–277), edited by Birger A. Pearson and James E. Goehring. Philadelphia, PA: Fortress, 1986.

Verbrugghe, Gerald P., and John M Wickersham. *Berossos and Manetho, Introduced and Translated: Native Traditions in Ancient Mesopotamia and Egypt.* Ann Arbor: University of Michigan Press, 1996.

Waaijman, K. *Spirituality: Forms, Foundations, Methods.* Translated by John Vriend. Leuven, Belgium: Peeters, 2002.

Wand, John W. *History of the Early Church to AD 500.* London: Routledge, 1937; reprint, 1994.

Waszink, J.H. "Tertullian's Principles and Methods of Exegesis." In *Early Christian Literature and the Classical Intellectual Tradition* (16–31), edited by William R. Schoedel and Robert L. Wilken. Paris: Editions Beauchesne, 1979.

Welborn, L.L. "The Preface to 1 Clement: The Rhetorical Situation and the traditional Date." In *Encounters with Hellenism: Studies on the First Letter of Clement* (196–216), edited by Cilliers Breytenbach and Laurence L. Welborn. Leiden: Brill, 2004.

Werner, Eric. *The Sacred Bridge: The Interdependence of Liturgy and Music in Synagogue and Church During the First Millennium.* New York: KTAV, 1989.

White, Carolinne. *Christian Friendship in the Fourth Century.* Cambridge: Cambridge University Press, 1992; paperback edition, 2002.

———. "General Introduction." In *Early Christian Lives* (xi-xli), edited by Caroline White. London: Penguin Group, 1998.

White, L. Michael. *From Jesus to Christianity: How Four Generations of Visionaries & Storytellers Created the New Testament and Christian Faith.* New York: HarperCollins, 2004.

Wiles, Maurice. "Attitudes to Arius in the Arian Controversy." In *Arianism after Arius: Essays on the Development of the Fourth Century Trinitarian Conflicts* (31–42), edited by Michel R. Barnes and Daniel H. Williams. Edinburgh: T & T Clark, 1993.

Wilfong, Terry G. "'Friendship and Physical Desire': The Discourse of Female Homoeroticism in Fifth Century C.E. Egypt." In *Among Women: From the Homosocial to the Homoerotic in the Ancient World* (304–330), edited by Nancy Sorkin Rabinowitz and Lisa Auanger. Austin: University of Texas Press, 2002.

Williams, Frank. *The Panarion of Epiphanius of Salamis (Books II and III).* Leiden, Netherlands: Brill, 1994.

Williams, Michael A. *The Immoveable Race: A Gnostic Designation and the Theme of Stability in Late Antiquity.* Leiden, Netherlands: Brill, 1985.

Williamson, G. *Eusebius: From Christ to Constantine.* Revised ed. London: Penguin, 1989.

Wills, Garry. *Saint Augustine's Childhood.* New York: Viking, 2001.

———. *Why I Am a Catholic.* New York: Houghton Mifflin/Mariner edition, 2003.

Wilson, Katharina M., and Elizabeth M. Makowski. *Wykked Wyves and the Woes of Marriage: Misogamous Literature from Juvenal to Chaucer.* Albany: State University of New York Press, 1990.

Wilson, Marvin R. *Our Father Abraham: Jewish Roots of the Christian Faith.* Grand Rapids, MI: Wm. B. Eerdmans, 1989.

Witherington, Ben. *The Gospel of Mark: A Socio-Rhetorical Commentary.* Grand Rapids, MI: Wm. B. Eerdman, 2001.

Wolfram, Herwig. *History of the Goths.* Berkeley: University of California Press. 1988; paperback edition, 1990.

———. *The Roman Empire and Its Germanic Peoples.* Berkeley: University of California Press, 1997.

Worth, Roland H., Jr. *Messiahs and Messianic Movements through 1899.* Jefferson, NC: McFarland, 2005.

———. *The Seven Cities of the Apocalypse & Roman Culture.* Mahwah, NJ: Paulist Press, 1999.

Wright, David. "Tertullian." In *The Early Christian World*, Volume 2, edited by Philip K. Esler, 1027–1047. London: Routledge, 2000.

Wurthwein, Ernst. *The Text of the Old Testament: An Introduction to the Biblia Hebraica.* English translation of 5th German ed. Grand Rapids, MI: Wm. B. Eerdmans, 1995.

INTERNET RESOURCES

Attributed Material

Arbea, Antonio. *Carmen Sacrum of Faltonia Betitia Proba, the First Christian Poetess.* Google translation of the Spanish. Available online at http://www.translate.google.com/translate?hl=en&sl=es&u=http://www.conocereisdeverdad.org/website/index.php%3Fid%3D2591&prev=/search%3Fq%3DFaltonia%2BProba%26start%3D80%26hl%3Den%26lr%3D%26sa%3DN (accessed December 2005).

Armstrong, Dave. "Exposition on the Christian Veneration of Images." Available online at http://www.bringyou.to/apologetics/a121.htm (accessed December 2005).

Aumann, Jordan. *Christian Spirituality in the Catholic Tradition.* Chapter 4, "Monasticism in the West." Available online at http://www.op.org/domcentral/study/aumann/cs/cs04.htm (accessed December 2005).

Blackhurst, R. "Astrology, Autochony and Salvation." Copyright 2003–2004. Available online at http://www.religioperennis.org/documents/blacks/Astrology.pdf (accessed December 2005).

Campion, Nick. "The Concept of Destiny in Islamic Astrology and Its Impact on Medieval European Thought." Reprinted from *Aram: The Journal for Syro-Mesopotamian Culture*: 2 (Summer 1989): 281–289. Available online at http://www.nickcampion.com/nc/history/articles/islamic.htm (accessed December 2005).

Clark, Elizabeth A. "Jesus the Hero in the Vergilian *Cento* of Faltonia Betitia Proba." Abstract of a paper presented at the Sixth Annual Byzantine

Studies Conference, October 24–26, 1980, at Oberlin College and the College of Wooster, Oberlin, Ohio. Available online at http://www.byzconf.org/1980abstracts.html (accessed December 2005).

Detering, Hermann. "1 Clement and the Ignatiana in Dutch Radical Criticism." Translated by Frans-Joris Fabri. Available online at http://www.hermann-detering.de/clem_engl.htm (accessed February 2006).

DiMaio, Michael, Jr., and Robert Frakes. "Constantius II (A.D. 337–361)" In *Online Encyclopedia of Roman Rulers,* May 16, 1998. Available online at http://www.roman-emperors.org/constaii.htm (accessed February 2006).

Disse, Dorothy. "Proba/Faltonia Betitia Proba (c.322–c.370)." *Other Women's Voices: Translations of Women Writing before 1700* Website. Available online at http://www.home.infionline.net/~ddisse/proba.html (accessed December 2005).

Hines, Michael. "Barbarian Breakthrough." Available online at http://www.christianchronicler.com/history1/barbarian_breakthrough.html (January 2006).

Huning, Matthias. "The Gothic Bible Translation." Available online at http://www.ned.univie.ac.at/publicaties/taalgeschiedenis/en/gotbibel.htm (accessed January 2006).

Hunter, David D. "Sex, Sin, and Salvation: What Augustine Really Said." Lecture at the Washington Theological Union. Available online at http://www.wtu.edu/news/lectures/Augustine_Lec1_text.htm (accessed December 2005).

Keck, Karen Rae. "Epiphanius of Salamis (Cyprus)." *Ecole Initiative* Website. Available online at http://www2.evansville.edu/ecoleweb/glossary/salamis.html (accessed December 2005).

"Lady Alchima" [pseudonym]. "The Battle for the Soul." Available online at http://www.mugglenet.com/editorials/editorials/edit-ladyalchymia01.shtml (accessed December, 2005).

McCann, David. "Julius Firmicus Maternus: Profile of a Roman Astrologer." *The Traditional Astrologer* (Autumn 1994). Available online at http://www.skyscript.co.uk/firmicus.html (accessed December 2005).

Metzger, Bruce M. "Theories of the Translation Process." *Bibliotheca Sacra* 150:598 (1993): 140–150. Available online at http://www.biblicalstudies.org.uk/article_trans_metzger2.html (accessed December, 2005).

Moreschini, Claudius. "Jerome and His Learned Lady Disciples." *The City and the Book,* International Congresses in Florence's Certosa, 30–31 May, 1 June 2001. Google translation of the Italian. Available online at http://www.translate.google.com/translate?hl=en&sl=it&u=http://www.florin.ms/aleph2.html&prev=/search%3Fq%3DPammachius%26start%3D60%26hl%3Den%26lr%3D%26sa%3DN (accessed December 2005).

Muller, Bernard D. "The Epistles of Ignatius: Are They All Forgeries?" Available online at http://www.geocities.com/b_d_muller/ignatius.html (accessed February 2006).

Noy, David. "Women in Latin Love Poetry." Available online at http://www.lamp.ac.uk/~noy/roman5.htm (accessed December 2005).

Pingree, David. "Astrology." In *The Dictionary of the History of Ideas.* Available online at http://www.etext.lib.virginia.edu/cgi-local/DHI/dhi.cgi?id=dv1-20 (accessed December 2005).

Power, Kim E. "The Rehablitation of Eve." Originally appeared in *Religion in the Ancient World: New Themes and Approaches,* edited by M. Dillon. Amsterdam: Hakkert, [n.d.]. Available online at http://www.womenpriests.org/theology/power3.asp (accessed December 2005).

Rust, John. "Validation of the Orpheus Minor Scales in a Working Population," *Social Behavior and Personality* (1998). Available online at http://www.looksmartweightloss.com/p/articles/mi_qa3852/is_199801/ai_n8797744 (accessed December 2005).

Wider, Laurance. "Review of *Hymns of Prudentius.*" *First Things* 74 (June-July, 1997). Available online at http://www.firstthings.com/ftissues/ft9706/reviews/wieder.html (accessed December 2005).

Wishart, Alfred W. *A Short History of Monks and Monasteries.* (No publication data for original book appearance provided.) Available online at http://www.historion.net/a.w.wishart-short-history-monks-monasteries/page-30.html (accessed December 2005).

Unattributed Material

"Aurelius Clemens Prudentius, 348-c. 413." *Cyber Hymnal* Website. Available online at http://www.cyberhymnal.org/bio/p/r/prudentius_ac.htm (accessed December 2005).

"Constantine the Great." *Catholic Encyclopedia.* Available online at http://www.newadvent.org/cathen/04295c.htm (accessed September 2005).

"Felicissimus." *Catholic Encyclopedia.* Available online at http://www.newadvent.org/cathen/06027c.htm (accessed December 2005).

"Firmicus Maternus." *Catholic Encyclopedia.* Available online at http://www.newadvent.org/cathen/06080a.htm (accessed December 2005).

"Flavius Julius Constantius." *Catholic Encyclopedia.* Available online at http://www.newadvent.org/cathen/16027c.htm (accessed August 2005).

"Julian the Apostate." *Catholic Encyclopedia.* Available online at http://www.newadvent.org/cathen/08558b.htm (accessed September 2005).

"Ostia." *Ostia—The Harbor District: Ostia.* Available online at http://www.ostia-antica.org/portus/remainsn.htm (accessed December 2005).

"Prudentius, Aurelius Clemens, 348-c. 413." *Evan-*

gelical Lutheran Hymnary Handbook: Biographies and Sources, P-Z Website. Available online http://www.blc.edu/comm/gargy/gargy1/ELH.biographies.P...Z.html (accessed December 2005).

"Saint Pammachius." *Catholic Encyclopedia*. Available online at http://www.newadvent.org/cathen/11436a.htm (accessed December 2005).

"Saint Pammachius." *Catholic Online Saints*. Available online at http://www.catholic.org/saints/saint.php?saint_id=807 (accessed December 2005).

"The Sign of the Cross." Available online at http://www.latin-mass-society.org/2005/signofthecross.html (accessed December 2005).

Index

Ades Pater Supreme 70–71
Adrianople 41, 110
Aelia Capitolina 58
Aeneas 67
aeons 130
Africanus, Julius 4
Against Aunomius 106
Against Marcion 127
Against the Heresies 33
Against the Pagans 98
Alexander (Bishop of Alexandria) 97, 134
Alexander of Cappadocia 37
Alexandria, Egypt 35, 37, 45, 48, 58, 60, 80, 97, 101, 134, 136, 152, 157, 159
Alypius 117
Ambrose (theologian) 5, 47, 70, 86, 107–111, 117, 137, 146, 148, 158, 159, 160
Anicetus (Bishop of Rome) 25, 31
Anti-Christ 114
Antioch 14, 111, 162
Antony 5, 98, 117, 149–154, 156
Aphraetes 78
Apollinaris, Sidonius 137
Apollo 141
Apology 126, 127
"Apostolic Fathers" 7–8
Aquila (Bible translator) 82, 83
Arianism 4, 5, 19, 45–46, 64–65, 99–100, 102, 106, 108–110, 113, 114, 127, 133–134, 136–138, 160
Arius 5, 100, 134–136, 153
Armenia 50, 53, 78
asceticism 20–21, 75–76, 88, 122, 123, 127, 139, 145, 148, 149, 153, 161
astrology 68
Athanasius 5, 48, 49, 64, 97–103, 133, 136, 151, 153, 155, n. 29 175, n. 48 175
Athens, Greece 37, 50, 103, 105
Augustine of Hippo 5, 34, 36, 56, 59, 71, 80, 90, 100, 114–120, 144, 145–146, 147, 150
Augustus (emperor) 43, 53, 58
Auxentius (Bishop of Milan) 108, 114, 136

baptism 49, 95–96
Bardesanes 72
Basil the Great 5, 61, 103, 105–107, 150
Bethlehem 162, 163
Bible translations 3
Blastus 31
Blessila 161
Bonosus 5, 147–148
Bordeaux 113
Bucolis, Bishop 24
Bulgaria 84
Byzantium 41

Caecilian 143, 144
Caesarea, Palestine 62, 81, 105
Canonical Letter 61
canonicity 8
Cappadocia 37
"Caraphrygian heresy" 138
Carthage 34, 36, 44, 92, 93, 115–116, 125, 126, 143, 144
Cassius, Dio 53
catechumens 35, 108, 126
celibacy 37, 43, 161
charity 52, 55–56, 155
choirs 72
Chrysostom, John 5, 47, 73–74, 111–113, 158
Church/Basilica of St. Peter (Rome) 55, 159
Church of the Holy Sepulcher 162
Cicero 116
cithara 72
City of God 120
Clemens, Titus Flavius 8
Clement *see* Clement of Rome; First Clement; Second Clement
Clement of Alexandria 37–39, 80, 129, 131, 147
Clement of Rome 8–9
Codex Alexandrius 8
Codex Fuldensis 78
Codex Sinaiticus 8
Colombanus 147
Commentary on Matthew 88
Confessions 120
Constans 48, 67
Constantine the Great 4, 36, 40–47, 63, 64, 84, 101, 103

Constantine II 48
Constantinople 41, 48, 88, 104, 105, 108, 111, 112, 115, 136
Constantius, Flavius Julius 4, 47–49, 51, 97, 101, 113, 136
Contra Celsum 80, 82
Corinth 35
Cornelius (Bishop of Rome) 93, 95
Council of Antioch 48, 101
Council of Constantinople 106, 114
Council of Nicaea 45–46, 47, 64, 71, 86, 97, 99, 101, 103, 135–136
Council of Philippopolis 48
Council of Serdica 48
Council of Sirium 101
Council of Tyre 63, 101
courts 44
Cybele 141
Cyprian 5, 80, 92–96, 131, 132, n. 74 177
Cyprus 128, 129, 162
Cyril of Jerusalem 138

Damascus (Bishop of Rome) 88, 161
De errore profanarum religionum (The Error of the Pagan Religions) 67–68, 69
De fide 110
De Principiis 56–57
De synodis 113
De Trinitate 114
Decius (emperor) 61, 81, 93, 132
Defense of Origen 63
Demetrius (Bishop of Alexandria) 81
Demonstration (Proof) of Apostolic Teaching 33
Diatessaron 72, 76, 77–79
Didache 7
Diocletian (emperor) 40, 41, 63, 159
Diogenes 101
Dionysius of Alexandria (Bishop) 8, 23, 93
divination 43
docetism 131
Doctrine of Addai 78

Domitian (emperor) 19
Donatus and Donatism 5, 44–45, 56, 87, 139, 143–144
dreams 19, 20, 42, 128

Easter 30, 31
Edessa 72, 78, 79
Edict of Milan 42
Eleusinian mysteries 50
Emmaus, Palestine 59
encraticism 76–77, 78, n. 10 173
Ephraem 4, 71–72, 78
Epiphanius 72–74, 98, 129, 147, 148
Epiphanius of Salamis 4, 82
Erasmus 91
Eudoxia 112
Eulalia (martyr) 70
Eusebius' *Chronicle* 65
Eusebius' *Church/Ecclesiastical History* 24–25, 63, 65, 78, 122
Eusebius of Caesarea 4, 12, 19, 20, 22, 23, 27–28, 30, 38, 43–44, 53, 59, 62–65, 75, 83, 135, 138
Eusebius of Cremona 88
Eusebius of Nicomedia 45, 48, 84, 135
Eustathius of Sebaste 106, 107
Evangelium Veritatis (Gospel of Truth) 130
Exhortation to Chastity 128
Exhortation to Martyrdom 80
Exhortation to the Greeks 38
exorcisms 125, 126

Fabian (Bishop of Rome) 93
Fabiola, Saint 55, 56
Faustus 117
Felicissimus 5, 93, 131–133
Felicity 34–37
First Clement 7, 8–10
Florinus 129
Fortanus 133
Fortunatus 95
Fretela 89
Fulgentius of Ruspe 137

Galerius (emperor) 40
"Galileans" 52, 97
Gallican Psalter 90
Gallus (half-brother of Julian the Apostate) 47
Gaul 108, 114, 121, 129, 137, 159
Gaza, Palestine 72
Gelasius (Bishop of Rome) 66
George of Cappadocia 101–102
Gnosticism 5, 33, 38, 68, 75–76, 122, 139, 153, 157
Gospel of the Hebrews 22
Gospel of Thomas 76, 78
Gospel of Truth 130
Gothic Bible translation 85–86
Goths 84, 85, 86
Gratian (emperor) 108
Gratius (emperor) 109–110

Gregory I (Bishop of Rome) 147
Gregory of Cappadocia 101
Gregory of Nazianzus 5, 97, 103–105, 107, 136, 150
Gregory of Neocaesarea 60–62
Gregory of Nyssa 61–62

Hadrian (emperor) 58
Helena (sister of emperor Constantius) 50
Hermas *see* Shepherd of Hermas
hermits 150, 161
Herod the Great 58, 81
Hexapla 4, 82–83, 89, 90
Hilary of Poitiers 5, 49, 108, 113–114
Hippo, Algeria 118, 120
Hippolytus 15, 73, 123, 140
History of the Arians 97
History of the Patriarchs of Alexandria 97
Horsiesios 156, 157
hospitals 55, 107, 163, n. 67 169
Hymn to King Helios 50
hymns 69, 70, 71, 114, 150
Hymns Against Julian 71

Ignatius 7, 12–15, 25–26, n. 36 165
images (veneration of) 74
In Constantium 114
"Inner Mountain" 152
Irenaeus 18–19, 24, 30, 31, 32–34, 73, 75, 130

Jacob (Bishop of Nisibis) 71
Jerome 3, 5, 16, 20, 28, 32, 55, 56, 57, 66, 72, 73, 82, 83, 87–91, 114, 126, 141, 145, 146, 147, 150, 156, 160, 161, 162, 163, 164
Jerusalem 58
Jesus 12, 22–23, 52, 58–59, 67, 74, 78, 124, 125, 131, 139
John (Patriarch of Jerusalem) 73, 74
Jovian (emperor) 102
Jovinian/Jovinianus 5, 56, 145–147, n. 180 179
Judaism 51–52, 89, 111, 123, 124
Julian "the Apostate" 4, 49–53, 71–72, 101, 102, 103–104
Julius (Bishop of Rome) 48
Julius Africanus 58–60, 65
Justin Martyr 15–18, 23, 75, 121
Justinian I (emperor) 157

Lactantius 68
Lausiac History 153, 157
leprosy/lepers 107
Liber Peristephanon 70
Liberius (Bishop of Rome) 159
libraries 58, 81
Licinius, Augustus (emperor) 40–41
Life of Antony 98, 151–152, 153

Life of Polycarp 24
liturgy 77
"Longer and Shorter Rules" 107
Lyons 32
lyre 72

Macedonius (Bishop of Constantinople) 48
magical arts 60
Magnentius 49
Magus, Simon 33
Manichaeanism 78, 116, 117, 118–119
Marcella 159
Marcellina 5, 158–160
Marcellinus 5, 143
Marcellus 143
Marcion 5, 15–16, 32, 72, 75, 95, 121–125
marriage 76, 145
martyrdom 80, 117
Martyrdom of Polycarp 26–27
Mary (Jesus' mother) 5, 56, 91, 147–148
Mary (Pachomius' sister) 157
Maternus, Firmicus 67–69
Matheseos Libri Octo (Eight Books of Astrology) 68
Maxentius 40, 41–42
Maximianist theology 144
Maximila 5, 142
Maximus of Ephesus 50
medicine 55, 60, 86
Melania 162
Melitius of Lycopolis and the Melitians 91 98–99
Melito 27–30
Mesopotamia 75, 77
Milan, Italy 56, 107, 116, 160
"Milan Fragments" 83
Millennialism 59; *see also* premillennialism
miracles 138
Moesia 84, 85
monasticism and monasteries 66, 69, 73, 98, 106–107, 117, 118, 119, 137, 149–150
Montanism 5, 25, 37, 94, 125, 127–128, 138–140
Montanus 5, 95, 141
Mount Ararat 58
Mount of Olives 162
Muratorian Fragment 18

Nag Hammadi codices 157
Neocaesarea (Turkey) 61
Neoplatonism 50
New Prophetic Movement *see* Montanism
Nicene Creed 46, 64, 97, 102, 153, 160
Nicopolis, Palestine 59
Nile River 149, 154
Novatianism 93–96
Novatus 131, 133
nudity 20–21

Numidia 56

Oceanus 57
Olympics 60
On the Holy Spirit 106
On the Lapsed 95
On Virginity 160
Onqelos 82
Opus Imperfectum 86
Oration and Panegyric Addressed to Origen 60–61
Oration to the Greeks 77
Origen 4, 18, 37, 56–57, 58, 60, 61, 63, 73, 79–83, 89, 90, 134, 161, 163
"original sin" 110
Ossius (Bishop of Cordova) 43, 46, 64
Ostia, Italy 55, 117
"Outer Mountain" 152

Pachomius 5, 154–158
Palamon 154
Palladius (Bishop) 136, 153, 157
Pammachius 4, 54–57, 90, 98, 146
Pamphilus 62–63
Pantaenus 37
Papias 22–23
Paranion (Medicine Chest) 73
Passion of Perpetua and Felicity 34
Paul (Bishop of Constantinople) 48
Paula 5, 88, 146, 160–164, n. 98 180
Paulinus 55, 73, 109
Penitentials 147
Peri Pascha (Homily on the Passover) 28–29
Perpetua 34–37, 138, n. 170 168, n. 177 168
persecution (of Christians) 26–27, 34–37, 41, 61, 63, 81
Persia/Persian Empire 41, 48, 52, 71
Peter (Bishop of Alexandria) 99
Petronios 156
philosophy 63, 73, 111, 119–120
Philostorgius 85
Photius 38
Phrygia 22, 140
"Phrygian heresy" 138
Pispir 152

Pius, Bishop of Rome (140–154) 18
plague 62
Plotinus 38
poetry 66–67, 69–71, 104
Polycarp 7, 14, 23–27, 30, 31, 122
Polycrates of Ephesus 30
Pontifex Maximus 51
Pontius 60, 61, 62
Possidius 119
poverty 52
premillennialism 22–23
Priscilla 5, 142–143
Proba, Flatonia 4, 66–67
Prudentius, Aurelius Clemens 4, 69–71
Pseudo-Barnabas 7, 8, 17
Pseudo-Clementine literature 8
Psychomachia 70

Rabbula (Bishop of Edessa) 79
Refutations 72
Rhodo 75
Roman Psalter 90
Rome 58, 75, 77, 81, 107, 108, 116, 128
Rufinus 56–57, 82, 162

Sardis 28
Satan 119
Saturus 36
Second Clement 7, 8, 10–12
Secundus of Ptolemais 64, 136
Senate (Roman) 47, 68
Septuagint (LXX) 83, 89
Severus, Septimus 32, 35
Shapur (Persian king) 41
Shepherd of Hermas 7, 8, 18–21, 138
sign of the cross 71
Silvanus 113
Sinope, Pontus 121
Siricius (Bishop of Rome) 56, 147
Sisinius (Bishop) 111
Smyrna 23, 32
Socrates (church historian) 30
soldiers 44, 53–54, 55, 110
Sophia 130
Sorer, Bishop of Rome 11
Sotheris 159
Sozomen (church historian) 30–31

Stephen (Bishop of Rome) 96
stoicism 113
Stridon, Yugoslavia 87
Stromata 38
Sunday closing laws 44
Sunnia 89
Symmachus (Bible translator) 82, 83
Symmachus (Roman senator) 54
Synod of Antioch 64
Synod of Aries 113
Synod of Beziers 113
Synod of Milan 113
Synod of Tyre 101

Tabennisis 154
Tatian 4, 21, 75–79, n. 4 173
Teaching of the Twelve Apostles 7
Tertullian 5, 21, 28, 37, 42, 43, 53, 68, 92, 95, 123, 125–128, 129, 138, 140, 147
"Tertullianists" 127
Tetrapla 83
Thagaste, Algeria 115, 117
Thebes 154
Theodore 156, 157
Theodoret 79
Theodosius I (emperor) 105, 111
Theodotion (Bible translator) 83
Theognis of Nicaea 135
Theonas of Marmarcia 64
"Thundering Legion" 4, 53–54
To the Nations 126, 127
Tobit 91
Trajan (emperor) 12, 19
Trinity 127, 133, 134, 141
Trypho 15, 16–18, n. 50 166
Tutor (Paedagogus) 38

Ulfilas 4–5, 84–87, n. 70 173

Valens (emperor) 102, 106, 108
Valentinian I (emperor) 102, 108
Valentinian II (emperor) 108
Valentinus and the Valentinian heresy 5, 25, 33–34, 76, 128–131
Valerius (Bishop of Hippo) 118
Victor (Bishop of Rome) 30–32, 129
Virgil 66, 67
visions 19–20, 36
Vulgate 5, 88–91

www.ingramcontent.com/pod-product-compliance
Ingram Content Group UK Ltd.
Pitfield, Milton Keynes, MK11 3LW, UK
UKHW050525150426
5217IPUK00026B/1796